Introduction to Python® Programming and Developing GUI Applications with PyQT

B.M. Harwani

Course Technology PTR
A part of Cengage Learning

COURSE TECHNOLOGY
CENGAGE Learning

Australia • Brazil • Japan • Korea • Mexico • Singapore • Spain • United Kingdom • United States

COURSE TECHNOLOGY
CENGAGE Learning®

**Introduction to Python®
Programming and Developing
GUI Applications with PyQT**
B.M. Harwani

**Publisher and General Manager,
Course Technology PTR:**
Stacy L. Hiquet

Associate Director of Marketing:
Sarah Panella

Manager of Editorial Services:
Heather Talbot

Marketing Manager: Mark Hughes

Senior Acquisitions Editor:
Mitzi Koontz

Project Editor: Kim Benbow

Technical Reviewer: Keith Davenport

Copy Editor: Gene Redding

Interior Layout: MPS Limited,
a Macmillan Company

Cover Designer: Mike Tanamachi

Indexer: BIM Indexing Services

Proofreader: Brad Crawford

For product information and technology assistance, contact us at
Cengage Learning Customer & Sales Support, 1-800-354-9706

For permission to use material from this text or product,
submit all requests online at
www.cengage.com/permissions

Further permissions questions can be emailed to
permissionrequest@cengage.com

Python and the Python logos are trademarks or registered trademarks of the Python Software Foundation.

All other trademarks are the property of their respective owners.

All images © Cengage Learning unless otherwise noted.

Library of Congress Control Number: 2011936040

ISBN-13: 978-1-4354-6097-3

ISBN-10: 1-4354-6097-9

Course Technology, a part of Cengage Learning
20 Channel Center Street
Boston, MA 02210
USA

Cengage Learning is a leading provider of customized learning solutions with office locations around the globe, including Singapore, the United Kingdom, Australia, Mexico, Brazil, and Japan. Locate your local office at: **international.cengage.com/region**

Cengage Learning products are represented in Canada by Nelson Education, Ltd.

For your lifelong learning solutions, visit **courseptr.com**

Visit our corporate website at **cengage.com**

Printed in the United States of America
1 2 3 4 5 6 7 13 12 11

This book is dedicated to my mother, Mrs. Nita Harwani, and American inventor and entrepreneur, the late Steve Jobs.

My mother is next to God for me, and whatever I am today is because of the moral values taught by her.

Steve Jobs, co-founder, chairman, and chief executive officer of Apple Inc. has been and will always be a great inspiration for me.

ACKNOWLEDGMENTS

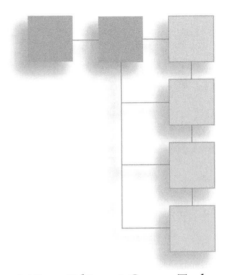

I owe a debt of gratitude to Mitzi Koontz, Senior Acquisitions Editor at Course Technology, Cengage Learning for her initial acceptance and giving me an opportunity to create this work. I am highly grateful to the whole team at Cengage for their constant cooperation and contribution to create this book.

I must thank Keith Davenport, the technical editor for his excellent, detailed review of the work and the many helpful comments and suggestions he made. He offered a significant amount of feedback that helped to improve the book's content. He played a vital role in improving its structure and the quality of information.

Special thanks to Gene Redding, the copy editor for first class structural and language editing. I appreciate his efforts in enhancing the contents of the book and giving it a polished look.

Big and ongoing thanks to Kim Benbow, my project editor, for doing a great job and her sincere efforts to get the book published on time.

A great big thank you goes to the production staff who worked tirelessly to produce this book. I enjoyed working with each of you.

I am also thankful to my family (my small world): Anushka (my wife) and my two little darlings, Chirag and Naman, for always inspiring me and giving me the courage to work harder.

I should not forget to thank my dear students who have been good teachers for me, as they help me to understand the basic problems they face with a subject, which enables me to directly teach those topics. Their endlessly interesting queries help me to write books with a practical approach.

About the Author

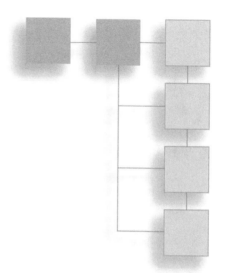

B.M. Harwani is founder and owner of Microchip Computer Education (MCE), based in Ajmer, India, which provides computer education on all programming and web developing platforms. Harwani graduated with a BE in computer engineering from the University of Pune, and also has a C Level (master's degree) in computer technology from DOEACC, Government of India. Being involved in the teaching field for over 16 years, he has developed the art of explaining even the most complicated technical topics in a straightforward and easily understandable fashion. He has written several books on various subjects that include JSP, JSF, EJB, PHP, .NET, Joomla, jQuery, and smartphones. His latest books include *Beginning Web Development for Smartphones* (Shroff, 2011), *Core Data iOS Essentials* (Packt Publishing, 2011) and *Blogging with WordPress 3 for Beginners* (CreateSpace, 2011). He also writes articles on a variety of computer subjects, which can be seen on a number of websites. To find out more, visit his blog at http://bmharwani.com/blog.

Contents

Introduction xii

Chapter 1   Python and Its Features 1

Python 1

   Python Implementations. 2

   Features of Python 2

Installing Python. 3

   Installing Python on Microsoft Windows 3

   Installing Python on the Mac 5

   Installing Python on UNIX 6

Interacting with Python 7

   Command Line Mode. 7

   IDLE (Integrated DeveLopment Environment). 7

Writing Your First Python Program 8

   Running Python Programs from the Command Prompt 9

Data Types in Python 9

Basic Elements in a Program. 10

   Literals 10

   Variables 11

   Keywords 11

Comments 12

Continuation Lines 12

Printing 12

Summary 14

Chapter 2   **Getting Wet in Python 17**

Performing Arithmetic Operations 17

   Division Operator 18

   Exponentiation 20

   Multiple Assignment Statement 21

   Using Escape Sequences 21

Bitwise Operations 26

Complex Numbers 28

Making Decisions 29

   if...else statement 30

   if-elif-else statement 32

Logical Operators 32

Chaining Comparison Operators 34

Loops 35

   The while Loop 36

   The for Loop 40

Summary 44

Chapter 3   **Sequences 45**

Sequences 45

Strings 46

   How Characters Are Stored in a String 47

   Arrays 59

Lists 63

   Finding the Length of the List 64

   List Slicing 66

Tuples 70

Sets 74

   Union (|) 74

   Intersection (&) 74

   Difference (-) 75

Summary 77

Chapter 4   **Functions and Modules 79**

Functions 79

   The def Statement 80

   The return Statement 81

   Default Value Parameters 82

   Keyword Arguments 83

Local and Global Variables 84

Lambda Functions 86

Applying Functions to Sequences 87

Function Attributes 90

Documentation String 91

Recursion 92

Iterators 94

Generators 95

Generator Expression 96

Modules 97

The math Module 100

Summary 103

Chapter 5   **Classes** **105**

The class Statement 105

Attributes of Class Objects 106

Built-In Class Attributes 107

Defining Functions in a Class 108

Instances. 109

Class Methods. 114

Static Methods 115

Garbage Collection. 118

Inheritance. 120

Types of Inheritance. 120

Multilevel Inheritance. 125

Two Classes Inheriting from the Same Base Class 128

Multiple Inheritance. 131

Operator Overloading 135

Overloading the Comparison Operator (==) 136

Descriptors 139

The __setattr__ Method 141

The __getattr__ Method. 141

The __delattr__ Method 141

Summary 142

Chapter 6   **File Handling** **143**

Exception Handling 159

Using a try/except Block 160

Using a try/finally Block 164

Raising an Exception 165

Summary 167

Chapter 7   **PyQt** **169**

Qt Toolkit 170

PyQt 170

Installing PyQt 170

Window and Dialogs 172

   Ways of Creating GUI Applications 173

Creating a GUI Application with Code 173

Using Qt Designer 175

   Widget Box 179

   Toolbar 186

Understanding Fundamental Widgets 188

   Displaying Text 189

   Entering Single-Line Data 189

   Displaying Buttons 190

Event Handling in PyQt 191

First Application in Qt Designer 191

   Connecting to Predefined Slots 193

Using Custom Slots 199

Converting Data Types 202

Defining Buddies 206

   Setting Tab Order 207

Summary 211

Chapter 8   **Basic Widgets** **213**

Using Radio Buttons 213

Using Checkboxes 218

   Initiating Action Without Using a Push Button 223

Entering Integer and Float Values Using a Spin Box 226

ScrollBars and Sliders 231

   ScrollBars 231

   Sliders 233

Working with a List Widget 237

   Adding Items to a List Widget 237

   Performing Operations on a List Widget 241

Summary 247

Chapter 9   **Advanced Widgets** **249**

Displaying System Clock Time in LCD Format 249

   Displaying LCD Digits 250

Working with Calendar and Displaying Dates in Different Formats 253

   Displaying Calendar 253

            QDate Class 255
            Using the Date Edit Widget 256
        Using Combo Box. 259
        Displaying a Table 264
            Displaying Items in the Table 265
        Displaying Web Pages 268
        Displaying Graphics 271
        Summary 276

Chapter 10   Menus and Toolbars. **277**
        Understanding Menus 277
            Action Editor 279
            Creating a Menu 280
        Creating a Toolbar 287
            Creating a Resource File 287
        Dock Widget 295
        Tab Widget 302
            Working with the Style Sheet Editor 303
        Converting a Tab Widget 309
            Converting a Tab Widget into a Tool Box 310
            Converting Tab Widget into Stacked Widget 311
        Summary 315

Chapter 11   Multiple Documents and Layouts. **317**
        Multiple-Document Interface 317
        Layouts. 327
            Horizontal Layout. 328
            Using a Group Box 332
            Vertical Layout 333
            Using the Grid Layout 334
        Summary 339

Chapter 12   Database Handling. **341**
        Why MySQL? 342
            MySQLdb 343
            Installation of MySQLdb. 343
        Creating a Database. 344
            Creating a Database Table 345
        Database Maintenance Through Console-Based Programs 349
            Inserting Rows in a Database Table 349

Database Maintenance Through GUI Programs 359
       Displaying Rows 360
     Summary 375

Index **377**

INTRODUCTION

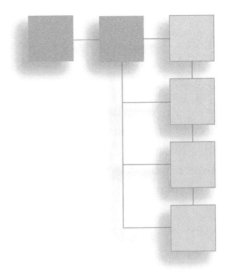

Python is an interpreted, general-purpose, high-level programming language that is very popular among developers and professionals because of its vast library of add-on modules. It is a platform-independent scripted language that is supported by many individuals as an open-source project. The fact that it is freely available and runs on all platforms makes it ever more popular.

The goal of *Introduction to Python Programming and Developing GUI Applications with PyQT* is to teach the Python programming language through practical examples. Whether you are new to computers or are an experienced programmer, this book is intended to help you develop your programming skills. It is written with the requirements of all levels in mind—developers, professionals, and beginners. The book begins with a solid introduction of Python from scratch—loops, control structures, sequences, functions, classes, and exception handling. Thereafter, the book explains persistence through file handling and targets developers by introducing GUI application development in PyQT.

As you read through the book, you will acquire the skills needed for building practical Python programming applications and will learn how these skills can be put into use in real-world scenarios.

Like any good book, *Introduction to Python Programming* explains the more basic concepts, one step at a time, by writing small programs to demonstrate each step. Gradually, once the reader is acquainted with logical blocks, the book explains using the blocks for understanding more complex concepts. By the time you finish the book, you will understand how to break problems down into manageable chunks, and then refine your code into applications.

HOW THIS BOOK IS ORGANIZED

This book starts with a discussion of Python's basics, beginning with easy examples, and then gradually going deeper to uncover the more complex topics of GUI programming in Python. By the end of the book, readers will also have an understanding of using back-end databases for storing and fetching information.

Chapter 1, "Python and Its Features": In this chapter, you will have a detailed introduction to Python and its features, such as installing Python on different platforms, interacting with Python through Command Line mode and the IDLE IDE. You will also learn to write your first Python program. The chapter also introduces the Python basics, like its different data types, literals, variables, and keywords. Finally, the chapter explains how to write comments, continuation lines, and print messages.

Chapter 2, "Getting Wet in Python": In this chapter, you will learn to apply arithmetic operations and different logical and membership operators in Python programs. You will see the use of escape sequences. You will learn to get data from the user as well as process incoming data. You will also see how to convert data into different types, learn to display octal and hexa values, perform bitwise operations, and use complex numbers. You will also learn how to use the `if...else` statement in making decisions. Finally, the chapter explains how to use `while` and `for` loops for doing repetitive tasks.

Chapter 3, "Sequences": This chapter focuses on using different containers. You will learn to perform different operations on strings, including concatenating strings, splitting strings, and then converting them into different cases, such as uppercase, title case, and lowercase, etc. Also, you will learn to do list slicing, searching elements in tuples, and performing operations on sets, such as finding their union, intersection, and differences. You will learn how key/value pairs are maintained in a dictionary and how to append, delete, or and modify key/value pairs. Finally, the chapter explains how to create one- and two-dimensional arrays.

Chapter 4, "Functions and Modules": In this chapter, you will learn about different statements that define and return values from functions. Also, you will learn to use default value parameters and keyword arguments in a function, as well as use local and global variables. The chapter explains how to create lambda functions for smaller expressions. Also, you will learn how to apply functions to sequences using different function attributes and implement recursion. For accessing collections of data, the chapter explains how to use iterators, generators, and generator expressions. You will learn to import and use modules for built-in functions. The chapter also explains how to pass command-line arguments to a Python program.

Chapter 5, "Classes": This chapter focuses on classes. You will learn how to define a class, define functions for it, initialize its instance variables, and use class and static methods. You will also learn to use class attributes to display specific information related to the class. You will learn the concept of garbage collection and its role in freeing up memory consumed by objects that are out of scope. Also, you will learn to apply single, multilevel, and multiple inheritance through running practical examples. You will learn the use of private and public access specifiers and how to apply method overriding and operator overloading to perform arithmetic operations on instances. Finally, the chapter explains polymorphism and setting and getting values of instance attributes through properties and descriptors.

Chapter 6, "File Handling": In this chapter, you will learn to perform different operations on files. You will learn to open a file in different modes and to read its contents, update existing content, delete content, and append new content. You will also see how to copy a file, read a file sequentially or randomly, and read only specific content. You will learn to create a binary file as well as pickle and unpickle objects. Finally, the chapter explains how to implement exception handling and the procedure for raising exceptions.

Chapter 7, "PyQt": In this chapter, you will be introduced to the Qt toolkit, Qt Designer, and PyQt. You will learn about different Qt Designer components, such as the toolbar, the Object Inspector, the Property Editor, and the Widget Box. You will also learn to create a GUI application through coding. Also, you will learn about the fundamental Label, Line Edit, and Push Button widgets as well as learn to develop applications using them. You will also learn about signal/slot connection in the Qt Designer and how to connect signals to both predefined slots and to custom slots.

Chapter 8, "Basic Widgets": This chapter demonstrates how to create a GUI application using Radio Buttons, which enable the user to select one option out of several. You will also learn how to select more than one option by using CheckBoxes and specify integers as well as float values using Spin Boxes. Also, you will learn to use ScrollBars and Sliders to display large documents and represent integer values. Finally, the chapter explains how to display options with a List widget, add items to a List widget, and delete and edit existing items in a List widget.

Chapter 9, "Advanced Widgets": This chapter explains how to access and display system clock time in LCD digits. You also will see how to display a calendar and display a selected date in different formats. You will learn to create an application that displays options with a Combo Box, displays information with a Table widget, displays web pages, and displays graphics.

Chapter 10, "Menus and Toolbars": In this chapter, you will learn to create menus and toolbars. Also, you will learn about the Action Editor and how it can help you define actions for menus and toolbars. You will also learn how to manage application resources in one place through a resource file. You will see how to create dockable windows and how to display information in small chunks with the Tab widget. Finally, the chapter explains how to convert a Tab widget into a Tool Box or Stacked widget.

Chapter 11, "Multiple Documents and Layouts": In this chapter, you will learn to manage multiple documents in a main window through an MDI. You will see how child windows in MdiArea can be arranged in cascading and tile fashions. You will also learn to place a collection of widgets that do similar tasks in a Group Box. You will also learn to organize widgets in different layouts.

Chapter 12, "Database Handling": In this chapter, you will learn to install and use the MySQLdb module, which is required in order to access the MySQL Database Server through Python. Also, you will learn to maintain a database through console-based programs and through GUI programs. You will also learn to write Python scripts to insert, fetch, delete, search, and update rows in a database table.

COMPANION WEBSITE DOWNLOADS

You may download the companion website files from www.courseptr.com/downloads. Please note that you will be redirected to the Cengage Learning website.

CHAPTER 1

PYTHON AND ITS FEATURES

This chapter covers the following:

- Introduction to Python and its features
- Installing Python on different platforms
- Interacting with Python through Command Line Mode and IDLE
- Writing Your First Python Program
- Understanding data types and basic elements in Python
- Writing comments and continuation lines and printing messages

PYTHON

Python is a very powerful high-level, dynamic object-oriented programming language created by Guido van Rossum in 1991. It is implemented in C, and relies on the extensive portable C libraries. It is a cross-platform language and runs on all major hardware platforms and operating systems, including Windows, Linux/UNIX, and Macintosh. Python has an easy-to-use syntax and is quite easy to learn, making it suitable for those who are still learning to program. Python has a rich set of supporting libraries, and many third-party modules are available for it. Python is a programming language that also supports scripting, making it suitable for rapid application development. Python comes with a powerful and easy to-use graphical user interface (GUI) toolkit that makes the task of developing GUI applications in Python quite easy. It is freely available.

Python Implementations

Python currently has three implementations, known as CPython, Jython, and Iron-Python. In this book, you will be using CPython, the most widely used implementation, which I will refer to as just Python for simplicity. A small description of all three implementations is as follows:

- **CPython.** Classic Python (often just called Python) is the fastest, most up-to-date, and complete implementation of Python. It is implemented in C (i.e., its libraries and modules are all coded in standard C). It is cross-platform and runs on almost all platforms.

- **Jython.** Jython is a Python implementation that is Java Virtual Machine (JVM) compliant. With Jython, we can use all Java libraries and frameworks.

- **IronPython.** IronPython is a Python implementation for the Microsoft designed Common Language Runtime (CLR), popularly known as .NET. With Iron Python, you can use all CLR libraries and frameworks.

Features of Python

As mentioned earlier, Python is a scripting language that includes a vast library of add-on modules. It supports integration of pre-built components for creating complex applications. Python has full access to operating system (OS) services. Following are a few of its features:

- **Python is easy to learn**. Programmers familiar with traditional languages will find all the familiar constructs, such as loops, conditional statements, arrays, and so on.

- **It has easier to read syntax**. It avoids the use of punctuation characters like { } $ / and \.

- **It uses white space** to indent lines for defining blocks instead of using brackets.

- **Python is free**. You can download and install any version of Python and use it to develop software for commercial or personal applications without paying a penny. Python is developed under the open-source model. You can copy Python, modify it, and even resell it.

- **It comes with a large number of libraries included**, and there are many more that you can download and install.

- **Python can be integrated with other languages,** like C, C++, and Java. That is, the components written in these languages can be embedded with Python programs, thus making it easier to develop complex solutions.

- **Python is an interpreted language**, therefore it supports a complete debugging and diagnostic environment making the job of fixing mistakes much faster. Also, the software development is quite rapid and flexible in it.

- **Python is a good choice for web development**, networking, games, data processing, and business applications.

- **For efficient memory management**, Python uses garbage collection, so you don't have to worry about memory leaks. The Python run-time environment handles garbage collection of all Python objects. Each object has a reference counter to make sure that no live objects are removed. Only the object with a reference counter value equal to 0 is garbage collected.

- **Python supports exception handling**. That is, errors are raised as exceptions so that you can take corrective measures. Python signals almost all errors with an exception.

However, you cannot take advantage of Python's features unless you install it and begin using it. So, read on to understand how Python is installed on different platforms.

INSTALLING PYTHON

To install Python, you will need to download its most recent distribution from the following URL: www.python.org. Don't worry if you already have an earlier version of Python installed on your machine. You can have multiple versions of Python on the same computer. The new version of Python is installed in a separate location and will not interfere with the older version on your computer. Many Linux distributions and Mac OS X come with Python 2.x as part of the operating system. Let's have a look at the steps for installing Python on Microsoft Windows.

Installing Python on Microsoft Windows

For Microsoft Windows, download the latest Python installer program from its site. This book is based on Python version 3.2, and its installer program is python-3.2.msi. Download it, and then double-click on it to begin the installation wizard.

Note

You need to be logged in as the administrator to run the install.

The first dialog box of the installation wizard, shown in Figure 1.1, asks whether you want to install this Python version for all the users or only for one user (i.e., the administrator). Select the option Install For All Users, followed by selecting the Next button.

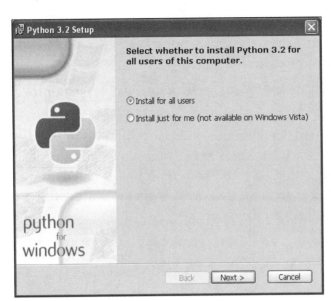

Figure 1.1
Python installation wizard.

In the next dialog, you will be asked for the destination folder where you want to install Python files. The wizard also displays a folder name by default that represents the Python version being installed. In this case, the default folder will be C:\Python32\. You can either keep the default folder or specify a new folder for your Python installation. Select the Next button to continue. If you have a previous installation, then you will be asked whether you wish to back up replaced files. The option to make backups is already selected, and the default folder for the backup appears as C:\Python32\BACKUP. Click Next to continue. The next dialog is to specify the Python features (i.e., the components) that you want to install, as shown in Figure 1.2. You can select or unselect the features as per your requirement. On selecting a feature, the hard disk space needed by its files will be displayed. Keeping the default components selected, click Next to continue.

The installer program will copy the Python files to the selected folder, and you will be asked to select the Finish button to exit the installation wizard. On successful installation of Python, you will find a new group, called Python 3.2, added to your Windows system that you can see by selecting the Start > All Programs option. The Python 3.2 group shows several options, such as IDLE (Python GUI), Module Docs, Python (Command Line), Python Manuals, and Uninstall Python.

On selecting the Python (Command Line) menu item, you see the Python Command Line window displaying the Python prompt (>>>), as shown in Figure 1.3. The

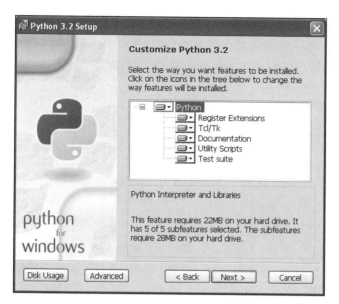

Figure 1.2
Selecting Python components to install.

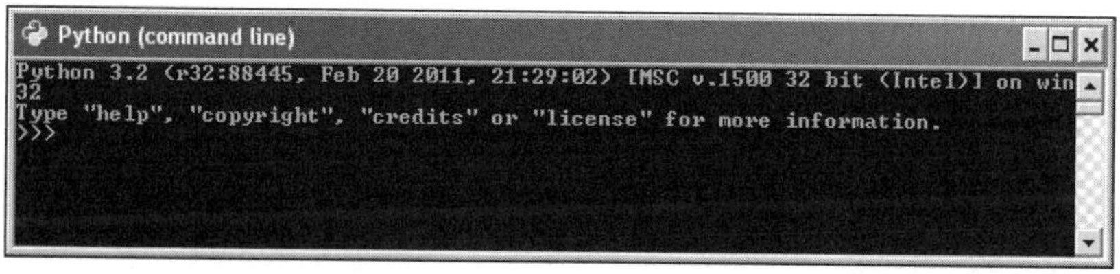

Figure 1.3
Python Command Line window.

window informs you which version of Python is running, the date the version was released, and a few hints for viewing copyright, credits, and license information. Below the hints messages is displayed the Python prompt (>>>) where you can issue Python commands. To execute Python commands, you write them at the prompt followed by pressing the Enter key. To close the Python Command Line window, press Ctrl+Z followed by the Enter key.

Congratulations for successfully installing Python on Windows! Now I'll show you how to install Python on Mac OS X.

Installing Python on the Mac

Python is part of the Mac OS environment. Tiger (Mac OS 10.4) includes Python 2.3.5 and IDLE (Integrated DeveLopment Environment). Leopard (Mac OS 10.5) includes Python 2.5.1. Snow Leopard (Mac OS 10.6) includes Python 2.6. The Python files can be found in the /System/Library/Frameworks/Python.framework/Versions folder. To install or upgrade to Python 3.2, download the pre-built Mac OS X installer from www.python.org. The file name will be python-3.2.macosx.dmg. To initiate the installation procedure, double-click the file. It will create a disk image named Universal MacPython 3.2. The disk image will contain a license, a ReadMe file, and the MacPython.mpkg file. You need to double-click the MacPython.mpkg file to install Python on your computer. The installer will take you through a few steps that include agreeing to the license terms and conditions for using Python, specifying a destination folder, and selecting installation type (e.g., whether it is an upgrade or a fresh installation).

To test whether the upgraded version of Python is successfully installed on your Mac platform, open the Terminal window and type **python** followed by the Enter key. The Python command invokes Python and displays its prompt (>>>) along with the version information. If the prompt displays the version as 3.2, it confirms that the upgraded version of Python is successfully installed on your computer, and you can execute Python commands at the prompt. To close the prompt and exit Python, press Ctrl+D.

Installing Python on UNIX

To install Python on the UNIX platform, the first step, as usual, is to download and extract its installer program from www.python.org. The next step is to give the following command to configure options for your UNIX system:

```
./configure
```

Thereafter, the following commands are needed to begin the installation procedure:

```
make
make install
```

The preceding commands will install Python files in the /usr/local/bin folder and install its libraries in /usr/local/lib/python32 folder. Since the make install command can overwrite your previous Python installation, it is better to use the make altinstall command:

```
make altinstall prefix=~ exec-prefix=~
```

prefix=~ installs all platform-independent files in the ~/lib folder, and exec-prefix=~ installs all binary and other platform-specific files in the ~/bin folder. The make altinstall command creates ${prefix}/bin/python, which refers to the new python installation.

INTERACTING WITH PYTHON

There are two ways to work with Python interactively:

- Using Command Line Mode
- Using IDLE IDE

Command Line Mode

In command line mode, you type Python instructions one line at a time. You can also import code from other files or modules. To open Python's command line mode in Windows, select Start > All Programs > Python 3.2 to open the Python 3.2 group. The group shows several options, such as IDLE (Python GUI), Module Docs, Python (command line), Python Manuals, and Uninstall Python. Select the Python (command line) option from the group. Alternatively, you can open a command prompt window and type **python** followed by pressing the Enter key. If you get an error message saying that the Python program couldn't be found, it means that your operating system could not find the path for the Python installation. To define the correct path for the Python installation, right-click on the My Computer icon and select Properties from the shortcut menu that appears. Select the Advanced tab from the dialog that appears, and click the Environment Variables button at the bottom. A list of environment variables will be displayed. Double click the Path variable to edit it. In the Edit box, add the location of your Python installation (i.e., **;C:\python32**) at the end of the line, and select OK. Also, click the OK button in all of the windows that are open until you get back to your desktop. Open another command prompt window (because the old window will still have the old path settings) and invoke Python by typing **python** followed by Enter.

On Mac OS X, open the Terminal window and type **python3** followed by the Enter key. On UNIX, open a new shell window and type **python3.2** at a command prompt.

After typing the appropriate command in the respective platform, Python's command line mode is invoked, displaying a window (refer to Figure 1.3). While working in command line mode, a history of the commands given is maintained. You can use the up and down arrows, as well as the Home, End, Page Up, and Page Down keys, to scroll through the commands used previously. Since whatever you type in command line mode is not saved, it is better to save code in a file and then execute it. The following section shows you how to use this method, too.

IDLE (Integrated DeveLopment Environment)

IDLE is a simple IDE that comes with the standard Python distribution. IDLE combines an interactive interpreter with code editing, debugging tools, and several specialized

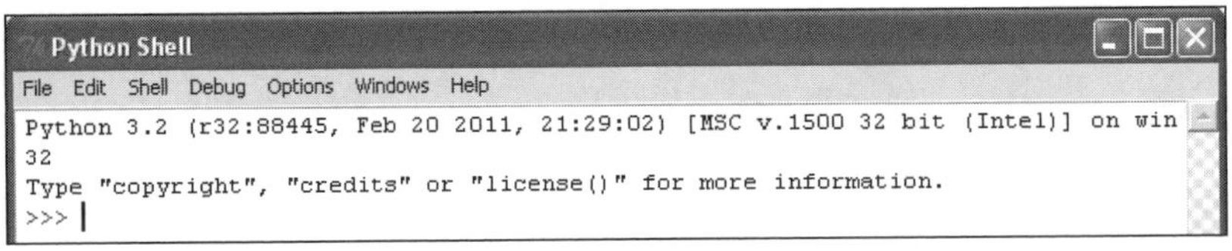

Figure 1.4
Python Shell window.

browsers/viewers built into it. It provides automatic indentation and colors to the code based on Python syntax types, making your program more readable. Also, you can navigate to the previously given commands that are in the buffer using the mouse, arrow keys, or Page Up and Page Down keys. You can also toggle up and down through the previously given commands using the Alt+P and Alt+N key commands. You can also complete Python keywords or user-defined values by pressing Alt+/.

To start IDLE on Windows, select Start > All Programs > Python 3.2 > IDLE (Python GUI). On Mac OS X, navigate to the Python 3.2 subfolder in the Applications folder, and run IDLE from there. On UNIX, type **idle3.2** at a command prompt. The Python Shell window opens upon invoking IDLE, as shown in Figure 1.4.

Besides executing individual Python commands in the Python Shell window, you can also write and edit Python programs in any editor and execute them through IDLE. You can use any text editor, like Notepad on Windows or ed on Linux, for writing and editing Python programs. Besides using external editors, you can also use IDLE's built-in editor for the same purpose. To open IDLE's editor, select File > New Window. A blank window appears where you can type a Python program. To save the program, select File > Save As. The program will be saved with extension .py. The .py extension shows that it is a Python program. To execute the program, select Run > Run Module or press the F5 key. While running a program, IDLE will display the line(s) where errors, if any, occur. You can also open and edit programs written in other editors by selecting File > Open. Alternatively, you can right-click on the program name in an Explorer window and select Edit with IDLE to open it in IDLE's editor.

WRITING YOUR FIRST PYTHON PROGRAM

As mentioned earlier, you can write your first Python program either through IDLE's built-in editor or through any editor. I will be using IDLE's editor throughout the book for writing programs. You can launch IDLE by selecting Start > All Programs > Python 3.2 > IDLE (Python GUI). Then select the File > New Window option to open IDLE's built-in editor and write the following small program:

```
arearect.py
# The program calculates area of rectangle
```

```
l=8
b=5
a=l*b
print ("Area of rectangle is ", a)
```

Save it to your computer in any desired folder by any name, for example, arearect.py.

Note

Remember to add the .py extension when saving the file, as IDLE does not add the extension automatically.

The program consists of two variables, l and b, initialized to values 8 and 5, respectively. The l and b variables here represent the length and breadth of a rectangle. The l and b are multiplied, and the result is stored in a third variable, a, that is then displayed as the area of a rectangle. To run the program, select Run > Run Module from the menu or just press F5. You will get the following output:

```
Area of rectangle is 40
```

Congratulations! You have successfully written and executed your first Python program.

Running Python Programs from the Command Prompt

You can run Python programs from the command prompt, too. Open the command prompt and type **python arearect.py** followed by the Enter key to open Python and tell it to run the script file, arearect.py. You will get the output of the program as previously shown. You might have noticed that variables l, b, and a are of integer types. What are other data types in Python? Go to the next section for a brief overview of different data types in Python.

DATA TYPES IN PYTHON

Python has a rich set of fundamental data types. The operations that are applicable on an object depend on its data type (i.e., an object's data type determines which operations are applicable on it). The list of data types are as follows:

- **Integers:** Integers are 32 bits long, and their range is from -2^{32} to $2^{32} - 1$ (i.e., from –2,147,483,648 to 2,147,483,647).

- **Long Integers:** It has unlimited precision, subject to the memory limitations of the computer.

- **Floating Point Numbers:** Floating-point numbers are also known as double-precision numbers and use 64 bits.

■ **Boolean:** It can hold only one of two possible values: True or False.

■ **Complex Number:** A complex number has a real and an imaginary component, both represented by float types in Python. An imaginary number is a multiple of the square root of minus one, and is denoted by j. For instance, 2+3j is a complex number, where 3 is the imaginary component and is equal to $3 \times \sqrt{-1}$.

■ **Strings:** Sequences of Unicode characters.

■ **Lists:** Ordered sequences of values.

■ **Tuples:** Ordered, immutable sequences of values.

■ **Sets:** Unordered collections of values.

■ **Dictionaries:** Unordered collections of key-value pairs.

Note

Unicode is a standard that uses 16-bit characters to represent characters on your computer. Unlike ASCII (American Standard Code for Information Interchange), which consists of 8 bits, Unicode uses 16 bits and represents characters by integer value denoted in base 16.

A number does not include any punctuation and cannot begin with a leading zero (0). Leading zeros are used for base 2, base 8, and base 16 numbers. For example, a number with a leading 0b or 0B is binary, base 2, and uses digits 0 and 1. Similarly, a number with a leading 0o is octal, base 8, and uses the digits 0 to 7, and a number with a leading 0x or 0X is hexadecimal, base 16, and uses the digits 0 through 9, plus a, A, b, B, c, C, d, D, e, E, f, and F.

Note

An object that can be altered is known as a *mutable* object, and one that cannot be altered is an *immutable* object.

BASIC ELEMENTS IN A PROGRAM

Every program consists of certain basic elements, a collection of literals, variables, and keywords. The next few sections explain what these terms mean.

Literals

A *literal* is a number or string that appears directly in a program. The following are all literals in Python:

```
10   # Integer literal
```

```
10.50   # Floating-point literal
10.50j  # Imaginary literal
'Hello' # String literal
"World!" # String literal
'''Hello World!
It might rain today          # Triple-quoted string literal
Tomorrow is Sunday'''
```

In Python, you can use both single and double quotes to represent strings. The strings that run over multiple lines are represented by triple quotes.

Variables

Variables are used for storing data in a program. To set a variable, you choose a name for your variable, and then use the equals sign followed by the data that it stores. Variables can be letters, numbers, or words. For example,

```
l = 10
length = 10
length_rectangle = 10.0
k="Hello World!"
```

You can see in the preceding examples the variable can be a single character or a word or words connected with underscores. Depending on the data stored in a variable, they are termed as *integer*, *floating point*, *string*, *boolean*, and *list* or *tuple* variables. Like in above examples, the variables l and length are integer variables, length_rectangle is a floating-point variable, and k is a string variable. Following are examples of boolean, list, and tuple variables:

```
a=True   # Boolean variable
b=[2,9,4] # List variable
c=('apple', 'mango', 'banana') # tuple variable
A tuple in python language refers to an ordered, immutable (non changeable) set of
values of any data type.
```

Keywords

Python has 30 keywords, which are identifiers that Python reserves for special use. Keywords contain lowercase letters only. You cannot use keywords as regular identifiers. Following are the keywords of Python:

```
and assert break class continue def del elif else except exec finally for from global if
import in is lambda not or pass print raise return try while with yield
```

COMMENTS

Comments are the lines that are for documentation purposes and are ignored by the interpreter. The comments inform the reader what the program is all about. A comment begins by a hash sign (#). All characters after the # and up to the physical line end are part of the comment. For example,

```
# This program computes area of rectangle
a=b+c  # values of b and c are added and stored in a
```

CONTINUATION LINES

A *physical* line is a line that you see in a program. A *logical* line is a single statement in Python terms. In Python, the end of a physical line marks the end of most statements, unlike in other languages, where usually a semicolon (;) is used to mark the end of statements. When a statement is too long to fit on a single line, you can join two adjacent physical lines into a logical line by ensuring that the first physical line has no comment and ends with a backslash (\). Besides this, Python also joins adjacent lines into one logical line if an open parenthesis (( ), bracket ([ ), or brace ({) is not closed. The lines after the first one in a logical line are known as *continuation* lines. The indentation is not applied to continuation lines but only to the first physical line of each logical line.

PRINTING

For printing messages and results of computations, the print() function is used with the following syntax,

```
print(["message"][variable list])
```

where message is the text string enclosed either in single or double quotes. The variable list may be one or more variables containing the result of computation, as shown in these examples:

```
print ("Hello World!")
print (10)
print (1)
print ("Length is ", 1)
```

You can display a text message, constant values, and variable's values through the print statement, as shown in the preceding examples.

After printing the desired message/value, the print() function also prints the newline character, meaning the cursor moves onto the next line after displaying the required message/value. As a result, the message/value displayed through the next print() function appears on the next line. To suppress printing of the newline character, end the print line with end=' ' followed by a comma (,) after the expression so that the print() function prints an extra space instead of a newline character. For example, the strings displayed via the next two print() functions will appear on the same line with a space in between:

```
print('Hello World!', end=' ')
print('It might rain today')
```

You can also concatenate strings on output by using either a plus sign (+) or comma (,) betweens strings. For example, the following print function will display the two strings on the same line separated by a space:

```
print('Hello World!', 'It might rain today')
```

The following statement merges the two messages and displays them without any space in between:

```
print('Hello World!'+'It might rain today')
```

In order to get a space in between the strings, you have to concatenate a white space between the strings:

```
print('Hello World!'+ ' '+ 'It might rain today')
```

You can also use a comma for displaying values in the variables along with the strings:

```
print ("Length is ", l, " and Breadth is ", b)
```

Assuming the values of variables l and b are 8 and 5, respectively, the preceding statement will display the following output:

```
Length is 8 and Breadth is 5
```

You can also use format codes (%) for substituting values in the variables at the desired place in the message:

```
print ("Length is %d and Breadth is %d" %(l,b))
```

where %d is a format code that indicates an integer has to be substituted at its place. That is, the values in variables l and b will replace the respective format codes.

Note

If the data type of the values in the variables doesn't match with the format codes, auto conversion takes place.

Table 1.1 Frequently Used Format Codes

Format Code	Usage
%s	Displays in string format.
%d	Displays in decimal format
%e	Displays in exponential format.
%f	Displays in floating-point format.
%o	Displays in octal (base 8) format.
%x	Displays in hexadecimal format.
%c	Displays ASCII code.

The list of format codes is as shown in Table 1.1. You will be learning to apply format codes in the next chapter.

The following program demonstrates using the `print()` function for displaying different output:

```
printex.py
print (10)
print('Hello World! \
It might rain today. \
Tomorrow is Sunday.')
print('''Hello World!
It might rain today.
Tomorrow is Sunday.''')
```

Output:

```
10
Hello World! It might rain today. Tomorrow is Sunday.
Hello World!
It might rain today.
Tomorrow is Sunday.
```

SUMMARY

In this chapter, you had a detailed introduction to Python and its features. You saw the procedure of installing Python on different platforms. You saw how to interact with Python through command line mode and through the IDLE IDE. You also learned to write your first Python program. I also introduced you to the Python basics, like its different data types, literals, variables, and keywords. Finally, you saw how to write comments, continuation lines, and print messages.

In the next chapter, you will learn to apply different arithmetic operations in Python programs, use escape sequences in a program, and get data from a user and convert it into the desired data type. Also, you will learn to deal with octal and hexa values. You will also learn to perform bitwise operations, use complex numbers, and take decisions through an `if...else` statement. Finally, you will learn to use different loops, like `while` and `for` loops.

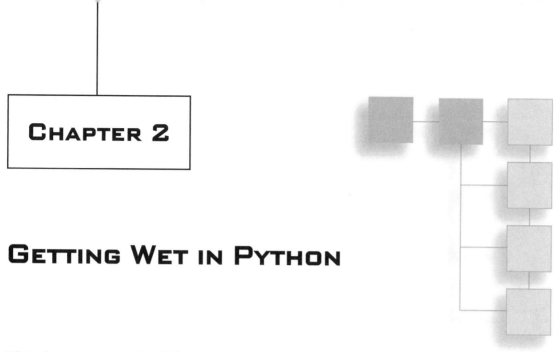

CHAPTER 2

GETTING WET IN PYTHON

This chapter covers the following:

- Performing Arithmetic Operations
- Using Escape Sequences
- Displaying Octal and Hexa Values
- Performing Bitwise Operations
- Using Complex Numbers
- Making Decisions: if...else Statement
- Using Loops: while and for Loops
- Breaking and Continuing a Loop
- Using Operators: Logical Operators and Membership Operators

PERFORMING ARITHMETIC OPERATIONS

Arithmetic operators play a major role in programming, and it is essential to understand the use of different operators for efficient programming. Python provides several arithmetic operators for performing different operations on numerical data. The list of arithmetic operators used in Python is shown in Table 2.1.

Table 2.1 displays the usual arithmetic operators such as addition, subtraction, and multiplication. The multiplication and division operators have higher precedence

Table 2.1   Arithmetic Operators

Operation	Description
x + y	Addition
x - y	Subtraction
x * y	Multiplication
x / y	Division
x // y	Truncating division
x ** y	Exponentiation. Sets x to the power y; i.e., x^y
x % y	Modulo operator
-x	Unary minus
+x	Unary plus

than the addition and subtraction operators. The modulo operator returns the remainder of the division operation. What is the difference between the division operator and the truncating division operator? Let's see.

Division Operator

The truncating division operator (//), also known as floor division, truncates the result to an integer (ignoring the remainder) and works with both integers and floating-point numbers. The true division operator (/) also truncates the result to an integer if the operands are integers. It also means that the true division operator returns a floating-point result if either operand is a floating-point number.

Note

When both operands are integers, the / operator behaves like //.

The following program uses the true division operator for calculating the area of a triangle.

```
areatriangle.py
b=17
h=13
```

```
a=1.0/2.0*b*h
print ("Area of triangle is", a)
print ("Base= %d, Height is %d, Area of triangle is %f" %(b,h,a))
Output:
Area of triangle is 110.5
Base= 17, Height is 13, Area of triangle is 110.500000
```

In this program, you are using the true division operator, /, which returns an integer if both the operands are integers. To get the correct result, 1/2 is converted into a float, 1.0/2.0, so that the result from the true division operator comes out to be a float. One thing to observe in the program's output is that the %f directive returns the float value up to six decimal places. Can it be rounded to 2 or 3 decimal places? Let's see.

The following program calculates the average of three values and displays the result rounded up to the desired number of decimal places:

```
average1.py
p=q=r=10
a=1.0/3.0*(p+q+r)
print ("Average of three variables is", a)
print ("Average of three variables is %.2f" %a)
print ("Average of three variables is %d" %a)
Output:
Average of three variables is 10.0
Average of three variables is 10.00
Average of three variables is 10
```

In this program, you see that the floating-point result is rounded to 2 places by using %.2f. Also, you see that the floating-point value is truncated to a decimal value when %d format code is applied to it.

While using the true division operator, /, you need to ensure that either operand is a floating-point number to avoid getting an incorrect truncating integer. While using the true division operator, it's better to begin the source file with this statement:

```
from __future__ import division
```

This statement ensures that the true division operator works without truncation on operands of any type. Basically, the from __future__ statement ensures that the script uses the new-style floating-point division operator.

```
average2.py
from __future__ import division
p=q=r=10
```

```
a=(p+q+r)/3
print ("Average of three variables is", a)
Output:
Average of three variables is 10.0
```

Exponentiation

To apply exponentiation, use double asterisks: `**`. For example, `a**b` means a^b. You get an exception if a is less than zero and b is a floating-point value with a nonzero fractional part. You can also use the built-in `pow()` function for applying exponentiation. For example, `pow(a, b)` is the same as `a**b`.

You will learn about exception handling in Chapter 6, "File Handling."

Let's write a program to calculate the volume of a sphere. The formula is `4/3*pi*r3`, where the value of radius r is known to be 3.

```
volsphere.py
from __future__ import division
r=3
pi=22/7
v=4/3*pi*pow(r,3)
print ("Volume of sphere is %.2f" %v)
Output:
Volume of sphere is 113.14
```

In this program, you can see that r3 is computed through `pow()`. The expression `pow(r,3)` can also be replaced by `r**3`, as both do the same task. Is there any way to get the value of pi instead of computing it manually as 22/7?

Yes, the math module, besides other important functions, also provides the value of pi to use directly in arithmetic expressions. You will learn about the math module in detail in Chapter 4, "Functions and Modules."

For now, let's see how the value of pi can be used through the math module. Rewrite the program above to use the pi value provided by the math module.

```
from __future__ import division
from math import pi
r=3
v=4/3*pi*pow(r,3)
print ("Volume of sphere is %.2f" %v)
```

The statement `from math import pi` imports the value of pi from the math module to be used directly in the arithmetic expression. The value represented will be `3.1415926535897931`.

Multiple Assignment Statement

The basic assignment statement can do more than assign the result of a single expression to a single variable. It can also assign multiple variables at one time. The rule is that the left and right sides must have the same number of elements, and the values will be assigned on a one-to-one basis.

```
Examples
p,q,r=10,20,30
sum, avg=p+q+r,(p+q+r)/3
```

The values on the right side of the assignment operator will be assigned on a one-to-one basis; for example, 10 will be assigned to the p variable, 20 will be assigned to the q variable, and so on. Similarly, in the second example, the result of the expression p+q+r will be assigned to the sum variable, and the result of the expression (p+q+r)/3 will be assigned to the variable avg.

Using Escape Sequences

Escape sequences are special characters that represent nonprinting characters such as tabs, newlines, and such. These special characters begin with a backslash. When Python sees a backslash, it interprets the next character with a special meaning. Table 2.2 shows a list of escape characters that can be used in Python scripts.

Table 2.2 Escape or Non-Printable Characters

Escape Character	Description
\a	Bell (beep)
\b	Backspace
\f	Form feed
\n	Newline
\r	Carriage return
\t	Tab
\v	Vertical tab
\\	Literal backslash
\'	Single quote
\"	Double quote

Note

In a double-quoted string, an escape character is interpreted; in a single-quoted string, an escape character is preserved.

The following program demonstrates using escape sequences in a program:

```
escapeseq.py
print('Hello World\nIt\'s hot today')
print('Festival Discount\b\b\b\b\b\b\b\b\b Offer')
print("Isn't it?")
print('Isn\'t it?')
print("He said: \"I am going \"")     -
print('\\Text enclosed in back slashes\\')
print ('Bell sound \a')
print('Name\tEmail Address\tContact Number')
```

Output is shown in Figure 2.1.

In the output you see that the text Hello World and It's hot today appear on two different lines because of the newline character between. The text Festival Discount appears as Festival Offerunt because after displaying the term Festival Discount when the cursor was standing after the character t of the word Discount, the cursor is shifted back nine characters where the D is. At the location of character D, the text Offer is displayed, overwriting the first five characters of the word Discount and leaving unt to appear after Offer. Displaying of the text Isn't it twice reveals that the single quote can be displayed either when enclosed within double quotes or when preceded by \ when enclosed within single quotes. Similarly, you use \ to display the text I am going enclosed within double quotes. Similarly, Text enclosed in back slashes appears with \ on either side because of \\. The \a escape character makes a bell sound, and \t makes Name, Email Address, and Contact Number appear at the tab stops.

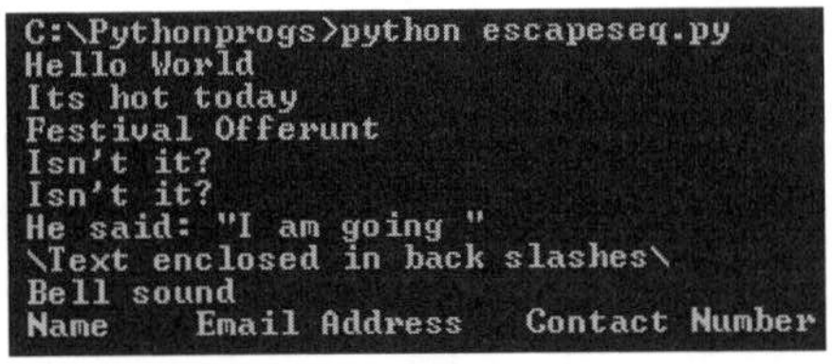

Figure 2.1
Output of escape sequence program.

Note

The IDLE (Python GUI) doesn't recognize a few escape sequence characters, including \a and \b. Therefore, when you run the preceding program in IDLE instead of the command prompt, no bell sound will appear and you will get the following output:

```
Hello World
It's hot today
Festival Discount•••••••• Offer
Isn't it?
Isn't it?
He said: "I am going "
\Text enclosed in back slashes\
Bell sound •
Name   Email Address   Contact Number
```

You can see that \b and \a appear as some unusual symbols.

Finding a Data Type

To find the data type of the specified object, you use the type() function, which returns the data type of the object passed to it.

```
Syntax:
type(x)
```

where x is the object whose data type will be returned. The function accepts all types of parameters, such as integers, strings, lists, dictionaries, tuples, functions, classes, and modules.

Examples:

```
type(10)
type('Hello')
```

The following program displays data types integers, floats, strings, Booleans, and so on.

```
typeexample.py
a=10
b=15.5
c="Hello"
d=[2,9,4]
e=('apple', 'mango', 'banana')
f=True
print (type(a))
print (type(b))
print (type(c))
print (type(d))
```

```
print (type(e))
print (type(f))
Output:
<class 'int'>
<class 'float'>
<class 'str'>
<class 'list'>
<class 'tuple'>
<class 'bool'>
```

This program initializes variables a, b, c, d, e, and f to data type integer, floating-point, string, list, tuple, and Boolean, respectively. Thereafter, the data type of these variables is determined and displayed using the type() function.

Displaying Octal and Hexa Values

To assign an octal value to a variable, the number should be preceded by 0o. Similarly, if a number is preceded by 0x, it is considered a hexa value. The following program demonstrates conversion of a decimal value into octal and hexa and vice versa.

```
octhex.py
a=0o25
b=0x1af
print ('Value of a in decimal is', a)
c=19
print ('19 in octal is %o and in hex is %x' %(c,c))
d=oct(c)
e=hex(c)
print ('19 in octal is', d, 'and in hexa is', e)
Output:
Value of a in decimal is 21
19 in octal is 23 and in hex is 13
19 in octal is 0o23 and in hexa is 0x13
```

In this program, variables a and b are assigned octal and hexa values, respectively. The octal value is converted and displayed as a decimal. Similarly, the decimal value 19 is converted to octal and hexa and displayed using the directives %o and %x, respectively. Also, by using the oct() and hex() functions, the number 19 is converted to octal and hexa, respectively.

Getting Data

To get input from the user, you use the input method. It prompts the user to enter data and reads one line from the standard input and returns it as a string that can be consequently assigned to a variable.

```
Syntax:
variable=input ('Message')
```

The data entered by the user is assigned to the variable in string format. If you want the data in another format (integer, float, etc.), it has to be converted explicitly. Before you see explicit conversion, let's talk about auto conversion (coercion) in Python.

Coercion

In Python, if you do some arithmetic operations on the operands of the same data type, no auto conversion or coercion takes place. When operands of different data types are computed, coercion takes place. Python converts the operand with the "smaller" type to the "larger" type. For example, if either of the operands is a floating number, then the other operand is also converted to float point. If either argument is a complex number, the other is also converted to complex. Similarly, if either is of type long, the other is converted to long. An integer operand is converted to float by adding .0 to it. A non-complex type is converted to a complex number by adding a zero imaginary component, 0j, to it.

For explicit conversion, the functions that you will be frequently using are int(), float(), and str(). The function that is needed for the next program is an int() function.

Converting Explicitly into integer Type

To convert the specified numerical or string into an integer data type, you use the int() function.

```
int()
```

The data to be converted into the integer is passed as an argument to the int() function.

```
Syntax:
int([x[, base]])
```

The specified x object is converted into integer format. The base parameter can be any value in the range 2 to 26 and refers to the base for the conversion. The default value of the base is 10. If the argument contains some fractional part, it is dropped. For example, int(7.5) will return 7.

The following program computes and displays the area of a rectangle. The area of a rectangle is the multiplication of length and width, and their values will be supplied by the user. The values supplied by the user will be through the input() function, which returns the supplied values in string format and hence will be converted into the integer data type using the `int()` function.

```
arearectinput.py
l=input("Enter length: ")
b=input("Enter width: ")
a=int(l)*int(b)
print ("Area of rectangle is",a)
Output:
Enter length: 9
Enter width: 5
Area of rectangle is 45
```

In this program, you can see that the user is asked to enter values for length and width through the `input()` method. The values entered by the user will be assigned to the variables l and b, respectively. As said earlier, the input method returns data in string format, hence the values in variables l and b are first converted from string to integer format through the `int()` function before they are used in any arithmetic operation.

The following program computes and returns the area of a circle. The formula is pi*r^2. The r in the formula refers to radius, and its value will be supplied by the user.

```
areacircleinput.py
from math import pi
r=int(input("Enter radius: "))
a=pi*r*r
print ("Area of the circle is", a)
print ("Area of the circle is %.2f" %a)
Output:
Enter radius: 5
Area of the circle is 78.53981633974483
Area of the circle is 78.54
```

BITWISE OPERATIONS

Every numerical that is entered in a computer is internally represented in the form of binary digits. For instance, the decimal value 25 is internally represented in the form of binary digits as 11001. The bitwise operators operate on these binary digits to give desired results.

Note

The shifting and bitwise operators can only be applied to integers and long integers.

Considering x and y as two operands, following are the shifting and bitwise operators:

- x << y (binary shift left): Returns x with the bits shifted to the left by y places. The digit is padded with 0s on the right side. This operation is the same as multiplying x by 2**y.

- x >> y (binary shift right): Returns x with the bits shifted to the right by y places. This operation is the same as dividing x by 2**y.

- x & y (bitwise AND): Corresponding bits of x and y are compared. It returns 1 if the corresponding bit of x AND y is 1; otherwise 0 is returned.

- x | y (bitwise AND): Corresponding bits of x and y are compared. It returns 0 if the corresponding bit of x and of y is 0; otherwise it returns 1. That is, if either x or y is 1, the operator returns 1.

- x ^ y (bitwise exclusive AND): Corresponding bits of x and y are compared. It returns 1 if either x or y is 1; otherwise it returns 0. That is, the operator returns 0 if the corresponding bits of x and y are the same.

- ~ x (bitwise inversion): It returns the complement of x; i.e., binary digit 1 is converted to 0, and 0 is converted to 1.

The following program demonstrates the application of AND, OR, EXCLUSIVE AND, and left and right shift operators.

```
bitwise.py
a=10
b=7
c=a&b
d=a ^ b
e= a | b
print ('The result of 10 and 7 operation is', c)
print ('The result of 10 exclusive or 7 operation is', d)
print ('The result of 10 or 7 operation is', e)
g=a<<2
print ('Left shifting - Multiplying 10 by 4 becomes:', g)
h=a>>1
print ('Right shifting - Dividing 10 by 2 becomes:',h)
Output:
The result of 10 and 7 operation is 2
The result of 10 exclusive or 7 operation is 13
The result of 10 or 7 operation is 15
Left shifting - Multiplying 10 by 4 becomes: 40
Right shifting - Dividing 10 by 2 becomes: 5
```

```
10 ⇨ 0 0 0 0 1 0 1 0          10 ⇨ 0 0 0 0 1 0 1 0          10 ⇨ 0 0 0 0 1 0 1 0
 7 ⇨ 0 0 0 0 0 1 1 1           7 ⇨ 0 0 0 0 0 1 1 1           7 ⇨ 0 0 0 0 0 1 1 1

10&7 ⇨ 0 0 0 0 0 0 1 0  (2)   10^b ⇨ 0 0 0 0 1 1 0 1  (13)   a|b ⇨ 0 0 0 0 1 1 1 1  (15)
         (a)                           (b)                           (c)
```

Figure 2.2
(a) Result of the AND operator. (b) Result of the EXCLUSIVE OR operator. (c) Result of the OR operator.

```
10    ⇨      0 0 0 0 1 0 1 0          10    ⇨  0 0 0 0 1 0 1 0

10<<2 ⇨      0 0 1 0 1 0 0 0  (40)    10>>1 ⇨  0 0 0 0 0 1 0 1  (5)
              (a)                              (b)
```

Figure 2.3
(a) Result of left-shifting the number by 2. (b) Result of right-shifting the number by 1.

The integers 10 and 7 and the result of application of the & (AND) operator on them are shown in Figure 2.2(a). The figure shows that the AND operator returns 1 if both the integers are 1; otherwise it returns 0. Figure 2.2(b) shows the result of applying the EXCLUSIVE OR operator on the two integers, 10 and 7. You can see that the EXCLUSIVE OR operator returns 1 if either of the two integers is 1. Figure 2.2(c) shows the result of applying the OR operator; it returns 1 if either or both of the integers are 1.

Figure 2.3(a) shows the result of left shifting the value 10 by 2. You can see that two 0s are added to the right in the number. On every left shift, the value of the number is multiplied by 2. That is, on left shifting the number by two, the number is multiplied by 4, giving the result as 40. Figure 2.3(b) shows the number 10 shifted one bit to the right. The right-most bit of the number is dropped, and a 0 is added to its left, dividing the number by 2 and giving the result as 5.

COMPLEX NUMBERS

A complex number is the combination of a real and an imaginary component, where both are represented by floating-point data type. The imaginary component of the complex number is a multiple of the square root of minus one and is denoted by j.

Example:
3+1.2j

In this example, 3 is a real component, and 1.2 is the imaginary component and is equal to $1.2 \times \sqrt{-1}$.

The real and imaginary components of a complex object can be accessed by using its real and imag attributes.

The following program shows the addition of two complex numbers:

```
complex.py
a = 3.0 + 1.2j
b= -2.0 - 9.0j
print ('The two complex numbers are', a, 'and', b)
c=a+b
print ('The addition of two complex numbers is:', c)
print ('The addition of two real numbers is:', a.real+b.real)
print ('The addition of two imaginary number is:', a.imag+b.imag)
Output:
The two complex numbers are (3+1.2j) and (-2-9j)
The addition of two complex numbers is: (1-7.8j)
The addition of two real numbers is: 1.0
The addition of two imaginary number is: -7.8
```

This program defines two complex numbers, a and b. The real and imaginary components of the complex number a are 3.0 and 1.2, respectively. Similarly, the real and imaginary components of the complex number b are -2.0 and -9.0, respectively. While adding the complex numbers, the respective real and imaginary components of the two complex numbers are added, as shown in Figure 2.4. The program also accesses the real and imaginary components of the two complex numbers by adding their real and imag attributes.

Note

The complex numbers are displayed enclosed in parentheses ( ).

When writing programs, you come across a situation where you want to execute a block statement out of the two blocks. That is, you need to control flow of the program and execute a block statement out of available choices, depending on the prevalent conditions. Let's see how to make decisions in Python.

MAKING DECISIONS

The statement that helps in making decisions and controlling flow of the program is the if...else statement.

```
  3.0 +  1.2 j
- 2.0 -  9.0 j
─────────────
  1.0 -  7.8 j
```

Figure 2.4
Addition of two complex numbers.

if...else statement

The if...else statement decides which block of statements to execute on the basis of the logical expression included. A block of statements is attached with if as well as with else, and when the logical expression is evaluated, either the if or the else block statement is executed.

Syntax:

```
if (logical expression):
statement(s)
else:
statement(s)
```

If the logical expression evaluates to true, then the if statement is executed; otherwise, the else statement is executed.

Note
_____

The else statement is optional.
_____

Let's write a program that asks the user to enter a student's grades. If the grades are greater than or equal to 60, the program should display a message, First Division. If not, it should display the message Second Division.

```
ifelse1.py
m=int(input("Enter grades: "))
if(m >=60):
        print ("First Division")
else:
        print ("Second Division")
Output:
Enter grades: 75
First Division

Enter grades: 50
Second Division
```

You can see in this program that the user enters grades through an input() method. Since the value entered by input() is in string format, it is converted to an integer and assigned to the variable m. Using an if...else statement, you check the value in variable m. If the value in variable m is greater than or equal to 60, the if block will be executed, displaying the message First Division. If the value entered is less than 60, the else block will be executed, displaying the text Second Division. The output of the program confirms this.

Table 2.3 Comparison Operators

Operator	Meaning
<	Less than
>	Greater than
<=	Less than or equal to
>=	Greater than or equal to
==	Equal to
!=	Not equal to

In this program, greater than or equal to (>=) compares the value of the variable m with 60. Table 2.3 lists the comparison operators.

In the next program, again you ask the user to enter a student's grades. If the grades entered are greater than or equal to 60, a message First Division will be displayed. If the grades entered are greater than or equal to 45 but less than 60, the message Second Division will be displayed. If the grades entered are less than 45, Third Division will be displayed. For such programs, you nest an if...else block within the else block of the outer if...else statement. Let's see how this nesting is done in the following program:

```
ifelse2.py
m=int(input("Enter grades: "))
if(m >=60):
      print ("First Division")
else:
      if(m >=45):
            print ("Second Division")
      else:
            print ("Third Division")
Output:
Enter grades: 75
First Division

Enter grades: 50
Second Division

Enter grades: 40
Third Division
```

You can see in this program that an if...else statement is written within an else statement of the outer if...else statement. The if...else statement within the else statement will be executed if the logical expression included in the outer if statement evaluates to False. That is, if the user enters a value less than 60, the inner if...else statement will be executed to check if the entered value is greater than 45, and the appropriate message will be displayed.

if-elif-else statement

If you have multiple logical expressions to evaluate, and on the basis of those logical expressions you want to execute a specific set of code block, you need to use an if-elif-else statement.

```
Syntax:
if (logical expression):
   statement(s)
elif (logical expression 1):
   statement(s)
[elif (logical expression n):
   statement(s)]
else:
   statement(s)
```

You can see that the else statement and the if statement nested in it are merged to form an elif statement. An elif statement is helpful in avoiding excessive indentation. The program ifelse2.py that you wrote earlier can be rewritten with an if-elif-else statement as shown here:

```
ifelif.py
m=int(input("Enter grades: "))
if(m >=60):
      print ("First Division")
elif (m >=45):
      print ("Second Division")
else:
      print ("Third Division")
```

What if you need to combine more than one logical expression? You use logical operators for connecting logical expressions. Let's have a quick look at logical operators.

LOGICAL OPERATORS

In writing logical expressions, you sometimes need to combine two or more logical expressions. The logical expressions are usually combined with the logical operators

Table 2.4 Logical Operators

Logical Operator	Description
AND	The logical expression connected with the AND logical operator returns true if all the logical expressions evaluate to true.
or	The logical expression connected with the or logical operator returns true if any of the logical expressions evaluates to true.
not	The logical expression preceded by the not logical operator is negated. That is, the logical expression that evaluates to true becomes false when preceded by the logical not operator and vice versa.

AND, or, and not. The list of logical operators with a brief description is shown in Table 2.4.

Consider the logical expressions x and y connected with the logical AND operator as shown below:

```
x and y
```

On combining the logical expressions by the logical AND operator, first the logical expression x is evaluated, and if it returns false, the result of the combination will be x; otherwise, the result will be y.

Similarly, on combining the logical expressions x and y by the logical or operator, first the logical expression x is evaluated, and if it results in true, the result of the combination will be x; otherwise, the result will be y.

The program ifelse2.py that you wrote earlier can be rewritten by combining the logical expressions with logical operators:

```
ifelse3.py
m=int(input("Enter grades: "))
if(m >=60):
     print ("First Division")
if(m >=45 and m<60):
     print ("Second Division")
if (m<45):
     print ("Third Division")
```

You see that if the grade entered is greater than 60, the first if block will be executed, displaying the message First Division. If the grade entered is greater than

45 and less than 60, both logical expressions, m>=45 and m<60, are true, and the message in the second if block, Second Division, will be displayed. If the grade entered is less than 45, the third if block will be executed, displaying the message Third Division.

CHAINING COMPARISON OPERATORS

Consider the following comparison operators, which are connected with the AND operator:

x<=y and y<=z

These comparison operators can be chained as:

x<=y <=z

As expected, if the logical expression x<=y is true, then only the logical expression y<=z will be evaluated.

For example, the statement used in the program above, m>=45 and m<60, can be chained to appear as 45 <=m <60.

Let's rewrite the program by chaining comparison operators.

ifelschaining.py

```
m=int(input("Enter grades: "))
if(m >=60):
        print ("First Division")
if(45<= m <60):
        print ("Second Division")
if(m<45):
        print ("Third Division")
```

If the grade entered is greater than or equal to 45, the next part of the chained operators is evaluated to see if the value entered is less than 60.

The following program asks the user to enter a value between 1 and 10 and prints a message based on the value entered:

```
opr1.py
m=int(input("Enter a number between 1 and 10: "))
if 1<= m <=10:
        print ("Number is within range")
else:
        print ("Number is out of range")
Output:
Enter a number between 1 and 10: 3
```

```
Number is within range
```

```
Enter a number between 1 and 10: 15
Number is out of range
```

You can see that the program prints the message Number is within range if the entered value is between 1 and 10; otherwise it prints the message Number is out of range.

The following program determines if the value entered is even or odd. The program uses the modulo operator, %. Remember that the modulo operator returns the remainder of the division.

```
evenodd.py
m=int(input("Enter a number "))
n = m%2
if n ==0:
      print ("Number is even")
else:
      print ("Number is odd")
Output:
Enter a number 6
Number is even

Enter a number 9
Number is odd
```

In this program, the user is asked to enter a number that is assigned to variable m. Variable m is divided by 2, and if the remainder is 0, meaning the number is a multiple of 2, a message Number is even is displayed. Similarly, if the remainder of the division operation is not 0, the number is not a multiple of 2, and Number is odd is displayed.

Note

> Python provides a divmod function, which takes two numeric arguments and returns the quotient and the remainder, so you don't have to use both // for the quotient and % for the remainder.

When writing programs, sometimes you want to execute some statements several times. For such situations, you use loops. Let's see how to use loops in Python.

Loops

Loops are used to execute a set of statements while a logical expression is true. You will learn two loops in this section: the while loop and the for loop.

The while Loop

A while loop is repeatedly executes a block of code as long as a specified logical expression remains true. The logical expression in a while loop is evaluated first, and if it evaluates to false, the body of the while loop will not execute. If the logical expression evaluates to true, the block of code in the while loop is executed. After executing the body, control jumps back to the beginning of the loop to confirm if the logical expression is still true. The loop will continue to execute until the logical expression evaluates to false, in which case the execution of the program continues from the statement following the while loop.

```
Syntax:
while expression :
      statement1
      statement2
      statement3
```

Here you see that the block of code in the while loop is indented. Why is that?

Indentation

Python uses indentation to express the block structure of a program. Unlike other languages, Python does not use braces or begin/end delimiters to denote blocks. Instead it uses indentation to represent blocks of statements.

A block is a contiguous sequence of logical lines, all indented by the same amount, and a logical line with less indentation ends the block. The first statement in a block must have no indentation—it must not begin with any white space. You can use tabs or spaces to indent statements. Python replaces each tab with up to eight spaces.

Note

Don't mix spaces and tabs for indentation, as tabs may be treated differently by different editors.

The following program displays numbers from 1 to 10 using the while loop:

```
whileloop.py
k=1
while k <=10 :
      print (k)
      k=k+1
Output:
1
2
3
```

```
4
5
6
7
8
9
10
```

You can see that the while loop is set to execute as long as the value in variable k is less than or equal to 10. In the loop, you print the value of variable k and increment its value by 1 to print the next successive value.

You also see that the while loop terminates when the logical expression evaluates to false. Is there any other way to terminate a loop? Also, what if you want to skip the loop on occurrence of some condition? The following section explains how to terminate and skip a loop.

Breaking and Continuing a Loop

There are two situations when a loop terminates and you exit from a loop: when the logical expression evaluates to false, and on occurrence of a break statement in the loop.

The break Statement   The break statement terminates and exits from the current loop and resumes execution of the program from the statement following the loop. It is typically used in an infinite loop.

```
Syntax:
break
```

The following program demonstrates using a break statement to terminate an infinite while loop to print 10 numbers:

```
breakex1.py
k=1
while 1 :
      print (k)
      k=k+1
      if(k>10):
            break
Output:
1
2
3
4
5
```

```
6
7
8
9
10
```

You initialize the variable k to value 1. Also, you set a while loop to run infinitely. In the loop, you display variable k and then increment its value by 1. When k becomes more than 10, you exit from the infinite loop through the break statement.

Remember that value 1 represents the Boolean value true. You can also replace while 1 by while true to create an infinite loop.

Now let's look at the statement that tells Python to skip the part of the current loop and begin with the next iteration.

The continue Statement   The continue statement stops execution of the current iteration by skipping the rest of the loop and continuing to execute the loop with the next iterative value.

```
Syntax:
continue
```

The following program prints numbers from 1 to 10 except for the value 7:

```
continueex.py
k=1
while k <=10 :
        if k==7:
                k+=1
                continue
        print (k)
        k=k+1
Output:
1
2
3
4
5
6
8
9
10
```

First, initialize variable k to 1. Then, set the while loop to execute as long as k is less than or equal to 10. In the while loop, print the value of k and then increment its value by 1. Also, skip the body of the loop through a `continue` statement when the value of k is 7. That is, you don't print k but just increment its value by 1 to execute the loop with the next value in sequence.

The pass Statement   The `pass` statement is used in Python to indicate an empty block of statements. It is also used as a placeholder for code that you want to write later and acts as a reminder of where a program can be expanded.

You can rewrite the previous program to display the numbers from 1 to 10 except for 7 by using the `pass` statement as shown here:

```
passex1.py
k=1
while k <=10 :
        if k==7:
                pass
        else:
                print (k)
        k+=1
```

Output:

```
1
2
3
4
5
6
8
9
10
```

You can see that value of k is initialized to 1. The `while` loop will execute until k becomes larger than 10. In the `while` loop, the value of k is displayed and its value incremented by 1. When the value of k is equal to 7, the `pass` statement is executed; k is not displayed and is incremented by 1 to execute the loop with the next value in sequence.

The range() Function   The `range()` function generates and returns a sequence of integers and is very commonly used in looping statements. There are three variations of the `range()` function, depending on the number of parameters passed to it:

- **range(x):** Returns a list whose items are consecutive integers from 0 (included) to x (excluded).

- **range(x, y)**: Returns a list whose items are consecutive integers from x (included) to y (excluded). The result is an empty list if x is greater than or equal to y.

- **range(x, y, step)**: Returns a list of integers from x (included) to y (excluded), and the difference between each successive value is the value defined by step. If step is less than 0, range counts down from x to y. The function returns an empty list when x is greater than or equal to y and step is greater than 0, or when x is less than or equal to y and step is less than 0. If 0 is specified as the step value, the range() function raises an exception. When step is not specified, its default value is 1.

The for Loop

The for loop iterates through a sequence of objects. A sequence is a container object that may be in the form of a list, tuple or string.

Note

Containers in Python means sets, sequences such as lists, tuples, and strings, and mappings such as dictionaries. You will learn about these containers in detail in Chapter 3, "Sequences."

```
Syntax:
for iterating_var in sequence:
      statement1
      statement2
      statement3
```

The first item in the sequence is assigned to the iterating variable iterating_var, and the statement block is executed. One by one, each item in the sequence is assigned to iterating_var, and the statement block is executed until the entire sequence is finished.

The following program displays numbers from 1 to 10:

```
forloop.py
for i in range(1,11):
      print (i)
```

This prints a sequence of numbers, which are generated from 1 to 10 using the built-in range() function. Since the value for step is not indicated, the default value of 1 is the step value.

The following program displays the odd numbers between 1 and 10. The two successive odd values differ by 2, so you use the step value of 2 in the range() function.

```
forloop2.py
print ("Odd numbers between 1 and 10 are:")
for i in range(1,11,2):
      print (i)
Output:
Odd numbers between 1 and 10 are:
1
3
5
7
9
```

The range(1,11,2) function will first generate a value 1. To this value, the step value 2 is added to generate the next value in the list, 3. The process will continue until the generated value is less than or equal to 10.

A for loop can be used to print random values from a tuple. We will discuss tuples in detail in the next chapter. For now it is sufficient to know that a tuple is an immutable object that can be used to represent a set of values of any data type. The values or elements of a tuple are enclosed in parentheses, ( ). An immutable object is one that cannot be changed once it is created. You will be using membership operators to display elements from the tuple.

Membership Operators

A membership operator tests for membership in a sequence, such as strings, lists, or tuples. There are two membership operators, as shown in Table 2.5.

Here are some examples:

- ab in abcde—Returns true because the string ab is found in the string abcde.

- 2 in (10,3,5,2,1)—Returns true because the value 2 exists in the tuple.

- bob not in ab—Returns true because the string bob is not found in the string ab.

Table 2.5 Membership Operators

Operator	Description
in	Returns Boolean value true if it finds the specified variable in the given sequence; otherwise it returns false.
not in	Returns Boolean value true if it does not find the specified variable in the given sequence; otherwise it returns false.

The following program displays the random values included in a tuple using the membership operator `in` through a `for` loop:

```
for i in ( 7, 3, 8, 1, 4 ):
    print i
```

Here you provide a tuple of values in the `for` loop. The first value from the tuple will be assigned to the variable `i`, and the loop will be executed. Then the next value in the tuple will be assigned to `i` and the loop executed. The loop will be executed with each value in the tuple. In the body of the loop you display just the value assigned to `i`, displaying all the values in the tuple one by one.

The following program displays a random value between 1 and 9. To get random values, you will use a `choice()` function.

The choice() Function

The `choice()` function picks and returns a random item from a sequence. It can be used with lists, tuples, or strings.

```
Syntax:
choice(sequence)
```

where `sequence` can be a list, tuple, or string.

Note

> To use the `choice()` function in a program, you need to import a random module.

```
Example:
k=choice([2,4,6,8,10])
```

You will get a random value picked from the specified sequence, which may be 2, 6, or some other value from the list.

```
randomnumber.py
from random import choice
k=choice(range(1,10))
print ("Random number is",k)
Output:
Random number is 4
Random number is 1
```

In this program, the `range()` function will return values between 1 and 9. The `choice()` function will pick up any value at random from these nine values and assign it to the variable k, which is then displayed on the screen. Every time you execute the program, the choice() function returns a random value.

The following prints the prime numbers between 1 and 100.

```
primes.py
print (1)
for i in range(2,101):
        x=1
        for j in range(2, i):
                n=i%j
                if n==0:
                        x=0
                        break
        if x==1:
                print (i)
Output:
1
2
3
5
7
11
13
17
19
23
29
31
37
41
43
47
53
59
61
67
71
73
79
83
89
97
```

This program displays value 1, knowing it is a prime number. Then it uses a `for` loop to generate values from 2 to 100, and each value is assigned to variable `i`. The value in variable `i` is divided by 2 through `i-1` values. If it divides by any of these values, it is not a prime number and is not displayed. The value in variable `i` is displayed when it does not divide by any value between 2 and `i-1`.

SUMMARY

In this chapter you learned to apply arithmetic operations and different logical and membership operators in Python programs. You also saw the use of escape sequences. To enhance interaction with the user, you learned to get data from the user and process the incoming data. You saw conversion of data into different types. You also learned to display octal and hexa values, perform bitwise operations and use complex numbers. You also saw usage of `if...else` statement in making decisions. Finally you saw using `while` and `for` loops for doing repetitive tasks.

In the next chapter, you are going to learn about containers: sequences, mappings, and sets. A sequence includes strings, lists, and tuples, and mappings include dictionaries. You will also learn to perform operations on sequences through their respective methods. Also, you will learn about one- and two-dimensional arrays. Finally, you will learn to apply operations to sets such as unions, intersections, and differences.

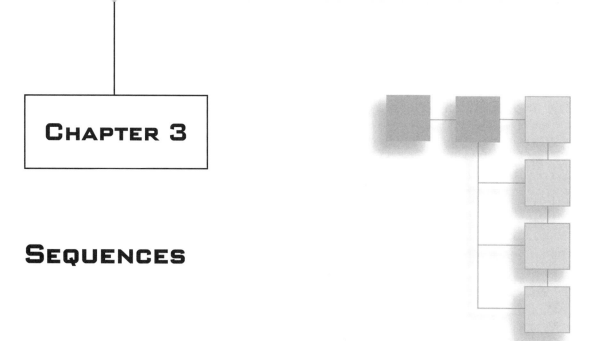

CHAPTER 3

SEQUENCES

This chapter covers the following:

- How data is stored in a string
- Creating and displaying one- and two-dimensional arrays
- List slicing and its methods
- Creating tuples and searching for elements
- Key/value pairs and their methods
- Union, intersection, and difference operators

SEQUENCES

A sequence contains objects that are kept in a specific order. You can identify an object in a sequence by its index location. Also, you can extract from a sequence with the slicing operation. In this chapter you will look at three examples of sequences: lists, tuples, and strings.

- Strings use quotes, such as `'Hello'`, `"Hello"`, `'"Hello"'`, `"""Hello"""`.
- Lists use square brackets, such as `[Tiger, Coffee, 1,'a', 10.50, 'b']`.
- Tuples use parentheses, such as `(Tiger, Coffee, 1,'a',10.50, 'b')`.

Tuples and strings are immutable—they cannot be modified after they are created. A copy of a string or a tuple is created when you apply an operation to the original string or tuple. A list is mutable; you can append elements, remove existing elements, or rearrange elements. All modifications in a list are made without creating a new list object.

The three operations that are commonly applied to sequences are these:

+ will concatenate sequences to make longer sequences.

* is used with a numerical digit to repeat the sequence several times.

[ ] fetches a particular element from the sequence (indexing) or a subset of elements from the sequence (slicing).

Note

Positions are numbered from zero in sequences; that is, the first element in a sequence is at index value 0.

STRINGS

A string is a sequence of characters used to store and represent text information. A string literal can be enclosed in single ('), double (") or triple quotes ('''). Strings are immutable in Python; you cannot modify an existing string object. When you perform an operation on a string object, you create a new string object.

Examples of strings in single, double, and triple quotes are as follows:

```
k='Hello World!'
k="Hello World!"
k='''
Hello World!
It\'s hot today
Let\'s party'''
```

To make the string appear on two lines, you can embed a newline in the string:

```
k="Hello World!\nIt's hot"
```

If the string literal spans multiple lines, use a backslash as the last character of a line to indicate that the next line is a continuation:

```
k="Hello World!\
It's hot"
```

To display a single quote in a string, you need to use the escape character:

```
k='Isn\'t it?'
```

There is no need to use an escape character to display a single quote within a double-quoted string.

```
k="Isn't it?"
```

A triple-quoted string may be enclosed in matching triplets of quote characters (''' or """). The string literal above can also be written as:

```
k="""
Hello World!
It's hot today
Let's party"""
```

In a triple-quoted string literal, line breaks in the literal are preserved as newline characters. You cannot use a backslash in a triple-quoted string.

Note

> Unlike other programming languages, there is no separate character data type in Python. A character is considered a string of length one.

How Characters Are Stored in a String

When text is assigned to a string, each of its characters is stored at a specific index location. For example, the statement k="David" will assign the text David to the variable k. Internally, the characters will be stored in variable k, as shown in Figure 3.1.

Where 0,1... are the index. A string is terminated by a NULL character, \0. You can access any character of the string through its index. For example, k[0] accesses the first character, D, k[1] accesses the second character, a, and so on.

Python strings support several methods and functions. What is the difference between functions and methods?

Differences Between Functions and Methods

A function is a module of code that is called by name. You can pass data to the function in the form of arguments, and it can return some value. The data to be passed to the function needs to be passed explicitly. A method also is called by name and may return a value. The main difference between a method and a function is that a method is associated with an object, and the object for which it is called is implicitly passed to it. Also, a method is able to operate on data that is contained within the class. The list of methods and functions is given in Table 3.1.

D	a	v	i	d	\0
k[0]	k[1]	k[2]	k[3]	k[4]	k[5]

Figure 3.1
Characters stored in a string.

Table 3.1   String Methods and Functions

Method/Function	Description
str()	Returns a string representation of the object. If the argument is a string, the returned value is the same object.
max()	Returns the maximum alphabetical character in the string.
min()	Returns the minimum alphabetical character in the string.
len()	Counts and returns the number of characters in the sequence (string, tuple, or list) or in the mapping (dictionary).
sorted()	Returns the string's characters in sorted order. After it is expanded into a list of individual characters, the string is sorted and returned.
reversed()	Returns the string's characters in reverse order.
capitalize()	Returns the string with its first character in uppercase.
lower()	Returns the string converted to lowercase.
upper()	Returns the string converted to uppercase.
swapcase()	Returns the string with uppercase characters converted to lowercase and vice versa.
title()	Returns the string with first character of each word converted to uppercase characters and the rest all characters in lowercase.
join(sequence)	Returns a string that is the concatenation of the strings in the sequence.
ljust(width)	Returns the string left-justified in a string of length width. The string is padded using spaces.
rjust(width)	Returns the string right-justified in a string of length width. The string is padded using spaces.
center(width)	Returns the string centered in a string of length width. The string is padded with spaces.
lstrip()	Returns the string with leading white space removed.
rstrip()	Returns the string with trailing white space removed.
strip()	Returns the string with leading and trailing white space removed.
isalnum()	Returns true if all characters in the string are alphanumeric, otherwise returns false.
isalpha()	Returns true if all characters in the string are alphabetic, otherwise returns false.

Method/Function	Description
isdigit()	Returns true if all characters in the string are digits, otherwise returns false.
islower()	Returns true if all characters in the string are lowercase, otherwise returns false.
istitle()	Returns true if the string is title cased (the first character of each word is in uppercase and the rest all in lower case). The function returns false otherwise.
isupper()	Returns true if all characters in the string are in uppercase, otherwise returns false.

Finding the Length of a String   To find the number of characters in a string, use the len() function. As indicated in Table 3.1, the len() function counts and returns the number of characters in a sequence (string, tuple, or list). The program for doing so is shown here:

```
string1.py
n=input("Enter your name: ")
l=len(n)
print ("The name entered is", n, "and its length is", l)
Output:
Enter your name: John
The name entered is John and its length is 4
```

In this program, you ask the user to enter a string that is temporarily stored in a variable n. Then, through the len() function, you find out the length of the string and display it.

The following program checks if the entered value is numeric or non-numeric:

```
ifelse4.py
m=input("Enter marks: ")
if m.isdigit():
   print ("Entered data is numeric")
else:
   print ("Entered data is not numeric")
Output:
Enter marks: 50
Entered data is numeric

Enter marks: fifty
Entered data is not numeric
```

The program uses the isdigit() method to know if the entered value is a numeric value or not. The isdigit() method returns the Boolean value true if the referenced object is numerical; otherwise it returns false.

The following program demonstrates the use of the upper(), lower(), title(), capitalize(), and swapcase() methods. A string, Hello World!, is converted to uppercase, lowercase, capitalized, and swapcase (the uppercase letters are switched to lowercase and vice versa).

```
string2.py
s="Hello World!"
print ("Original String is", s)
print('String after toggling the case:', s.swapcase())
print ("String in uppercase is", s.upper())
if (s.istitle()):
   print("String in lowercase is", s.lower())
print("String,", s, "is in title case:", s.istitle())
print ("String in capitalized form is", s.capitalize())
Output:
Original String is Hello World!
String after toggling the case: hELLO wORLD!
String in uppercase is HELLO WORLD!
String in lowercase is hello world!
String, Hello World! is in title case: true
String in capitalized form is Hello world!
```

The following program displays the first character of the entered string. Also, the entered string is displayed characterwise—each character is displayed one by one.

```
characterwise.py
s=input("Enter a string: ")
n=len(s)
print ("The first character of", s, "is", s[0])
print ("The entered string will appear character wise as:")
for i in range(0,n):
   print (s[i])
print ("The entered string will appear character wise as:")
for i in s:
   print (i)
print ("String with its characters sorted is", sorted(s))
print ("String in reverse form is", "".join(reversed(s)))
Output:
Enter a string: katherine
The first character of katherine is k
The entered string will appear character wise as:
```

k
a
t
h
e
r
i
n
e
The entered string will appear character wise as:
k
a
t
h
e
r
i
n
e
String with its characters sorted is ['a', 'e', 'e', 'h', 'i', 'k', 'n', 'r', 't']
String in reverse form is enirehtak

Knowing that a string's index is zero-based, you display the first character of the string by accessing its 0th index location. The program also finds the length of the entered string and prints each of its characters through its index. Also, the program uses the membership operator in to access and display each character of the string. The program displays the characters of the string after sorting them alphabetically. Finally, the string is reversed and displayed using the reversed() function.

The following program displays the maximum and minimum alphabetical character in an entered string. Also, the program converts an entered number into string data type, counts the number of digits, and displays its first digit by applying string functions to it.

```
string3.py
s=input('Enter a string: ')
print ('The string entered is:', s)
print('The maximum alphabetical character from the string is:', max(s))
print('The minimum alphabetical character from the string is:', min(s))
n=int(input('Enter a number: '))
m=str(n)
print('The number in string form is', m, 'its length is', len(m), 'and its first digit
is', m[0])
Output:
```

```
Enter a string: enormous
The string entered is: enormous
The maximum alphabetical character from the string is: u
The minimum alphabetical character from the string is: e
Enter a number: 53
The number in string form is 53 its length is 2 and its first digit is 5
```

The program asks the user to enter a string and displays its maximum and minimum alphabetical characters. The maximum and minimum characters are those that have the highest and lowest ASCII values, respectively. Also, the program demonstrates how a numerical value is converted intro string type using the str() function. Once the number is converted into string type, you can apply a string function such as len() to count the number of digits in it. You also see the first digit of the number is accessed by accessing the content at index location 0.

The following program demonstrates string concatenation, the application of the * operator to repeat a string several times and join the strings:

```
stringconcat1.py
s="Hello World!"
t="Nice Day"
print (s+t)
print (s+" "+t)
print (s*3)
u="#"
print('The string after joining character # to the string', t,':', u.join(t))
u="hello"
print('The string after joining word, hello to the string',t,':', u.join(t))

Output:
Hello World!Nice Day
Hello World! Nice Day
Hello World!Hello World!Hello World!
The string after joining character # to the string Nice Day : N#i#c#e# #D#a#y
The string after joining word, hello to the string Nice Day : Nhelloihellochelloehello
helloDhelloahelloy
```

In this program, the two strings Hello World! and Nice Day are concatenated without a space and with a space. Then, the string Hello World! is displayed three times using the * operator. The join() method is used to demonstrate joining a character to all the characters of the specified string. Also, a complete string is joined to each character of the given string.

The following program asks the user to enter two strings and then joins a string to each of the characters of another string:

```
stringjoin.py
p=input("Enter a string: ")
q=input("Enter another string: ")
print ("The first string is:", p)
print ("The second string is:", q)
print ("The combination is", p.join(q))
Output:
Enter a string: Hello
Enter another string: ABC
The first string is: Hello
The second string is: ABC
The combination is AHelloBHelloC
```

You can see that the two strings entered are Hello and ABC. The string Hello is joined to each character of the string ABC.

Do strings in Python support methods that help in searching or finding a substring in a string? Yes. Table 3.2 displays the string methods that help in finding substrings in a string.

The following program demonstrates the use of different functions to count the number of vowels in a sentence:

```
countvowel.py
s=input('Enter a sentence: ')
n=len(s)
c=0
```

Table 3.2 String Methods Used to Find Substrings in a String

Method	Description
count(s, [start], [end])	Returns the number of occurrences of substring s in a string. If start or end is specified, the substring s is searched and counted within the index range.
find(s, [start], [end])	Returns the lowest index in a string where substring s is found. The function returns -1 if the substring is not found.
index(s, [start], [end])	Returns the lowest index in a string where substring s is found. The function raises ValueError if the substring is not found.
rfind(s, [start], [end])	Returns the highest index in a string where substring s is found. It returns -1 if the substring is not found.

```
for i in range(0,n):
    if(s[i]=='a' or s[i]=='A' or s[i]=='e' or s[i]=='E' or s[i]=='i' or s[i]=='I' or s[i]
    =='o' or s[i]=='O' or s[i]=='u' or s[i]=='U'):
        c+=1
print ('The number of vowels in the sentence is', c)
t=s.count('a', 0, n)+ s.count('A', 0, n)+ s.count('e', 0, n)+s.count('E', 0, n)+
s.count('i', 0, n)+ s.count('I', 0, n)+ s.count('o', 0, n)+ s.count('O', 0, n)+
s.count('u', 0, n)+s.count('U', 0, n)

print ('The number of vowels in the sentence is', t)

v=s.count('a')+      s.count('A')+      s.count('e')+s.count('E')+      s.count('i')+
s.count('I')+ s.count('o')+ s.count('O')+ s.count('u')+s.count('U')
print ('The number of vowels in the sentence is', v)
Output:
Enter a sentence: amazing day in alaska
The number of vowels in the sentence is 8
The number of vowels in the sentence is 8
The number of vowels in the sentence is 8
```

In this program, the user is asked to enter a sentence. Using the index, every character of the sentence is accessed to see if it is a vowel. A variable c that is initialized to 0 is incremented by 1 every time a vowel is found in the sentence. The program also displays the two ways of using the count() function for counting vowels in the sentence.

The following program uses membership operators to see if an entered substring is in a string:

```
checkstr.py
m=input("Enter a string: ")
n=input("Enter a substring: ")
if n in m:
    print (n, "is found in the string", m)
else:
    print (n,"does not exist in the string", m)
Output:
Enter a string: education
Enter a substring: cat
cat is found in the string education

Enter a string: education
Enter a substring: cari
cari does not exist in the string education
```

The following program is one step ahead of the previous program. It not only informs if a substring is found in a string or not but also displays where the substring appears in the given string if it is found. The program uses the find() method.

```
searchstr1.py
p=input("Enter a string: ")
print ("Entered String is ", p)
q=input("Enter the substring to search: ")
r=p.find(q)
if r==-1:
    print (q, "not found in", p)
else:
    print (q, "found in", p, "at location", r+1)
Output:
Enter a string: katherine
Entered String is katherine
Enter the substring to search: her
her found in katherine at location 4
```

Here you ask the user to enter a main string and a substring and assign them to the variables p and q, respectively. Then, the find() method is used to search the substring q in the string p. The find() method returns either the value -1 if the substring is not found in the string or the lowest index location where the substring occurs in the string. On the basis of the value returned by the find() method, either a message saying the substring is not found in the string or the location of the occurrence of the substring in the string is displayed.

You can use the find() method for finding the occurrence of the substring in the given string, but you cannot use it for counting the occurrences of the substring in the string. For this, you use the count() method, as demonstrated in the following program:

```
searchstr2.py
p=input("Enter a string: ")
print ("Entered String is", p)
q=input("Enter the substring to search: ")
r=p.count(q)
if r==0:
    print (q, "not found in", p)
else:
    print (q, "occurs in", p, r, "times")
Output:
Enter a string: alabalabalab
Entered String is alabalabalab
Enter the substring to search: la
la occurs in alabalabalab 3 times
```

This program accepts a string and a substring from the user and uses the count() method to count the occurrences of the substring in the given string. The count is then displayed.

Are there any string methods to see if a string begins or ends with a given prefix or suffix? Yes, and they are these:

startswith(s, [start], [end])—Returns true if the string starts with the specified prefix, otherwise returns false. The prefix can be a single string or a sequence of individual strings.

endswith(suffix, [start], [end])—Returns true if the string ends with the specified suffix; otherwise false is returned. The suffix can be a single string or a sequence of individual strings.

The following program asks the user to enter a sentence and then checks to see if it begins or ends with the given prefix or suffix.

```
stringfunc2.py
s=input("Enter a sentence: ")
print ('The original sentence is:', s)
if s.startswith('It'):
   print('The entered sentence begins with the word It')
if s.startswith('It', 0, 2):
   print('The entered sentence begins with the word It')
if s.endswith('today'):
   print('The entered sentence ends with the word today')
if s.endswith('today', 10, 15):
   print('The entered sentence ends with the word today')
```

```
Output:
Enter a sentence: It is hot today
The original sentence is: It is hot today
The entered sentence begins with the word It
The entered sentence begins with the word It
The entered sentence ends with the word today
The entered sentence ends with the word today
```

In this program, the sentence entered by the user is checked to see if it begins with the prefix It or ends with the suffix today; then the appropriate message is displayed. The program demonstrates the use of the startswith() and endswith() methods.

You might need to split a string into parts. Or you might need to replace certain specific characters or a substring in a string with other data. Python provides string methods for this. Table 3.3 displays the string methods for breaking a string and replacing substrings.

Table 3.3   Methods for Breaking a String and Replacing Substrings

Method	Description
partition(separator)	Partitions and returns the string in three parts: the text prior to the first occurrence of separator in the string, the separator, and the text after the first occurrence of the separator. If the separator doesn't occur, the complete string is returned as the first part, and the other parts are returned as empty strings.
split(separator, [n])	Splits the string on the basis of the specified separator and returns an array of strings. The string is split wherever the separator occurs in the string. If the optional value n is specified, the string will be split into at most n parts. If separator is not specified, white space is considered a default separator. The white space includes the escape characters \n (carriage return) and \t (tab character).
splitlines(boolean)	Splits the string on line boundaries and returns the list of lines. The line breaks are not included in the resulting list unless boolean value true is specified in the function.
expandtabs([tabsize])	Returns the string with all tabs expanded using spaces. If tabsize is not given, a tab size of 8 characters is assumed.
replace(s1, s2, n)	Returns the string with all occurrences of substring s1 replaced by s2. If the optional argument n is specified, only the first n occurrences are replaced.

The following program breaks the sentence entered into words and returns:

```
splitting.py
p=input("Enter a sentence: ")
print ("The sentence entered is:", p)
print ("The words in the sentence are")
print (p.split())
Output:
Enter a sentence: It is a great day
The sentence entered is: It is a great day
The words in the sentence are
['It', 'is', 'a', 'great', 'day']
```

This program looks for white spaces in the sentence and splits it into words at occurrence of white spaces. The words of the sentence are returned as an array of strings.

The following program asks the user to enter a name consisting of a first and a last name and then displays it after interchanging the two:

```
interchangenme.py
n=input('Enter your first name and last name: ')
k=n.partition(' ')
print('The name after interchanging first and last name:', k[2], k[0])
Output:
Enter your first name and last name: Caroline Stevens
The name after interchanging first and last name: Stevens Caroline
```

In this program, the first and last names entered by the user are assigned to variable n. The name in variable n is partitioned into three parts on occurrence of the white space, using the partition() method: the first name, white space, and the last name. To interchange the first and last name, you display the third part, followed by the first part of the string.

The following program demonstrates three methods: partition(), replace(), and split():

```
breaking.py
s='education'
k=s.partition('cat')
print('The word', s, 'is partitioned into three parts')
print('The first part is', k[0], 'separator is', k[1], 'and the third part is',k[2])
t=input('Enter a sentence: ')
print('The original sentence is', t)
print('The sentence after replacing all the characters "a" by "#" is:', t.replace('a',
'#'))
print('The sentence after replacing first three "a" characters by "#" is:',
t.replace('a', '#', 3))
u=t.split(' ')
print('The words in the entered sentence are', u)
print('The words in the entered sentence are')
for i in range(0, len(u)):
    print(u[i])
u=t.split(' ',1)
print('The sentence is split into two parts:', u[0], 'and', u[1])
Output:
The word education is partitioned into three parts
The first part is edu separator is cat and the third part is ion
Enter a sentence: amazing day in alaska
The original sentence is amazing day in alaska
The sentence after replacing all the characters "a" by "#" is: #m#zing d#y in #l#sk#
The sentence after replacing first three "a" characters by "#" is: #m#zing d#y in alaska
```

```
The words in the entered sentence are ['amazing', 'day', 'in', 'alaska']
The words in the entered sentence are
amazing
day
in
alaska
The sentence is split into two parts: amazing and day in Alaska
```

The string education is partitioned into three parts at the substring cat using the partition() method. The three parts will be edu, cat, and ion. Also, the program uses replace() to replace the character a in the sentence by #. The program uses replace() to replace only the first three occurrences of character a by #. The program splits the entered sentence into an array of strings using split()and displays its words. Finally, the program splits the sentence into two parts on occurrence of a white space.

You have seen examples that deal with arrays of characters. Now let's look at examples that deal with arrays of numbers.

Arrays

Numerical arrays are used for storing numerical data. Since they don't have NULL characters, numerical arrays are not terminated by NULL characters as with strings, but the index concept still applies to them for accessing their elements. The arrays are of two types, one- and two-dimensional arrays.

One-Dimensional Arrays

Consider a numerical array, p, which has five numerical values: 8, 3,1, 6, and 2. These values will be represented by the structure shown in Figure 3.2.

The values are the indices that can be used to access the elements in the array. That is, p[0] will access the first element of the array, 8, p[1] will access the second element of the array, 3, and so on.

The following program demonstrates creation of a numerical array of five elements:

```
numericarr.py
p= [ 0 for i in range(5) ]
```

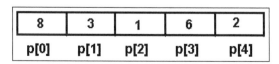

Figure 3.2
Numbers stored in a one-dimensional array.

```
print ("Enter five numbers")
for i in range(5):
     p[i]= int(input())
print ("Numbers entered in the array are", p)
print ("Numbers entered in the array are")
for n in p:
   print (n)
Output:
Enter five numbers
8
3
1
6
2
Numbers entered in the array are [8, 3, 1, 6, 2]
Numbers entered in the array are
8
3
1
6
2
```

The first line of the program declares that p is an array of 5 numbers. Using a for loop, the user is asked to enter five numbers that will be stored in the respective indexes, p[0], p[1], p[2], p[3], and p[4]. The numerical values in the array p are then displayed.

Now let's see how two-dimensional arrays are created in Python.

Two-Dimensional Arrays

Two-dimensional arrays are divided into rows and columns. The indices of row and column begin at value 0. To access each element of the array, you have to specify two indices; one represents the row, and the other represents the column. Both are enclosed in square brackets.

In Figure 3.3 you see that every location in the array is represented by a row and column location. The index p[0][0] refers to the element stored at 0th row and 0th column position. Similarly, the index p[0][1] refers to the element that is stored at 0th row and 1st column position in the two-dimensional array.

The following program creates a two-dimensional array of 3 rows and 3 columns. The program also computes and displays the sum of elements of the array.

	0	1	2
0	p[0][0]	p[0][1]	p[0][2]
1	p[1][0]	p[1][1]	p[1][2]
2	p[2][0]	p[2][1]	p[2][2]

Figure 3.3
Two-dimensional array showing the index values.

```
matrix1.py
table= [ [ 0 for i in range(3) ] for j in range(3) ]
print ("Enter values for a matrix of order 3 x 3")
for d1 in range(3):
    for d2 in range(3):
        table[d1][d2]= int(input())
print ("Elements of the matrix are", table)
print ("Elements of the matrix are")
for row in table:
    print (row)
s=0
for row in table:
    for n in row:
        s+=n
print ("The sum of elements in matrix is",s)
Output:
Enter values for a matrix of order 3 x 3
1
2
3
4
5
6
7
8
9
Elements of the matrix are [[1, 2, 3], [4, 5, 6], [7, 8, 9]]
Elements of the matrix are
[1, 2, 3]
[4, 5, 6]
[7, 8, 9]
The sum of elements in matrix is 45
```

Figure 3.4
Numerical values stored in a two-dimensional array.

The data supplied by the user is entered in the two-dimensional array in row major form (see Figure 3.4). When the first row is full, the elements will be stored in the second row, and so on.

The first line declares table as a two-dimensional array of three rows and three columns. The values entered by the user are stored in the two-dimensional array through two nested for loops. On displaying a row of the two-dimensional array, the row will appear with its elements enclosed in square brackets. The program also adds and displays the sum of the elements.

The following program demonstrates addition of elements of two-dimensional arrays. The elements in the two arrays consisting of three rows and three columns will be added and displayed.

```
matrix2.py
m1 = [ [1, 2], [3, 4], [5, 6], [7, 8] ]
m2 = [ [9, 8], [7, 6], [5, 4], [3, 2] ]
m3= [ 2*[0] for i in range(4) ]
print("Addition of two matrices is")
for i in range(4):
   for j in range(2):
      m3[i][j]= m1[i][j]+m2[i][j]
for row in m3:
   print (row)
Output:
Addition of two matrices is
[10, 10]
[10, 10]
[10, 10]
[10, 10]
```

The elements in the two-dimensional arrays m1 and m2 are arranged as shown in Figure 3.5.

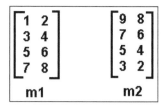

Figure 3.5
Numerical values stored in two-dimensional arrays.

$$\begin{bmatrix} 1 & 2 \\ 3 & 4 \\ 5 & 6 \\ 7 & 8 \end{bmatrix} + \begin{bmatrix} 9 & 8 \\ 7 & 6 \\ 5 & 4 \\ 3 & 2 \end{bmatrix} = \begin{bmatrix} 10 & 10 \\ 10 & 10 \\ 10 & 10 \\ 10 & 10 \end{bmatrix}$$

m1   m2   m3

Figure 3.6
Addition of two-dimensional arrays.

For storing the addition of the elements of the two-dimensional arrays m1 and m2, you declare another two-dimensional array, m3. Using nested for loops, you access the elements at the respective row and column position of the two two-dimensional arrays and store their addition in the third array, m3. The addition of m1 and m2 is computed and stored in array m3 (see Figure 3.6), which is then displayed.

This finishes our discussion on arrays. Next comes another sequence, lists.

LISTS

A list is a collection of elements, which might include other lists. Lists begin and end with a square bracket, and the elements inside are separated with commas.

```
["John", "Kelly", 1, 2, [Sugar, Butter, 10]]
```

The first element of the list is at index 0, the second is at index value 1, and so on. The last element is at index -1.

The following example displays the first and last elements of a list:

```
list1.py
names=['John', 'Kelly', 'Caroline', 'Paula']
print (names[0])
print (names[-1])
Output:
```

```
John
Paula
```

The index values 0 and -1 refer to the first and last elements of the list, John and Paula.

Finding the Length of the List

To find the length of a list, you use the len() function, which returns the length as an index location of the last element plus one. From this, you can say that the index location of the last element of the list is len(list)-1. Similarly, the index location of the second to last element of the list is computed as len(list)-2. Besides using the len() method for finding the index location of the last element, there is one more way: the index location of the last element is defined as -1 by default. This way, you can compute the index location of the second-to-last element as -2 and so on. In other words, list[len(list)-1] and list[-1] are the same and will display the last element of the list. Thus any element in the list can be indexed in two ways: from the front (using the len() function) and from the back (using -1).

The following example displays all the elements of the list:

```
list2.py
names=['John', 'Kelly', 'Caroline', 'Paula']
for i in range(0,len(names)):
    print (names[i])
Output:
John
Kelly
Caroline
Paula
```

Here, the len() function will return the length of the list as 4. range(0,4) will return values 0 through 3 (excluding 4), so all the elements of the list from index location 0 through 3 will be displayed.

You can also access the elements of the list using the membership in operator as shown in the following program:

```
list3.py
names=['John', 'Kelly', 'Caroline', 'Paula']
for n in names:
    print (n)
Output:
John
Kelly
```

```
Caroline
Paula
```

The in operator with an if statement can be used to search for an element in the list. The following example searches for the desired content in the list:

```
list4.py
names=['John', 'Kelly', 'Caroline', 'Paula']
n=input("Enter a name: ")
if n in names:
   print ("Entered name is present in the list")
else:
   print ("Sorry the entered name is not in the list")
Output:
Enter a name: Susan
Sorry the entered name is not in the list

Enter a name: Caroline
Entered name is present in the list
```

The next program asks the user to enter a numerical value for a month and displays the name of the month in text form. For instance, if the user enters 1, the program will display the output as January. If the user enters 2, the program will print February, and so on.

```
list5.py
months = ['January', 'February', 'March', 'April', 'May', 'June', 'July', 'August',
'September', 'October', 'November', 'December']
n = int(input("Enter a value between 1 and 12: "))
if 1 <= n <= 12:
   print ("The month is", months[n-1])
else:
   print ("Value is out of the range")
Output:
Enter a value between 1 and 12: 5
The month is May

Enter a value between 1 and 12: 13
Value is out of the range
```

The elements in the months list will be stored as shown in Figure 3.7.

January	February	March	----------	December
months[0]	months[1]	months[2]		months[11]

Figure 3.7
Elements in the months list.

When a user enters a value, it will be assigned to the variable n. You decrement the value in n by 1 because the index locations in the list begin at 0 and not 1. Its value will become 4, and you print the element at index location 4, which is the desired output, May. To avoid entering a value above the given range, you validate the value entered by applying chaining of comparison operators to ensure that the value entered by the user is between 1 and 12.

Next let's see how lists can be divided or sliced into parts.

List Slicing

You can slice a list into parts to get desired elements. To slice a list, you specify the index locations from which you want to extract elements.

```
Syntax:
list[first_index:following_index]
```

This returns the elements from first_index to the index before following_index is returned.

Note

> If first_index is not specified, then the beginning of the list is assumed. If following_index is not specified, then the rest of the list is assumed.

To better understand the concept of slicing, let's assume you have a list named tmplist with these contents:

```
tmplist=['John', 'Kelly', 10, 'Caroline', 15, 'Steve', 'Katheline']
```

Now observe the output of the following examples:

tmplist[0:3] will return the elements at the index value 0 through 2 ['John', 'Kelly', 10].

tmplist[2:4] will return the elements at the index value 2 through 3 [10, 'Caroline'].

tmplist[-4] will return the fourth element from the last ['Caroline'].

tmplist[-4:-2] will return the fourth element from the last through the third element from the last ['Caroline', 15].

tmplist[-5:5] will return the fifth element from the last through the fourth element from the beginning [10, 'Caroline', 15].

tmplist[:3] will return the first three elements of the list ['John', 'Kelly', 10].

Table 3.4 List Methods

Method	Description
append(object)	Appends the specified object to the end of the list.
insert(index, object)	Inserts the specified object before the index position. If index is greater than the length of the list, object is appended to the list. If index is less than zero, object is prepended.
pop([index=-1])	Removes and returns the last item from the list. That is, the element at index location -1 is returned. An exception is raised if the list is empty.
del[n]	Deletes item with the n index number from the list. That is, the element at index location n is removed from the list.
remove(value)	Removes the first occurrence of value from the list. An exception is raised if the value is not found in the list.
reverse()	Reverses the elements in the list.
extend(list)	Takes a single argument, which is always a list, and adds the elements on that list to the original list.
count(value)	Returns the number of occurrences of value in the list.
index(value)	Returns the index of the first occurrence of value in the list.

tmplist[3:] will return the elements at index value 3 to the end of the list ['Caroline', 15, 'Steve', 'Katheline'].

tmplist[:-3] will return the element from index value 0 through the third element from the last [' John', 'Kelly', 10, 'Caroline'].

tmplist[-3:] will return the third element from the last to the end of the list [15, 'Steve', 'Katheline'].

Table 3.4 shows some of the methods that can be applied to lists.

The following program performs list slicing to display the first four elements in the list, finds the length of the list, appends the new elements to the list, deletes an element from the list, and displays elements in the list.

```
list6.py
tmplist=['John', 'Kelly', 10, 'Caroline', 15, 'Steve', 'Katheline']
print ("The original list is", tmplist)
print ("The first four elements in the list are:", tmplist[0:4])
print ("The number of elements in the list are", len(tmplist))
m=input ("Enter a name to add to the list ")
```

```
tmplist.append(m)
print ("The elements in the list now are", tmplist)
n=int(input ("Enter the element number to delete "))
del tmplist[n-1]
print ("The elements in the list now are", tmplist)
print ("The elements in the list can also be displayed as shown:")
for i in range(0, len(tmplist)):
    print (tmplist[i])
Output:
The original list is ['John', 'Kelly', 10, 'Caroline', 15, 'Steve', 'Katheline']
The first four elements in the list are: ['John', 'Kelly', 10, 'Caroline']
The number of elements in the list are 7
Enter a name to add to the list Rebecca
The elements in the list now are ['John', 'Kelly', 10, 'Caroline', 15, 'Steve', 'Kathe-
line', 'Rebecca']
Enter the element number to delete 2
The elements in the list now are ['John', 10, 'Caroline', 15, 'Steve', 'Katheline',
'Rebecca']
The elements in the list can also be displayed as shown:
John
10
Caroline
15
Steve
Katheline
Rebecca
```

This program defines seven elements by the name tmplist. You first display all the elements of the list. Then, with the slicing method, you display the first four elements of the list.

Print the count of the elements in the list using the len() function. Then ask the user to enter an element that is to be appended to the list. The data entered by the user is appended to the list through the append() method.

Then you ask the user to enter the location of the element that is required to be removed from the list. Knowing that the user will count the location beginning from value 1, whereas the elements in the list begin at index value 0, decrement the location entered by the user by 1 so that it matches the index location of the element the user wishes to remove from the list. Finally, with the del() method, the element at that index location is removed from the list.

The following program demonstrates adding new elements to the list, searching for an element in the list, and updating the element.

```
list7.py
names=[]
n=int(input("How many names? "))
print("Enter", n, "names")
for i in range (0,n):
   m=input()
   names.append(m)
print ("The original list of names is", names)
p=input ("Enter the name to search: ")
if p in names:
   print ("The name", p, "is found in the list at location ", names.index(p)+1)
else:
   print ("The name", p, "is not found in the list ")
q=input ("Enter the name to update/change: ")
if q in names:
   loc=names.index(q)
   r=input("Enter the new name: ")
   names[loc]=r
   print ("The name", q, "in the list is changed to", r)
else:
   print ("The name", q, "is not found in the list")
names.sort()
print ("Sorted names are", names)
Output:
How many names? 4
Enter 4 names
Kelly
Caroline
David
Beth
The original list of names is ['Kelly', 'Caroline', 'David', 'Beth']
Enter the name to search: David
The name David is found in the list at location 3
Enter the name to update/change: Caroline
Enter the new name: Candace
The name Caroline in the list is changed to Candace
Sorted names are ['Beth', 'Candace', 'David', 'Kelly']
```

The program creates an empty list, names, and asks the user to add the desired number of names (any text) to it. After some names are added to the list, its original content is displayed. Then you ask the user to enter the name to search for. The name entered is searched in the list using the membership in operator. If the name is found in the list, its location is displayed; otherwise, the message name not found is displayed. After searching comes updating. The program asks the user to enter the name to update. If the name entered is found, its index location is accessed using the index() method, and the new name is stored at that index location, replacing the old name. Finally, the program displays all the names in the list after sorting them alphabetically using sort().

TUPLES

Tuples are a type of sequence, like strings. But unlike strings, which can contain only characters, tuples can contain elements of any type. A tuple is an *immutable* object that cannot be changed once it is created. As with every sequence, tuple indices are zero based; the first element is at index 0, and the last element is at index -1.

The following program demonstrates how a tuple is defined and how its elements are accessed and displayed:

```
tup1.py
names=('John', 'Kelly', 'Caroline', 'Steve', 'Katheline')
print ("The names in the tuple are:", names)
print ("The first name in the tuple is", names[0])
print ("The last name in the tuple is", names[len(names)-1])
print ("The names in the tuple are")
for n in names:
    print (n)
Output:
The names in the tuple are: ('John', 'Kelly', 'Caroline', 'Steve', 'Katheline')
The first name in the tuple is John
The last name in the tuple is Katheline
The names in the tuple are
John
Kelly
Caroline
Steve
Katheline
```

In this program, a tuple names is defined that contains five elements: John, Kelly, Caroline, Steve, and Katheline. All the elements of the tuple are displayed, followed by the first and last elements. The program also shows how elements of a tuple are accessed using the membership in operator.

The next program demonstrates searching for an element in a tuple and concatenating two tuples.

```
tup2.py
names=('John', 'Kelly', 'Caroline', 'Steve', 'Katheline')
n=input("Enter the name to search: ")
```

```
if n in names:
    print ("The name", n, "is present in the tuple")
else:
    print ("The name", n, "does not exist in the tuple")
countries=('U.S.', 'U.K', 'India')
names+=countries
print ("The tuples are concatenated. The concatenated tuple is", names)
Output:
Enter the name to search: Beth
The name Beth does not exist in the tuple
The tuples are concatenated. The concatenated tuple is ('John', 'Kelly', 'Caroline',
'Steve', 'Katheline', 'U.S.', 'U.K', 'India')
```

Here, names is defined as consisting of five elements. The user is asked to enter a name to search for. Using the membership in operator, the name entered is searched for in the names tuple, and a message is displayed. Also, one more tuple, countries, is defined to include three elements. The elements in countries are added to the names tuple. The elements in the concatenated tuple, names, are then displayed.

Mappings are mutable objects that are used for mapping values to objects. The standard mapping type that we discuss next is the dictionary.

Dictionary

A dictionary is a combination of key/value pairs in which every key has to be unique. Key/value pairs are separated by a colon, and the pairs are separated by commas. The key/value pairs are enclosed in a curly brackets.

```
Syntax:
d = {key1 : value1, key2 : value2 }
```

Dictionaries are mutable, which means a dictionary can be modified, and you don't have to create a copy of it to modify it. Dictionary keys are case sensitive and immutable because Python associates them with a unique number called a *hash*. Also, dictionary keys can be of mixed data types: strings, integers, and others. Table 3.5 shows some of the methods that can be applied to the dictionary.

The following program demonstrates how to fetch a value from the dictionary by supplying a key. Also, the program shows how to add a key/value pair to an existing dictionary and delete an existing key/value pair. The program demonstrates the use of the dictionary in accessing the capital of the country whose name is entered by the user.

Table 3.5 Dictionary Methods

Method	Description
clear()	Removes all items from the dictionary.
pop(key, [default])	Returns and removes the value associated with the specified key from the dictionary. If the key does not exist, the method returns the default value provided. If the key does not exist and no default value is provided, a KeyError exception is raised.
update(new, [key=value…])	Merges the new key/value pairs in the dictionary. The existing key/value pairs are updated.
copy()	Makes a copy of the dictionary. The objects in the new dictionary are references to the objects in the original dictionary.
get(key, [default])	Returns the value associated with the given key. If key is not present and default is provided, the method returns the default value. If key is not present and no default is provided, a KeyError exception is raised.
items()	Returns all the items in the dictionary as a sequence of key/value tuples.
keys()	Returns all the keys in the dictionary as a sequence of keys.
values()	Returns all the values from the dictionary as a sequence.

```
dict1.py
countrycap={'U.S.' : 'Washington D.C.', 'U.K.' : 'London', 'India' : 'New Delhi', }
n=input('Enter country: ')
if n in countrycap:
    print ('The capital of', n , 'is', countrycap[n])
else:
    print ('Sorry the country', n, 'does not exist in our dictionary')
countrycap['Australia']='Sweden'
print ('The dictionary after adding a country:')
for country, capital in countrycap.items():
    print ('Capital of', country, 'is', capital)
m=input('Enter the country to delete:')
del countrycap[m]
print ('The dictionary after deleting a country:')
for country, capital in countrycap.items():
    print ('Capital of', country, 'is', capital)
```

```
Output:
Enter country: U.S.
The capital of U.S is Washington D.C.
The dictionary after adding a country:
Capital of U.S. is Washington D.C.
Capital of Australia is Sweden
Capital of India is New Delhi
Capital of U.K. is London
Enter the country to delete: U.K.
The dictionary after deleting a country:
Capital of U.S. is Washington D.C.
Capital of Australia is Sweden
Capital of India is New Delhi
```

This program defines a dictionary named countrycap with three key/value pairs in it. The keys are the country names U.S., U.K., and India, and the values of these keys are the respective capitals of the countries. You ask the user to enter the country name whose capital is required. Taking the entered country name as the key, its respective value is accessed and displayed. One key/value pair is added to the dictionary, with Australia as its key and Sweden as its value. The program also displays the dictionary elements, each country with its respective capital. The program also deletes the desired country/capital pair from the dictionary.

The following program demonstrates the use of items(), keys(), values(), and get() methods of the dictionary. Also, it shows how two dictionaries are merged.

```
dictexample.py
student1={'John' : 60, 'Kelly' : 70, 'Caroline': 80}
student2=dict([('David', 90), ('John',55)])
print ('The items in dictionary student1 are:', student1.items())
print ('The keys in student1 dictionary are:', student1.keys())
print ('The values in student1 dictionary are:', student1.values())
student1.update(student2)
print ('The items in dictionary student1 after merging with student2 dictionary are:',
student1.items())
n=input('Enter name whose marks you want to see: ')
if n in student1:
   print ('The marks of', n , 'are', student1.get(n))
else:
   print ('Sorry the name', n, 'does not exist in student1 dictionary')
Output:
The items in dictionary student1 are: dict_items([('Kelly', 70), ('John', 60),
('Caroline', 80)])
The keys in student1 dictionary are: dict_keys(['Kelly', 'John', 'Caroline'])
```

```
The values in student1 dictionary are: dict_values([70, 60, 80])
The items in dictionary student1 after merging with student2 dictionary are: dict_items
([('Kelly', 70), ('John', 55), ('Caroline', 80), ('David', 90)])
Enter name whose marks you want to see: Caroline
The marks of Caroline are 80
```

The program defines two dictionaries, student1 and student2. The student2 dictionary is created by applying the dict() function to the pairs of values. All the key/value pairs of the student1 dictionary are displayed using the items() function. Also, the keys and values of the student1 dictionary are accessed through the keys() and values() functions and displayed. The key/value pairs of the dictionary student2 are merged with the dictionary student1. While merging, the values of the keys in dictionary student1 will be updated with the values of the matching keys in dictionary student2. The merged key/value pairs are displayed. Also, the user is asked to enter a student's name whose marks are required. Using the get() function, the supplied name is accessed and displayed.

Let's finish the chapter by discussing one more container object, sets.

SETS

A set is a collection of certain values. You can perform a number of set operations, including union (|), intersection (&), difference (-), and symmetric difference (^). Let's begin with the union operation.

Union (|)

In a union operation, an element appears in the union if it exists in one set or the other. For example, consider the two sets S1 and S2 with the following elements:

```
S1=set([3,5,6,10,11,100])
S2=set([1,3,5,6,11,15])
```

S1 | S2 will display the union as:

```
set([1,3,5,6,10,11,15,100])
```

Intersection (&)

In an intersection operation, the elements that appear in both sets appear in the intersection.

S1 & S2 will display the intersection as:

```
set([3, 5, 6, 11])
```

Difference (-)

In a difference operation, all the elements that are in the left set but not in the right set will appear in the difference operation.

S1-S2 will display the difference as :

```
set([10, 100])
```

Similarly, S2-S1 will display the difference as:

```
set([1, 15])
```

Let's look at the methods and functions that can be applied to sets. Remember that a function is a module of code that is called by name, and data is passed to it explicitly. It can return a value. A method is associated with an object, and the object for which it is called is passed to it implicitly. The list of methods and functions that can be applied to sets is given in Table 3.6.

Table 3.6 Set Methods/Functions

Method/Function	Description
len()	Returns the number of items in the set. Duplicate items are considered as one item.
max()	Returns the maximum item in the set.
min()	Returns the minimum item in the set.
sum()	Returns the sum of items in the set. Duplicate items are added only once.
any()	Returns true if any item in the set is true. false and 0 are considered as false, and every other value is considered as true.
all()	Returns true if all items in the set are true.
sorted()	Returns the set items in sorted order.
clear()	Removes all the items from the set.
pop()	Removes and returns an arbitrary item from the set. If the set is empty, the function will raise a KeyError exception.
add(item)	Adds the specified item to the set. If the item is already in the set, nothing happens.
remove(item)/discard (item)	Removes the specified item from the set. If the item does not exist in the set, a KeyError exception is raised.
update(set)	Merges values from the specified set into the original set.

The following program demonstrates the use of set methods such as max(), min(), any(), all(), sum(), and sorted(). The program also demonstrates the application of union, intersection, difference, and merging operations on the sets.

```
setexample.py
S1=set([3,5,6,10,11,100])
S2=set([1,3,5,6,11,15])
print ('Length of set S1 is:', len(S1))
print ('Maximum value in set S1 is:', max(S1))
print ('Minimum value in set S2 is:', min(S2))
print ('Sum of items in set S1 is:', sum(S1))
print ('Applying any() to set S1 results into:', any(S1))
print ('Union of the two sets is:', S1 | S2)
print ('Intersection of the two sets is:', S1 & S2)
print ('Difference of S1-S2 is:', S1 - S2)
print ('Difference of S2-S1 is:', S2 - S1)
S1.add(0)
print ('The items in set S1 after adding an item are:', sorted(S1))
print ('As set S1 now has a value 0, so all() will result into:', all(S1))
S1.update(S2)
print ('The items in set S1 after merging set S2 are:', sorted(S1))
Output:
Length of set S1 is: 6
Maximum value in set S1 is: 100
Minimum value in set S2 is: 1
Sum of items in set S1 is: 135
Applying any() to set S1 results into: true
Union of the two sets is: {1, 3, 100, 5, 6, 10, 11, 15}
Intersection of the two sets is: {11, 3, 5, 6}
Difference of S1-S2 is: {10, 100}
Difference of S2-S1 is: {1, 15}
The items in set S1 after adding an item are: [0, 3, 5, 6, 10, 11, 100]
As set S1 now has a value 0, so all() will result into: false
The items in set S1 after merging set S2 are: [0, 1, 3, 5, 6, 10, 11, 15, 100]
```

This program displays the count of the number of elements in the set, the highest value, the lowest value, and the sum of the values in the set. The application of the any() function on set S1 returns true as it contains several non-zero values. The program also displays the union, intersection, and difference of the sets. A value 0 is added to the set S1 by using the add() method. Also, the set S1 is displayed after sorting its elements. The application of the all() function on set S1 returns false as it now contains a 0 value. The elements in set S2 are merged to the elements of set S1, and the merged set is displayed after sorting its elements.

SUMMARY

This chapter focused on different containers. You learned to perform different operations on strings, including concatenating, splitting, and converting them into different cases such as uppercase, title case, and lowercase. You also learned about list slicing and searching elements in tuples. You performed operations on sets such as finding their union, intersection, and difference. You saw how key/value pairs are maintained in a dictionary and how to append, delete, and modify key/value pairs. Finally, you created one- and two-dimensional arrays.

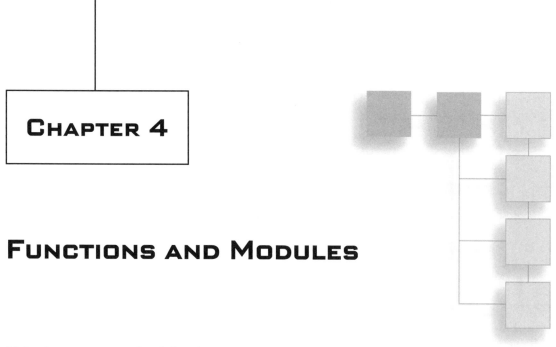

CHAPTER 4

FUNCTIONS AND MODULES

This chapter covers the following:

- Creating and using functions
- Using default value parameters and keyword arguments
- Using local and global variables
- Creating lambda functions
- Applying functions to the sequences
- Using function attributes
- Implementing recursion
- Using iterators, generators, and generator expressions
- Importing and using modules
- Using command-line arguments

Let us begin the chapter with functions and their statements.

FUNCTIONS

A function is a group of statements that can be invoked any number of times. Besides the built-in functions, you can define your own functions. The statement that invokes a function is known as a *function call*. In calling a function, you can pass arguments to it to perform the desired computation. In Python, a function always returns a value that may be either None or that represents the task performed by the function.

In Python, functions are treated as objects, and so you can pass a function as an argument to another function. Similarly, a function can return another function. Also, a function, just like any other object, can be bound to a variable, an item in a container, or an attribute of an object.

Let's look at the statements used in defining a function.

The def Statement

The `def` statement is used to define a function.

```
Syntax:
def function-name(parameters):
statement(s)
```

where `function-name` is an identifier to recognize the function. `parameters` is an optional list of identifiers that are bound to the values supplied as arguments while calling the function.

When calling a function, the data you send to the function is called *arguments*, and the variables in the function that receive the arguments are called *parameters*. Hence, while calling a function, you should pass the same number of arguments as there are parameters listed in the function definition. The parameters are local variables of the function, and each call to the function binds these local variables to the corresponding values passed as arguments. The function body can contain zero or more occurrences of the `return` statement.

The following program demonstrates the addition of two numerical values using a function.

```
func1.py
def sum(a, b):
        return a + b

k=sum(10,20)
print ("Sum is", k)
Output:
Sum is 30
```

In this program, a `sum()` function is called, passing two arguments 10 and 20. The arguments 10 and 20 will be assigned to the parameters a and b, defined in the `sum()` function. The `sum()` function computes the addition of the values assigned to the parameters a and b and returns the result to the main program. The result is assigned to the variable k in the main program, which is then displayed.

The return Statement

The `return` statement is used for returning output from the function. The statement is optionally followed by an expression. When `return` executes, the function terminates, and the value of the expression is passed to the caller. When there is nothing to be returned to the caller, the function returns `None`.

If a function doesn't require any external data to process, it can be defined with no parameters. The following program demonstrates a function that takes no parameter and returns a value:

```
func3.py
def quantity():
        return 10

print (quantity())
q=quantity()
print (q)
Output:
10
10
```

In this program, a `quantity()` function is defined that takes no parameters. On calling the function in a `print` statement, it prints the value 10 that is returned. In the next function call, you assign the value returned to the variable q, which is then displayed.

The following program asks the user to enter a numerical value between 1 and 4 and displays it in text form. For example, if the user enters 1, the program will display one. If the user enters 2, the program will display two, and so on.

```
func4.py
def conv(x):
        if x==1:
                return "one"
        if x==2:
                return "two"
        if x==3:
                return "three"
        if x==4:
                return "four"

n=int(input("Enter a number between 1 and 4: "))
print (n, "in words is", conv(n))
Output:
Enter a number between 1 and 4: 3
3 in words is three
```

The program asks the user to enter a value between 1 and 4 that is converted to integer data type and assigned to a variable n. The variable n is then passed as an argument to the function conv(). In conv(), n is assigned to the parameter x. Using if statements, the value in parameter x is analyzed, and its text form is returned.

Sometimes you want a function to return a value of None. Consider a situation when the value passed to the function's parameter is not within the expected range. That is, the data passed is not suitable for performing any processing on it. You want the function to skip its body and return None. The following program displays the text form of the number passed between 1 and 4. If the number passed is 0, the output will be None.

```
passex2.py
def conv(x):
     if x==0:
          pass
     if x==1:
          return "one"
     if x==2:
          return "two"
  if x==3:
          return "three"
     if x==4:
          return "four"

print (conv(2))
print (conv(0))

Output:
two
None
```

You can see that when value 2 is passed as an argument to the conv() function, the respective if statement is executed to display the text two. When 0 is passed to the conv() function, the first if statement in the function is executed. It does nothing because it contains the pass statement, so None is returned. Remember that the pass statement indicates an empty block of statements. It is usually used as a placeholder for code you plan to write later.

Default Value Parameters

The parameters listed in the function definition may be mandatory or optional. The mandatory parameters are those whose value has to be supplied in the form of arguments when calling the function. The optional parameters are those whose value may or may not be passed when calling the function. An optional parameter is defined with the following syntax:

```
identifier=expression
```

The expression is evaluated and is assigned as the default value for the identifier. When a function call does not supply an argument corresponding to an optional parameter, the call binds the parameter to its default value.

The following program demonstrates the use of a default parameter. In this program, you define a function that has two parameters; one is mandatory, and the other is optional or the default. When the function call passes the value for the default parameter, the passed value is applied; otherwise the default value is applied.

```
func2.py
def sum(x, y=10):
     return x+y

print (sum(10))
print (sum(5,8))
Output:
20
13
```

In this program, the sum( ) function is called twice. In the first call, only one argument, 10, is passed and is assigned to parameter x. The function will take the default value of the parameter y (10) while executing the function. In the second call to the sum( ) function, arguments 5 and 8 are passed and are assigned to the parameters x and y, respectively. The default value of y, 10, is ignored, and the value passed as an argument (8) is applied.

Keyword Arguments

If when calling a function you want to supply arguments for only a few of its parameters, you do so by naming the parameters when passing arguments. A value passed to a parameter by referring to its name is known as a *keyword argument.* The advantage of using this approach is that you don't have to worry about the order of the arguments.

The following program demonstrates using keyword arguments when calling a function.

```
keywordarg.py
def volume(l, b=5, h=10):
    print ('l is', l, 'and b is', b, 'and h is', h, 'and volume is', l*b*h)

volume(2, 4)
volume(3, h=6)
```

```
volume(h=7, 1=2)
Output:
1 is 2 and b is 4 and h is 10 and volume is 80
1 is 3 and b is 5 and h is 6 and volume is 90
1 is 2 and b is 5 and h is 7 and volume is 70
```

The volume() function has three parameters, one that has no default value and two parameters that do. In the first function call, volume(2,4), the 1 parameter gets the value 2, the b parameter gets the value 4, and h gets its default value, 10. In the second function call, volume(3, h=6), the 1 parameter gets the value 3 due to the position of the argument. Then, the h parameter gets the value 6 as a keyword argument. The b parameter gets its default value, 5. In the third function call, volume (h=7, 1=2), you use keyword arguments to specify the values of the h and 1 parameters. The h parameter will get 7, 1 will get 2, and b will get the default 5.

The scope of variables in a function is determined by whether it is locally or globally defined.

Local and Global Variables

Local variables have scope within the body of the function in which they are defined. That is, local variables are accessible inside the function. Global variables are accessible inside and outside of functions.

Note

You get an error if you try to access a local variable outside the function.

Global Variables

Global variables are not bound to any particular function and can be accessed within the body of the function, outside the body of the function, or by any other function. The changes made to a global variable by any function will be visible by other functions. If a function needs global variables, the first statement of the function must be this:

```
global identifiers
```

where identifiers is one or more identifiers separated by commas. Identifiers listed in a global statement are referred to as *global variables*.

You use the keyword global to define a global variable; otherwise, an UnboundLocal-Error exception is raised because the variable is an uninitialized (unbound) local variable.

The following program explains the concept of global variables. The main thing to observe in this program is how the changes made in the global variable by one function can be seen in another function.

```
globalvar.py
def compute():
        global x
        print ("Value of x in compute function is", x)
        x += 5
        return None
def dispvalue():
        global x
        print ("Value of x in dispvalue function is", x)
        x -=2
        return None

x=0
compute()
dispvalue()
compute()
Output:
Value of x in compute function is 0
Value of x in dispvalue function is 5
Value of x in compute function is 3
```

In this program, you define two functions, compute() and dispvalue(). Both functions define a global variable, x. Remember, global variables are accessible in every part of the program, in the main program as well as functions. Changes made in global variables are visible in other parts of the program. You can see that the global variable x is initialized to 0 in the main program. The main program calls the compute() function to print the value of the global variable and modify its value. The value of the global variable x being 0, the compute() function prints 0, increments its value by 5, and returns to the main program. The main program then calls the dispvalue() function to display and modify the global variable. The value of the global variable x was set to 5 by the compute() function and so the dispvalue() function prints its value as 5 and decrements its value by 2, making it 3, and returns to the main program. The main program calls the compute() function again to see if the changes made to x in the dispvalue() function are visible in compute(). The compute() function displays the current value of x (3) and increments the value of x by 5, making it 8, and returns to the main program. This confirms that the global variable is accessible in every part of the program, and changes made to the global variable in one part of the program will be seen in another part.

Let's now see how local variables are defined and accessed in a function.

Local Variables

By default, any variable that is bound within a function body is a local variable. Each function has its own copy of a local variable, and its value is not accessible or modifiable outside the body of the function.

The following program demonstrates the use of local variables:

```
localvar.py
def compute(x):
        x += 5
        print ("Value of x in function is", x)
        return None

x=10
compute(x)
print ("Value of x is still", x)
Output:
Value of x in function is 15
Value of x is still 10
```

The main program initializes the value of the local variable x at 10. The variable x is then passed to the compute() function as an argument. In the compute() function, the value of the parameter x is incremented by 5, making its value 15. But x being local to the function, the modified value of x (15) is visible only within the body of the compute() function. When you display the value of x in the compute() function, it will print the modified value 15, but when you return to the main program, the program picks up the older value of x (10). Hence, the main program prints the old value of x, 10.

Sometimes you need to create very small functions, consisting of just a single line. Can you handle such small functions in Python? Yes. Let's see how.

Lambda Functions

For functions that are small enough (a single line expression) and that are going to be used only once, you generally don't define function objects. Instead, you use lambda functions.

A lambda function is an anonymous and one-use-only function that can have any number of parameters and that does some computation. The body of the lambda function is small, a single expression. The result of the expression is the value when the lambda is applied to an argument. There is no need for a return statement in lambda functions.

Note

The scope of a lambda function is limited. It exists only in the scope of a single statement's execution.

Consider a small function that multiplies a passed argument by 2 and returns, as shown here:

```
def f(x):
return x*2

f(3)
6
```

You can see that a function f takes a parameter x that it returns by multiplying it by 2. On calling the function with argument 3, it will return 6 as output. You can rewrite this function as a lambda function:

```
g = lambda x: x*2
g(3)
6
```

You can see that the lambda function has no name and is called through the variable it is assigned to.

You can use a lambda function without even assigning it to a variable. The following is a lambda function with no name that accepts a single argument. It multiplies the argument by 2 and returns the result:

```
(lambda x: x*2)(3)
6
```

You can see that there are no parentheses around the argument list, and the return keyword is missing. The return is implied in the lambda function as the entire function consists of a single expression.

Note

A lambda function cannot contain commands and cannot contain more than one expression.

Applying Functions to Sequences

Now that you know about defining and calling functions, let's apply them to sequences. In the previous chapter, you learned about the three types of sequences: strings, lists, and tuples. The three methods in this section are filter(), map(), and reduce(). To implement these methods, you use functions.

```
filter(function, sequence)
```

The filter() method returns a sequence consisting of those elements for which the included function returns true, those that satisfy the criteria given in the specified function. If the included function is None, the method returns those elements of the sequence that are supposed to be returned when the function returns true. Let's examine the use of this method through an example. The following program filters out the odd values and returns only the even values using the filter() method.

```
def evenval(x):
        return x % 2 ==0

evens=filter(evenval, range(1,11))
print(list(evens))
Output:
[2,4,6,8,10]
```

In this example, you see that the filter() method uses an evenval() function and a range() method. The range(1,11) method will generate numerical values from 1 to 10, which are then passed to the evenval() function as arguments. The evenval() function divides the parameter value by 2, compares the remainder with 0, and returns True or False. The function will return True if the result of the mod operation is 0, indicating that the parameter's value is even. The function will return False if the result of the mod operation is 1, indicating that the parameter's value is odd. Since the filter() method will return only those values for which the included function returns True, the program will display only even values.

```
map(function, sequence)
```

The map method calls the included function for each of the elements in the sequence and returns a list of the returned values.

The following example displays the square values of the first 10 sequence numbers using the map() method:

```
def square(x):
        return x*x

sqr=map(square, range(1, 11))
print(list(sqr))

Output:
[1, 4, 9, 16, 25, 36, 49, 64, 81, 100]
```

In this example, the map() method includes a square() function and a range() method. The range(1,11) method will generate numerical values from 1 to 10, which are then passed to the square() function as arguments. The square() function simply returns the square of the supplied parameter. The program will display the square values of the first 10 sequence numbers.

Let's see an example of the map() method that converts the elements of the supplied sequence into integer values.

```
k=map( int, [ 5, 10.15, 20, 25.628, 7 ] )
print (list(k))
Output:
[5, 10, 20, 25, 7]
```

In this program, you see that the map() method includes an int() function and a list of values. The list includes values of different types, including integers, floating-point and long integers. The int() function truncates the elements of the list to integers.

Note

You can also pass more than one sequence in a map() method. The function included in map() is then set to accept multiple arguments. The corresponding elements from each sequence are provided as arguments to the function. If any sequence falls short, None is used for the missing values.

reduce(function, sequence)

The reduce() method returns a single value that is produced by calling the function on the first two elements of the sequence. The function then is called on the result of the function and the next element in the sequence, and so on. For example, the following reduce() method computes the sum of the numbers 1 through 10:

```
import functools
def add(x,y):
        return x+y

r=functools.reduce(add, range(1, 11))
print(r)

Output:
55
```

Here, the reduce() method, which is the part of functools module, includes an add() function and a range() method. The range(1,11) method will return values from 1 to 10. The first two values generated by the range() method are passed to the specified function, add(), and the result (3) and the next value in the sequence (3) are again passed to the add() function. Again, the result of addition (6) and the next value in sequence (4) are passed to the add() function. When all the values generated by the range() method are applied, the final result is returned by the add() function for display.

Note

The functools module is imported at the top because the reduce() method is defined in that module. You will learn more about modules later in this chapter.

Python provides a facility to access more specific information of a function—function attributes.

FUNCTION ATTRIBUTES

A `function` object has a number of attributes that you can use to get more information about a function. Also, you can change these attributes. A list of function attributes is shown in Table 4.1.

Note

You can set and get your own function attributes, too.

The following program demonstrates using function attributes to display specific information of the function, such as its version, author, docstring, and default arguments.

```
funcattrib.py
def sum(a, b=5):
        "Adds the two numbers"
        return a + b

sum.version= "1.0"
sum.author= "bintu"
k=sum(10,20)
print ('Sum is', k)
```

Table 4.1 Function Attributes

Attribute	Description
functionname.__doc__	Represents the docstring from the first line of the function's body.
functionname.__name__	Represents the function name.
functionname.__module__	Represents the name of the module in which the function is defined.
functionname.__defaults__	Represents the tuple with default values to be assigned to the default arguments of the function.
functionname.__code__	Represents the actual code object, the statements in the body of the function.
functionname.__dict__	Represents the dictionary that defines the local namespace for the attributes of the function.

```
print('The documentation string is', sum.__doc__)
print('The function name is', sum.__name__)
print('The default values of the function are', sum.__defaults__)
print('The code object of the function is', sum.__code__)
print('The dictionary of the function is', sum.__dict__)
Output:
Sum is 30
The documentation string is Adds the two numbers
The function name is sum
The default values of the function are (5,)
The code object of the function is <code object sum at 0x00F11250, file "D:\python\
funcattrib.py", line 1>
The dictionary of the function is {'version': '1.0', 'author': 'bintu'}
```

In this program, the version and author information of the sum() function is set in the form of a dictionary, in the *key/value* pattern. Thereafter, the sum() function is called with two arguments, 10 and 20, which are assigned to the parameters a and b, respectively. The first line in the body of the function is the docstring. That is, the docstring or __doc__ attribute of the function, sum(), is set to the text Adds the two numbers. Thereafter, the docstring and its default arguments are displayed by printing the __doc__, __name__, and __defaults__ attributes. Finally, the code object and dictionary of the function are displayed through the __code__ and __dict__ attributes.

Documentation String

The documentation string (docstring) helps to document the program better and makes it easier to understand. A string on the first logical line of a function is the docstring for that function. To display a documentation string, you use the following attribute:

__doc__

This displays the documentation of the function, class, or module.

Note

The docstring also applies to modules and classes that we will discuss later. If the first statement in the class body is a string literal, the compiler binds that string as the documentation string attribute for the class.

The following program displays the multiline documentation string of a function:

```
docstr.py
def rect(l,b):
        '''Computes the area of rectangle
        Values for length and breadth are passed to the function for computation'''
        print ('Area of rectangle is', l*b)
```

```
rect(5,8)
print (rect.__doc__)
Output:
Area of rectangle is 40
Computes the area of rectangle
        Values for length and breadth are passed to the function for computation
```

The attribute __doc__ displays the docstring of the function.

Can a function call itself? Yes—the procedure is called *recursion*.

RECURSION

Recursion is said to occur when a function calls itself. As expected, a function calling itself will generate recursive function calls and result in an infinite loop. When implementing recursion, an exit condition must be included in the function.

Note

Recursion is implemented with the help of a structure known as a *stack*.

Let's examine the concept of recursion through an example. The following program calculates the sum of 10 numbers using recursion:

```
recurfunc.py
def addseq(x):
        if x == 1: return 1
        else: return x + addseq(x-1)

print ('The sum of first 10 sequence numbers is', addseq(10))
Output:
The sum of first 10 sequence numbers is 55
```

The addseq() function is called, passing value 10 to it, which will be assigned to its x parameter. In the body of the function, you see that the first line defines the exit condition. The function terminates or exits, returning 1, if the value of the x parameter is 1. Since the current value of the parameter is 10, an else statement is executed, which is 10+addseq(9).

The else statement calls the addseq() function recursively, passing value 9 to the x parameter. Again the else statement is called, which executes the statement 9+ addseq(8).

Again, the addseq() function is called, passing 8 to its x parameter, resulting in an else statement being executed. The process continues until the value of the x parameter becomes 1, in which case the function exits, returning 1. The execution of the function is shown here:

```
10+addseq(9)
     9+ addseq(8)
         8+ addseq(7)
           ...

           ...
               2+ addseq(1)
                  1
```

The final expression returned from the addseq(10) function call is 10+9+8+7+6...+1. The program displays 55, which is the sum of the 10 numbers.

Let's write one more program on recursion. The following program calculates the factorial of 5 through recursion.

```
factorial.py
def fact(x):
        if x == 1: return 1
        else: return x * fact(x-1)

print ('The factorial of 5 is', fact(5))
```

```
Output:
The factorial of 5 is 120
```

The fact(5) function call passes 5 to the fact() function, which will be assigned to its x parameter. The first statement in the function is an exit condition that ensures that the function will terminate, returning 1 if the value of the x parameter becomes 1. Since the value of the x parameter in the first call to the function is 5, the else statement is executed and returns the following statement:

```
5 * fact(4)
```

The call to the fact(4) function will pass 4 to the x parameter, and again the else statement will be executed and return the following statement:

```
4* fact(3)
```

Again the call to the fact(3) function will pass 3 to the x parameter, resulting in execution of the else statement again. The process continues until the value assigned to the x parameter is 1, in which case the function exits, returning 1. The complete expression that results in execution of the program is this:

```
5*4*3*2*fact(1) or
5*4*3*2*1
```

The program prints the result as 120, which is the factorial of 5.

ITERATORS

Iterators are used for looping through collections of data. Every time you use a for loop in a list, iterators are invoked in the background for retrieving data. An iterator has a next() method that can be called to get each value in the sequence. When all the values are applied, a StopIteration exception is raised. You will learn about exception handling in Chapter 6, "File Handling." For the time being it is enough to know that raising an exception means an occurrence of some kind of error.

To create an iterator object, you need to call the iter() method.

```
iter(object)
```

The iter() method is used to get an iterator object. The iter(object) method calls that object's __iter__ method to get an iterator object. Once, you get an iterator object, you can iterate over the object using its next() method.

The following program displays all the elements of a list using the iterator object:

```
createiter.py
names=['John', 'Kelly', 'Caroline', 'Paula']
i = iter(names)
print (i.__next__())
print (i.__next__())
print (i.__next__())
print (i.__next__())
print (i.__next__())
Output:
John
Kelly
Caroline
Paula
Traceback (most recent call last):
  File "D:\python\createiter.py", line 7, in <module>
    print (i.__next__())
StopIteration
```

In this program, a list is defined, names, that contains four elements: John, Kelly, Caroline, and Paula. An iterator object, i, is created from the list names by invoking the iter() method. Thereafter, you iterate over the object i by using its next() method and display all the four elements of the list. The last call to next() is made deliberately to raise the StopIteration exception and to display the error message that it generates.

The two ways of creating iterators that we are going to discuss next are using generators and using generator expressions.

Generators

A *generator* is a function that creates an iterator. For a function to become a generator, it must return a value using the yield keyword. In other words, the generator function uses the yield keyword to get the next value in the container.

yield

The yield statement is used only when defining a generator function and is used only in the body of the generator function. The presence of a yield statement in a normal function definition converts it into a generator function. When a generator function is called, it returns an iterator known as a *generator iterator*, or just a generator. The body of the generator function is executed by calling the generator's __next__() method repeatedly until it raises an exception.

```
generatorex.py
def fruits(seq):
        for fruit in seq:
                yield '%s' % fruit

f=fruits(['Apple', 'Orange', 'Mango', 'Banana'])
print ('The list of fruits is:')
print (f.__next__())
print (f.__next__())
print (f.__next__())
print (f.__next__())
f=fruits(['Apple', 'Orange', 'Mango', 'Banana'])
print ('The list of fruits is:')
for x in f:
    print (x)
Output:
The list of fruits is:
Apple
Orange
Mango
Banana
The list of fruits is:
Apple
Orange
Mango
Banana
```

In this program, the fruits() function has become a generator function because it contains a yield keyword. The generator that the fruits() function returns is assigned to a variable, f. On calling the __next__() method of the generator f, the first string in the list, Apple, is yielded. When the __next__() method is called for the first time in the generator, execution of the fruits generator function begins and continues until the yield keyword is encountered. On every successive call of the __next__() method, execution of the generator function will continue on the statement following the yield keyword, resulting in yielding the next string in sequence. Since the yield statement occurs within a loop, execution will continue within the loop. The program also displays all the strings through the generator object.

If you call __next__() after that, you get an exception:

```
Traceback (most recent call last):
  File "D:\python\generatorex.py", line 12, in <module>
    print (f.__next__())
StopIteration
```

Beside generators, there is one more way to create iterators, and that is through generator expression.

Generator Expression

A generator expression is an expression in parentheses that creates an iterator object. On getting the iterator object, you can call the __next__() method to get the next value from the iterator as you have seen in the previous two programs. The generator expression is like an anonymous function that yields values and usually consists of at least one for clause and zero or more if clauses. The generator expression you are going to use in the following program consists of one for loop:

```
(squarenum(x) for x in range(6))
```

This generator expression will produce an iterator object.

genexpression.py

```
def squarenum(x):
    return x*x

iteratorobj = (squarenum(x) for x in range(6))
print('The squares of first five sequence numbers')
print (iteratorobj.__next__())
print (iteratorobj.__next__())
print (iteratorobj.__next__())
print (iteratorobj.__next__())
print (iteratorobj.__next__())
print (iteratorobj.__next__())
```

```
Output:
The squares of first five sequence numbers
0
1
4
9
16
25
```

In this program, you can see that the generator expression (squarenum(x) for x in range(6)) creates an iterator object, which is then assigned to iteratorobj. The generator expression calls the squarenum() function and uses a for loop to yield the squares of the numerical values from 0 to 5. Thereafter, using the __next__(), you access the square values from the iterator object one by one.

MODULES

A module is a file consisting of a few functions and variables used for a particular task. A module can be reused in any other program that imports it. The functions and variables of the module become available in the current program and can be used in it. The filename of the module must have a .py extension.

To import a module to a program, you use the import statement. You can use import in several forms. Consider a calendar module that displays a calendar of a specified month and year. Let's have a look at different ways of importing a calendar module in the current program. The first way is through this statement:

```
import calendar
```

Python looks for the calendar.py file in the disk drive. If the file is found, then the statements in the main block of that module are executed so that its functions can be reused in the current program. That is, all the functions of the calendar module become accessible in the current program. To refer a prcal() function of the calendar module, write the following statement:

```
calendar.prcal()
```

The second way of importing a calendar module to the current program is through this statement:

```
from calendar import prcal
```

This imports the prcal() function from the calendar module. Now you can directly refer to the prcal() function in the current program without prefixing the module name calendar to it:

```
prcal()
```

The third way of importing a `calendar` module to the current program is through this statement:

```
from calendar import *
```

This imports all objects from the `calendar` module. You can access any function of the `calendar` module directly without prefixing the module name to the function. To refer to the `prcal()` function of the `calendar` module, you can write:

```
prcal()
```

The fourth way of importing a `calendar` module to the current program is through this statement:

```
import calendar as cal
```

It imports the `calendar` module in the current program and makes it accessible through the term `cal`. Its `prcal()` function can now be accessed by prefixing it with the term `cal`:

```
cal.prcal()
```

The following program imports a `calendar` module in the program and displays the calendar of the specified year, using its `prcal()` function.

```
module1.py
import calendar
year = int(input("Type in the year number:"))
calendar.prcal(year)
```

You can also rewrite the program as shown here:

```
from calendar import prcal
year = int(input("Type in the year number:"))
prcal(year)
```

The output of the program will be the calendar of the year entered, as shown in Figure 4.1.

This program displays the calendar of the year entered by the user. The technique of calling the `prcal()` function changes according to the method used in importing the `calendar` module to the program.

The following program prints the system clock time infinitely:

```
module2.py
from time import time, ctime

prev_time = ""
while(True):
```

```
Type in the year number:2011
                          2011

        January                 February                   March
Mo Tu We Th Fr Sa Su     Mo Tu We Th Fr Sa Su     Mo Tu We Th Fr Sa Su
               1  2              1  2  3  4  5  6            1  2  3  4  5  6
 3  4  5  6  7  8  9      7  8  9 10 11 12 13      7  8  9 10 11 12 13
10 11 12 13 14 15 16     14 15 16 17 18 19 20     14 15 16 17 18 19 20
17 18 19 20 21 22 23     21 22 23 24 25 26 27     21 22 23 24 25 26 27
24 25 26 27 28 29 30     28                       28 29 30 31
31

         April                    May                      June
Mo Tu We Th Fr Sa Su     Mo Tu We Th Fr Sa Su     Mo Tu We Th Fr Sa Su
            1  2  3                          1            1  2  3  4  5
 4  5  6  7  8  9 10      2  3  4  5  6  7  8      6  7  8  9 10 11 12
11 12 13 14 15 16 17      9 10 11 12 13 14 15     13 14 15 16 17 18 19
18 19 20 21 22 23 24     16 17 18 19 20 21 22     20 21 22 23 24 25 26
25 26 27 28 29 30        23 24 25 26 27 28 29     27 28 29 30
                         30 31

         July                   August                   September
Mo Tu We Th Fr Sa Su     Mo Tu We Th Fr Sa Su     Mo Tu We Th Fr Sa Su
            1  2  3       1  2  3  4  5  6  7               1  2  3  4
 4  5  6  7  8  9 10      8  9 10 11 12 13 14      5  6  7  8  9 10 11
11 12 13 14 15 16 17     15 16 17 18 19 20 21     12 13 14 15 16 17 18
18 19 20 21 22 23 24     22 23 24 25 26 27 28     19 20 21 22 23 24 25
25 26 27 28 29 30 31     29 30 31                 26 27 28 29 30

        October                 November                 December
Mo Tu We Th Fr Sa Su     Mo Tu We Th Fr Sa Su     Mo Tu We Th Fr Sa Su
                  1  2       1  2  3  4  5  6               1  2  3  4
 3  4  5  6  7  8  9      7  8  9 10 11 12 13      5  6  7  8  9 10 11
10 11 12 13 14 15 16     14 15 16 17 18 19 20     12 13 14 15 16 17 18
17 18 19 20 21 22 23     21 22 23 24 25 26 27     19 20 21 22 23 24 25
24 25 26 27 28 29 30     28 29 30                 26 27 28 29 30 31
31
```

Figure 4.1
Calendar of the year 2011.

```
    curr_time = ctime(time())
    if(prev_time != curr_time):
        print ("The time is:",ctime(time()))
        prev_time = curr_time
Output:
The time is: Wed Feb 02 10:16:33 2011
The time is: Wed Feb 02 10:16:34 2011
The time is: Wed Feb 02 10:16:35 2011
The time is: Wed Feb 02 10:16:36 2011
The time is: Wed Feb 02 10:16:37 2011
```

In this program, you want to display the system clock infinitely and don't want the same time to be repeated again. Remember, CPU machine cycles are much faster than a clock and execute a loop or a program several times in a second. Hence, the same time will be displayed again and again. To avoid this, you use two variables— one stores the current system clock time, and the other waits for the time to change.

First the program imports the `time` and `ctime` functions of the `time` module in the current program. Then an infinite loop is executed. In the loop, the current system clock time is accessed and stored temporarily in the variable `curr_time`. The time in `curr_time` is displayed and assigned to another variable, `prev_time`. In the next iteration of the `while` loop, the system clock time is again fetched and stored in the `curr_time` variable. Until the time in `curr_time` differs from the time in `prev_time`, the new time fetched in `curr_time` will not be displayed. After displaying the new time in `curr_time`, it is assigned to the `prev_time` variable, and the loop continues.

The math Module

The `math` module contains not only common trigonometric functions but also several constants and functions:

- **math.pi**—Returns the value of pi, 3.1415926535897931.
- **math.e**—Returns the value of e, 2.7182818284590451.
- **ceil(x)**—Displays the next larger whole number.
- **floor(x)**—Displays the next smaller whole number.

The `math` module is made available to the program through this statement:

```
import math
```

The following program computes and displays the next larger and smaller whole numbers of the specified float value using the `ceil()` and `floor()` functions of the `math` module.

```
mathmethod.py
import math
print (math.ceil(7.3))
print (math.ceil(-7.3))
print (math.floor(7.9))
print (math.floor(-7.9))

Output:
8
-7
7
-8
```

In this program, you import the `math` module and use its `ceil()` and `floor()` methods to display the next larger and smaller whole numbers.

Does Python provide a function that you can use to see all the identifiers defined in a module? Yes, and the function name is `dir()`.

The dir() Function

The `dir()` function is used to list the identifiers defined by a module. The identifiers are the functions, classes, and variables defined in that module.

When you supply a module name to the `dir()` function, it returns a list of the names defined in that module. When no argument is applied to it, the `dir()` function returns a list of the names in the current local scope.

The following program displays the list of identifiers defined in the `sys` and `calendar` modules:

```
direx.py
import sys, calendar
print("The list of methods and attributes in the local scope:",dir())
print ("\nThe list of methods and attributes in the calendar module:", dir(calendar))
print ("\nThe list of methods and attributes in the sys module:", dir(sys))
```

```
Output:
The list of methods and attributes in the local scope: ['__builtins__', '__doc__',
'__name__', '__package__', 'calendar', 'sys']

The list of methods and attributes in the calendar module: ['Calendar', 'EPOCH', 'FRI-
DAY', 'February', 'HTMLCalendar', 'IllegalMonthError', 'IllegalWeekdayError', 'Janu-
ary', 'LocaleHTMLCalendar', 'LocaleTextCalendar', 'MONDAY', 'SATURDAY', 'SUNDAY',
'THURSDAY', 'TUESDAY', 'TextCalendar', 'WEDNESDAY', '_EPOCH_ORD', '__all__',
'__builtins__', '__cached__', '__doc__', '__file__', '__name__', '__package__',
'_colwidth', '_locale', '_localized_day', '_localized_month', '_spacing', 'c', 'cal-
endar', 'datetime', 'day_abbr', 'day_name', 'different_locale', 'error', 'firstweek-
day', 'format', 'formatstring', 'isleap', 'leapdays', 'main', 'mdays', 'month',
'month_abbr', 'month_name', 'monthcalendar', 'monthrange', 'prcal', 'prmonth',
'prweek', 'setfirstweekday', 'sys', 'timegm', 'week', 'weekday', 'weekheader']

The list of methods and attributes in the sys module: ['__displayhook__', '__doc__',
'__excepthook__', '__name__', '__package__', '__stderr__', '__stdin__',
'__stdout__', '_clear_type_cache', '_current_frames', '_getframe', '_xoptions',
'api_version', 'argv', 'builtin_module_names', 'byteorder', 'call_tracing', 'call-
stats', 'copyright', 'displayhook', 'dllhandle', 'dont_write_bytecode', 'exc_info',
```

```
'excepthook', 'exec_prefix', 'executable', 'exit', 'flags', 'float_info', 'float_
repr_style', 'getcheckinterval', 'getdefaultencoding', 'getfilesystemencoding',
'getprofile', 'getrecursionlimit', 'getrefcount', 'getsizeof', 'getswitchinterval',
'gettrace', 'getwindowsversion', 'hash_info', 'hexversion', 'int_info', 'intern',
'maxsize', 'maxunicode', 'meta_path', 'modules', 'path', 'path_hooks', 'path_impor-
ter_cache', 'platform', 'prefix', 'setcheckinterval', 'setprofile', 'setrecursionli-
mit', 'setswitchinterval', 'settrace', 'stderr', 'stdin', 'stdout', 'subversion',
'version', 'version_info', 'warnoptions', 'winver']
```

Command-Line Arguments

Command-line arguments are used to pass arguments to a program while running it. Each command-line argument that you pass to the program will be stored in the sys.argv variable. The sys.argv variable is a list that always has a length of at least 1. The item at index 0 is the name of the Python program you are running.

Note

Command-line arguments are separated by spaces.

The following program lists the command-line arguments passed to the program, their count, and the path of the Python installation.

```
commandline1.py
import sys
print ('There are %d arguments' % len(sys.argv))
print ('The command line arguments are:')
print (sys.argv)
for i in sys.argv:
    print(i)
print ('Path of the Python is', sys.path)
```

Output is shown in Figure 4.2.

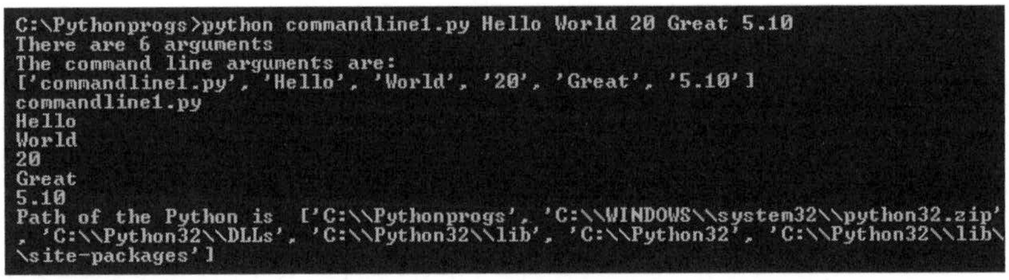

Figure 4.2
Command-line arguments passed to the program.

Summary

In this chapter you learned about different statements that define and return values from functions. You also learned to use default value parameters and keyword arguments in a function. You learned to use local and global variables. For smaller expressions, you learned to create lambda functions. Also, you saw how to apply functions to sequences using different function attributes and implement recursion. For accessing collections of data, you learned to use iterators, generators, and generator expressions. To use built-in functions, you learned to import and use modules. Finally, you saw how to pass command-line arguments to a Python program.

The next chapter will discuss object-oriented programming (OOP). You will learn to define classes, define functions in a class, and use class attributes. You will learn to initialize instance variables through the __init__ method. You will learn to define and use class and static methods. You will see how Python removes the objects that go out of scope through garbage collection. The chapter also covers an important topic in OOP, inheritance. You will learn to apply single, multilevel, and multiple inheritance. You will also learn to apply method overriding and arithmetic operations to instances through operator overloading. The chapter will also explain the concept of polymorphism and the use of properties and descriptors.

CHAPTER 5

CLASSES

This chapter covers the following:

- Defining classes
- Using class attributes
- Defining functions in a class
- Accessing class variables in instance methods
- Creating instances and initializing instance variables through the __init__() method
- Using class and static methods
- Understanding garbage collection
- Understanding inheritance—single, multilevel, and multiple inheritance
- Using access control specifiers
- Method overriding
- Operator overloading
- Polymorphism
- Using properties and descriptors

THE CLASS STATEMENT

Python supports object-oriented programming and provides reusable code in the form of classes. It is always better to use old code than to start from scratch because existing code has already been used and tested, so it saves time in debugging a project.

A *class* is like a template or blueprint for data and operations. It consists of a number of attributes that include variables and methods. The variables are called *data members*, and methods are called *member functions*. The functions define the operations that can be applied to data members. From classes, you create *instances*, also known as *objects*. The instances automatically get access to data members and methods.

To create a class, you use the `class` statement, an executable statement that is used for creating a class object. It not only creates a new class object but also assigns it the name specified.

```
Syntax:
class classname(base-classes):
statement(s)
```

where `classname` is an identifier that is bound to the class object. You can create either an independent class or one that inherits from other classes. The class that inherits is also known as a *derived* class or a *sub-class*, and the class that is inherited from is known as a *super or base class*. When creating a derived class, you specify the comma-delimited base classes from which the new class is going to be derived. The base classes are also known as the *parents* of the new class being created. The new class inherits the attributes of its parent classes. It can override any of the parent's attributes and can add attributes of its own. Base classes are optional. To create a class without bases, you can omit `(base-classes)`, placing the colon right after `classname`.

The sequence of statements that follows the class statement is known as the *class body*, where you specify the functions and other attributes of the class.

Attributes of Class Objects

To specify an attribute of a class object, you bind a value to an identifier within the class body. For example:

```
class rect:
     l = 8
print (rect.l)
```

In this example, `rect` is a class object with an attribute named `l` that is bound to the value 8, and `rect.l` refers to that attribute.

The following example shows a class object, `rect`, with two attributes, `l` and `b`, bound to the values 8 and 5.

```
rectclass1.py
class rect:
    l=8
    b=5
print ("Length is %d, Breadth is %d" %(rect.l, rect.b))
Output:
Length is 8, Breadth is 5
```

You can see that when referring to the attributes, the class object is prefixed to the attributes.

You also can have a class that does nothing, as is shown in the following example:

```
passex.py
class rect(object):
    pass

rect.l = 10
print (rect.l)
Output:
10
```

The pass statement does nothing and represents an empty block of statements. It acts as a placeholder for code that you plan to write later. In this program, you can see that the l attribute of the rect class object is bound to value 10 outside the body of the class that is then displayed.

Built-In Class Attributes

A class statement implicitly sets some class attributes. You can use these class attributes to get information about a class. A list of class attributes is shown in Table 5.1.

The following program displays the class's name, base class, dictionary object, and so on using the class attributes:

```
rectclass2.py
class rect:
    l=8
    b=5
print ("Length is %d, Breadth is %d" %(rect.l, rect.b))
print ("Class name is ", rect.__name__, " and Base class is ",rect.__bases__)
print ("Attributes of this class are ", rect.__dict__)
Output:
Length is 8, Breadth is 5
Class name is rect and Base class is (<class 'object'>,)
```

Table 5.1   Class Attributes

Attribute	Description
__name__	The class name identifier used in the class statement.
__bases__	The tuple of class objects specified as the base classes in the class statement.
__dict__	The dictionary object that the class uses to hold its other attributes. To assign a value to an attribute, you use the dictionary object. The following example assigns value 8 to the l attribute of the rect class object: `rect.__dict__['l']=8`
__doc__	The class documentation string.
__module__	The name of the module in which the class is defined.

```
Attributes of this class are {'__module__': '__main__', 'b': 5, 'l': 8, '__dict__':
<attribute '__dict__' of 'rect' objects>, '__weakref__': <attribute '__weakref__' of
'rect' objects>, '__doc__': None}
```

This program defines and initializes two attributes of the rect class object, l and b, to values 8 and 5. The l and b attributes, class name, and base class name are then displayed. The program also displays the attributes of the class through a dictionary object.

Note

If you don't specify a base class, the default is object.

Defining Functions in a Class

The functions defined in a class are known as *methods*. A method defined in a class always has a mandatory first parameter named self that refers to the instance on which you call the method. The self parameter plays a special role in method calls. The methods that you will be defining in the class are called *instance methods*. Later you will see how to define class methods in a class. The format of the class with methods added is this:

```
class classname(base-classes):
  class variable(s)
  def method 1(self):
    instance variable(s)
```

```
    statement(s)
[def method n(self):
    instance variable(s)
    statement(s)]
```

A class can have two types of data members:

Class variable—The data member that is outside of any method of the class is known as a *class variable*. All instances of the class share the class variables, and changes made in the class variable by one instance will be seen by other instances.

Instance variable—The variables that are defined inside a method belong only to the current instance of the object and are known as *instance variables*. Changes made to instance variables by any instance are limited to that particular instance and don't affect the instance variables of other instances.

Let's see how to create an instance method and how it can be used to access class variables.

Accessing Class Variables in Instance Methods

To access class variables, the methods defined in a class body must use a fully qualified name; the class object must be prefixed with the class variables. The following example demonstrates accessing class variables in an instance method:

```
class rect:
    l = 8
    b=5
    def area(self):
        print rect.l*rect.b
```

Two class variables, l and b, are initialized to 8 and 5. The area() instance method refers to the class l and b variables, using the fully qualified names rect.l and rect.b.

You cannot understand the concept of instance variables until you know about instances of a class and how to create them.

Instances

A class is a template or blueprint of data and operations; to use the data and operations independently, you need to create instances. An instance is a variable that acts as a replica of a class. You can create as many instances of a class as desired. Each instance gets a separate copy of the methods and attributes defined in the class. Each instance can access the methods and attributes of the class independently, and an attribute of one instance doesn't interfere with an attribute of another instance. It also means that through instances, you can use a class for performing operations with several different sets of data. To create an instance of a class, you call the class object as if it were without parameters, as shown here:

```
r=rect()
```

You can see that the class object rect is called as if it is a function. Each call returns a new instance of that class. The above statement returns a new instance of the class, rect, and assigns it to the variable r.

The following program computes the area of a rectangle by creating an instance of the class and invoking a method through the instance:

```
rectclass3.py
class rect:
    l=8
    b=5
    def rectarea(self):
        return rect.l * rect.b
r=rect()
print ("Area of rectangle is ", r.rectarea())
Output:
Area of rectangle is 40
```

In this program, an instance of class rect is created with the name r. The class has two class variables, l and b, initialized to 8 and 5. The rectarea() method of the class is invoked through the instance r, which computes and returns the area of a rectangle. Remember, you need to specify self explicitly when defining the method, whereas you do not specify it when calling the method, as Python adds it automatically.

Note

> Python adds the self argument automatically when calling the methods via instance, so you don't have to include the term self when you call the methods of the class.

In this program, the variables l and b defined in the class rect are the class variables, and class variables are implicitly shared by all instances of the class. It also means that changes applied to the class variables by one instance can be seen by another instance of the class. This problem will be solved when creating instance variables.

The method we are going to discuss next helps in initializing variables of an instance.

The __init__() Method

The __init__ method is the first method to be executed after creation of an instance. This method is like a constructor in C++ and Java languages and is used to perform initialization. Arguments may or may not be passed to the __init__ method.

Note

> The instance is already constructed by the time __init__ is called.

The first argument of every class method is a reference to the current instance of the class. This first argument is named self. In the __init__ method, self refers to the newly created instance; in other class methods, it refers to the instance whose method was called. When defining __init__, you must remember to call the ancestor's __init__ method explicitly if it is there.

For example:

```
class rect:
   def __init__(self):
      self.l = 8
      self.b = 5


r=rect()
```

In this example, an instance is created for the rect class by name r. The __init__ method will be automatically executed to perform the task of initializing the variables of the instance. Here, the __init__ method initializes the variables l and b of the instance r to 8 and 5. The variables l and b defined in the class are instance variables.

Note

> The __init__ method must not return a value, or a TypeError exception is raised.

The following program demonstrates the __init__ method in initializing instance variables and also calculates the area of a rectangle:

defaultcons.py

```
class rect:
   def __init__(self):
      self.l = 8
      self.b = 5
   def rectarea(self):
      return self.l * self.b
```

```
r=rect()
print ("Area of rectangle is ", r.rectarea())
Output:
Area of rectangle is 40
```

An instance of the rect class object is created by name r. The __init__ method will be automatically executed to initialize the variables of the instance r. The variables 1 and b of the instance r will be initialized to 8 and 5. Finally, the rectarea() method is called through instance r and calculates and returns the area of the rectangle.

After the creation of an instance, the __init__ method is automatically executed. Can you pass arguments to the __init__ method for initializing instance variables?

Passing Arguments to the __init__ Method The following program demonstrates passing arguments to the __init__ method:

```
paramcons.py
class rect:
   def __init__(self, x,y):
      self.1 = x
      self.b = y
   def rectarea(self):
      return self.1 * self.b

r=rect(5,8)
print ("Area of rectangle is ", r.rectarea())
Output:
Area of rectangle is 40
```

An instance of the rect class object is created by name r. The two arguments, 5 and 8, which are supplied during creation of the instance, r will be passed to the __init__ method as arguments. That is, the values 5 and 8 will be assigned to parameters x and y of the __init__ method from where they will be assigned to the instance variables 1 and b. Finally, the rectarea() method is called through instance r that calculates and returns the area of rectangle.

Note

The arguments to be passed to the __init__ method if any have to be supplied when initializing of the instance.

Can you have default value parameters in __init__ method as in normal functions? Yes.

Defining Default Value Parameters in the __init__ Method This example shows how default values are specified for the parameters of the __init__ method so that if the value of any parameter is not supplied when initializing an instance, its default value is used.

The following program demonstrates using default value parameters in the __init__ method. The program demonstrates creates two instances: one that supplies the arguments and another that doesn't supply any argument. The default values will be considered for the instance that doesn't supply arguments. Here is the code:

```
constructor.py
class rect:
   def __init__(self,x=8, y=5):
      self.l = x
      self.b = y
   def rectarea(self):
      return self.l * self.b

r=rect()
s=rect(10,20)
print ("Area of rectangle is ", r.rectarea())
print ("Area of rectangle is ", s.rectarea())
Output:
Area of rectangle is 40
Area of rectangle is 200
```

You can see that the __init__ method defines the default values for its parameters x and y as 8 and 5. The two instances of rect are created as r and s. The instance r has no arguments for the __init__ method and hence, the default values 8 and 5 in the parameters x and y will be used to initialize its instance variables l and b. The s instance supplies the arguments 10 and 20 when it's initialized and will be assigned to the parameters x and y from where they will be assigned to its instance variables l and b. The rectarea() method when invoked by the two instances will calculate and return the area of a rectangle on the basis of the values assigned to their instance variables, l and b.

By now, you know how to create an instance and how to initialize its variables through __init__. Now let's see the procedure for printing the instance. Remember, you are not printing the instance variables but the instance itself. When printing an instance, it is converted into a string.

String Representation of an Instance The __str__ method is called by the str() and print statements to display the string representation of an instance.

```
classstr.py
class rect:
   def __init__(self, x,y):
      self.l = x
      self.b = y
   def __str__(self):
      return 'Length is %d, Breadth is %d' %(self.l, self.b)
   def rectarea(self):
      return self.l * self.b
r=rect(5,8)
print (r)
print ("Area of rectangle is ", r.rectarea())
Output:
Length is 5, Breadth is 8
Area of rectangle is 40
```

This program creates an instance r of class rect and passes values 5 and 8 to the __init__ method for assigning them to its instance variables l and b. Then, instance r is passed to a print statement that results in creation of the string representation of the instance and hence invokes the __str__ method. The __str__ method returns a message displaying values of the instance variables l and b, so the whole instance is returned in the form of a string. The program also computes and displays the area of rectangle through rectarea().

Besides the instance methods, you can also create class methods and static methods in a class. Let's learn about them.

CLASS METHODS

A class method has no self argument and receives a class as its first argument. By convention, the argument to the class method is called cls. That is, in a class method, the class on which it is called is passed to it as the first argument. The class method can also be called directly through the class object without instantiating the class. A class method is defined using the @classmethod decorator. A decorator provides a convenient method to insert and modify code in functions or classes.

```
Syntax:
@classmethod
def f(cls, parm1, parm2, ...):
      body of the method
```

This shows a class method, f, with few parameters parm1, parm2, and so on.

The following program creates a class as well as an instance method and accesses them to display the content of instance and class variables.

```
classmethod.py
class book:
   price=100
   @classmethod
   def display(cls):
      print (cls.price)
   def show(self,x):
      self.price=x
      print (self.price)

b=book()
c=book()
book.display()
b.display()
b.show(200)
c.show(300)
Output:
100
100
200
300
```

This program defines a class object, book, which contains a class variable, price, initialized to 100. Also, the class contains a class method, display(), and an instance method, show(). Two instances, b and c, are created of the class book. The class method display() is called through the class object, book, which displays the value of the price class variable, 100. The class method display() is called through the instance b, which again displays the value of the class variable price as 100. Then the instance method show() is called through instance b, passing value 200 to it, which is assigned to its parameter x and which is finally assigned to its instance variable, price. Now there are two price variables, a class variable initialized to value 100, which is common for all instances, and an instance variable of the instance b set to 200. The show() instance method is called through the instance c, passing value 300 as an argument to be assigned to its instance variable, price.

There is an alternative to the class method known as the static method.

STATIC METHODS

A static method is an ordinary function that is built using the @staticmethod decorator and that binds its result to a class attribute. The difference between a static method and a class method is that a static method has no cls parameter. It doesn't use the self parameter, either. There is one more difference—the class method is automatically inherited by any child classes, whereas the static method is not. Also, the definition of a static method is immutable via inheritance. A static method can be called on a class or on any instance of a class.

```
Syntax:
@staticmethod
def name (parm...) :
     body of the method
```

This shows a static method, name, with parameters parm....

The following program defines a class that contains a static method and accesses it via a class object as well as through an instance.

```
staticmethod.py
class rect:
   @staticmethod
   def disp_message():
      l=50
      print ("Length is ", l)

rect.disp_message()
r=rect()
r.disp_message()
Output:
Length is 50
Length is 50
```

The program creates a rect class with a disp_message() static method in it. First, disp_message() is called through the class object rect. The method initializes an attribute l to value 50 and displays it. Then, an instance r is created of rect, and disp_message() is called through the instance r. In disp_message(), again, the value of the attribute l will be set to 50 and displayed. Hence, the program confirms that the static method can be called on a class as well as on an instance of a class.

The following program creates a class that contains both a static method and a class method and shows how a class variable is displayed through the two methods:

```
staticlassmethod.py
class product:
   count = 0
   def __init__(self, name):
    self.name=name
    product.count += 1
```

```
@staticmethod
def prodstatcount():
   return product.count

@classmethod
def prodclasscount(cls):
   print('Class info: ', cls)
   print ('Class method - The product count is: ', cls.count)

p1=product('Camera')
p2=product('Cell')
print('Static method - The product count is: ', product.prodstatcount())
p2.prodclasscount()
Output:
Static method - The product count is: 2
Class info: <class '__main__.product'>
Class method - The product count is: 2
```

The program defines a product class that contains a class variable, count, initialized to 0. The class contains a static method and a class method, prodstatcount() and prodclasscount(). An instance, p1, of class product is created that passes the string 'Camera' to the __init__ method to be assigned to its instance variable, name. The __init__ method also increments the value of the class variable count by 1. Similarly, another instance, p2, is created that passes the string 'Cell' to the __init__ method to be assigned to its instance variable, name. The __init__ method again increments the value of the class variable count by 1, making its value 2. Thereafter, the static method prodstatcount() is called on the product class object, which returns the value of the class count variable, 2. Finally, the class method prodclasscount() is called on instance p2, passing the product class to it via the cls parameter. The information of the class is displayed by printing the cls parameter, and the value of the count class variable is displayed.

Assigning One Instance to Another

Python provides a facility to assign one instance to another. Assigning an instance to another results in creation of a new instance if it doesn't exists. For example, assuming inst1 and inst2 are instances of some class, then the following statement:

```
inst1=inst2
```

will create the instance inst1 if it doesn't exist, and all the instance variables of inst1 will be initialized to values equal to those in instance variables of inst2.

The following program demonstrates how an instance is assigned to another and results in assigning the attributes of an instance to another instance.

```
assignobj.py
class rect:
   def __init__(self, x,y):
      self.l = x
      self.b = y
   def rectarea(self):
      return self.l * self.b
r=rect(5,8)
s=r
print ("Area of rectangle is ", r.rectarea())
print ("Area of rectangle is ", s.rectarea())
Output:
Area of rectangle is 40
Area of rectangle is 40
```

In this program, an object r is created of class rect. The arguments 5 and 8 are passed to the __init__ method, and then are assigned to the l and b variables of the r instance. The content of instance r is assigned to instance s. That is, the instance s will also have its instance variables initialized to 5 and 8. This is proved by computing the area of a rectangle by invoking rectarea() through both the instances, and the area comes out the same.

GARBAGE COLLECTION

Garbage collection is a procedure of freeing up the memory that is used by the variables or instances that are no longer required. The memory that is used by the instances is usually freed up automatically when the variables assigned to them go out of scope. That's why memory leaks are rare in Python.

For garbage collection, Python uses a reference countering mechanism. Each object has a reference count that indicates the number of references that exist for that object. The reference count increases for each reference added to the object and is decreased by removing the reference to that object. When the refer count reaches zero, the object is garbage collected.

The following program demonstrates the concept of garbage collection. It creates two instances. A class variable is incremented by 1 on creation of an instance and is decremented by 1 on deleting an instance.

```
destructor.py
class rect:
```

```
    n=0
    def __init__(self,x,y):
            rect.n +=1
            self.l=x
            self.b=y
    def __del__(self):
            rect.n -=1
            class_name = self.__class__.__name__
            print(class_name,' destroyed')
    def rectarea(self):
        print ('Area of rectangle is ', self.l * self.b)
    def noOfObjects(self):
        print ('Number of objects are: ', rect.n)

r=rect(3,5)
r.rectarea()
s=rect(5,8)
s.rectarea()
r.noOfObjects()
del r
s.noOfObjects()
del s
Output:
Area of rectangle is 15
Area of rectangle is 40
Number of objects are: 2
rect destroyed
Number of objects are: 1
rect destroyed
```

In this program, an instance r is created and passes values 3 and 5 as arguments to the __init__ method for assigning them to its instance variables l and b. On creation of the instance r, the class variable that was initially set to 0 will be incremented by 1. Similarly, another instance, s, is created, passing arguments 5 and 8 to its __init__ method for assignment to its instance variables l and b. Again, the value of the class variable n is incremented by 1, making its value 2. The area of a rectangle is computed on instances r and s. The noOfObjects() method displays the value of the class variable n (2), which confirms the existence of two instances of the class. When the instance r is deleted, the __del__ method is executed, the value of the class variable n is decremented, and a message is displayed confirming destruction of the instance. After deleting the instance r, when you call the noOfObjects() method, the value of the class variable n is displayed as 1, confirming that only a single instance of the rect class is left. Finally, s is also deleted, which decrements the value of the class variable to 0.

INHERITANCE

Inheritance is a technique of copying the data members and member functions of an existing class into another class. That is, instead of beginning from scratch, an existing class can be inherited, and additional data members and member functions can be defined. The class that is being inherited is called the base class or the super class, and the inheriting class is called the derived class or sub-class. The sub-class inherits all the properties of the base class and hence results in saving time and effort.

Types of Inheritance

I will discuss three types of inheritance:

- Single inheritance
- Multilevel inheritance
- Multiple inheritance

Single Inheritance

This is the simplest type of inheritance, where one class is derived from another single class, as shown in Figure 5.1.

Class B inherits class A, or class B is derived from class A. A derived class has to identify the class from which it is derived. Suppose, for example, you want to derive the triangle class from the rect class. The class definition of triangle will appear like this:

```
class triangle(rect):
```

This statement indicates that rect is a base class, and triangle is a derived class.

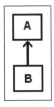

Figure 5.1
Single inheritance.

Consider the following program of single inheritance. In this program, a triangle class inherits the base class, rect, as a result of which the instance of the triangle class can access the public member functions of the rect class (beside its own member functions).

```
inherit1.py
from __future__ import division

class rect:
    def __init__(self):
        self.l = 8
        self.b = 5
    def rectarea(self):
        return self.l * self.b

class triangle(rect):
    def __init__(self):
        rect.__init__(self)
        self.x = 17
        self.y = 13
    def trigarea(self):
        return 1/2*self.x * self.y

r=triangle()
print ("Area of rectangle is ", r.rectarea())
print ("Area of triangle is ", r.trigarea())
Output:
Area of rectangle is 40
Area of triangle is 110.5
```

Note

If you have __init__ in both classes, the base class's __init__ method must be made from the __init__ method of the derived class.

This program defines a rect class consisting of an __init__ and a rectarea() method. One more class, triangle, is defined in the program that is derived from rect. The triangle class consists of __init__ and trigarea() methods.

An instance r of triangle is created. Since the triangle class derives the rect, the instance r can invoke the methods of the rect base class, as well as that of its own class. After creation of the instance r, the __init__ method of triangle is executed, which in turn invokes the __init__ method of its base class, rect. Recall that the __init__ method must explicitly call the ancestor's __init__ method if it is there. The __init__ method of the rect class initializes the values of the instance variables 1 and b to 8 and 5. After the execution of the __init__ method of the rect class, the __init__ method of the triangle class will be executed, which initializes the values of the instance variables x and y to 17 and 13. Being able to call methods of both the classes, the instance r invokes the rectarea() and trigarea() methods to compute and display the area of the rectangle and the triangle.

Access Control Specifiers

Access control specifiers define the visibility of the members of the class. All the members of the class are assigned a boundary in which they can be accessed using these control specifiers. There are two keywords, public and private.

> **Public member**—Accessed from inside as well as outside of the class.
>
> **Private member**—Cannot be accessed from outside the body of the class. A private member is preceded by a double underscore (__).

Accessing public Members   The following program shows how to define and access public members

```
publicaccess.py
class rect:
   def __init__(self, x,y):
      self.l = x
      self.b = y
   def rectarea(self):
      return self.l * self.b

r=rect(5,8)
print ("Area of rectangle is ", r.rectarea())
print ("Area of rectangle is ", r.l* r.b)
Output:
Area of rectangle is 40
Area of rectangle is 40
```

The program creates an instance r of rect and passes 5 and 8 as arguments to the __init__ method to be assigned to its instance variables, 1 and b. The program calculates the area of a rectangle by invoking the rectarea()method on instance r as well as by accessing and multiplying the instance variables 1 and b outside the body of the class, which confirms that the instance variables 1 and b are publicly accessible.

Accessing private Members   When in a method of a class body, an identifier is defined starting with two underscores but not ending with underscores, it is considered a private identifier of the class. The private identifiers cannot be accessed from outside the body of the class.

The following program demonstrates how to define private accessible variables in a class:

```
privateaccess.py
class rect:
   def __init__(self, x,y):
      self.__l = x
      self.__b = y
   def rectarea(self):
      return self.__l * self.__b
r=rect(5,8)
print ("Area of rectangle is ", r.rectarea())
print ("Area of rectangle is ", r._rect__l* r._rect__b)
Output:
Area of rectangle is 40
Area of rectangle is 40
```

This program defines two private instance variables, l and b, represented by __l and __b. These can be accessed within the body of the class. If you try to access the private members such as r.__l * r.__b, you will get AttributeError: 'rect' has no attribute '__l'. To access private variables from outside the body of the class, you need to use the class name, along with the instance name such as r._rect__l.

A derived class can access the public data members and member functions of the base class. Perhaps the derived class needs to access a member function of the base class but with slight modification. For example, suppose the base class has a member function named commission() that computes commission equal to 5% of an amount, whereas the derived class needs a member function that computes commission of 10%. In this case, the derived class needs to redefine the commission() member function that computes the commission of 10% in its own body, overriding the member function of the base class. Let's see the concept in detail.

Method Overriding   If in a derived class you have a member function with the same signature as that of the base class, then you say that the member function of the derived class is *overriding* the member function of the base class. If the member function is invoked by the instance of the derived class, the member function of the derived class will be executed (and not the member function of the base class).

The following program demonstrates the concept of method overriding. A triangle class inherits from the class rect and overrides the area()method of the base class by redefining it. Here is the code:

```
override.py
from __future__ import division
class rect:
   def __init__(self):
      self.l = 8
      self.b = 5
   def area(self):
      return self.l * self.b

class triangle(rect):
   def __init__(self):
      rect.__init__(self)
      self.x = 17
      self.y = 13
   def area(self):
      return 1/2*self.x * self.y
r=triangle()
print ("Area of triangle is ", r.area())
Output:
Area of triangle is 110.5
```

The program creates an instance r of the triangle class. Since the triangle class inherits from the rect class, its instance can execute the methods of rect as well as those of triangle. On creation of the instance, the __init__ method of triangle is invoked, which in turn invokes the __init__ method of rect, initializing the instance variables l, b, x, and y to values 8, 5, 17, and 13. triangle overrides the area() method, so when the area() method on instance r is invoked, it will execute the area() method of the triangle class, computing and returning the area of triangle instead of the area of rectangle.

What if I want to get the area of rectangle as well as the area of triangle? For this, you need to call the method of the base class from the derived class.

Accessing Methods of a Base Class from a Derived Class   You can access methods of the base class from the derived class by using a fully qualified name, by prefixing the class name to the method name. The following program shows how to access a method of the base class from the derived class:

```
inherit2.py
from __future__ import division

class rect:
   def __init__(self):
      self.l = 8
      self.b = 5
```

```
    def area(self):
        print ("Area of rectangle is ", self.l * self.b)

class triangle(rect):
    def __init__(self):
        rect.__init__(self)
        self.x = 17
        self.y = 13
    def area(self):
        rect.area(self)
        print ("Area of triangle is ", 1/2*self.x * self.y)

r=triangle()
r.area()
Output:
Area of rectangle is 40
Area of triangle is 110.5
```

The program contains two classes, rect and triangle, both consisting of the methods __init__ and area(). The triangle class inherits from the rect class, hence it overrides the area() method of the base class, rect. An instance r of triangle is created, and area()is invoked on it. As expected, it will invoke the area() method of the derived class, triangle. In the area() method of the triangle class, the area() method of the base class, rect, is invoked, and the program prints the area of rectangle as well as the area of triangle.

Now let's learn about multilevel inheritance.

MULTILEVEL INHERITANCE

When a class inherits a class that in turn is inherited by some another class, you call it *multilevel inheritance*, as shown in Figure 5.2.

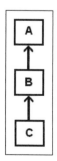

Figure 5.2
Multilevel inheritance.

The B class inherits from the A class, which in turn is inherited by class C. B can access the public members of A, and C can access the public members of B and hence of A.

For example, consider the following:

```
class worker:
...
...
class officer(worker):
...
...
class manager(officer):
...
...
```

The manager class inherits from the officer class, which is a derived class of the worker class. In this scenario, worker is the base class, officer is an intermediate base class, and manager is a derived class. manager inherits the properties of officer directly and the properties of the worker class indirectly via the officer class. The manager class can access the public members of the officer class, which in turn can access the public members of the worker class.

Let's examine the concept through a program.

multilevel.py

```
from __future__ import division

class worker:
   def __init__(self, c, n, s):
      self.code = c
      self.name= n
      self.salary = s
   def showworker(self):
      print ("Code is ", self.code)
      print ("Name is ", self.name)
      print ("Salary is ", self.salary)

class officer(worker):
   def __init__(self, c,n,s):
      worker.__init__(self,c,n,s)
      self.hra = s*60/100
   def showofficer(self):
      worker.showworker(self)
      print ("HRA - House Rent Allowance is ", self.hra)
```

```
class manager(officer):
    def __init__(self, c,n,s):
        officer.__init__(self,c,n,s)
        self.da = s*98/100
    def showmanager(self):
        officer.showofficer(self)
        print ("DA - Dearness Allowance is ", self.da)

w=worker(101, 'John', 2000)
o=officer(102, 'David', 4000)
m=manager(103, 'Ben', 5000)
print ("Information of worker is ")
w.showworker()
print ("\nInformation of officer is ")
o.showofficer()
print ("\nInformation of manager is ")
m.showmanager()
Output:
Information of worker is
Code is 101
Name is John
Salary is 2000

Information of officer is
Code is 102
Name is David
Salary is 4000
HRA - House Rent Allowance is 2400.0

Information of manager is
Code is 103
Name is Ben
Salary is 5000
HRA - House Rent Allowance is 3000.0
DA - Dearness Allowance is 4900.0
```

The program contains three classes: worker, officer, and manager. officer inherits from worker. The manager class inherits from officer. The manager class can access the methods of officer, which in turn can access the methods of the worker class. The instances of worker, officer, and manager are created by the names w, o, and m. worker is supposed to display code, name, and salary. The officer class is supposed to display code, name, salary, and hra. manager is supposed to display code, name, salary, hra, and da.

In multilevel inheritance, one class is inherited by another class that in turn is inherited by a third class. Can a class be inherited by two or more classes?

Two Classes Inheriting from the Same Base Class

Consider a situation in which you want to create two classes, A and B, having attributes in common. Class A consists of attributes p, q, and r, and B consists of attributes p, q, and s. You can see that both the classes have p and q in common. In this situation it is better to create a third class C with two attributes p and q and let A and B inherit from C. This approach helps reduce the code and effort because you only need to write code for the r attribute for A and for the s attribute for B.

In the following program, two classes inherit from the same base class. You want to store the code, name, and salary information of officers and managers. The attributes required for storing information for officers are code, name, salary, and hra, and that for managers is code, name, salary, hra, and da. Both classes have three attributes in common: code, name, and salary. So, to save time and effort, it is better to create a class named worker consisting of three attributes: code, name, and salary and let both officer and manager inherit from this class. Here is the complete code:

```
inherit3.py
from __future__ import division

class worker:
   def __init__(self, c, n, s):
      self.code = c
      self.name= n
      self.salary = s
   def showworker(self):
      print ("Code is ", self.code)
      print ("Name is ", self.name)
      print ("Salary is ", self.salary)

class officer(worker):
   def __init__(self, c,n,s):
      worker.__init__(self,c,n,s)
      self.hra = s*60/100
   def showofficer(self):
      worker.showworker(self)
      print ("HRA - House Rent Allowance is ", self.hra)
```

```
class manager(worker):
   def __init__(self, c,n,s):
      worker.__init__(self,c,n,s)
      self.hra=s*60/100
      self.da = s*98/100
   def showmanager(self):
      worker.showworker(self)
      print ("HRA - House Rent Allowance is ", self.hra)
      print ("DA - Dearness Allowance is ", self.da)

w=worker(101, 'John', 2000)
o=officer(102, 'David', 4000)
m=manager(103, 'Ben', 5000)
print ("Information of worker is ")
w.showworker()
print ("\nInformation of officer is ")
o.showofficer()
print ("\nInformation of manager is ")
m.showmanager()
Output:
Information of worker is
Code is 101
Name is John
Salary is 2000

Information of officer is
Code is 102
Name is David
Salary is 4000
HRA - House Rent Allowance is 2400.0

Information of manager is
Code is 103
Name is Ben
Salary is 5000
HRA - House Rent Allowance is 3000.0
DA - Dearness Allowance is 4900.0
```

This program defines a worker class consisting of three attributes: code, name, and salary. The officer class inherits from the worker class and its __init__ method, and, besides calling the __init__ method of the worker class, also computes the attribute hra. Similarly, the manager class inherits from the worker class, and its __init__ method, after calling the __init__ method of the worker class, computes the hra and da attributes. The idea is that the common attributes be dealt with by one common class and the others be dealt with by the inheriting class, reducing the code and effort.

Let's look at one more program that demonstrates one class being inherited by two classes. Suppose you want to store the information of science and arts students. The attributes that you want to store for science students are roll, name, physics, and chemistry. For the arts students you want to store roll, name, history, and geography. Both classes have two attributes in common, roll and name. A student class is created with these two common attributes, roll and name, and both classes will inherit from the student class. Here is the complete code:

```
inherit4.py
class student:
    def __init__(self, r, n):
        self.roll = r
        self.name= n
    def showstudent(self):
        print ("Roll : ", self.roll)
        print ("Name is ", self.name)

class science(student):
    def __init__(self, r,n,p,c):
        student.__init__(self,r,n)
        self.physics = p
        self.chemistry=c
    def showscience(self):
        student.showstudent(self)
        print ("Physics marks : ", self.physics)
        print ("Chemistry marks : ", self.chemistry)

class arts(student):
    def __init__(self, r,n,h,g):
        student.__init__(self,r,n)
        self.history = h
        self.geography=g
    def showarts(self):
        student.showstudent(self)
        print ("History marks : ", self.history)
        print ("Geography marks : ", self.geography)

s=science(101, 'David', 65, 75)
a=arts(102, 'Ben', 70, 60)
print ("Information of science student is ")
s.showscience()
```

```
print ("\nInformation of arts student is ")
a.showarts()
Output:
Information of science student is
Roll : 101
Name is David
Physics marks : 65
Chemistry marks : 75

Information of arts student is
Roll : 102
Name is Ben
History marks : 70
Geography marks : 60
```

The program creates two instances of science and arts class, s and a, and both of them pass information for the student as an argument to their __init__ methods. Since both classes inherit from the student class, their __init__ method invokes the __init__ method of the student class to initialize the instance variables, roll and name, which are common to both instances. After that, the __init__ methods of the science and arts classes are invoked to assign the marks for the rest of the attributes such as physics and chemistry marks of science students and history and geography marks of arts students. To display the information of the science student, the showscience() method on instance s is invoked, which in turn invokes the showstudent() method of the student class to print the common attributes, roll and name. The information of the other attributes, physics and chemistry, is displayed through the showscience() method. Similarly, the information of the arts student is displayed through the showarts() method, which invokes the showstudent() method to display the common attributes, roll and name.

Can a class inherit one or more classes? Yes! And the procedure is called multiple inheritance.

Multiple Inheritance

If a class is derived from more than one base class, you call it multiple inheritance, as shown in Figure 5.3. Usually when you need to use the members of two or more classes (having no connection) via another class, you combine the features of all those classes by inheriting them.

The class C inherits from both A and B. Now C can access the public members of A and B.

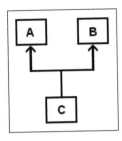

Figure 5.3
Multiple inheritance.

For example, consider the following:

```
class worker
{
...
...
}
class officer
{
...
...
}
class manager(worker,officer)
{
...
...
}
```

You see that, with no connection between them, the two base classes, worker and officer, are inherited from by the manager class. Now manager can access the public members of worker as well as officer.

Note

All the base classes that are to be inherited have to be separated by commas.

The following program explains multiple inheritance. Two classes, student and science, are inherited by a third class, results.

```
multiple.py
from __future__ import division
```

```python
class student:
    def __init__(self, r, n):
        self.roll = r
        self.name= n
    def showstudent(self):
        print ("Roll : ", self.roll)
        print ("Name is ", self.name)

class science:
    def __init__(self, p,c):
        self.physics = p
        self.chemistry=c
    def showscience(self):
        print ("Physics marks : ", self.physics)
        print ("Chemistry marks : ", self.chemistry)

class results(student,science):
    def __init__(self, r,n,p,c):
        student.__init__(self,r,n)
        science.__init__(self,p,c)
        self.total = self.physics+self.chemistry
        self.percentage=self.total/200*100

    def showresults(self):
        student.showstudent(self)
        science.showscience(self)
        print ("Total marks : ", self.total)
        print ("Percentage marks : ", self.percentage)

s=results(101, 'David', 65, 75)
print ("Result of student is ")
s.showresults()
```

```
Output:
Result of student is
Roll : 101
Name is David
Physics marks : 65
Chemistry marks : 75
Total marks : 140
Percentage marks : 70.0
```

student is defined by two attributes, r and n, representing roll and name. One more class, science, is defined that has attributes p and c, representing physics and chemistry. A results class is defined that inherits from both student and science, so results can access the attributes of student and science: r, n, p, and c. The results class calculates total and percentage from p and c (psychics and chemistry) and displays all six attributes.

In case of multiple inheritance, a confusing state may arise.

Two Base Classes Having a Method with the Same Name and Signature

What will happen if the two classes that are derived by a third class contain a method with the same signature? Suppose there are two classes, A and B, that have a method with the same name and signature, area(), and a third class C inherits from both A and B. The instance of C will have two copies of the area() method. Which area() method will it execute, the one from A or the one from B?

The answer is that the method of the class A will be executed. The following program confirms that the method of the first class will be accessed if two classes have a method of the same signature in multiple inheritance:

```
basefunc.py
from __future__ import division

class rect:
    def __init__(self):
        self.l = 8
        self.b = 5
    def area(self):
        return self.l * self.b

class triangle:
    def __init__(self):
        self.x = 17
        self.y = 13
    def area(self):
        return 1/2*self.x * self.y

class both(rect, triangle):
    pass

r=both()
print ("Area of rectangle is ", r.area())
Output:
Area of rectangle is 40
```

The program contains two classes, rect and triangle, both consisting of __init__ and area() methods. Both classes are accessed by a class named both. both has no methods of its own. Also, its r instance will have two copies of the area() method. On accessing area() through r, you observe that it accesses the area() method of rect, displaying the area of the rectangle.

You can apply arithmetic operations on the class instances in the same way as you apply them on numbers. Let's learn more about it.

OPERATOR OVERLOADING

To overload a standard operator means that you apply arithmetic operators to a class instance to perform the desired operations. You can add, subtract, multiply, and divide instances using the standard operators in the same way they are used with numbers. For example, the __add__ method is used to add instances just as the plus operator (+) does.

When you use an operator such as +, Python calls the special method __add__ in the background. All you need to do is implement __add__ to add two instances.

The following program adds the instances r1 and r2 of the class rect through the + operator:

```
operatorovr1.py
class rect:
    def __init__(self, x,y):
        self.l = x
        self.b = y
    def __str__(self):
        return 'Length is %d, Breadth is %d' %(self.l, self.b)
    def __add__(self, other):
        return rect(self.l+ other.l, self.b+other.b)
    def rectarea(self):
        return self.l * self.b
r1=rect(5,8)
r2=rect(10,20)
r3=r1+r2
print (r3)
print ("Area of rectangle is ", r3.rectarea())
Output:
Length is 15, Breadth is 28
Area of rectangle is 420
```

In this program, r1 and r2 are created of class rect. The instance variables 1 and b of instance r1 are initialized to values 5 and 8. 1 and b of instance r2 are initialized to values 10 and 20. Then, r1 and r2 are added through the + operator, and the result is stored in the newly created instance r3. The + operator will be invoked through r1 instances, passing itself and the second instance, r2, to the __add__ method, where the 1 and b of both instances are added, returned, and assigned to the instance r3. The __str__ method is invoked by calling a print statement to display the string representation of the instance r3. The __str__ method displays the values of the instance variables of r3. The program also computes and displays the area of rectangle on the added instance.

Overloading the Comparison Operator (==)

The following program explains how to overload the comparison operator (==) to see if the two instances have instance variables with the same value.

```
operatorovr2.py
class rect:
   def __init__(self, x,y):
      self.l = x
      self.b = y
   def __str__(self):
      return 'Length is %d, Breadth is %d' %(self.l, self.b)
   def __eq__(self, other):
      return ((self.l== other.l) and (self.b==other.b))
   def rectarea(self):
      return self.l * self.b
r1=rect(5,8)
r2=rect(10,20)
if r1==r2 :
   print('The two instances are equal')
else:
   print('The two instances are not equal')
Output:
The two instances are not equal
```

The program creates two instances of class rect, r1 and r2. The instance variables 1 and b of instance r1 are initialized to 5 and 8. The instance variables 1 and b of instance r2 are initialized to 10 and 20. The instances r1 and r2 are compared through the equal to (==) operator to see if they are the same. Since the values of the instance variables of the two instances are not the same, the program displays a message, The two instances are not equal.

Polymorphism

Poly means many, and *morph* means change. Through polymorphism, you can have a method with the same name in different classes to perform different tasks. You can handle objects of different types in the same way.

To implement polymorphism, you define a number of classes or subclasses that have method(s) with the same name. These classes or subclasses are polymorphic. You can access the polymorphic methods without knowing which class or subclass is invoked.

For example, the commission percentage from selling a book may be different for a stockist, a distributor, and a retailer. You can define a commission() method in three classes—stockist, distributor, and retailer, where each method computes a different percentage of commission. On execution of the program, the respective commission() method is called on each instance. Here is a complete program that demonstrates polymorphism.

```
polymorphism.py
class book:
   def __init__(self,x):
      self.price = x

class stockist(book):
   def __init__(self,x):
      book.__init__(self,x)
   def commission(self):
      self.comm=self.price*5/100
      print ("Commission of Stockist is %.2f" %self.comm)

class distributor(book):
   def __init__(self,x):
      book.__init__(self,x)
   def commission(self):
      self.comm=self.price*8/100
      print ("Commission of Distributor is %.2f" %self.comm)

class retailer(book):
   def __init__(self,x):
      book.__init__(self,x)
   def commission(self):
      self.comm=self.price*10/100
      print ("Commission of Retailer is %.2f" %self.comm)

r = stockist(100)
s = distributor(100)
```

```
t = retailer(100)
prncomm = [r,s,t]
for c in prncomm:
   c.commission()
```

```
Output:
Commission of Stockist is 5.00
Commission of Distributor is 8.00
Commission of Retailer is 10.00
```

The program creates r, s, and t instances of stockist, distributor, and retailer. All three classes, stockist, distributor, and retailer, inherit the book class. The three instances initialize their instance variable price by invoking the __init__ method of the book class. A prncomm list is created that contains the three instances. One instance at a time is accessed from prncomm, and its commission() method is accessed to compute and display the commission of the respective class. From the output, you observe that the commission() method of each class calculates and displays the commission accordingly, hence implementing polymorphism.

Properties

Properties are used to manage attributes with get/set methods. In earlier versions of Python, management of attributes was done by overriding __getattr__ and __setattr__ methods. To avoid the overhead of overriding these two methods, properties are used. You use properties to reroute an attribute's set, get, or even delete operation to a function.

```
propertyex.py
class product(object):
   def __init__(self, name):
      self._name = name
   def set_name(self, name):
      print ('Setting product name: %s' % name)
      self._name = name
   def get_name(self):
      return self._name
   def del_name(self):
     del self._name

   name = property(get_name, set_name)

p = product('Camera')
print('Getting product name ', p.name)
```

```
p.name='Cell'
print('Getting product name ', p.name)
Output:
Getting product name Camera
Setting product name: Cell
Getting product name Cell
```

This program creates a name property that consists of two methods, get_name and set_name, in the product class. An instance of products, p, is created that initializes its instance variable _name to Camera by invoking its __init__ method. On accessing the name property on p, the get_name method of the property will be invoked automatically and return the value of the _name instance variable. Similarly, on assigning value to the name property, the set_name method will be invoked, assigning the value passed to the property to the instance variable, _name.

There is another way to manage instance attributes, *descriptors*. A descriptor is a superset of properties.

DESCRIPTORS

Descriptors are classes that enable us to manage instance attributes efficiently. To manage instance attributes, three methods are used: __set__, __get__, and __delete__. The descriptors are of two types:

- **Non-data descriptor**—The class that implements only the __get__ method for an object is known as a *non-data* descriptor.

- **Data descriptor**—The class that implements __delete__ and __set__ methods as well as the __get__ method for an object is known as a *data descriptor*.

When you access an instance attribute, Python obtains the attribute's value by calling __get__ on the corresponding descriptor. Similarly, when you assign some value to an instance attribute with a corresponding descriptor, the value of that attribute is set by calling __set__ on the descriptor.

The syntax for coding descriptors is this:

```
class Descriptor:
    def __get__(self, instance, owner):
        ...
    def __set__(self, instance, value):
        ...
    def __delete__(self, instance):
        ...
```

The following program demonstrates using the __set__ and __get__ methods in setting and getting instance attributes:

```
descript.py
class product:
    def __init__(self, name, x=5):
        self.name = name
        self.price=x
    def __set__(self, obj, value):
        print ('Setting attribute' , self.name)
        self.price = value
    def __get__(self, obj, objtype):
        print ('Getting attribute',self.name)
        return self.price

class cart:
    p = product('butter',7)

k=cart()
print(k.p)
k.p=10
print(k.p)
Output:
Getting attribute butter
7
Setting attribute butter
Getting attribute butter
10
```

A product class is defined, consisting of three methods, __init__, __set__, and __get__. Another class, cart, is defined that contains an instance p of product. p initializes its instance variables, name and price, to butter and 7.

A k instance of the cart class is created. The p instance of product is accessed via k in a print statement. The __get__ method is automatically invoked on accessing an instance. The __get__ method returns the values of the instance variables name and price to display the information in them. Also, the program assigns 10 to the p instance of the k instance. As expected, the __set__ method is invoked on assigning a value to any instance variable. The __set__ method assigns the passed value 10 to the instance variable price of the instance p.

To read and write class attributes, you can use the __getattr__ and __setattr__ methods.

The __setattr__ Method

The __setattr__ method is called whenever you try to assign a value to an instance variable. When assigning a value to an attribute, you should take care that the value not be assigned in the usual way as shown here:

```
self.name = value,
```

This will result in an infinite number of recursive calls to __setattr__. Hence, you use dictionary to assign values to the instance variables:

```
def __setattr__(self, name, value):
    self.__dict__[name] = value
```

The __setattr__ method can also be used to perform type checking on values before assigning them to instance variables.

The __getattr__ Method

The __getattr__ method fetches an attribute of an instance using a string object and is called when attribute lookup fails, that is, when you try to access an undefined attribute. The __getattr__ method should either return the value (of any type) of the instance variable or raise an AttributeError exception.

```
def __getattr__(self, name):
    return self.name
```

The __delattr__ Method

The __delattr__ method is called when an attribute of an instance is deleted via the del statement.

```
def __delattr__(self, name):
    del self.name
```

The following program demonstrates using __setattr__ and __getattr__ methods for setting and getting instance attributes:

getsetattr.py

```
class product:
    price=25
    def __init__(self, name):
        self.name=name
    def __setattr__(self,name,value):
        self.__dict__[name]=value
```

```
    def __getattr__(self,name):
       return self.name

p=product('Camera')
print (p.price)
print (p.name)
p.price=15
p.name="Cell"
print (p.name)
print(p.price)
Output:
25
Camera
Cell
15
```

A product class is defined using three methods: __init__, __setattr__, and __getattr__. The class contains a class attribute, price, initialized to 25. A p instance of product is created that initializes its name instance variable to Camera. Then the price and name attributes of the instance are accessed, which results in invoking __getattr__. The __getattr__ method returns the value of the name instance variable. Also, the program assigns the values 15 and Cell to price and name, resulting in __setattr__ being invoked. In the __setattr__ method, the values are assigned to the instance variables using dictionary to avoid recursive calls.

SUMMARY

This chapter focused on classes. You learned to define a class, define functions for it, initialize its instance variables, and use class and static methods. You also learned to use class attributes to display specific information related to the class. We looked at garbage collection and its role in freeing up memory consumed by objects that are out of scope. You learned to apply single, multilevel, and multiple inheritance through running examples. You learned the use of private and public access specifiers and how to apply method overriding and operator overloading to perform arithmetic operations on instances. Finally, you learned about polymorphism and setting and getting values of instance attributes through properties and descriptors.

In the next chapter you will learn about file handling. You will learn to open files in different modes and perform different tasks such as reading, updating, deleting, and appending content to a file. You will learn to copy content from one file to another.

CHAPTER 6

FILE HANDLING

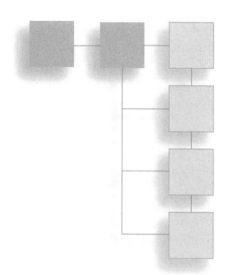

This chapter covers the following:

- Opening a file
- Performing actions on a file
- Displaying information of a file object
- Reading from a file
- Appending content to a file
- Copying a file
- Deleting content from a file
- Updating content of a file
- Reading content of a file randomly
- Accessing specific content of a file
- Creating a binary file
- Serialization (pickling)
- Exception handling
- Using a `try/except` block
- Using a `try/finally` block
- Raising exceptions

A file is a container for a sequence of data objects, represented as sequences of bytes. *File handling* is a technique by which you can store data and can retrieve it later. When you run a program, it asks you to enter some data (for processing), and the processed information is displayed on the screen. The data that you enter while running a program is stored in RAM, which is temporary in nature, so if later you want to see the data that was entered, you can't get it. To retrieve the data in the future, you need to make it persistent.

You will be dealing with three types of files: text, binary, and pickled objects:

Text files are encoded and stored in a format that is viewable by many programs as well as people. Text files are difficult to update in place.

Binary files are formatted to optimize processing speed. A binary file will typically place data at known offsets, making it possible to access any particular byte using the seek() method.

Pickled files are formatted to store objects. The objects are stored in binary format to optimize performance.

The following three steps are required for working with files:

- Opening a file
- Performing actions on the file (reading, writing, updating contents)
- Closing the file

Opening a File

The syntax for opening a file is this:

```
open(file_name, mode)
```

file_name represents the name of the file, and mode specifies the purpose for opening the file. The open() method returns a file handler that represents the file on the disk drive. The file handler can also be positioned at desired byte locations in the file to read or write specific contents from the file. Table 6.1 shows the mode options for opening a file.

For example:

```
f = open('xyz.txt', 'w')
```

This creates the file xyz.txt in write mode and returns the file handler to variable f. Any earlier content in xyz.txt will be erased.

Table 6.1 Mode Options

Mode	Description
R	Opens the file for reading. This is the default.
W	Creates a file for writing. It overwrites the earlier contents if a file already exists with the same name.
A	Opens the file for appending contents. It creates a new file if it does not already exist.
r+	Opens the file for reading and writing. The file must already exist.
w+	Creates a new file for reading and writing. It overwrites the contents if a file already exists with the same name.
a+	Opens the file for reading and for appending the contents to the end of the file. It creates a new file if it does not already exist.

Performing Actions on a File

After opening a file, the next step is to perform some task on the file such as writing, reading, setting the file handler at a specific location, or getting the location of the file handler. Let's have a quick look at different file methods. Table 6.2 shows methods used for operating a file in Python.

Table 6.2 File Methods Used in Python

Method	Purpose
close()	Closes the file, flushing all data.
read([n])	Reads the n number of characters or bytes from the file. If the optional value n is negative or omitted, the rest of the file is read.
readline([n])	Reads the next line from the file. If n is negative or omitted, the next complete line is read. The positive value of parameter n is if provided will read n number of characters from the file. If a complete line is read, it includes the trailing newline character, \n.
readlines([n])	Reads the next lines from the file. If the optional value n is provided, the method reads the next lines from the next n characters from file. If n is negative or omitted, the rest of the file is read. All lines will include the trailing newline character, \n.
flush()	Flushes all data from the internal buffers to the OS file.

Table 6.2 File Methods Used in Python (*Continued*)

Method	Purpose
`write(string)`	Writes the given string to the file.
`writelines(list)`	Writes the list of strings to the file.
`seek(offset, location)`	Sets the location of file handler at the specified offset. The location defines whether the offset relates to the current position of the file handler, beginning of the file, or the end of the file. The default value of the location is 0. Examples: `f.seek(0)` moves the file handler to the beginning of the file. `f.seek(10, 1)` moves the file handler 10 bytes from its current position. If `offset` is negative, the file handler will move backwards from its current position. `f.seek(10, 2)` moves the file handler to the 10th byte from the end of the file. `f.seek(0, 2)` moves the file handler at the 0th byte from the end of the file. This positions the file handler at the end of the file, making it possible to append contents to the file.
`tell()`	Returns the position of the file handler.

To understand the use of these methods, let's write some programs. The following program creates a file named `aboutbook.txt` and writes a couple of lines in it. The text written in the file is then accessed and displayed on the screen.

```
createfile1.py
matter = '''Python is a great language
Easy to understand and learn
Supports Object Oriented Programming
Also used in web development '''
f = open('aboutbook.txt', 'w')
f.write(matter)
f.close()
f = open('aboutbook.txt')
while True:
    line = f.readline()
    if len(line) == 0:
        break
    print (line,)
f.close()
Output:
Python is a great language
```

```
Easy to understand and learn

Supports Object Oriented Programming

Also used in web development
```

Multiline text is assigned to the `matter` variable. A file named `aboutbook.txt` is opened in write mode, deleting its contents, if any. The file handler for the `aboutbook.txt` file is assigned to variable `f`. The multiline text in the `matter` variable is written into the file using the `write()` method, and the file is closed. To confirm the content is written in the file, it is opened in read mode, and the text lines in the file are accessed and assigned to a `line` variable, which is then displayed on the screen.

Note

A blank line carries a newline character `\n` and is considered a string of length `1`.

Displaying Information from a File Object

On creation of a file object, you can use different methods and attributes to get detailed information about the object's status. Methods and attributes of the file object are shown in Table 6.3.

Following is a program that displays the attributes of a file object:

```
fileattrib.py
f = open("aboutbook.txt", "r")
```

Table 6.3   Methods and Attributes of a File Object

Method/Attribute	Description
fileno()	Returns the internal file descriptor used by the OS library when working with this file.
isatty()	Returns true if the file is connected to the console or keyboard.
closed	This attribute is true if the file is closed.
mode	This attribute is the mode of the file that was used to create the file object through the open() function.
name	This attribute is the filename that was passed to the open() function when creating the file object.

```
print ("Name of the file:", f.name)
print ("Closed?", f.closed)
print ("Opening mode:", f.mode)
print ("File number descriptor is:", f.fileno())
f.close()
Output:
Name of the file: aboutbook.txt
Closed? False
Opening mode: r
File number descriptor is: 3
```

The program opens aboutbook.txt in write mode. The file handler of the file is represented by a variable f. The filename, its mode, its file descriptor, and its status (open or closed) are displayed by calling the respective methods and attributes.

Reading from a File

In the program createfile1.py you used readLine() in a loop to access one line at a time from the file to display on the screen. The following program shows how to read the entire contents of the file.

```
fileread.py
f = open('aboutbook.txt', 'r')
lines = f.read()
print (lines)
f.close()
Output:
Python is a great language
Easy to understand and learn
Supports Object Oriented Programming
Also used in web development
```

The program opens the file aboutbook.txt that you created in the previous program in read mode. The content of the file is accessed through read()and assigned to the variable lines, which is then displayed on the screen. Finally, the file is closed.

In this program, you opened the file aboutbook.txt in read mode. What if the file aboutbook.txt doesn't exist? Python displays a technical error message when it tries to open a file that doesn't exist, as shown here:

```
Traceback (most recent call last):
  File "C:\pythonprograms\fileread.py", line 1, in <module>
    f = open('aboutbook.txt', 'r')
IOError: [Errno 2] No such file or directory: 'aboutbook.txt'
```

The error message is displayed through the default Python error handler. You can make the error message more readable through *exception handling*. You will learn exception handling in detail in the next section, but here's a small example:

```
filereadtry.py
import sys
try:
     f = open('aboutbook.txt', 'r')
     lines = f.read()
except IOError:
    print ('File aboutbook.txt does not exist')
    sys.exit(1)
f.close()
print (lines)
Output:
File aboutbook.txt does not exist
Traceback (most recent call last):
  File "C:\pythonprograms\filereadtry.py", line 7, in <module>
    sys.exit(1)
SystemExit: 1
```

When opening a file for reading, an IOError exception is raised if the file doesn't exist. Without a try/except block, Python just prints out the error message in technical language, as you saw in an earlier program. When using the same approach with a try/except block, the IOException is caught by the except clause, and the statement in the except clause is executed to display readable error message(s) so as to guide the user to take corrective measures. The except clause will be ignored if the file that you are trying to open already exists. The contents of the file will be displayed without any error message in that case.

The stdin, stdout, and stderr variables contain stream objects corresponding to the standard I/O streams. You can use them to have better control over streams. The following program demonstrates using stdout for displaying contents on the screen:

```
fileread2.py
import sys
f = open('aboutbook.txt', 'r')
lines = f.readlines()
f.close()
print('The contents in the file are:', lines)
print('\nThe contents in the file are:')
for line in lines:
    sys.stdout.write(line)
print('\n\nThe contents in the file are:')
```

```
for i in range(0, len(lines)):
    sys.stdout.write(lines[i])
```
Output:
The contents in the file are: ['Python is a great language\n', 'Easy to understand and learn\n', 'Supports Object Oriented Programming\n', 'Also used in web development ']

The contents in the file are:
Python is a great language
Easy to understand and learn
Supports Object Oriented Programming
Also used in web development

The contents in the file are:
Python is a great language
Easy to understand and learn
Supports Object Oriented Programming
Also used in web development

The sys module is imported into the program. The aboutbook.txt file is opened in read mode. All the text in the file is accessed and stored in a lines variable. lines is a list in which each element represents a line of the file. Then stdout is used to display each element in lines.

Appending Content to a File
The following program shows how to append content to a file:

```
fileappend.py
import sys
matter2 = '''Its very hot today
Lets have a Cold drink '''
f = open('aboutbook.txt', 'a')
f.write("\n%s" %matter2)
f.close()
f = open('aboutbook.txt', 'r')
lines = f.readlines()
f.close()
print('The contents in the file are:')
for line in lines:
    sys.stdout.write(line)
```
Output:
The contents in the file are:
Python is a great language
Easy to understand and learn
Supports Object Oriented Programming

```
Also used in web development
Its very hot today
Lets have a Cold drink
```

Multiline text is assigned to a variable, `matter2`. An `aboutbook.txt` file is opened in append mode so that its file handler will be positioned at the end of file. The text in `matter2` will be added to the end of `aboutbook.txt`. The file is then closed. To confirm if the text is really appended to the file, you can open it in read mode, and its contents are accessed and stored in a variable `lines`. On displaying the contents in `lines`, you observe that the contents in `matter2` are added to the previous contents in `aboutbook.txt`.

Copying a File

The following program shows how to make a copy of the file `aboutbook.txt` and name it `copyaboutbook.txt`:

```
filecopy.py
f = open('aboutbook.txt', 'r')
lines = f.read()
f.close()
g = open('copyaboutbook.txt', 'w')
g.write(lines)
g.close()
print('The copy of the file is made')
g = open('copyaboutbook.txt', 'r')
lines = g.read()
print (lines)
g.close()
Output:
The copy of the file is made
Python is a great language
Easy to understand and learn
Supports Object Oriented Programming
Also used in web development
```

The program opens `aboutbook.txt` in read mode, reads its content, and stores it in the variable `lines`. The file is then closed. After that, a file named `copyaboutbook.txt` is opened in write mode. The content of the file `aboutbook.txt` in `lines` is written into `copyaboutbook.txt`. To confirm if the content is correctly copied to `copyaboutbook.txt`, you can open it in read mode, and its contents are accessed and displayed.

Deleting Content from a File

The following program shows the procedure of deleting content from a file. The procedure is quite simple. First the file is opened in read mode, and its existing content is temporarily copied into a list. Then the contents to be deleted are deleted from the list. The file is then opened in write mode, deleting all its content. The content in the list that represents the desired data and from which the unwanted content is already removed is then copied into the file. The code for deleting content in a file appears as shown here:

```
delfilecontent.py
import sys
f = open('aboutbook.txt', 'r')
lines = f.readlines()
print('Original content of the file:')
for line in lines:
    sys.stdout.write(line)
f.close()
del lines[1:3]
f = open('aboutbook.txt', 'w')
f.writelines(lines)
f.close()
print('\nThe content of the file after deleting second and third line:')
f = open('aboutbook.txt', 'r')
lines = f.read()
print (lines)
f.close()
Output:
Original content of the file:
Python is a great language
Easy to understand and learn
Supports Object Oriented Programming
Also used in web development
The content of the file after deleting second and third line:
Python is a great language
Also used in web development
```

The program opens `aboutbook.txt` in read mode and fetches and stores its contents in `lines`. The file is then closed. The content that is to be deleted from the file is deleted from `lines`. `aboutbook.txt` and is opened in write mode, erasing its existing content. The content in `lines` is written into `aboutbook.txt`, and the file is closed. To confirm that the data is deleted from the file, you can open it in read mode, and its content is displayed. The output confirms that the undesired content is removed from the file.

Updating the Content of a File

The following program demonstrates the task of updating the content of a file. First the file is opened in read mode, and its existing content is temporarily copied into a variable, lines. The original content in the file is displayed from lines. The user is then asked to specify the line number to update. The new content entered by the user is stored at the location in lines specified by the user, replacing its previous content. The file is then opened in write mode, deleting all its content. The content in the list that represents the updated data is then copied into the file. The code for updating content in a file appears here:

```
updatefilecont.py
import sys
f = open('aboutbook.txt', 'r')
lines = f.readlines()
print('Original content of the file:')
for line in lines:
    sys.stdout.write(line)
f.close()
n=int(input ("\n\nEnter the line number to change: "))
if n <=len(lines):
    r=input("Enter the new content: ")
    lines[n-1]=r+"\n"
    f = open('aboutbook.txt', 'w')
    f.writelines(lines)
    f.close()
    print('The content of the file after updating line', n)
    f = open('aboutbook.txt', 'r')
    lines = f.read()
    print (lines)
    f.close()
else:
    print ("The line number", n, "is not found in the file")
Output:
Original content of the file:
Python is a great language
Easy to understand and learn
Supports Object Oriented Programming
Also used in web development
Enter the line number to change: 2
Enter the new content: Easy to develop applications
The content of the file after updating line 2
Python is a great language
Easy to develop applications
```

```
Supports Object Oriented Programming
Also used in web development
```

The program opens aboutbook.txt in read mode and fetches and stores its contents in lines. The original contents of the file are displayed by displaying elements in lines. The file is then closed. The user is asked to specify the line number(s) to modify and their new content. The new content entered by the user is stored in the list at the specified index locations, replacing the previous content. The content in lines is written into aboutbook.txt, followed by closing the file. To confirm that the data is updated in the file, it is opened in read mode, and its content are displayed. The output confirms that the content in the file is updated.

Reading the Content of a File Randomly

Can you read the content of the file randomly? That is, instead of reading the file content from the beginning, can you read from any location you want? Yes! This program does that.

```
filerandomread.py
f = open('aboutbook.txt', 'r')
line=f.readline()
print('A line from file is:', line)
f.seek(5)
line=f.readline()
print('The line from character 6 till end of line is:', line)
print ('The pointer is at location', f.tell())
f.seek(10)
line=f.read(15)
print ('The fifteen characters starting at location 11 are as:', line)
Output:
A line from file is: Python is a great language
The line from character 6 till end of line is: n is a great language
The pointer is at location 28
The fifteen characters starting at location 11 are as: a great language
```

The program opens aboutbook.txt in read mode. On opening the file, the file handler is positioned at the beginning of the file by default. Hence, reading a line from the file when the file handler is at the beginning of the file will display the first line of the file. Then the file handler is positioned at the fifth byte from the beginning of the file with the seek() method to read the entire line beginning at the sixth character. Again, the file handler is positioned at the tenth byte from the beginning of the file to read 15 characters beginning from the eleventh character.

Accessing Specific Content in a File

Is there any way to access a specific line of text from the file instead of accessing the complete file? Yes, and here is the code for doing so. The following program accesses and displays the third line from aboutbook.txt.

```
fileanyline.py
import linecache
line=linecache.getline('aboutbook.txt', 3)
print ('The content of the third line is:', line)
Output:
The content of the third line is: Supports Object Oriented Programming
```

This assumes that aboutbook.txt has the following contents:

```
Python is a great language
Easy to understand and learn
Supports Object Oriented Programming
Also used in web development
```

This program imports the linecache module and uses its getline method to access the third line from aboutbook.txt, which is then displayed on the screen.

Now let's see how to create a numerical file. The following program creates a file and stores numbers in it:

```
filenumerical.py
f = open('numbers.txt', 'w')
n=int(input('How many numbers? ' ))
print('Enter', n, 'numbers')
for i in range(0,n):
    m=input()
    f.write("%s\n" %m)
f.close()
f = open('numbers.txt')
lines = f.readlines()
f.close()
print('The numbers stored in the file are')
for line in lines:
    print (int(line),)
print('The numbers in the file multiplied by 2')
for line in lines:
    print (int(line)*2,)
Output:
How many numbers? 5
Enter 5 numbers
1
```

```
2
3
4
5
The numbers stored in the file are
1
2
3
4
5
The numbers in the file multiplied by 2
2
4
6
8
10
```

This program opens a `numbers.text` file in write mode and prompts the user to specify how many numbers are to be stored in it. The numbers entered by the user are stored in the file and the file is closed. To confirm that the file was created and has the content entered, it is opened in read mode, and its content is accessed and displayed on the screen. To confirm that the content in the file is of numerical type, the program displays all the numbers in it after multiplying them by 2.

Creating a Binary File

The following program creates a binary file and stores a string in it:

```
binaryfile1.py
str = 'Hello World!'
f = open("filebinary.bin","wb")
f.write(str.encode('utf-8'))
f.close()
f = open("filebinary.bin","rb")
fcontent=f.read()
f.close()
print('The content in the file is:')
print (fcontent.decode('utf-8'))
Output:
The content in the file is:
Hello World!
```

The program opens a file named `filebinary.bin` in write mode and stores a string, `Hello World!`, in it. The string is first encoded into UTF-8 before being written into the file. The file is then closed. To confirm if the string is stored correctly in the file, it is opened in read mode, and the string stored in it is fetched, decoded, and displayed on the screen.

Serialization (Pickling)

Serialization (also known as *pickling*) is a process of converting structured data into data stream format. Through serialization, structures such as lists, tuples, functions, and classes are preserved using ASCII characters between data values. The serialized data format is standardized, so structures serialized with serialization can be deserialized with cPickle and vice versa.

Serialization is done when storing data, and deserialization is done when retrieving data. For pickling, you can use either module, Pickle or cPickle. Both modules function the same, except that the cPickle module is written in the C language and is faster and results in better performance. The following program uses the Pickle module to store an instance into a file:

```
pickleprog.py
import pickle

class rect:
    def __init__(self, x,y):
        self.l = x
        self.b = y
    def rectarea(self):
        return "Area of rectangle is", self.l * self.b

r=rect(5,8)
f = open('studentinfo.bin', 'wb')
pickle.dump(r, f)
f.close()
del r
f = open('studentinfo.bin','rb')
storedobj = pickle.load(f)
print (storedobj.rectarea())
Output:
('Area of rectangle is', 40)
```

The program defines a rect class consisting of two methods, __init__ and rectarea(). An instance r of class rect is created, and its instance variables, l and b, are initialized to 5 and 8. A binary file, studentinfo.bin, is opened in write mode, and r is pickled and dumped into it. The file is then closed. r is deleted after it is copied into the binary file. To read r from the file and set it back into useable form, the file is opened in read mode, and the instance is read from the file with `pickle.load()`, unpickled, and assigned to `storedobj`. The area of the rectangle is calculated and displayed by calling `rectarea()` on the `storedobj` object.

This program demonstrates pickling and unpickling an instance from a file. Let's use the process to pickle and unpickle more than one instance. The following program stores information by pickling an instance of the `user` class. Also, the program unpickles the instances to display the stored information.

```
pickleprog2.py
import pickle

class user:
    def __init__(self, x,y,z):
        self.id = x
        self.name = y
        self.emailadd=z
    def dispuser(self):
        print('User ID:', self.id)
        print('User Name:', self.name)
        print('Email Address:', self.emailadd)

f = open('UsersInfo.bin', 'wb')
n=int(input('How many users? ' ))
print('Enter', n, 'numbers')
for i in range(0,n):
    u=input('User ID: ')
    n=input('User Name: ')
    e=input('Email Address: ')
    usrobj=user(u,n,e)
    pickle.dump(usrobj,f)
f.close()
print('\nInformation of the users is:')
f = open('UsersInfo.bin','rb')
while True:
    try:
        usrobj = pickle.load(f)
    except EOFError:
        break
    else:
        usrobj.dispuser()
f.close()
Output:
How many users? 3
Enter 3 numbers
```

```
User ID: johny111
User Name: John
Email Address: johny@gmail.com
User ID: kelly222
User Name: Kelly
Email Address: kelly@hotmail.com
User ID: bintu333
User Name: Bintu
Email Address: bintu@yahoo.com

Information of the users is:
User ID: johny111
User Name: John
Email Address: johny@gmail.com
User ID: kelly222
User Name: Kelly
Email Address: kelly@hotmail.com
User ID: bintu333
User Name: Bintu
Email Address: bintu@yahoo.com
```

The program defines a `user` class consisting of two methods, `__init__` and `dispuser()`. The `__init__` method is for initializing the instance variables of the respective instance of the `user` class `id`, `name`, and `emailadd`. The `dispuser()` method is for displaying information stored in the instance variables. A `UsersInfo.bin` binary file is opened in write mode. The user is asked to specify the number of users whose information has to be stored in the file. With the help of a loop, the user ID, name, and email address information of a specified number of users is entered and used to initialize the `id`, `name`, and `emailadd` instance variables of the instance `usrobj` of `user` class. The `usrobj` instance containing information of a user is pickled and dumped into the binary file. The file is then closed. To read the instances from the file and set them back into a useable form, the file is opened in read mode and, through `pickle.load()`, the instances are read from the file one by one, unpickled, and assigned to `usrobj`. The information in `usrobj` is displayed by calling `dispuser()` on the `usrobj` object.

EXCEPTION HANDLING

Exceptions occur when certain situations arise in a program. For example, dividing a value by 0, accessing a list element out of its index range, or reading a file that does not exist are situations that cause exceptions. When an exception occurs, Python usually displays a technical message that is a bit hard to understand. To make it easier for a user to understand what went wrong and provide an opportunity to correct the mistake, you can catch specific exceptions and display user-friendly messages. Syntax errors are different from exceptions in that syntax errors occur when any statement doesn't match the grammar of the Python interpreter. Misspelling in a statement or a missing parenthesis or quotation mark are all syntax errors.

To handle exceptions, you write the code in a block that begins with the word `try`. There are two kinds of `try` blocks:

try/except: The code that might raise an error is written in the `try` block, and all the errors and exceptions are handled through the `except` clause. The `except` clause can handle a single specified error or exception. If you don't specify any error name or exception, `except` will handle all errors and exceptions that appear in the code written in the `try` block. There has to be at least one `except` clause associated with every `try` block. If any error or exception is not handled, then the default Python handler is invoked, which stops the execution of the program and displays the error message.

try/finally: The code written in the `finally` block always executes whether an exception occurs or not. That is, the code that you want to execute in all situations is written in a `finally` block. Most commonly, the statements for closing open files, releasing memory, and such are written in a `finally` block.

Using a try/except Block

For handling exceptions through a `try/except` block, you specify the code that might result in an exception along with a group of `except` clauses. Each `except` clause names a class of exception and provides the statements to execute in response to that exception.

```
Syntax:
try:
    statement(s)
except SomeException:
    code for handling exception
[else:
    statement(s)]
```

You can have an unlimited number of `except` clauses in a single `try` block. The body of each `except` clause is known as an exception handler. Exception handling with a `try/except` block is done as follows:

1. Python runs the statements in the `try` block.

2. If none of the statements in the `try` block raises an exception, the `except` clauses are ignored.

3. If any of the statements in the `try` block raise an exception, the rest of the statements in the `try` block are skipped, and each of the `except` clauses is examined to locate a clause that matches the exception raised. If there is a match, Python runs the `except` clause.

4. If the raised exception doesn't match any of the `except` clauses, Python looks for a matching exception handler in any code that the `try` block is nested in. If Python doesn't find a matching exception handler, then Python uses its built-in exception handler and prints the technical error message.

5. The `else` clause runs only if the `try` block runs successfully and completely. That is, if no exception is raised or no block-exiting statement is executed, the `else` clause executes. The statements that you want to run if the `try` clause doesn't raise an exception are written in the `else` clause.

Once an exception has been handled, the program continues its execution from the first line after the `try`/`except` block.

Note

You can nest `try` blocks.

Table 6.4 shows exceptions that you can handle while a program runs.

Table 6.4 Exceptions That Can Be Handled While Running a Program

Exception	Description
AssertionError	Raised when `Assertion` fails.
AttributeError	Raised when an attribute is not found in an object.
EOFError	Raised when you try to read beyond the end of a file.
FloatingPointError	Raised when a floating-point operation fails.
IOError	Raised when an I/O operation fails.
IndexError	Raised when you use an index value that is out of range.
KeyError	Raised when a mapping key is not found.
OSError	Raised when an OS system call fails.
OverflowError	Raised when a value is too large to be represented.
TypeError	Raised when an argument of inappropriate type is supplied.
ValueError	Raised when an inappropriate argument value is supplied.
ZeroDivisionError	Raised when a number is divided by 0 or when the second argument in a modulo operation is zero.

Let's see how an exception occurs and how it is handled to display a user-friendly message and to take corrective measures through a running example. The following program demonstrates occurrence and handling of an EOFError exception

```
try1.py
import sys
try:
     n = input('Enter your name ')
except EOFError:
     print ('EOF error has occurred' )
     sys.exit(1)
except:
     print ('Some error has occurred')
print ('The name entered is', n)
Output:
Enter your name
EOF error has occurred
Traceback (most recent call last):
  File "C:\pythonprograms\try1.py", line 6, in <module>
    sys.exit(1)
SystemExit: 1

Enter your name Bintu
The name entered is Bintu
```

This program prompts the user to enter a name. The statement asking for the user name is enclosed in a try block. If the user presses Ctrl+D instead of entering a name, an EOFError exception will be raised, displaying EOF error has occurred followed by exiting from the application. The program also displays Some error has occurred if some exception other than EOFError occurs. No error message will be displayed if the user enters a name. The name entered by the user is displayed on the screen when no exception occurs. You can rewrite the above program by using the else clause in the try/except block. Remember that the statement in the else block will be executed only when no exception occurs.

```
tryelse.py
import sys
try:
     n = input('Enter your name ')
except EOFError:
     print ('EOF error has occurred' )
     sys.exit(1)
except:
     print ('Some error has occurred')
```

```
else:
      print('The name entered is', n)
Output:
Enter your name
EOF error has occurred
Traceback (most recent call last):
 File "D:\pythonprograms\tryelse.py", line 6, in <module>
   sys.exit(1)
SystemExit: 1


Enter your name John
The name entered is John
```

The following program demonstrates how TypeError and ZeroDivisionError exceptions occur and how they are handled. Remember that a TypeError exception occurs when an argument of inappropriate type is supplied, and a ZeroDivisionError exception occurs when a number is divided by 0.

```
try2.py
from __future__ import division
import sys
n = input('Enter a number ')
if n.isdigit():
      n=int(n)
try:
      m=15/n
except TypeError as ex:
      print ('You have not entered a numeric value:', ex)
      sys.exit(1)
except  ZeroDivisionError as ex:
      print ('You have entered zero value:', ex)
      sys.exit(1)
print ('The result is', m)
Output:
Enter a number John
You have not entered a numeric value unsupported operand type(s) for /: 'int' and 'str'
Traceback (most recent call last):
 File "D:\pythonprograms\try2.py", line 11, in <module>
   sys.exit(1)
SystemExit: 1


Enter a number 0
You have entered zero value: division by zero
```

```
Traceback (most recent call last):
  File "C:\pythonprograms\try2.py", line 14, in <module>
    sys.exit(1)
SystemExit: 1
```

```
Enter a number 5
The result is 3.0
```

The program prompts the user to enter a number that is used in a division operation. If the entered number is not of numerical type, a TypeError exception occurs and You have not entered a numeric value is displayed on the screen, followed by exiting from the application. If the entered data is of numerical type and its value is 0, a ZeroDivisionError exception occurs and You have entered zero value is displayed, followed by exiting from the application. If neither of the two exceptions occurs, which means the user entered a non-zero numerical value, the result of the division operation is displayed on the screen.

Using a try/finally Block

When an exception is raised, the program usually stops execution and exits. There are certain essential statements that you want to be executed whether an exception is raised or not. These statements, which might include freeing up memory or closing an opened file, are written in a finally block.

The try/finally block follows these steps:

1. Python runs the statements in the try block.

2. If none of the statements in the try block raise an exception, the statements in the finally block are executed.

3. If there is a block exiting statement in the try block such as return, break, or continue, the finally clause is executed on the way out.

4. If an exception occurs in the try block, Python skips the rest of the block, runs the finally clause, and then raises the exception again.

The following program demonstrates using the finally block to execute the statements that you want to execute whether an exception occurs or not:

```
filetryfinal.py
import sys
```

```
try:
      f = open('aboutbook.txt', 'r')
      try:
            lines = f.read()
      finally:
            f.close()
except IOError:
      print ('File aboutbook.txt does not exist')
      sys.exit(1)
print (lines)
Output:
File aboutbook.txt does not exist
Traceback (most recent call last):
  File "D:\pythonprograms\filertryfinal.py", line 11, in <module>
    sys.exit(1)
SystemExit: 1
```

This program opens `aboutbook.txt` in read mode in the `try` block. If an `IOError` exception occurs while opening the file, then `File aboutbook.txt does not exist` is displayed, followed by exiting from the application. Also, the lines from the file are read through `read()`, and whether an exception occurs or not, the file is closed through the `finally` block.

RAISING AN EXCEPTION

Exceptions are automatically raised when some undesired situation occurs during program execution. You can raise an exception explicitly through the `raise` statement in a `try/except` block.

```
Syntax:
raise customException, statement for customException
```

When raising an exception in a `try` block, the format will be this:

```
try:
    if condition:
        raise customException, statement for customException
except customException, e:
    statements for customException
```

The following program demonstrates how to create and raise an exception:

```
raiseexcepclass.py
class myException(Exception):
  def __init__(self, quantity):
```

```
        Exception.__init__(self)
        self.quantity = quantity
try:
  s = int(input('Enter quantity '))
  if s <=0 :
    raise myException(s)
except EOFError:
   print ('You pressed EOF ')
except myException as ex:
   print ('myException: The quantity entered is %d, it must be some positive value' %
ex.quantity)
else:
   print ('No exception raised.')
Output:
Enter quantity -3
myException: The quantity entered is -3, it must be some positive value

Enter quantity 5
No exception raised.
```

The program creates a myException class that inherits from the Exception class. The class contains __init__, which initializes the quantity instance variable of the class and that calls the __init__ method of the super class, Exception. The user is asked to enter the quantity of an item that is assigned to variable s. If the value entered is less than zero, the custom exception myException is raised, invoking the class and passing the value of quantity to it. If the user presses Ctrl+D instead of providing a value for quantity, an EOFError exception is raised, displaying You pressed EOF. When myException is raised, myException: The quantity entered is _, it must be some positive value is displayed. If no exception is raised, the statement in the else block will be executed, displaying No exception raised.

The assert Statement

The assert statement is used to place an error-checking statement in the program. It is a convenient way to debug a program. Through an assert statement, you can check the values of the variables in the middle of the program. The assert statement returns true if all the values of the variables are as expected, no matter what inputs are provided. If something is wrong in the program, the assert statement returns false. The AssertionError exception is raised when the assert statement returns false.

```
assertex.py
n=int(input('Enter a positive value: '))
assert(n >=0), "Entered value is not a positive value"
Output:
Enter a positive value: -5
Traceback (most recent call last):
  File "D:\python\assertex.py", line 2, in <module>
    assert(n >=0), "Entered value is not a positive value"
AssertionError: Entered value is not a positive value

Enter a positive value: 5
```

SUMMARY

In this chapter you learned to perform different operations on files. You learned to open a file in different modes and to read its contents, update existing content, delete content, and append new content. You also saw how to copy a file, read a file sequentially or randomly, and read only specific content. You also learned to create a binary file and pickle and unpickle objects. Finally, you learned to implement exception handling and the procedure of raising exceptions.

In the next chapter you will learn to develop GUI applications in Python through PyQt. You will learn to install PyQt and use Qt Designer to develop GUI applications.

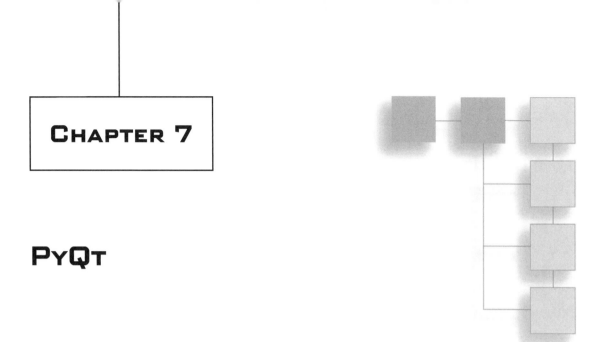

CHAPTER 7

PyQt

In the previous chapter you learned about file handling. You learned to open a file in different modes, read its contents, update existing content, delete content, append new content, and make a copy. You learned to read files sequentially as well as randomly. Besides this, you also learned to create binary files, pickle and unpickle objects, and implement exception handling.

The applications that you have created so far were console-based applications. From now on you will be learning to develop graphical user interface (GUI) applications in Python through PyQt. This chapter covers the following:

- Introduction to Qt toolkit and PyQt
- PyQt installation
- Window and dialogs
- Creating GUI Application through coding
- Using Qt Designer
- Understanding fundamental widgets—Label, Line Edit, and Push Button
- Event handling in PyQt
- First Application in Qt Designer
- Connecting to the predefined slots
- Using custom slots

- ■ Converting data types
- ■ Defining buddies and setting tab order

Let's begin the chapter with an introduction to Qt toolkit.

QT TOOLKIT

Qt toolkit, known simply as Qt, is a cross-platform application and UI framework developed by Trolltech that is used for developing GUI applications. It runs on several platforms, including Windows, Mac OS X, Linux, and other UNIX platforms. It is also referred to as a *widget toolkit* because it provides widgets such as buttons, labels, text boxes, pushbuttons, and list boxes, which are required in designing a GUI. It includes a cross-platform collection of classes, integrated development tools, and a cross-platform IDE.

PYQT

PyQt is a set of Python bindings for the Qt toolkit. PyQt combines all the advantages of Qt and Python. With PyQt, you can include Qt libraries in Python code, enabling you to write GUI applications in Python. In other words, PyQt allows you to access all the facilities provided by Qt through the Python code. Since PyQt depends on the Qt libraries to run, when you install PyQt, the required version of Qt is also installed automatically on your machine.

INSTALLING PYQT

You need to have Python Interpreter installed on your system before you install PyQt. Recall from Chapter 1, "Python and Its Features," that you have already installed Python 3.2 on your system, so you can go ahead and download PyQt from http://www.riverbankcomputing.co.uk/software/pyqt/download. The latest version at the time of this writing is PyQt version 4.8.5 for Python 3.2. The name of the downloaded file is `PyQt-Py3.2-x86-gpl-4.8.5-1.exe`. Just double-click the downloaded file to begin installation. The first screen that you see is a welcome screen to the PyQt Setup Wizard, as shown in Figure 7.1. The screen displays general information about the components that come with PyQt. Select Next to move forward.

Note

Your operating system may complain, saying the program is from an unknown publisher and may harm your computer. Select the Yes button to proceed with the installation. If you don't see a Yes button, select Actions to see the list of possible actions. In the dialog that appears, select the More Options drop-down and select Run to begin with the installation procedure.

Figure 7.1
PyQt Setup Wizard dialog.

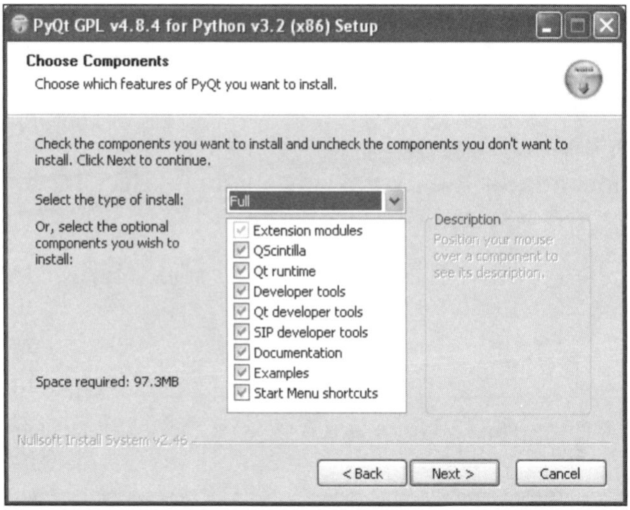

Figure 7.2
Selecting the features of PyQt to install.

The next screen shows the License Agreement, which you need to read and agree to before installing PyQt. Select I Agree to continue installation. Next, you get a screen that shows the list of components that you can install with PyQt (see Figure 7.2). You can select or deselect any component. The dialog also shows the disk space that will be required for installing the selected components.

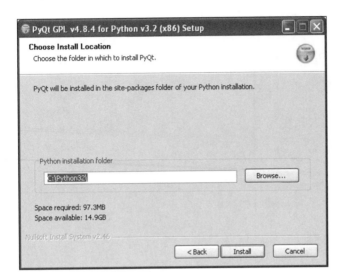

Figure 7.3
Specifying a location for PyQt installation.

Let's go ahead with Full Installation and select Next to move on. The next screen will prompt you to specify the name and location of the folder where Python 3.2 is installed. The reason is that PyQt is installed in the `site-packages` folder of the Python installation. The wizard auto-detects and shows the location of the Python installation by default, as shown in Figure 7.3. You can also select Browse to modify the folder name. After specifying the location of the Python installation, select Install to begin copying and installing the PyQt files.

When PyQt files are copied and installed, you will be prompted to select Finish to close the wizard.

Note

Don't forget to set the path of the PyQt folder so that you can access it from any folder on your computer.

Congratulations! You successfully installed PyQt on your computer. You can now begin creating your GUI applications. When doing so, you might be prompted to specify whether you want to create a main window application or a dialog application. What does this mean? Let's see.

WINDOW AND DIALOGS

A GUI application may consist of a main window with several dialogs or just dialogs. A small GUI application usually consists of at least one dialog. A dialog application contains buttons. It doesn't contain a menu bar, toolbar, status bar, or central widget, whereas a main window application normally has all of those. A central widget is one that contains other widgets.

Dialogs are of two types: *modal* and *modeless*. A modal dialog is one that blocks the user from interacting with other parts of the application. The dialog is the only part of the application that the user can interact with. Until the dialog is closed, no other part of the application can be accessed. The modeless dialog is the opposite of a modal dialog. When a modeless dialog is active, the user is free to interact with the dialog and with the rest of the application.

Ways of Creating GUI Applications

There are two ways to write a GUI application:

From scratch using a simple text editor.

With Qt Designer, a visual design tool that comes with PyQt.

Obviously, you will be using Qt Designer for developing GUI applications in PyQt. Before you do that, to understand the structure of a GUI application, let's create one through coding.

CREATING A GUI APPLICATION WITH CODE

The application that you are going to create will display a pushbutton with the text Close on it. When you click the Close button, the application will terminate. Type the code below in any text editor and save the file with the extension .pyw. However, don't include the line numbers in the code, as they are just meant to identify each statement individually to explain their role.

Note

> The console applications that you created before this chapter were saved with the .py extension. The GUI applications that you are going to develop now will be saved with the .pyw extension. This is to invoke the Pythonw.exe interpreter instead of the Python.exe interpreter so that no console window appears on executing a Python GUI application.

```
1. import sys
2. from PyQt4 import QtGui, QtCore
3. class demowind(QtGui.QWidget):
4.    def __init__(self, parent=None):
```

```
5.      QtGui.QWidget.__init__(self, parent)
6.      self.setGeometry(300, 300, 200, 200)
7.      self.setWindowTitle('Demo window')
8.      quit = QtGui.QPushButton('Close', self)
9.      quit.setGeometry(10, 10, 70, 40)
10.      self.connect(quit, QtCore.SIGNAL('clicked()'), QtGui.qApp,
            QtCore.SLOT('quit()'))
11. app = QtGui.QApplication(sys.argv)
12. dw = demowind()
13. dw.show()
14. sys.exit(app.exec_())
```

Before running this application, let's see what the code in different lines does.

1, 2. Imports the necessary modules. The basic GUI widgets are located in the QtGui module.

3. QWidget is the base class of all user interface objects in PyQt4, so you are creating a new demowind class that inherits from the base class, QWidget.

4, 5. Provides the default constructor for QWidget. The default constructor has no parent, and a widget with no parent is known as a window.

6. setGeometry() sets the size of the window and defines where to place it. The first two parameters are the x and y locations at which the window will be placed. The third is the width, and the fourth is the height of the window. A window 200 pixels high and wide will be positioned at coordinates 300,300.

7. This statement sets the window title to Demo Window. The title will be visible in the title bar.

8. Creates a pushbutton with the text Close.

9. Defines the width and height of the pushbutton as 70 and 40 pixels, respectively, and positioning it on the QWidget (window) at coordinates 10,10.

10. Event handling in PyQt4 uses signals and slots. A signal is an event, and a slot is a method that is executed on occurrence of a signal. For example, when you click a pushbutton, a clicked() event, also known as a signal, occurs, or is said to be *emitted*. The QtCore.QObject.connect() method connects signals with slots. In this case, the slot is a predefined PyQt4 method: quit (). That is, when the user clicks the pushbutton, the quit() method will be invoked. You will learn about event handling in detail soon.

11. Creates an application object with the name app through the QApplication() method of the QtGui module. Every PyQt4 application must create an

application object. sys.argv, which contains a list of arguments from the command line, is passed to the method while creating the application object. sys.argv helps in passing and controlling the startup attributes of a script.

12. An instance of the demowind class is created with the name dw.

13. The show() method will display the widget on the screen.

14. Begins the event handling loop for the application. The event handling loop waits for an event to occur and then dispatches it to perform some task. The event-handling loop continues to work until either the exit() method is called or the main widget is destroyed. The sys.exit() method ensures a clean exit, releasing memory resources.

Note

The exec_() method has an underscore because exec is a Python keyword.

On executing the above program, you get a window titled Demo Window with a pushbutton with text Close on it, as shown in Figure 7.4. When the pushbutton is selected, the quit() method will be executed, terminating the application.

Now, let's see how the Qt Designer tool, which comes with PyQt, makes the task of creating user interfaces quicker and easier.

USING QT DESIGNER

Though you can write PyQt programs from scratch using a simple text editor, you can also use Qt Designer, which comes with PyQt. For developing GUI applications in PyQt, using Qt Designer is a quick and easy way to design user interfaces without writing a single line of code. To open Qt Designer, click the Start button and then select All Programs > PyQt GPL v4.8.5 for Python v3.2 (x86) > Qt Designer.

Figure 7.4
Output displaying the Close pushbutton.

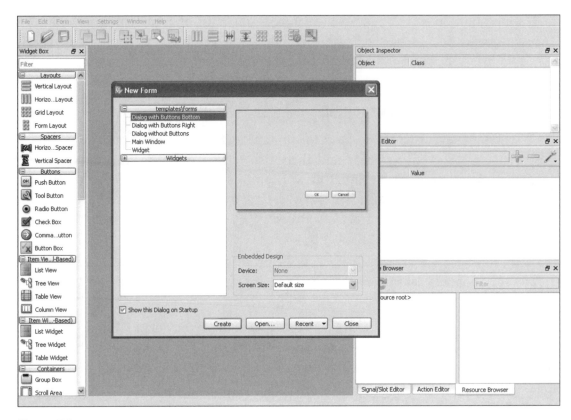

Figure 7.5
First screen on opening Qt Designer.

Qt Designer is for building graphical user interfaces. It makes it very easy for you to create dialogs or main windows using predefined templates, as shown in Figure 7.5.

Qt Designer provides predefined templates for a new application:

- **Dialog with buttons at the bottom:** Creates a form with OK and Cancel buttons in the right bottom corner.

- **Dialog with buttons on the right:** Creates a form with OK and Cancel buttons on the right side.

- **Dialog without buttons:** Creates an empty form on which you can place widgets. The superclass for dialogs is QDialog. You will learn more about these classes soon.

- **Main window:** Provides a main application window with a menu bar and a toolbar that can be removed if not required.

- **Widget:** Creates a form whose superclass is QWidget rather than QDialog.

Note

When creating a GUI application, you need to specify a top-level widget, which is usually `QDialog`, `Qwidget`, or `QMainWindow`. If you create an application based on the Dialog template, the top-level widget or the first class that you inherit is `QDialog`. Similarly, if the application is based on the Main Window template, the top-level widget will be `QmainWindow`, and if you use the Widget template for your application, the top-level widget will be `QWidget`. The widgets that you use for the user interface are then treated as child widgets of the classes.

Qt Designer displays a menu bar and toolbar at the top. It shows a Widget Box on its left that contains a variety of widgets used to develop applications, grouped in sections. All you have to do is drag and drop the widgets you want from the form. You can arrange widgets in layouts, set their appearance, provide initial attributes, and connect their signals to slots. The user interface that you create with Qt Designer is stored in a `.ui` file that includes all the form's information: its widgets, layout, and so on. The `.ui` file is an XML file, and you need to convert it to Python code. That way, you can maintain a clear separation between the visual interface and the behavior implemented in code. You will soon see the methods of converting `.ui` files into Python code.

Note

You can create widgets with code, also.

On the right side of Qt Designer you will find three windows by default, as shown in Figure 7.6.

- **Object Inspector:** Displays a hierarchical list of all the objects present on the form. You can select any object on a form by clicking on its corresponding name in the Object Inspector. Usually you select an object in Object Inspector window when you have overlapping objects. The window also displays the layout state of the containers. Containers are those widgets that can store other widgets or objects. Containers include frames, group boxes, stacked widgets, tab widgets, and tool box widgets.

- **Property Editor:** Used to view and change the properties of the form and widgets. It consists of two columns, Property and Value. The Property column lists property names, and the Value column lists the corresponding values. To change a property to the same value for a set of widgets, select all of them. To select a set of widgets, click one of the widgets and then Shift+Click the others one by one. When a set of widgets is selected, the Property Editor window will show the

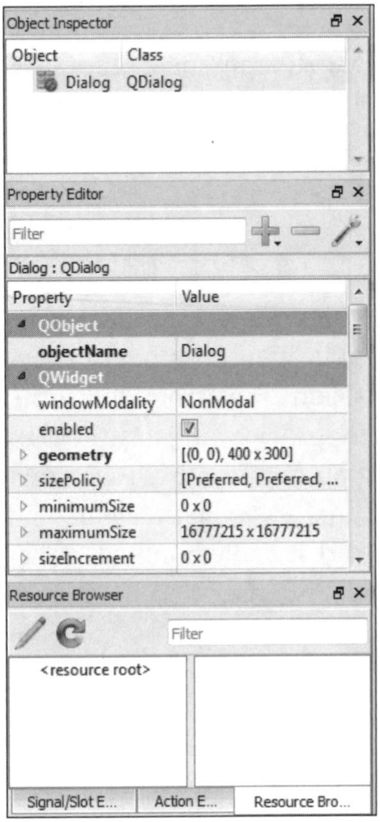

Figure 7.6
Three windows: Object Inspector, Property Editor, and Resource Browser.

properties that are common in all the selected widgets, and any change made to one property will be applied to the selected widgets.

- **Resource Browser**: Qt Designer enables you to maintain resources like images, audio, video, etc., of your applications through the Resource Browser. For each form of your application, a separate resource file is maintained. You can define, load, and edit resource files of your application through the Resource Browser. Below the Resource Browser window, you find two more tabs, the Signal/Slot Editor and Action Editor.

- **Signal/Slot Editor:** This window displays the signal/slot connections between objects. You can edit the signal/slot connections through this window.

- **Action Editor:** The Action Editor lets you to manage the actions of your applications. To initiate actions, the toolbar and menu bar are designed in an application. The respective action or task for each of the icons of the toolbar and menu items of the menu bar are defined through the Action Editor. You can create new actions, delete actions, edit actions, and define icons for the actions through the Action Editor. Also, you can associate respective actions with menu items and toolbars.

Note

For quick and handy actions, Qt Designer provides a context menu that you get by right-clicking an object.

The main component used for creating a user interface is widgets. Button, menus, and scrollbars are examples of widgets and are not only used for receiving user input but also for displaying data and status information. Widgets can be nested inside another in a parent-child relationship. A widget that has no parent widget is called a window. The class for widgets, QWidget, provides methods to render them on screen, receive user input, and handle different events. All UI elements that Qt provides are subclasses of QWidget. Qt Designer displays a list of widgets in a Widget Box displayed on the left side.

Widget Box

The Widget Box (see Figure 7.7) displays a categorized list of widgets and other objects that you can use for designing a user interface quickly and easily. Widgets with similar functions and uses are grouped into categories. It's very simple to create a graphical user interface by switching to Widget Editing mode. Select an icon from the toolbar and drag the desired widgets to the form.

You can also group widgets that you use often in a category you create, also known as a scratch pad category. To place widgets in the scratch pad category, simply drag them from the form and drop them into the category. These widgets can be used in the same way as any other widget. You can change the name of any widget and remove it from the scratch pad with the context menu.

Widgets are objects of their respective classes. (Qt Designer does not use class names for its widgets; the name of the widget signifies the class it refers to.)

The widgets in Widget Box are grouped into the following categories:

- Layouts
- Spacers
- Buttons
- Item Views (Model-Based)

Figure 7.7
Widget Box.

- Item Widgets (Item-Based)
- Containers
- Input Widgets
- Display Widgets
- Phonon

A description of the widgets in each category is as follows.

Layouts

Layouts are used for arranging widgets in a desired manner. The layout controls the size of the widgets within it, and widgets are automatically resized when the form is resized. The widgets in the Layouts group is shown in Table 7.1.

Table 7.1   Widgets in the Layouts Group

Widget	Description
Vertical Layout (QVBoxLayout)	Arranges widgets vertically, one below the other.
Horizontal Layout (QHBoxLayout)	Arranges widgets horizontally, one next to the other.
Grid Layout (QGridLayout)	Arranges widgets into rows and columns.
Form Layout (QFormLayout)	Arranges widgets in a two-column layout. The first column usually displays message(s) in labels, and the second column usually contains the widgets, enabling the user to enter/edit data corresponding to the labels in the first column.

Table 7.2   Widgets in the Spacers Group

Widget	Description
Horizontal Spacer (Spacer)	Inserts horizontal spaces between widgets.
Vertical Spacer (Spacer)	Inserts vertical spaces between widgets.

Spacers

Spacers are not visible while running a form and are used for inserting spaces between widgets or groups of widgets. The widgets in the Spacers group are shown in Table 7.2.

Buttons

Buttons are used to initiate an action. They are event or signal generators that can be used to perform tasks. The widgets in the Buttons group are shown in Table 7.3.

Item Views (Model-Based)

Item Views widgets are used for displaying large volumes of data. Model-based means that the widgets are part of a model/view framework and enable you to present data in different formats and through multiple views. The classes of these widgets implement the interfaces defined by the QAbstractItemView class to allow it to

Table 7.3   Widgets in the Buttons Group

Widget	Description
Push Button (`QPushButton`)	Displays a command button.
Tool Button (`QToolButton`)	Displays a button to access commands or options. Used inside a toolbar.
Radio Button (`QRadioButton`)	Displays a radio button with a text label.
Check Box (`QCheckBox`)	Displays a check box with a text label.
Command Link Button (`QCommandLinkButton`)	Displays a command link button.
Button Box (`QDialogButtonBox`)	A sub-class of `QWidget` that presents a set of buttons in a layout.

Table 7.4   Widgets in the Item Views (Model-Based) Group

Widget	Description
List View (`QListView`)	Used to display a list of items. Must be used with a `QAbstractItemModel` subclass.
Tree View (`QTreeView`)	Used to display hierarchical data. Must be used with a `QAbstractItemModel` subclass.
Table View (`QTableView`)	Used to display data in tabular form. Can display icons as well as text in every cell. Must be used in conjunction with a `QAbstractItemModel` subclass.
Column View (`QColumnView`)	Provides a model/view implementation of a column view. It displays data in a number of list views.

display data provided by models derived from the `QAbstractItemModel` class. The widgets in the Item Views (Model-Based) group are shown in Table 7.4.

Item Widgets (Item-Based)

Item Widgets have self-contained views. The widgets in the Item Widgets (Item-Based) group are shown in Table 7.5.

Table 7.5   Widgets in the Item Widgets (Item-Based) Group

Widget	Description
List Widget (QListWidget)	Used to display a list of items. It has a built-in model, so items can be added to it directly.
Tree Widget (QTreeWidget)	Used to display hierarchical data. It has a built-in model, so items can be added to it directly.
Table Widget (QTableWidget)	Used to display data in tabular form. Can display icons as well as text in every cell. It has a built-in model, so items can be added to it directly.

Table 7.6   Widgets in the Containers Group

Widget	Description
Group Box (QGroupBox)	Used to group together a collection of widgets of similar function.
Scroll Area (QScrollArea)	Used to display the contents of a child widget within a frame. If the child widget exceeds the size of the frame, scrollbars appear to enable you to view the entire child widget.
Tool Box (QToolBox)	Displays a series of pages or sections in a tool box.
Tab Widget (QTabWidget)	Displays tabs that can be used to display information. A large volume of information can be displayed by splitting it into chunks and displaying it under individual tabs
Stacked Widget (QStackedWidget)	Displays a stack of widgets where only one widget is visible at a time.
Frame (QFrame)	Used to enclose and group widgets. Can also be used as a placeholder in forms.
Widget (QWidget)	The base class of all user interface objects.
MdiArea (QMdiArea)	Provides an area for displaying MDI windows.
Dock Widget (QDockWidget)	Can be docked inside a main window or floated as an independent tool window.

Containers

Container widgets are used to control a collection of objects on a form. A widget dropped onto a container becomes a child object of the container. The child objects in a container can also be arranged in desired layouts. The widgets in the Containers group are shown in Table 7.6.

Table 7.7   Widgets in the Input Widgets Group

Widget	Description
Combo Box (QComboBox)	Displays a pop-up list.
Font Combo Box (QFontComboBox)	Displays a combo box that allows font selection.
Line Edit (QLineEdit)	Displays a single-line text box for entering/editing plain text.
Text Edit (QTextEdit)	Used to edit plain text or HTML.
Plain Text Edit (QPlainTextEdit)	Used to edit and display plain text.
Spin Box (QSpinBox)	Displays a spin box.
Double Spin Box (QDoubleSpinBox)	Displays a spin box for double values.
Time Edit (QTimeEdit)	Used for editing times.
Date Edit (QDateEdit)	Used for editing dates.
Date/Time Edit (QDateTimeEdit)	Used for editing dates and times.
Dial (QDial)	Displays a rounded range control.
Horizontal Scrollbar (QScrollBar)	Displays a horizontal scrollbar.
Vertical Scrollbar (QScrollBar)	Displays a vertical scrollbar.
Horizontal Slider (QSlider)	Displays a horizontal slider.
Vertical Slider (QSlider)	Displays a vertical slider.
QsciScintilla	Scintilla is an editing component that performs syntax styling, code completion, break points, auto indenting, and other tasks. It is very useful in editing and debugging source code. The Scintilla component is inside QsciScintilla and used in Qt Designer for developing GUI applications like any other Qt widget.

Input Widgets
Input Widgets are for used for interacting with the user. The user can supply data to the application through these widgets. The widgets in the Input Widgets group are shown in Table 7.7.

Display Widgets
Display widgets are used for displaying information or messages to the user. The widgets in the Display Widgets group are shown in Table 7.8.

Table 7.8 Widgets in the Display Widgets Group

Widget	Description
Label (QLabel)	Displays text or images.
Text Browser (QTextBrowser)	Displays a read-only multiline text box that can display both plain text and HTML, including lists, tables, and images. It supports clickable links as well as cascading style sheets.
Graphics View (QGraphicsView)	Used to displays graphics.
Calendar (QCalenderWidget)	Displays a monthly calendar allowing you to select a date.
LCD Number (QLCDNumber)	Displays digits in LCD-like display.
Progress Bar (QProgressBar)	Displays horizontal and vertical progress bars.
Horizontal Line (QFrame)	Displays a horizontal line.
Vertical Line (QFrame)	Displays a vertical line.
QDeclarativeView	A QGraphicsView subclass provided for displaying QML interfaces. To display a QML interface within QWidget-based GUI applications that do not use the Graphics View framework, QDeclarative is used. QDeclarativeView initializes QGraphicsView for optimal performance with QML so that user interface objects can be placed on a standard QGraphicsScene and displayed with QGraphics-View. QML is a declarative language used to describe the user interface in a tree of objects with properties.
QWebView	Used to view and edit web documents.

Phonon

Phonon is a multimedia API that provides an abstraction layer for capturing, mixing, processing, and playing audio and video. The widgets in the Phonon group are shown in Table 7.9.

Qt Designer displays a toolbar at the top that shows icons for frequently used tasks such as opening and saving files, switching modes, and applying layouts. Let's look at the toolbar.

Table 7.9   Widgets in the Phonon Group

Widget	Description
Phonon::VideoPlayer	Used to display video.
Phonon::SeekSlider	Displays slider for setting positions in media stream.
Phonon::VolumeSlider	Displays slider to control volume of audio output.

Toolbar

At the top of Qt Designer is a toolbar with icons as shown in Figure 7.8.

The following is a brief description of icons shown in the toolbar:

- **New:** Displays a New Form dialog box (refer to Figure 7.5) showing different templates for creating a new form.

- **Open:** Opens the Open Form dialog box, which you can use to browse your disk drive to search and select a .ui file to work on.

- **Save:** Used to save the form.

- **Send to Back:** Sends the selected widget to the back in overlapping widgets, making it invisible. Consider two overlapping pushbuttons, PushButton1 and PushButton2. If you select PushButton1 and click Send to Back, Push-Button1 will be hidden behind PushButton2, as shown in Figure 7.9 (a).

- **Bring to Front:** Brings the selected widget to the front, making it visible. This icon works only when widgets overlap each other. If you select PushButton1 and click Bring to Front, it will become visible, as shown in Figure 7.9(b).

Figure 7.8
Qt Designer toolbar.

Figure 7.9
(a) PushButton1 sent back. (b) PushButton1 brought to the front.

- **Edit Widgets:** The Widget Editing mode allows you to edit widget properties. Also, you can drop widgets into existing layouts on the form in this mode. You can also drag widgets between forms. You can also clone a widget by dragging it with the Ctrl key pressed. To activate the Widget Editing mode, you can choose any of the three options: press F3, select the Edit > Edit Widgets from the menu, or click the Edit Widgets icon on the toolbar.

- **Edit Signals/Slots:** The Signals and Slots Editing mode is used for representing and editing signal/slot connections between objects on a form. To switch to the Signals and Slots Editing mode, you can press the F4 key, select the Edit > Edit Signals/Slots option, or select the Edit Signals/Slots icon from the toolbar. The mode displays all the signal and slot connections in the form of arrows so that you know which object is connected to what. You can also create new signal and slot connections between widgets in this mode and delete an existing signal. The signals and slots refer to different events and corresponding methods that are executed on occurrence of an event. To establish signal and slot connection between two objects in a form, select an object by clicking with the left mouse button and drag the mouse towards the object to which you want to connect and release the mouse button. You can also cancel the connection while dragging the mouse by pressing the Esc key. When you release the mouse over the destination object, a Connection Dialog box appears, prompting you to select a signal from the source object and a slot from the destination object. After selecting the respective signal and slot, select OK to establish the signal/slot connection. You can also select Cancel in the Connection dialog box to cancel the connection operation. The selected signal and slot will appear as labels in the arrow connecting the two objects. To modify a connection, double-click the connection path or one of its labels to display the Connection dialog box. From the Connection dialog you can edit a signal or a slot as desired. To delete a signal/slot connection, select its arrow on the form and press the Del key. The signal/slot connection can also be established between an object and the form; you can connect signals from objects to the slots in the form. To connect an object to the form, select the object, drag the mouse, and release the mouse button over the form. The end point of the connection changes to the electrical ground symbol. To come out of the Signals and Slots Editing mode, select Edit > Edit Widgets or press the F3 key.

- **Edit Buddies:** Buddy Editing mode is used for setting keyboard focus on the widgets that cannot accept keyboard input. That is, by making a widget that can accept keyboard input a buddy, widgets that cannot accept keyboard input will also gain keyboard focus. Arrows appear to show the relationships between widgets and their buddies. To activate the Buddy Editing mode, you can either select the Edit > Edit Buddies option from the menu, or click the Edit Buddies icon on the toolbar.

- **Edit Tab Order:** In this mode, you can specify the order in which input widgets can get keyboard focus. The default tab order is based on the order in which widgets are placed on the form.

- **Lay Out Horizontally:** Arranges selected widgets in a horizontal layout next to each other. Shortcut key is Ctrl+1.

- **Lay Out Vertically:** Arranges selected widgets in a vertical layout, one below another. Shortcut key is Ctrl+2.

- **Lay Out Horizontally in Splitter:** In this layout, the widgets are placed in a splitter, arranged horizontally and allowing you to adjust the amount of space allocated to each widget. Shortcut key is Ctrl+3.

- **Lay Out Vertically in Splitter:** The widgets are arranged vertically, allowing the user to adjust the amount of space allocated to each widget. Shortcut key is Ctrl+4.

- **Lay Out in a Grid:** Arranges widgets in a table-like grid (rows and columns). Each widget occupies one table cell that you can modify to span several cells.

- **Lay Out in a Form Layout:** Arranges selected widgets in a two-column format. The left column is usually for Label widgets displaying messages, and the right column shows widgets for entering/editing/showing data for the corresponding labels in the first column, such as Line Edit, Combo Box, and Date Edit.

- **Break Layout:** Once widgets are arranged in a layout, you cannot move and resize them individually, as their geometry is controlled by the layout. This icon is to break the layout. Shortcut key is Ctrl+0.

- **Adjust Size:** Adjusts the size of the layout to accommodate contained widgets and to ensure that each has enough space to be visible. Shortcut key is Ctrl+J.

In almost all applications, you need some very fundamental widgets such as Labels, Line Edits, and Push Buttons. These widgets are required to display text messages, to accept input from the user, and to initiate some action, respectively. Let's look at these fundamental widgets.

UNDERSTANDING FUNDAMENTAL WIDGETS

The first widget we will discuss is the Label widget, a very popular way of displaying text or information in a GUI application.

Table 7.10   Methods Provided by the QLabel Class

Methods	Usage
setText()	Assigns text to the Label widget.
setPixmap()	Assigns a pixmap, an instance of the QPixmap class, to the Label widget.
setNum()	Assigns an integer or double value to the Label widget.
clear()	Clears text from the Label widget.

Displaying Text

To display non-editable text or an image, Label widgets are used; a Label is an instance of the QLabel class. A Label widget is a very popular widget for displaying messages or information to the user. The methods provided by the QLabel class are shown in Table 7.10.

The default text of a QLabel is TextLabel. That is, when you add a QLabel to a form by dragging a Label widget and dropping it on the form, it will display "TextLabel." Besides using setText(), you can also assign text to a selected QLabel by setting its text property in the Property Editor window. For instance, if you set the text property to **Enter your name**, the selected QLabel will show the text "Enter your name" on the form.

You can also set any letter in the QLabel text to act as a shortcut key by preceding it with an ampersand symbol (&). For instance, if you set the text property of the selected QLabel to **&Enter your name**, the letter E will become a shortcut key, and you can access that QLabel with the Alt+E keys.

Entering Single-Line Data

To allow the user to enter or edit single-line data, you use the Line Edit widget, which is an instance of QLineEdit. The widget supports simple editing mechanisms such as undo, redo, cut, and paste. The methods provided by QLineEdit are shown in Table 7.11.

Signals emitted by the Line Edit widget are these:

textChanged(): The signal is emitted when text in the Line Edit widget is changed.

returnPressed(): The signal is emitted when Return or Enter is pressed.

Table 7.11   Methods Provided by QLineEdit

Method	Usage
setEchoMode()	Used to set the echo mode of the Line Edit widget to determine how the contents of the Line Edit widget are displayed. The available options are these: Normal: Default mode. Displays characters as they are entered. NoEcho: Doesn't display anything. Password: Displays asterisks as the user enters data. PasswordEchoOnEdit: Displays characters when editing; otherwise, asterisks are displayed.
maxLength()	Used to specify the maximum length of text that user can enter. For multiline editing, you use QTextEdit.
setText()	Assigns text to the Line Edit widget.
text()	Fetches the text entered in the Line Edit widget.
clear()	Clears the contents of the Line Edit widget.
setReadOnly()	Passes the Boolean value true to this method to make the Line Edit widget read-only. The user cannot edit the contents of the Line Edit widget but can copy it. The cursor will become invisible in read-only mode.
isReadOnly()	Returns true if the Line Edit widget is in read-only mode.
setEnabled()	The Line Edit widget will be blurred, indicating that it is disabled. You cannot edit content in a disabled Line Edit widget, but you can assign text via the setText() method.
setFocus()	Used to set the cursor on the specified Line Edit widget.

editingFinished(): The signal is emitted when focus is lost on the Line Edit widget, confirming the editing task is over on it.

The next widget is the most common way of initiating actions in any application.

Displaying Buttons

To display pushbuttons (usually command buttons) in an application, you need to create an instance of the QPushButton class. When assigning text to buttons, you can create shortcut keys by preceding any character in the text with an ampersand. For example, if the text assigned to a pushbutton is &Click Me, the character C will be underlined to indicate that it is a shortcut key, and the user can select the button by pressing Alt+C. The button emits a `clicked()` signal if it is activated. Besides text, an icon can also be displayed in the pushbutton. The methods for displaying text and an icon in a pushbutton are these:

`setText()`: Used to assign the text to the pushbutton.

`setIcon()`: Used to assign icon to the pushbutton.

The only concept left to examine before you begin with your first application in Qt Designer is event handling. Let's see how events are handled in PyQt.

EVENT HANDLING IN PYQT

In PyQt, the event-handling mechanism is also known as *signals and slots*. Every widget emits signals when its state changes. Whenever a signal is emitted, it is simply thrown. To perform a task in response to a signal, the signal has to be connected to a slot. A *slot* refers to the method containing the code that you want to be executed on occurrence of a signal. Most widgets have predefined slots, you don't have to write code for connecting a predefined signal to a predefined slot. To respond to the signals emitted, you identify the `QObject` and the signal it emits and invoke the associated method. You can use Qt Designer for connecting signals with built-in slots. How? Let's see by creating an application.

Note

Signals differ according to the widget type.

FIRST APPLICATION IN QT DESIGNER

Let's create an application in Qt Designer to demonstrate how to connect signals with built-in slots. On opening, Qt Designer asks you to select a template for your new application, as shown previously in Figure 7.5. Qt Designer provides a number of templates that are suitable for different kinds of applications. You can choose any of these templates and then select the Create button. Select Dialog with Buttons Bottom and click the Create button. A new form will be created with an "untitled" caption. The form contains a button box that has two buttons, OK and Cancel, as shown in Figure 7.10. The signal-slot connections of the OK and Cancel buttons are already set up by default.

In order to learn how to connect signals with slots manually, select the button box by clicking either of the buttons, and then delete it (which removes the buttons). Now you have an entirely blank form. Add a `QLabel`, `QLineEdit`, and `QPushButton` to

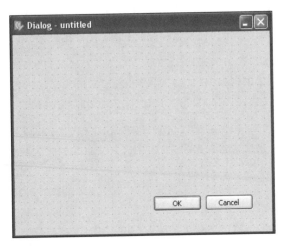

Figure 7.10
Dialog box with two buttons, OK and Cancel.

the form by dragging and dropping a Label, Line Edit, and Push Button widget from the Widget Box on the form. The default text property of Label is TextLabel, as shown in Figure 7.11(a). You can change it by changing the text property in the Property Editor. Select the Label widget and set its text property to Enter Text through the Property Editor. Similarly, set the text of the Push Button widget to Clear, as shown in Figure 7.11(b).

Note

To preview a form while editing, select either Form, Preview or Ctrl+R.

You want some action to happen when the user selects Clear on the form, so you need to connect Push Button's signal to Line Edit's slot.

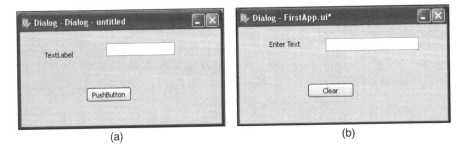

(a)   (b)

Figure 7.11
(a) Three widgets dropped on the form. (b) Widgets on the form with the text property set.

Connecting to Predefined Slots

Currently, you are in widget editing mode, and to apply signal/slot connections, you need to first switch to signals and slots editing mode. Select the Edit Signals/Slots icon from the toolbar to switch to signals and slots editing mode. On the form, select the Clear button and drag the mouse to the Line Edit widget and release the mouse button. The Configure Connection dialog will pop up, allowing you to establish a signal-slot connection between the Clear button and the Line Edit widget, as shown in Figure 7.12.

When the user selects the Clear button, you want any text in the Line Edit widget to be deleted. For this to happen, you have to connect the pushbutton's `clicked()` signal to the Line Edit's `clear()` slot. So, in the Configure Connection dialog, select the `clicked()` signal from the Push Button column and the `clear()` slot from the Line Edit column and select OK. On the form, you will see that an arrow appears, representing the signal-slot connection between the two widgets as shown in Figure 7.13.

Let's save the form with the name FirstApp. The default location where the form will be saved is C:\Python32\Lib\site-packages\PyQt4. The form will be saved in a file with the `.ui` extension. The `FirstApp.ui` file will contain all the information of

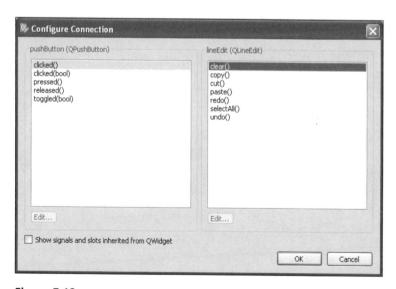

Figure 7.12
Configure Connection dialog displaying predefined slots.

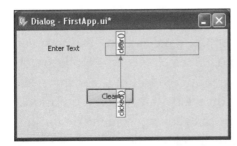

Figure 7.13
The signal-slot connection in widgets represented with arrows.

the form, its widgets, layout, and so on. The `.ui` file is an XML file, and it contains the following code:

```
FirstApp.ui
<?xml version="1.0" encoding="UTF-8"?>
<ui version="4.0">
 <class>Dialog</class>
 <widget class="QDialog" name="Dialog">
 <property name="geometry">
 <rect>
  <x>0</x>
  <y>0</y>
  <width>337</width>
  <height>165</height>
 </rect>
 </property>
 <property name="windowTitle">
 <string>Dialog</string>
 </property>
 <widget class="QPushButton" name="pushButton">
 <property name="geometry">
  <rect>
   <x>110</x>
   <y>90</y>
   <width>75</width>
   <height>23</height>
  </rect>
 </property>
 <property name="text">
  <string>Clear</string>
 </property>
 </widget>
 <widget class="QLineEdit" name="lineEdit">
```

```
    <property name="geometry">
     <rect>
      <x>140</x>
      <y>20</y>
      <width>151</width>
      <height>20</height>
     </rect>
    </property>
   </widget>
   <widget class="QLabel" name="label">
    <property name="geometry">
     <rect>
      <x>50</x>
      <y>20</y>
      <width>71</width>
      <height>16</height>
     </rect>
    </property>
    <property name="text">
     <string>Enter Text</string>
    </property>
   </widget>
  </widget>
  <resources/>
  <connections>
   <connection>
    <sender>pushButton</sender>
    <signal>clicked()</signal>
    <receiver>lineEdit</receiver>
    <slot>clear()</slot>
    <hints>
     <hint type="sourcelabel">
      <x>161</x>
      <y>103</y>
     </hint>
     <hint type="destinationlabel">
      <x>164</x>
      <y>24</y>
     </hint>
    </hints>
   </connection>
  </connections>
 </ui>
```

To use the file, you first need to convert it into Python script. The command utility that you will use for converting a .ui file into a Python script is pyuic4. In Windows, the pyuic4 utility is bundled with PyQt. To do the conversion, you need to open a command prompt window and navigate to the folder where the file is saved and issue this command:

```
C:\Python32\Lib\site-packages\PyQt4>pyuic4 FirstApp.ui -o FirstApp.py
```

Recall that you saved the form at the default location, C:\Python32\Lib\site-packages\ PyQt4.

The command shows the conversion of the FirstApp.ui file into a Python script, FirstApp.py.

Note

The Python code generated by this method should not be modified manually, as any changes will be overwritten the next time you run the pyuic4 command.

The Python script file FirstApp.py may have the following code. Your generated code may slightly vary when compared with the following code, as it depends on several factors, including window size, button location, and so on:

```
FirstApp.py
# Form implementation generated from reading ui file 'FirstApp.ui'

from PyQt4 import QtCore, QtGui

try:
    _fromUtf8 = QtCore.QString.fromUtf8
except AttributeError:
    _fromUtf8 = lambda s: s
class Ui_Dialog(object):
    def setupUi(self, Dialog):
        Dialog.setObjectName(_fromUtf8("Dialog"))
        Dialog.resize(337, 165)
        self.pushButton = QtGui.QPushButton(Dialog)
        self.pushButton.setGeometry(QtCore.QRect(110, 90, 75, 23))
        self.pushButton.setObjectName(_fromUtf8("pushButton"))
        self.lineEdit = QtGui.QLineEdit(Dialog)
        self.lineEdit.setGeometry(QtCore.QRect(140, 20, 151, 20))
        self.lineEdit.setObjectName(_fromUtf8("lineEdit"))
        self.label = QtGui.QLabel(Dialog)
        self.label.setGeometry(QtCore.QRect(50, 20, 71, 16))
        self.label.setObjectName(_fromUtf8("label"))
```

```
    self.retranslateUi(Dialog)
    QtCore.QObject.connect(self.pushButton, QtCore.SIGNAL(_fromUtf8("clicked()")),
self.lineEdit.clear)
    QtCore.QMetaObject.connectSlotsByName(Dialog)

  def retranslateUi(self, Dialog):
    Dialog.setWindowTitle(QtGui.QApplication.translate("Dialog", "Dialog", None,
QtGui.QApplication.UnicodeUTF8))
    self.pushButton.setText(QtGui.QApplication.translate("Dialog", "Clear", None,
QtGui.QApplication.UnicodeUTF8))
    self.label.setText(QtGui.QApplication.translate("Dialog", "Enter Text", None,
QtGui.QApplication.UnicodeUTF8))
```

This script is very easy to understand. A class with the name of the top-level object is created, with Ui_ prepended. Since, the top-level object used in our application is Dialog, the class Ui_Dialog is created and stores the interface elements of our widget. That class has two methods, setupUi() and retranslateUi(). The setupUi() method sets up the widgets; it creates the widgets that you used while defining the user interface in Qt Designer. The method creates the widgets one by one and also sets their properties. The setupUi() method takes a single argument, which is the top-level widget in which the user interface (child widgets) is created. In our application, it is an instance of QDialog. The retranslateUi() method translates the interface. The file imports everything from both modules, QtCore and the QtGui, as you will be needing them in developing GUI applications.

QtCore: The QtCore module forms the foundation of all Qt-based applications. It contains the most fundamental classes, such as QCoreApplication, QObject, and so on. These classes perform several important tasks, such as file handling, event handling through the event loop, implementing the signals and slot mechanism, concurrency control, and much more. The module includes several classes, including QFile, QDir, QIODevice, QTimer, QString, QDate, and QTime.

QtGui: The QtGUI module contains the classes required in developing cross-platform GUI applications. The module contains the majority of the GUI classes, including QCheckBox, QComboBox, QDateTimeEdit, QLineEdit, QPushButton, QPainter, QPaintDevice, QApplication, QTextEdit, and QTextDocument.

You will be treating the code as a header file, and you will import it to the source file from which you will invoke its user interface design. Let's create the source file with the name callFirstApp.pyw and import the FirstApp.py code to it. The code in the file is as shown here:

```
callFirstApp.pyw
import sys
```

```
from FirstApp import *
class MyForm(QtGui.QDialog):
    def __init__(self, parent=None):
        QtGui.QWidget.__init__(self, parent)
        self.ui = Ui_Dialog()
        self.ui.setupUi(self)
if __name__ == "__main__":
    app = QtGui.QApplication(sys.argv)
    myapp = MyForm()
    myapp.show()
    sys.exit(app.exec_())
```

The sys module is imported to enable you to access the command-line arguments stored in the sys.argv list. First you create an QApplication object. Every PyQt GUI application must have a QApplication object to provide access to information such as the application's directory, screen size, and so on. When creating an QApplication object, you pass the command-line arguments to it for the simple reason that PyQt can act on command-line arguments if required. You create an instance of MyForm and call its show() method, which adds a new event to the QApplication object's event queue: a request to paint the widgets specified in the class, MyForm. The method app.exec_() is called to start the QApplication object's event loop. Once the event loop begins, the top-level widget used in the class, MyForm, is displayed along with its child widgets. All the events that occur, whether through user interaction or system-generated, are added to the event queue. The application's event loop continuously checks to see if any event has occurred. If so, the event loop processes it and eventually passes it to the associated method. When you close the top-level widget being displayed, it goes into hidden mode, and PyQt deletes the widget and performs a clean termination of the application.

In PyQt, any widget can be used as a top-level window. To declare QDialog as a top-level window, all you need is to declare the parent of the class MyForm as None. So to the __init__() method of our MyForm class, you pass a default parent of None to indicate that the QDialog displayed through this class is a top-level window.

Note

A widget that has no parent becomes a top-level window.

Recall that the user interface design is instantiated by calling the setupUI() method of the class that was created in the Python code (Ui_Dialog). What you need is to create an instance of the class Ui_Dialog, the class that was created in the Python

Figure 7.14
Output of FirstApp application.

code, and invoke its setupUi() method. The Dialog widget will be created as the parent of all the user interface widgets and displayed on the screen.

Note

QDialog, QMainWindow, and all PyQt's widgets are derived from QWidget.

On running the above Python script, the application prompts for text to be entered in the Line Edit widget, as shown in Figure 7.14.

Any text in the Line Edit widget will be deleted when you select the Clear button.

Congratulations on successfully creating and executing your first GUI application.

In this application, you saw how to connect the built-in signals with slots. What if you want a custom method to execute an occurrence of an event?

USING CUSTOM SLOTS

The application you are going to create now will prompt a user to enter a name and select a pushbutton. When the pushbutton is selected, the application will display a welcome message to the user. This time let's use the Dialog without Buttons template, which provides a blank form ready to receive widgets. Recall that an instance of QDialog is the top-level widget in applications based on the Dialog template. Let's add two QLabels, a QlineEdit, and a QPushButton to the form by dragging and dropping two Label, Line Edit, and Push Button widgets from the Widget Box, as shown in Figure 7.15(a). Set the objectName property of the first and second Label to labelEnterName and labelMessage, respectively. Also, set the object-Name property of the Line Edit and Push Button widgets to lineUserName and ClickMeButton, respectively. Set the text property of the first Label widget to **Enter your name**. Also, delete the default text property, TextLabel, from the

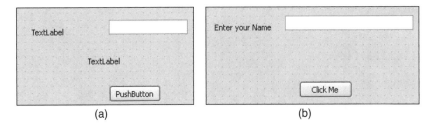

Figure 7.15
(a) Four widgets dropped on the form. (b) Widgets on the form with the `text` property set.

second Label as you will be setting its text through a Python script to display the welcome message to the user. The second Label will become invisible on deleting its `text` property. Also, set the text of the Push Button widget to **Click Me**, as shown in Figure 7.15(b).

Note

The `objectName` property helps in distinguishing widgets in the form, and it is only through the object names that the widgets are accessed in coding.

Save the form with the name `welcomemsg.ui`. You know that a `.ui` file is an XML file and has to be converted into Python code through the `pyuic4` command-line utility. The generated Python code is shown here:

```
welcomemsg.py
# Form implementation generated from reading ui file 'welcomemsg.ui'

from PyQt4 import QtCore, QtGui

try:
    _fromUtf8 = QtCore.QString.fromUtf8
except AttributeError:
    _fromUtf8 = lambda s: s

class Ui_Dialog(object):
    def setupUi(self, Dialog):
        Dialog.setObjectName(_fromUtf8("Dialog"))
        Dialog.resize(400, 300)
        self.ClickMeButton = QtGui.QPushButton(Dialog)
        self.ClickMeButton.setGeometry(QtCore.QRect(150, 120, 75, 23))
        self.ClickMeButton.setObjectName(_fromUtf8("ClickMeButton"))
        self.labelEnterName = QtGui.QLabel(Dialog)
        self.labelEnterName.setGeometry(QtCore.QRect(30, 30, 101, 21))
        self.labelEnterName.setObjectName(_fromUtf8("labelEnterName"))
        self.labelMessage = QtGui.QLabel(Dialog)
        self.labelMessage.setGeometry(QtCore.QRect(120, 75, 161, 21))
```

```
        self.labelMessage.setText(_fromUtf8(""))
        self.labelMessage.setObjectName(_fromUtf8("labelMessage"))
        self.lineUserName = QtGui.QLineEdit(Dialog)
        self.lineUserName.setGeometry(QtCore.QRect(130, 30, 181, 20))
        self.lineUserName.setObjectName(_fromUtf8("lineUserName"))
        self.retranslateUi(Dialog)
        QtCore.QMetaObject.connectSlotsByName(Dialog)

    def retranslateUi(self, Dialog):
        Dialog.setWindowTitle(QtGui.QApplication.translate("Dialog", "Dialog", None,
QtGui.QApplication.UnicodeUTF8))
        self.ClickMeButton.setText(QtGui.QApplication.translate("Dialog", "Click Me",
None, QtGui.QApplication.UnicodeUTF8))
        self.labelEnterName.setText(QtGui.QApplication.translate("Dialog", "Enter your
name", None, QtGui.QApplication.UnicodeUTF8))
```

As stated earlier, the top-level object used in the application is Dialog, hence the Ui_Dialog class is created that stores the interface elements of our widget. The class has two methods, setupUi() and retranslateUi(). The setupUi() method is for setting up the widgets and their properties, and the retranslateUi() method is for translating the interface.

The next task is to connect slots and write code for the slots to perform processing. For this, you need to write another Python script and import the previous Python code to invoke the user interface design. Let's create the source file, name it callwelcome.pyw, and import the Python code welcomemsg in it. The code in callwelcome.pyw is shown here:

```
callwellcome.pyw
import sys
from welcomemsg import *
class MyForm(QtGui.QDialog):
    def __init__(self, parent=None):
        QtGui.QWidget.__init__(self, parent)
        self.ui = Ui_Dialog()
        self.ui.setupUi(self)
        QtCore.QObject.connect(self.ui.ClickMeButton,  QtCore.SIGNAL('clicked()'),self.
dispmessage)

    def dispmessage(self):
        self.ui.labelMessage.setText("Hello "+ self.ui.lineUserName.text())

if __name__ == "__main__":
    app = QtGui.QApplication(sys.argv)
    myapp = MyForm()
    myapp.show()
    sys.exit(app.exec_())
```

Figure 7.16
Welcome message displayed on selecting the Click Me button.

As stated earlier, every PyQt GUI application must have a QApplication object to provide access to information such as the application's directory, screen size, and so on. You create an instance of MyForm and call its show() method, which adds a new event to the QApplication object's event queue. The app.exec_() method is called to start the QApplication object's event loop. Once the event loop begins, the top-level widget used in the class MyForm is displayed, along with its child widgets. On occurrence of an event, the event loop processes it and eventually passes it to the associated method. To the __init__() method of MyForm, you pass a default parent of None to cause the QDialog class to be treated as a top-level window.

Recall that the user interface design is instantiated by calling the setupUI() method of the class that was created in the Python code (Ui_Dialog). You need to create an instance of the class Ui_Dialog, the class that was created in the Python code, and invoke its setupUi() method. On calling the setupUi() method, the Dialog widget will be created as the parent of all the widgets and displayed on the screen.

To respond to the events, the clicked() signal (event) of the Click Me pushbutton with the ClickMeButton object name is connected to the dispmessage() slot (method). Hence, when the user selects the Click Me pushbutton, the code in dispmessage() will be executed. The code in dispmessage() retrieves the name entered by the user in the Line Edit widget, lineUserName, and displays it through the Label labelMessage after prefixing it with a string, Hello. In Figure 7.16, you can see that if the user enters the user name **Caroline** in Line Edit and selects the Click Me pushbutton, the welcome displayed via Label will be Hello Caroline.

Converting Data Types

The default data type in a Line Edit widget is string. What if you want to use the widget for numerical data? Let's think of an application where you want to add two integer values and print their sum through a Label widget. First you need to convert string data entered in the Line Edit widget to integer data type and then convert the sum of the numbers, which will be of integer data type, back to string type before being displaying through a Label widget.

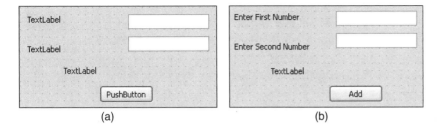

Figure 7.17
(a) Four widgets dropped on the form. (b) Widgets on the form with the text property set.

Let's create an application based on the Dialog without Buttons template and add three QLabels, two QlineEdits, and a QPushButton to the form by dragging and dropping three Labels, two Line Edits, and a Push Button on the form as shown in Figure 7.17(a). Set the text property of the two Label widgets to Enter First Number and Enter Second Number (Figure 7.17(b)). Set the objectName property of the three Labels to labelFirstNumber, labelSecondNumber, and labelAddition. Also, set the objectName property of the two Line Edit widgets to lineFirstNumber and lineSecondNumber. Set the objectName property of the Push Button to AddButton and also change its text property to Add. You don't need to change the third label's text property because the Python script will set the value and then display it when the two numerical values are added. Also, remember to drag the Label widget in the Designer to ensure it is long enough to display the text that will be assigned to it through the Python script. You can also increase the width of the Label widget by selecting Geometry > Width Property from the Property Editor.

Save the UI file as addtwonum.ui. The .ui file, which is in XML format when converted into Python code will appear as shown here:

```
addtwonum.py
# Form implementation generated from reading ui file 'addtwonum.ui'
from PyQt4 import QtCore, QtGui

try:
    _fromUtf8 = QtCore.QString.fromUtf8
except AttributeError:
    _fromUtf8 = lambda s: s

class Ui_Dialog(object):
    def setupUi(self, Dialog):
        Dialog.setObjectName(_fromUtf8("Dialog"))
        Dialog.resize(435, 255)
```

```
        self.lineFirstNumber = QtGui.QLineEdit(Dialog)
        self.lineFirstNumber.setGeometry(QtCore.QRect(190, 30, 113, 20))
        self.lineFirstNumber.setObjectName(_fromUtf8("lineFirstNumber"))
        self.lineSecondNumber = QtGui.QLineEdit(Dialog)
        self.lineSecondNumber.setGeometry(QtCore.QRect(190, 70, 113, 20))
        self.lineSecondNumber.setObjectName(_fromUtf8("lineSecondNumber"))
        self.labelSecondNumber = QtGui.QLabel(Dialog)
        self.labelSecondNumber.setGeometry(QtCore.QRect(50, 70, 111, 16))
        self.labelSecondNumber.setObjectName(_fromUtf8("labelSecondNumber"))
        self.AddButton = QtGui.QPushButton(Dialog)
        self.AddButton.setGeometry(QtCore.QRect(180, 130, 75, 23))
        self.AddButton.setObjectName(_fromUtf8("AddButton"))
        self.labelFirstNumber = QtGui.QLabel(Dialog)
        self.labelFirstNumber.setGeometry(QtCore.QRect(60, 30, 101, 16))
        self.labelFirstNumber.setObjectName(_fromUtf8("labelFirstNumber"))
        self.labelAddition = QtGui.QLabel(Dialog)
        self.labelAddition.setGeometry(QtCore.QRect(100, 100, 171, 21))
        self.labelAddition.setObjectName(_fromUtf8("labelAddition"))
        self.retranslateUi(Dialog)
        QtCore.QMetaObject.connectSlotsByName(Dialog)

    def retranslateUi(self, Dialog):
        Dialog.setWindowTitle(QtGui.QApplication.translate("Dialog", "Dialog", None,
QtGui.QApplication.UnicodeUTF8))
        self.labelSecondNumber.setText(QtGui.QApplication.translate("Dialog", "Enter
Second Number", None, QtGui.QApplication.UnicodeUTF8))
        self.AddButton.setText(QtGui.QApplication.translate("Dialog", "Add", None,
QtGui.QApplication.UnicodeUTF8))
        self.labelFirstNumber.setText(QtGui.QApplication.translate("Dialog", "Enter
First Number", None, QtGui.QApplication.UnicodeUTF8))
        self.labelAddition.setText(QtGui.QApplication.translate("Dialog", "TextLabel",
None, QtGui.QApplication.UnicodeUTF8))
```

Let's create a Python script named `calltwonum.pyw` that imports the Python code `addtwonum.py` to invoke a user interface design and that fetches the values entered in the Line Edit widgets and displays their addition. The code in the Python script `calltwonum.pyw` is shown here:

```
calltwonum.pyw
import sys
from addtwonum import *

class MyForm(QtGui.QDialog):
    def __init__(self, parent=None):
        QtGui.QWidget.__init__(self, parent)
        self.ui = Ui_Dialog()
```

```
    self.ui.setupUi(self)
    QtCore.QObject.connect(self.ui.AddButton,    QtCore.SIGNAL('clicked()'),    self.
dispsum)

  def dispsum(self):
    if len(self.ui.lineFirstNumber.text())!=0:
      a=int(self.ui.lineFirstNumber.text())
    else:
      a=0
    if len(self.ui.lineSecondNumber.text())!=0:
      b=int(self.ui.lineSecondNumber.text())
    else:
      b=0
    sum=a+b
    self.ui.labelAddition.setText("Addition: " +str(sum))
if __name__ == "__main__":
  app = QtGui.QApplication(sys.argv)
  myapp = MyForm()
  myapp.show()
  sys.exit(app.exec_())
```

Before we look at the code, let's consider the three functions used in it:

len(): Returns the number of characters in the string.

str(): Converts the passed argument into string data type.

int(): Converts the passed argument into integer data type.

The clicked() event of AddButton is connected to the dispsum() method to display the sum of the numbers entered in the two Line Edits. In the dispsum() method, you first validate lineFirstNumber and lineSecondNumber to ensure that if either Line Edit is left blank by the user, the value of that Line Edit is zero. The value entered in the two Line Edits is retrieved, converted into integers through int(), and assigned to the two variables a and b. The sum of the values in the variables a and b is computed and stored in the variable sum. The result in the variable sum is converted into string format through str()and displayed via labelAddition. You can see in Figure 7.18 that when the user selects the Add button after entering two numbers in the Line Edits, the addition is displayed through the Label widget.

Can you have a shortcut key for Line Edits? Consider a form with several Line Edit widgets that you want to access with a shortcut key. It is possible through buddies.

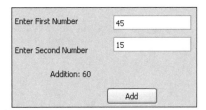

Figure 7.18
The sum of the numbers entered in Line Edit is displayed through a Label widget.

DEFINING BUDDIES

To establish a connection through between widgets or relate corresponding widgets, you create *buddies*. The benefit of using buddies is to have quick keyboard focus via shortcut keys on the widgets that do not accept focus. For example, to get focus on a Line Edit widget, you can set it as a buddy of a Label widget and assign a shortcut key to the Label widget. When the user presses the shortcut key for the Label widget, keyboard focus will be set on its Line Edit buddy widget.

Let's create a new application based on the Dialog without Buttons template. Add four QLabels, three QlineEdits, and a QPushButton to the dialog by dragging and dropping from the respective groups in the Widget Box. Set the text property of the three Label widgets to &Number of items, &Price per item, and &Discount Percentage. Recall that preceding any character in the text with an ampersand (&) will make it a shortcut key for the selected widget. Assigning the text &Number of items to the first Label (see Figure 7.19) will declare its first character, N, as its shortcut key. That also means that the Label will be accessed by

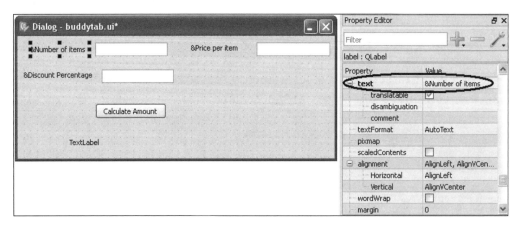

Figure 7.19
Setting a shortcut key for the Label.

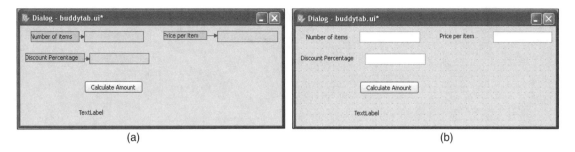

Figure 7.20
(a) Widgets on the form with the buddies set. (b) The dialog in Widget Editing mode.

Alt+N. Similarly, the shortcut keys for the next two Labels will be Alt+P and Alt+D. Set the text for the button to **Calculate Amount**. Set the objectName of the three Line Edit widgets to quantity, rate, and discount. Recall that it is through the object names that the widgets are distinguished and accessed in coding. Also set the objectName of the fourth Label to result and leave its default text property TextLabel as such because you will be setting its actual text in the program for displaying the result of computation. Also, increase the width of the fourth label either by dragging its nodes in the Designer or by selecing Geometry > Width Property in the Property Editor so that it can display all the information assigned to it by the script.

To begin setting buddies, select Edit > Edit Buddies or the Edit Buddies icon from the toolbar to switch to Buddy Editing mode. To go back to Widget Editing mode from Buddy Editing mode, you can choose any of the three options: press F3, select the Edit > Edit Widgets from the menu, or click the Edit Widgets icon on the toolbar. In Buddy Editing mode, select a Label widget and drag it to the Line Edit widget that you want to set as its buddy and release the mouse button. The Label and Line Edit widgets will become buddies. On defining a buddy for the Label widget, the & (ampersand) in its text becomes invisible. After setting the three Line Edit widgets as buddies of the Label widgets, the dialog will appear as shown in Figure 7.20(a). To switch from Buddy Editing to Widget Editing mode, either press F3 or select the Edit Widgets icon from the toolbar. The dialog in Widget Editing mode will appear as shown in Figure 7.20(b).

Before running the application, let's see how to set the tab order of the widgets.

Setting Tab Order

Tab order means the order in which the widgets will get focus when the Tab and Shift+Tab keys are pressed. The default tab order is based on the order in which widgets are placed on the form. To change this order, you need to switch to Tab Order

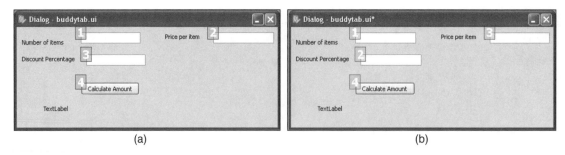

Figure 7.21
(a) Initial tab order of the widgets on the form. (b) Modified tab order of the widgets on the form.

Editing mode by either selecting the Edit, Edit Tab Order option or choosing the Edit Tab Order icon from the toolbar. In Tab Order Editing mode, each input widget in the form is shown with a number indicating its position in the tab order (see Figure 7.21(a)). If the user gives the first input widget the input focus and then presses the Tab key, the focus will move to the second input widget, and so on. You can change the tab order by clicking on each number in the correct order. When you select a number, it will change to red, indicating the currently edited position in the tab order chain. Clicking on the next number will make it the second in the tab order, and so on. In case of a mistake, you can restart numbering by choosing Restart from the form's context menu. To edit the tab order in the middle of the form, select a number with the Ctrl key pressed from where you want to change the tab order or choose Start from Here from the context menu. Let's set the tab order of the widgets on our dialog as shown in Figure 7.21(b).

Note

There is one more way to specify the tab order. Right-click anywhere on the form and select Tab Order List from the context menu that appears.

Save the application with the name `buddytab.ui`. Upon conversion to Python code, the XML file `buddytab.ui` will appear as shown here:

buddytab.py

```
# Form implementation generated from reading ui file 'buddytab.ui'

from PyQt4 import QtCore, QtGui

try:
    _fromUtf8 = QtCore.QString.fromUtf8
except AttributeError:
    _fromUtf8 = lambda s: s
```

```
class Ui_Dialog(object):
    def setupUi(self, Dialog):
        Dialog.setObjectName(_fromUtf8("Dialog"))
        Dialog.resize(490, 182)
        self.label = QtGui.QLabel(Dialog)
        self.label.setGeometry(QtCore.QRect(10, 20, 91, 16))
        self.label.setObjectName(_fromUtf8("label"))
        self.quantity = QtGui.QLineEdit(Dialog)
        self.quantity.setGeometry(QtCore.QRect(120, 10, 113, 20))
        self.quantity.setObjectName(_fromUtf8("quantity"))
        self.label_2 = QtGui.QLabel(Dialog)
        self.label_2.setGeometry(QtCore.QRect(280, 10, 71, 16))
        self.label_2.setObjectName(_fromUtf8("label_2"))
        self.rate = QtGui.QLineEdit(Dialog)
        self.rate.setGeometry(QtCore.QRect(370, 10, 113, 20))
        self.rate.setObjectName(_fromUtf8("rate"))
        self.label_3 = QtGui.QLabel(Dialog)
        self.label_3.setGeometry(QtCore.QRect(10, 50, 101, 16))
        self.label_3.setObjectName(_fromUtf8("label_3"))
        self.discount = QtGui.QLineEdit(Dialog)
        self.discount.setGeometry(QtCore.QRect(130, 50, 113, 20))
        self.discount.setObjectName(_fromUtf8("discount"))
        self.pushButton = QtGui.QPushButton(Dialog)
        self.pushButton.setGeometry(QtCore.QRect(120, 100, 111, 23))
        self.pushButton.setObjectName(_fromUtf8("pushButton"))
        self.result = QtGui.QLabel(Dialog)
        self.result.setGeometry(QtCore.QRect(50, 140, 351, 16))
        self.result.setText(_fromUtf8(""))
        self.result.setObjectName(_fromUtf8("result"))
        self.label.setBuddy(self.quantity)
        self.label_2.setBuddy(self.rate)
        self.label_3.setBuddy(self.discount)
        self.retranslateUi(Dialog)
        QtCore.QMetaObject.connectSlotsByName(Dialog)
        Dialog.setTabOrder(self.quantity, self.discount)
        Dialog.setTabOrder(self.discount, self.rate)
        Dialog.setTabOrder(self.rate, self.pushButton)

    def retranslateUi(self, Dialog):
        Dialog.setWindowTitle(QtGui.QApplication.translate("Dialog", "Dialog", None,
QtGui.QApplication.UnicodeUTF8))
        self.label.setText(QtGui.QApplication.translate("Dialog", "&Number of items",
None, QtGui.QApplication.UnicodeUTF8))
        self.label_2.setText(QtGui.QApplication.translate("Dialog", "&Price per item",
None, QtGui.QApplication.UnicodeUTF8))
```

```
        self.label_3.setText(QtGui.QApplication.translate("Dialog", "&Discount Per-
centage", None, QtGui.QApplication.UnicodeUTF8))
            self.pushButton.setText(QtGui.QApplication.translate("Dialog", "Calculate
Amount", None, QtGui.QApplication.UnicodeUTF8))
```

Let's create a Python script to import the Python code to invoke the user interface design and to compute the amount when number of items, price per item, and discount percentage are supplied by the user. Name the Python script callbuddytab.pyw; its code is shown below:

```
callbuddytab.pyw
from __future__ import division
import sys
from buddytab import *

class MyForm(QtGui.QMainWindow):
    def __init__(self, parent=None):
        QtGui.QWidget.__init__(self, parent)
        self.ui = Ui_Dialog()
        self.ui.setupUi(self)
        QtCore.QObject.connect(self.ui.pushButton, QtCore.SIGNAL('clicked()'), self.
calculate)

    def calculate(self):
        if len(self.ui.quantity.text())!=0:
            q=int(self.ui.quantity.text())
        else:
            q=0
        if len(self.ui.rate.text())!=0:
            r=int(self.ui.rate.text())
        else:
            r=0
        if len(self.ui.discount.text())!=0:
            d=int(self.ui.discount.text())
        else:
            d=0
        totamt=q*r
        disc=totamt*d/100
        netamt=totamt-disc
        self.ui.result.setText("Total Amount: " +str(totamt)+", Discount: "+str(disc)+",
Net Amount: "+str(netamt))

if __name__ == "__main__":
    app = QtGui.QApplication(sys.argv)
    myapp = MyForm()
    myapp.show()
    sys.exit(app.exec_())
```

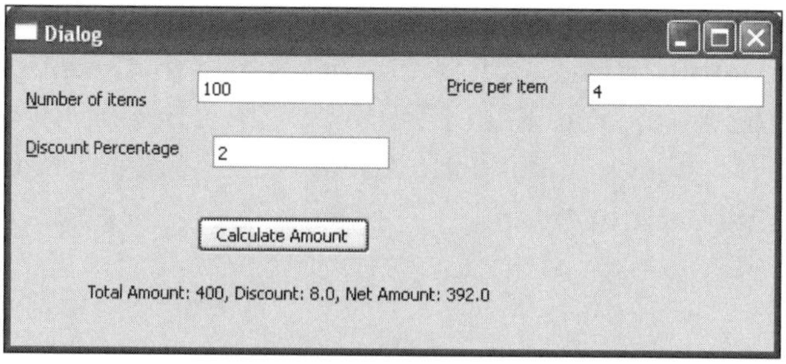

Figure 7.22
The characters acting as shortcut key appear underlined.

In this code, you can see that the Push Button's `clicked()` signal is connected to the `calculate()` function. After supplying the values for number of items, price per item, and discount percentage in the Line Edit widgets, when the user selects the Calculate Amount Push Button, the `calculate()` function will be invoked. In the `calculate()` function, you validate the Line Edit widgets to check if any Line Edit widget is left blank. The value of Line Edit that is left blank is assumed to be 0. Thereafter, you compute the net amount, which is total amount minus discount, where total amount is the product of number of items and price per item. The computed net amount is then converted to string data type to be displayed via a Label widget.

On running the application, you will find the underscored characters N, P, and D in the Label's texts, Number of items, Price per item, and Discount Percentage, as shown in Figure 7.22. The underscored characters mean that you can use Alt+N, Alt+P, and Alt+D shortcut keys for setting focus to the respective Line Edit widgets for entering values for number of items, price per item, and discount percentage. If you don't see the underscored characters in the Labels, just press Alt, and underscores will appear.

SUMMARY

In this chapter you had a brief introduction to the Qt toolkit and PyQt. You learned the procedure of installing PyQt. You learned about different Qt Designer components such as the toolbar, the Object Inspector, the Property Editor, and the Widget Box. You also learned to create a GUI application through coding. You learned about the fundamental Label, Line Edit, and Push Button widgets and developed applications using them.

You also had a good introduction to signal/slot connections in Qt Designer and learned to connect signals to the predefined slots and to custom slots. In the next chapter you will learn about basic widgets such as Radio Buttons, Checkboxes, Spin Boxes, Scroll Bars, Sliders, and Lists. To better understand these basic widgets, you will develop individual application using each of them.

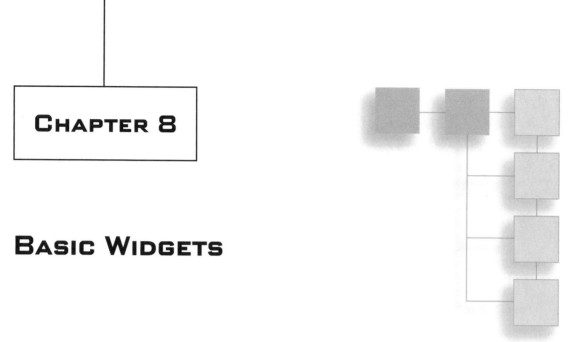

CHAPTER 8

BASIC WIDGETS

In this chapter, we will focus on a few basic widgets. These enable the user to choose one or more options and select integer or float values from a specified range. Not only will you learn how to display options to the user but also how to add, delete, or modify existing options. We will cover the following in this chapter:

- Using radio buttons
- Using checkboxes
- Entering integer and float values using a spin box
- Scroll bars and sliders
- Working with List widget

Let's begin the chapter with radio buttons.

USING RADIO BUTTONS

To display selectable options that are mutually exclusive (selecting one option automatically deselects other options in the group), you use Radio Button widgets, which are instances of the QRadioButton class. The class displays a radio button along with a text label. The radio button can be either in a selected (checked) or unselected (unchecked) state. If you want two or more sets of radio buttons, where each set allows exclusive selection of a radio button, put them into different button groups (instances of QButtonGroup). Button groups are explained in detail in Chapter 11, "Multiple Documents and Layouts." Methods provided by QRadioButton are shown in Table 8.1.

Table 8.1   Methods Provided by the QRadioButton Class

Method	Use
isChecked()	Returns true if the button is in selected state.
setIcon()	Used to display an icon with the radio button.
setText()	Used to set the text of the radio button. To specify a shortcut key for the radio button, precede the preferred character in the text with an ampersand (&).
setChecked()	Pass the Boolean value true to this method to make the radio button the default.

Table 8.2   Signals Emitted by the QRadioButton Class

Signal	Description
toggled()	Emitted whenever button changes its state from checked to unchecked or vice versa.
clicked()	Emitted when a button is activated (i.e., pressed and released) or when its shortcut key is pressed.
stateChanged()	Emitted when a radio button changes its state from checked to unchecked or vice versa.

Signals emitted by QRadioButton are shown in Table 8.2.

To understand the concept of radio buttons, let's create an application that asks the user to enter two numbers and displays four options—Add, Subtract, Multiply, and Divide—in the form of radio buttons. On selecting an option through Radio Button, the respective operation will be performed on the two numbers and the result displayed.

Let's create a new application based on the Dialog without Buttons template. Drag and drop three Label widgets, two LineEdit widgets, four radio buttons, and a push button onto the form. Set the text property of the first two Label widgets to Enter First Number and Enter Second Number. Leave the text property of the third Label at the default, TextLabel, as you will be setting its text through the program to display the result of computation. Also, set the text property of the four radio buttons to Add, Subtract, Multiply, and Divide. Set the objectName property of the three Label widgets to labelFirstNumber, labelSecondNumber, and labelResult. Set the objectName property of the two LineEdit widgets to

Figure 8.1
Form displaying four options to the user via radio buttons.

lineFirstNumber and lineSecondNumber. The default objectNames of the four Radio Buttons are radioButton, radioButton_2, radioButton_3, and radioButton_4. Change these to radioAdd, radioSubtract, radioMultiply, and radioDivide. Set the objectName of the push button to ComputeButton. The form will appear as shown in Figure 8.1.

Save the application with the name radiobtn.ui. On converting the .ui (XML) file into Python code through the pyuic4 command utility, you will get the code shown here:

```
radiobtn.py
# Form implementation generated from reading ui file 'radiobtn.ui'

from PyQt4 import QtCore, QtGui

try:
    _fromUtf8 = QtCore.QString.fromUtf8
except AttributeError:
    _fromUtf8 = lambda s: s

class Ui_Dialog(object):
    def setupUi(self, Dialog):
        Dialog.setObjectName(_fromUtf8("Dialog"))
        Dialog.resize(430, 448)
        self.labelResult = QtGui.QLabel(Dialog)
        self.labelResult.setGeometry(QtCore.QRect(60, 240, 171, 21))
        self.labelResult.setObjectName(_fromUtf8("labelResult"))
        self.lineSecondNumber = QtGui.QLineEdit(Dialog)
        self.lineSecondNumber.setGeometry(QtCore.QRect(170, 60, 113, 20))
```

```
        self.lineSecondNumber.setObjectName(_fromUtf8("lineSecondNumber"))
        self.labelSecondNumber = QtGui.QLabel(Dialog)
        self.labelSecondNumber.setGeometry(QtCore.QRect(50, 60, 111, 16))
        self.labelSecondNumber.setObjectName(_fromUtf8("labelSecondNumber"))
        self.labelFirstNumber = QtGui.QLabel(Dialog)
        self.labelFirstNumber.setGeometry(QtCore.QRect(60, 30, 101, 16))
        self.labelFirstNumber.setObjectName(_fromUtf8("labelFirstNumber"))
        self.ComputeButton = QtGui.QPushButton(Dialog)
        self.ComputeButton.setGeometry(QtCore.QRect(180, 280, 75, 23))
        self.ComputeButton.setObjectName(_fromUtf8("ComputeButton"))
        self.radioAdd = QtGui.QRadioButton(Dialog)
        self.radioAdd.setGeometry(QtCore.QRect(60, 110, 82, 17))
        self.radioAdd.setObjectName(_fromUtf8("radioAdd"))
        self.radioDivide = QtGui.QRadioButton(Dialog)
        self.radioDivide.setGeometry(QtCore.QRect(60, 200, 82, 17))
        self.radioDivide.setObjectName(_fromUtf8("radioDivide"))
        self.radioSubtract = QtGui.QRadioButton(Dialog)
        self.radioSubtract.setGeometry(QtCore.QRect(60, 140, 82, 17))
        self.radioSubtract.setObjectName(_fromUtf8("radioSubtract"))
        self.radioMultiply = QtGui.QRadioButton(Dialog)
        self.radioMultiply.setGeometry(QtCore.QRect(60, 170, 82, 17))
        self.radioMultiply.setObjectName(_fromUtf8("radioMultiply"))
        self.lineFirstNumber = QtGui.QLineEdit(Dialog)
        self.lineFirstNumber.setGeometry(QtCore.QRect(170, 30, 113, 20))
        self.lineFirstNumber.setObjectName(_fromUtf8("lineFirstNumber"))

        self.retranslateUi(Dialog)
        QtCore.QMetaObject.connectSlotsByName(Dialog)

    def retranslateUi(self, Dialog):
        Dialog.setWindowTitle(QtGui.QApplication.translate("Dialog", "Dialog", None,
QtGui.QApplication.UnicodeUTF8))
        self.labelResult.setText(QtGui.QApplication.translate("Dialog", "TextLabel",
None, QtGui.QApplication.UnicodeUTF8))
        self.labelSecondNumber.setText(QtGui.QApplication.translate("Dialog", "Enter
Second Number", None, QtGui.QApplication.UnicodeUTF8))
        self.labelFirstNumber.setText(QtGui.QApplication.translate("Dialog", "Enter
First Number", None, QtGui.QApplication.UnicodeUTF8))
        self.ComputeButton.setText(QtGui.QApplication.translate("Dialog", "Compute",
None, QtGui.QApplication.UnicodeUTF8))
        self.radioAdd.setText(QtGui.QApplication.translate("Dialog", "Add", None,
QtGui.QApplication.UnicodeUTF8))
        self.radioDivide.setText(QtGui.QApplication.translate("Dialog", "Divide",
None, QtGui.QApplication.UnicodeUTF8))
```

```
    self.radioSubtract.setText(QtGui.QApplication.translate("Dialog", "Subtract",
None, QtGui.QApplication.UnicodeUTF8))
    self.radioMultiply.setText(QtGui.QApplication.translate("Dialog", "Multiply",
None, QtGui.QApplication.UnicodeUTF8))
```

Let's import the code as a header file in the Python script that you are going to create next to invoke the user interface design. In the Python script, you will also write code to perform the arithmetic operation on the basis of the radio button selected by the user. Name the source file callradios.pyw; its code is shown here:

```
callradios.pyw
from __future__ import division
import sys
from radiobtn import *

class MyForm(QtGui.QDialog):
  def __init__(self, parent=None):
    QtGui.QWidget.__init__(self, parent)
    self.ui = Ui_Dialog()
    self.ui.setupUi(self)
    QtCore.QObject.connect(self.ui.ComputeButton, QtCore.SIGNAL('clicked()'),
self.calculate)
    self.ui.radioAdd.setChecked(1)

  def calculate(self):
    if len(self.ui.lineFirstNumber.text())!=0:
      a=int(self.ui.lineFirstNumber.text())
    else:

      a=0

    if len(self.ui.lineSecondNumber.text())!=0:
      b=int(self.ui.lineSecondNumber.text())
    else:
      b=0
    if self.ui.radioAdd.isChecked()==True:
      result=a+b
    if self.ui.radioSubtract.isChecked()==True:
      result=a-b
    if self.ui.radioMultiply.isChecked()==True:
      result=a*b
    if self.ui.radioDivide.isChecked()==True:
      result=a/b

    self.ui.labelResult.setText("Result: " +str(result))
```

Figure 8.2

(a) The addition operation applied to two numbers on selection of the Add radio button. (b) The division operation applied to the numbers on selection of Divide radio button.

```
if __name__ == "__main__":
    app = QtGui.QApplication(sys.argv)
    myapp = MyForm()
    myapp.show()
    sys.exit(app.exec_())
```

The clicked() event of ComputeButton is connected to the calculate() method, which will do the desired calculation. In the calculate() function, you set the default value of the LineEdits to 0, so if the user leaves either of the LineEdit widgets blank, its default value will be 0. The values entered in the two LineEdit widgets lineFirstNumber and lineSecondNumber are retrieved, converted into integers, and assigned to the variables a and b, respectively. After that, the state of the radio buttons is tested. Hence, if radioAdd is selected, the values in the variables a and b are added, and the addition is stored in the result variable. Similarly, if radioSubtract is selected, the values in variables a and b are subtracted, and the result is stored in result. Similarly, multiplication and division operations are performed when radioMultiply and radioDivide are selected. Finally, the result of the computation stored in result is displayed via labelResult. Figure 8.2 displays the addition and division operations applied to the number values entered in the LineEdit widgets.

Radio buttons display mutually exclusive options. You can select only one option from a set of available options. Selecting another option automatically deselects the earlier selected option. What if you want to select more than one option? Let's see.

Using Checkboxes

Where radio buttons allow only one option to be selected in a group, checkboxes allow you to select more than one option. That is, selecting a checkbox will not affect other checkboxes in the application. Checkboxes are displayed with a text label as an

Table 8.3   Methods Provided by the QCheckBox Class

Method	Use
isChecked()	Returns true if the checkbox is checked; otherwise returns false.
setTristate()	Pass Boolean value true to this method to use the "no change" state of the checkbox. With this state, you give the user the option of neither checking nor unchecking a checkbox.
setIcon()	Used to display an icon with the checkbox.
setText()	Used to set the text of the checkbox. To specify a shortcut key for the checkbox, precede the preferred character with an ampersand in the text.
setChecked()	Pass Boolean value true to this method to make the checkbox checked by default.

Table 8.4   Signals Emitted by the QCheckBox Class

Signal	Description
toggled()	The signal is emitted whenever a checkbox changes its state from checked to unchecked or vice versa.
clicked()	The signal is emitted when a checkbox is activated (i.e. pressed and released) or when its shortcut key is typed.
stateChanged()	The signal is emitted whenever a checkbox changes its state from checked to unchecked or vice versa.

instance of the QCheckBox class. A checkbox can be in any of three states: selected (checked), unselected (unchecked), or tristate (unchanged). Tristate is a *no change* state; the user has neither checked or unchecked the checkbox. The methods provided by QCheckBox are shown in Table 8.3.

The signals emitted by QCheckBox are shown in Table 8.4.

Note

The QAbstractButton class is the abstract base class of button widgets and provides functionality common to buttons. It provides support for pushbuttons, checkboxes, and radio buttons.

To understand the Checkbox widget, let's assume that you run a Food Corner where several food items such as pizzas, hot dogs, french fries, and chicken burgers are sold. The price of the food item is also mentioned with it. The user can select one or more food items. What you want is that when a food item is selected, the total price of the selected food items will be displayed. Begin by creating a new application based on the Dialog without Buttons template. Drag and drop two Label widgets, one LineEdit widget, four checkboxes, and a push button onto the form. Set the `text` property of the two Label widgets to `XYZ Food Corner` and `Total Amount`. Through the Property Editor, increase the font size of the first Label and make it bold to make it appear as a header in the application. Also, disable the LineEdit by unchecking its `enabled` property from the Property Editor because you will be displaying the result of computation with it and don't want it to be editable. Set the text of the four checkboxes to `Pizza $20`, `Hot Dog $5`, `French Fries $10`, and `Chicken Burger $15`. Also, set the text of the push button to `Calculate Amount`. The default `objectNames` of the four checkboxes are `checkBox`, `checkBox_2`, `checkBox_3`, and `checkBox_4`. Change these to `checkPizza20`, `checkHotDog5`, `check-Fries10`, and `checkBurger15`, respectively. Also set the `objectName` of the push button and LineEdit to `CalculateButton` and `lineAmount`, respectively. The form will appear as shown in Figure 8.3.

Save the application with the name `checkbx.ui`. The .ui (XML) file is then converted into Python code through the `pyuic4` command utility. The Python code is shown here:

```
checkbx.py
# Form implementation generated from reading ui file 'checkbx.ui'

from PyQt4 import QtCore, QtGui

try:
    _fromUtf8 = QtCore.QString.fromUtf8
except AttributeError:
    _fromUtf8 = lambda s: s
```

Figure 8.3
Form with four checkboxes, a push button, and a LineEdit widget in disabled mode.

```python
class Ui_Dialog(object):
    def setupUi(self, Dialog):
        Dialog.setObjectName(_fromUtf8("Dialog"))
        Dialog.resize(328, 270)
        Dialog.setWindowTitle(QtGui.QApplication.translate("Dialog", "Dialog", None,
QtGui.QApplication.UnicodeUTF8))
        self.label = QtGui.QLabel(Dialog)
        self.label.setGeometry(QtCore.QRect(110, 10, 141, 20))
        font = QtGui.QFont()
        font.setPointSize(11)
        font.setBold(True)
        font.setWeight(75)
        self.label.setFont(font)
        self.label.setText(QtGui.QApplication.translate("Dialog", "XYZ Food Corner",
None, QtGui.QApplication.UnicodeUTF8))
        self.label.setObjectName(_fromUtf8("label"))
        self.label_2 = QtGui.QLabel(Dialog)
        self.label_2.setGeometry(QtCore.QRect(40, 210, 81, 16))
        self.label_2.setText(QtGui.QApplication.translate("Dialog", "Total Amount",
None, QtGui.QApplication.UnicodeUTF8))
        self.label_2.setObjectName(_fromUtf8("label_2"))
        self.lineAmount = QtGui.QLineEdit(Dialog)
        self.lineAmount.setEnabled(False)
        self.lineAmount.setGeometry(QtCore.QRect(120, 210, 131, 20))
        self.lineAmount.setObjectName(_fromUtf8("lineAmount"))
        self.checkPizza20 = QtGui.QCheckBox(Dialog)
        self.checkPizza20.setGeometry(QtCore.QRect(110, 40, 91, 17))
        self.checkPizza20.setText(QtGui.QApplication.translate("Dialog", "Pizza  $20",
None, QtGui.QApplication.UnicodeUTF8))
        self.checkPizza20.setObjectName(_fromUtf8("checkPizza20"))
        self.checkHotDog5 = QtGui.QCheckBox(Dialog)
        self.checkHotDog5.setGeometry(QtCore.QRect(110, 70, 111, 17))
        self.checkHotDog5.setText(QtGui.QApplication.translate("Dialog", "Hot Dog  $5",
None, QtGui.QApplication.UnicodeUTF8))
        self.checkHotDog5.setObjectName(_fromUtf8("checkHotDog5"))
        self.checkFries10 = QtGui.QCheckBox(Dialog)
        self.checkFries10.setGeometry(QtCore.QRect(110, 100, 121, 17))
        self.checkFries10.setText(QtGui.QApplication.translate("Dialog", "French
Fries $10", None, QtGui.QApplication.UnicodeUTF8))
        self.checkFries10.setObjectName(_fromUtf8("checkFries10"))
        self.checkBurger15 = QtGui.QCheckBox(Dialog)
        self.checkBurger15.setGeometry(QtCore.QRect(110, 130, 121, 17))
        self.checkBurger15.setText(QtGui.QApplication.translate("Dialog", "Chicken
Burger $15", None, QtGui.QApplication.UnicodeUTF8))
```

```
    self.checkBurger15.setObjectName(_fromUtf8("checkBurger15"))
    self.CalculateButton = QtGui.QPushButton(Dialog)
    self.CalculateButton.setGeometry(QtCore.QRect(100, 170, 141, 23))
    self.CalculateButton.setText(QtGui.QApplication.translate("Dialog", "Calculate
Amount", None, QtGui.QApplication.UnicodeUTF8))
    self.CalculateButton.setObjectName(_fromUtf8("CalculateButton"))
    self.retranslateUi(Dialog)
    QtCore.QMetaObject.connectSlotsByName(Dialog)

  def retranslateUi(self, Dialog):
    pass
```

Let's import the code as a header file in our program to invoke the user interface design and to write code to calculate the total cost of food items selected and display the cost through a LineEdit widget when the user selects the push button. Let's name the program `callchecks.pyw`; its code is shown here:

```
callchecks.pyw
import sys
from checkbx import *

class MyForm(QtGui.QDialog):
   def __init__(self, parent=None):
     QtGui.QWidget.__init__(self, parent)
     self.ui = Ui_Dialog()
     self.ui.setupUi(self)
     QtCore.QObject.connect(self.ui.CalculateButton, QtCore.SIGNAL('clicked()'),
self.calculate)

   def calculate(self):
     amt=0
     if self.ui.checkPizza20.isChecked()==True:
       amt=amt+20
     if self.ui.checkHotDog5.isChecked()==True:
       amt=amt+5
     if self.ui.checkFries10.isChecked()==True:
       amt=amt+10
     if self.ui.checkBurger15.isChecked()==True:
       amt=amt+15
       self.ui.lineAmount.setText(str(amt))

if __name__ == "__main__":
   app = QtGui.QApplication(sys.argv)
   myapp = MyForm()
   myapp.show()
   sys.exit(app.exec_())
```

(a)   (b)

Figure 8.4
(a) The cost of two food items is displayed. (b) The cost of all four food items is displayed.

The clicked() event of CalculateButton is connected to the calculate() function, which will calculate the cost of the food items selected. In the calculate() function, you check the status of the checkboxes to know if they are checked or unchecked. The cost of the food items whose checkboxes are checked is added and stored in the amt variable. Finally, the addition of the amount stored in amt is displayed via lineAmount. To avoid any alterations in the amount displayed via LineEdit, LineEdit is disabled. On running the application, you get a dialog prompting you to select the food items that you want to order. Figure 8.4(a) shows the total cost for Hot Dog and French Fries, and Figure 8.4(b) shows the total for all food items.

Initiating Action Without Using a Push Button

In the previous application, you saw that the total cost of the food items selected by the user appears only when the CalculateButton push button is selected by the user. It is so because the calculate() function that does the computation is connected to the push button's clicked() signal. Now let's modify the application slightly. Instead of selecting the push button for getting the result, you want the amount to be displayed when the user checks or unchecks any checkbox, without the need to select the push button. It also means that you want the calculate() function to be fired every time the status of any checkbox changes and not on selecting the push button. To apply these modifications, you will remove the push button and connect the clicked() signal of each checkbox to the calculate() method. As a result, the total amount will be displayed via the lineAmount LineEdit, as soon as any checkbox is checked or unchecked. The application will appear as shown in Figure 8.5.

Save the modified application with a different name, checkbx2.ui. When the .ui (XML) file is converted into Python code through the pyuic4 command utility, it will appear as shown here:

Figure 8.5
Form with the push button removed and LineEdit disabled.

checkbx2.py

```
# Form implementation generated from reading ui file 'checkbx2.ui'
from PyQt4 import QtCore, QtGui

try:
    _fromUtf8 = QtCore.QString.fromUtf8
except AttributeError:
    _fromUtf8 = lambda s: s

class Ui_Dialog(object):
    def setupUi(self, Dialog):
        Dialog.setObjectName(_fromUtf8("Dialog"))
        Dialog.resize(328, 220)
        Dialog.setWindowTitle(QtGui.QApplication.translate("Dialog", "Dialog", None,
QtGui.QApplication.UnicodeUTF8))
        self.label = QtGui.QLabel(Dialog)
        self.label.setGeometry(QtCore.QRect(110, 10, 141, 20))
        font = QtGui.QFont()
        font.setPointSize(11)
        font.setBold(True)
        font.setWeight(75)
        self.label.setFont(font)
        self.label.setText(QtGui.QApplication.translate("Dialog", "XYZ Food Corner",
None, QtGui.QApplication.UnicodeUTF8))
        self.label.setObjectName(_fromUtf8("label"))
        self.label_2 = QtGui.QLabel(Dialog)
        self.label_2.setGeometry(QtCore.QRect(40, 170, 71, 16))
        self.label_2.setText(QtGui.QApplication.translate("Dialog", "Total Amount",
None, QtGui.QApplication.UnicodeUTF8))
        self.label_2.setObjectName(_fromUtf8("label_2"))
        self.lineAmount = QtGui.QLineEdit(Dialog)
```

```
    self.lineAmount.setEnabled(False)
    self.lineAmount.setGeometry(QtCore.QRect(120, 170, 131, 20))
    self.lineAmount.setObjectName(_fromUtf8("lineAmount"))
    self.checkPizza20 = QtGui.QCheckBox(Dialog)
    self.checkPizza20.setGeometry(QtCore.QRect(110, 40, 91, 17))
    self.checkPizza20.setText(QtGui.QApplication.translate("Dialog", "Pizza  $20",
None, QtGui.QApplication.UnicodeUTF8))
    self.checkPizza20.setObjectName(_fromUtf8("checkPizza20"))
    self.checkHotDog5 = QtGui.QCheckBox(Dialog)
    self.checkHotDog5.setGeometry(QtCore.QRect(110, 70, 111, 17))
    self.checkHotDog5.setText(QtGui.QApplication.translate("Dialog", "Hot Dog  $5",
None, QtGui.QApplication.UnicodeUTF8))
    self.checkHotDog5.setObjectName(_fromUtf8("checkHotDog5"))
    self.checkFries10 = QtGui.QCheckBox(Dialog)
    self.checkFries10.setGeometry(QtCore.QRect(110, 100, 121, 17))
    self.checkFries10.setText(QtGui.QApplication.translate("Dialog", "French
Fries  $10", None, QtGui.QApplication.UnicodeUTF8))
    self.checkFries10.setObjectName(_fromUtf8("checkFries10"))
    self.checkBurger15 = QtGui.QCheckBox(Dialog)
    self.checkBurger15.setGeometry(QtCore.QRect(110, 130, 121, 17))
    self.checkBurger15.setText(QtGui.QApplication.translate("Dialog", "Chicken
Burger  $15", None, QtGui.QApplication.UnicodeUTF8))
    self.checkBurger15.setObjectName(_fromUtf8("checkBurger15"))
    self.retranslateUi(Dialog)
    QtCore.QMetaObject.connectSlotsByName(Dialog)

  def retranslateUi(self, Dialog):
    pass
```

Import the code as a header file into the Python script to invoke the modified user interface design and to write code that initiates the calculation() method on checking or unchecking of the checkbox. Let's name the script callchecks2.pyw; its code is shown here:

```
callchecks2.pyw
import sys
from checkbx2 import *

class MyForm(QtGui.QDialog):
  def __init__(self, parent=None):
    QtGui.QWidget.__init__(self, parent)
    self.ui = Ui_Dialog()
    self.ui.setupUi(self)
    QtCore.QObject.connect(self.ui.checkPizza20, QtCore.SIGNAL('clicked()'),
self.calculate)
```

```
        QtCore.QObject.connect(self.ui.checkHotDog5, QtCore.SIGNAL('clicked()'),
self.calculate)
        QtCore.QObject.connect(self.ui.checkFries10, QtCore.SIGNAL('clicked()'),
self.calculate)
        QtCore.QObject.connect(self.ui.checkBurger15, QtCore.SIGNAL('clicked()'),
self.calculate)

    def calculate(self):
        amt=0
        if self.ui.checkPizza20.isChecked()==True:
            amt=amt+20
        if self.ui.checkHotDog5.isChecked()==True:
            amt=amt+5
        if self.ui.checkFries10.isChecked()==True:
            amt=amt+10
        if self.ui.checkBurger15.isChecked()==True:
            amt=amt+15
            self.ui.lineAmount.setText(str(amt))

if __name__ == "__main__":
    app = QtGui.QApplication(sys.argv)
    myapp = MyForm()
    myapp.show()
    sys.exit(app.exec_())
```

The clicked() signals in the four checkboxes are connected to the calculate() method; whenever any of the checkboxes is checked or unchecked, the calculate() function will be invoked. The calculate() function checks the status of each checkbox. The cost of the food items in the checked checkboxes is added and stored in amt, which is then displayed via lineAmount.

The next widget you are going to learn about is used in GUI applications for selecting integer or float values from a range of values.

ENTERING INTEGER AND FLOAT VALUES USING A SPIN BOX

The Spin Box widget is frequently used to display integer values, floating-point values, and text. It displays an initial value by default that can be increased or decreased by selecting the up/down button or up/down arrow key on the keyboard. You can choose a value that is being displayed by either clicking on it or typing it in manually. A spin box can be created via two classes, QSpinBox and QdoubleSpin-Box. The former displays only integer values, and the latter displays floating-point values. Methods provided by QSpinBox are shown in Table 8.5.

Table 8.5   Methods Provided by QSpinBox

Method	Use
value()	Returns the current integer value of the spin box.
text()	Returns the text displayed by the spin box.
setPrefix()	Sets the text that you want to be prepended to the value returned by the spin box.
setSuffix()	Sets the text that you want to be appended to the value returned by the spin box.
cleanText()	Returns the value of the spin box without a suffix, a prefix or leading or trailing white spaces.
setValue()	Sets the value of the spin box.
setSingleStep()	Sets the step size of the spin box. The value of the spin box will increase or decrease by this amount when the up or down button is pressed.
setMinimum()	Sets the minimum value of the spin box.
setMaximum()	Sets the maximum value of the spin box.
setWrapping()	Sets its value to true if you want wrapping behavior in the spin box. Wrapping or circular behavior means the spin box returns to the first value (minimum value) when the up button is pressed if the spin box is displaying the maximum value.

Signals emitted by the QSpinBox class are as follows:

valueChanged(): Emitted when the value of the spin box is changed either by selecting the up/down button or by the setValue() method.

editingFinished(): Emitted when focus is lost on the spin box confirming that editing is finished.

As stated earlier, the class used for dealing with float values is QDoubleSpinBox. The QDoubleSpinBox class also supports the methods above. It displays values up to 2 decimal places by default. To change the precision, you use setDecimals(), which displays the values up to the specified number of decimal places. The value will be rounded to the specified number of decimals.

Note

The default minimum, maximum, singleStep, and value properties of a spin box are 0, 99, 1, and 0, respectively. The default minimum, maximum, singleStep, and value properties of a double spin box are 0.000000, 99.990000, 1.000000, and 0.000000, respectively.

The next application allows the user to add two numbers; one will be an integer, and the other will be a floating-point value. You might think that this application is similar to the addtwonum.py application that you created earlier. But unlike that application, here the user will not enter values to be added through LineEdit widgets; instead he will select them through spin boxes.

As usual, let's create a new application based on the Dialog without Buttons template and drag and drop three Label widgets, a Spin Box, a Double Spin Box, two LineEdits, and a Push Button widget. The text property of the two labels is set to Select First value and Select Second value, and the objectName of the third label is set to labelAddition. The text property of the push button is set to Add. Set the objectNames of the two LineEdit widgets to lineFirstValue and lineSecond-Value and that of the push button to AddButton. Delete the default text property of the third label, TextLabel, as you will be setting its text in the program to display the sum of the numbers. The third label will become invisible on deleting its text property. Also, disable the two LineEdit widgets by unchecking their enabled property from the Property Editor window, as you want them to display non-editable values that are selected from the spin boxes. The form will appear as shown in Figure 8.6.

Save the application with the name spinner.ui. On using the pyuic4 command utility, the .ui (XML) file will be converted into Python code as shown here:

spinner.py

```
# Form implementation generated from reading ui file 'spinner.ui'

from PyQt4 import QtCore, QtGui

try:
    _fromUtf8 = QtCore.QString.fromUtf8
except AttributeError:
    _fromUtf8 = lambda s: s

class Ui_Dialog(object):
    def setupUi(self, Dialog):
        Dialog.setObjectName(_fromUtf8("Dialog"))
        Dialog.resize(389, 161)
```

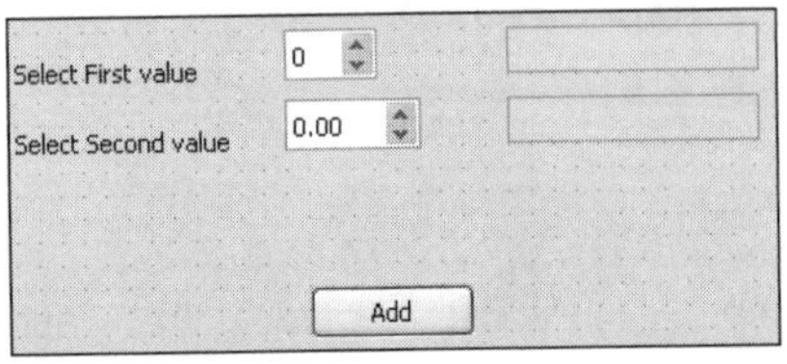

Figure 8.6
The form with a spin box, a double spin box, a push button, two labels, and two LineEdit widgets.

```
    self.spinBox = QtGui.QSpinBox(Dialog)
    self.spinBox.setGeometry(QtCore.QRect(140, 10, 42, 22))
    self.spinBox.setObjectName(_fromUtf8("spinBox"))
    self.lineSecondValue = QtGui.QLineEdit(Dialog)
    self.lineSecondValue.setEnabled(False)
    self.lineSecondValue.setGeometry(QtCore.QRect(240, 40, 113, 20))
    self.lineSecondValue.setObjectName(_fromUtf8("lineSecondValue"))
    self.labelAddition = QtGui.QLabel(Dialog)
    self.labelAddition.setGeometry(QtCore.QRect(130, 90, 121, 16))
    self.labelAddition.setText(_fromUtf8(""))
    self.labelAddition.setObjectName(_fromUtf8("labelAddition"))
    self.doubleSpinBox = QtGui.QDoubleSpinBox(Dialog)
    self.doubleSpinBox.setGeometry(QtCore.QRect(140, 40, 62, 22))
    self.doubleSpinBox.setObjectName(_fromUtf8("doubleSpinBox"))
    self.label_2 = QtGui.QLabel(Dialog)
    self.label_2.setGeometry(QtCore.QRect(20, 50, 101, 16))
    self.label_2.setObjectName(_fromUtf8("label_2"))
    self.lineFirstValue = QtGui.QLineEdit(Dialog)
    self.lineFirstValue.setEnabled(False)
    self.lineFirstValue.setGeometry(QtCore.QRect(240, 10, 113, 20))
    self.lineFirstValue.setObjectName(_fromUtf8("lineFirstValue"))
    self.AddButton = QtGui.QPushButton(Dialog)
    self.AddButton.setGeometry(QtCore.QRect(150, 120, 75, 23))
    self.AddButton.setObjectName(_fromUtf8("AddButton"))
    self.label = QtGui.QLabel(Dialog)
    self.label.setGeometry(QtCore.QRect(20, 20, 91, 16))
    self.label.setObjectName(_fromUtf8("label"))

    self.retranslateUi(Dialog)
    QtCore.QMetaObject.connectSlotsByName(Dialog)

def retranslateUi(self, Dialog):
    Dialog.setWindowTitle(QtGui.QApplication.translate("Dialog", "Dialog", None,
QtGui.QApplication.UnicodeUTF8))
    self.label_2.setText(QtGui.QApplication.translate("Dialog", "Select Second
value", None, QtGui.QApplication.UnicodeUTF8))
    self.AddButton.setText(QtGui.QApplication.translate("Dialog", "Add", None,
QtGui.QApplication.UnicodeUTF8))
    self.label.setText(QtGui.QApplication.translate("Dialog", "Select First value",
None, QtGui.QApplication.UnicodeUTF8))
```

Now let's create a Python script file that imports the code, enabling you to invoke the user interface design that displays the numbers selected through spin boxes in Line-Edit widgets and also compute their addition. The file will appear as shown here:

```
callspinner.pyw
import sys
from spinner import *

class MyForm(QtGui.QDialog):
    def __init__(self, parent=None):
        QtGui.QWidget.__init__(self, parent)
        self.ui = Ui_Dialog()
        self.ui.setupUi(self)
        QtCore.QObject.connect(self.ui.spinBox, QtCore.SIGNAL('editingFinished()'),
self.result1)
        QtCore.QObject.connect(self.ui.doubleSpinBox, QtCore.SIGNAL
('editingFinished()'), self.result2)
        QtCore.QObject.connect(self.ui.AddButton, QtCore.SIGNAL('clicked()'),
self.addvalues)

    def result1(self):
        self.ui.lineFirstValue.setText(str(self.ui.spinBox.value()))

    def result2(self):
        self.ui.lineSecondValue.setText(str(self.ui.doubleSpinBox.value()))

    def addvalues(self):
        sum=self.ui.spinBox.value()+self.ui.doubleSpinBox.value()
        self.ui.labelAddition.setText('Sum is '+str(sum))

    if __name__ == "__main__":
        app = QtGui.QApplication(sys.argv)
        myapp = MyForm()
        myapp.show()
        sys.exit(app.exec_())
```

In this code, you can see that the editingFinished() signal of the two spin boxes
is attached to the functions, result1() and result2(). It means that when focus
is lost on any of the spin boxes, the respective method will be invoked. Focus is lost
on a widget when the user moves onto other widget with the mouse or by pressing
the Tab key. In the result1() function, you retrieve the integer value from the Spin
Box widget and display it through the first LineEdit widget, lineFirstValue. Similarly, in result2(), you retrieve the floating-point value from the double spin box
and display it through the second LineEdit widget, lineSecondValue. The
clicked() signal of the push button is connected to addvalues(), which means
that, after selecting the values in the two spin boxes when the user selects the push
button, the addvalues() function will be invoked. In the addvalues() function,

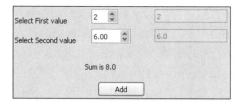

Figure 8.7
The spin box and double spin box values displayed through LineEdit along with their sum.

the values of the two spin boxes are added and displayed through the third Label widget, `labelAddition`, as shown in Figure 8.7.

The widgets that we are going to discuss next are helpful in viewing larger documents and in specifying integer values within a bounded range.

SCROLLBARS AND SLIDERS

Scrollbars are something that you usually come across while looking at large documents or images. Scrollbars appear horizontally or vertically, indicating your current position in the document or image and the amount that is not visible. Using the slider handle provided with these bars, you can access the hidden part of the document or image.

Sliders are a way of selecting an integer value between two values. That is, a slider can represent a minimum and maximum range of values, and the user can select a value within this range by moving the slider handle to the desired location in the slider. First let's look at ScrollBars.

ScrollBars

Scrollbars are used for viewing documents or images that are larger than the view area. To display horizontal or vertical scrollbars, you use the HorizontalScrollBar and VerticalScrollBar widgets, which are instances of the `QScrollBar` class. On applying scrollbars, you can move a slider handle to view the hidden area. The location of the slider handle indicates your location within the document or image so that you know how much of the document or image is hidden. A ScrollBar has the following controls:

- **Slider handle:** Used to move to any part of the document or image quickly.
- **Scroll arrows:** These are the arrows on either side of the scrollbars that are used to accurately navigate to a particular place in a document or image. On using these scroll arrows, the position of the slider handle also changes accordingly.

■ **Page control:** The page control is the background of the scrollbar over which the slider handle is dragged. When the background is clicked, the slider handle moves towards the click by one page. The amount the slider handle moves can be specified via the page step. The page step is the amount by which the value changes when the user presses the Page Up and Page Down keys, and is set with the setPageStep() method (explained next). The value of the page reresents the proportion of the document area shown in scrolling view. You can also move the slider handle by a value equal to page step by pressing Page Up or Page Down.

Methods used to set and retrieve values from ScrollBars are given in Table 8.6.

Note

QScrollBar provides only integer values.

The signals emitted through the QScrollBar class are shown in Table 8.7.

Let's take a brief look at sliders before you create an application using the two widgets.

Table 8.6   Methods Used to Set and Retrieve Values from ScrollBars

Method	Use
value()	Retrieves a value that indicates the distance of the slider handle from the start of the scrollbar. When the slider handle is at the top edge in a vertical scrollbar or at the left edge in a horizontal scrollbar, this method returns the minimum value. Similarly, when the slider handle is at the bottom edge in a vertical scrollbar or at the right edge in a horizontal scrollbar, this method returns the maximum value. The slider handle moves to the start (the minimum value) when the Home key is pressed and moves to the end (the maximum value) when the End key is pressed.
setValue()	Sets the value of the scrollbar and hence the location of the slider handle in the scrollbar.
minimum()	Returns the minimum value of the scrollbar.
maximum()	Returns the maximum value of the scrollbar.
setMinimum()	Sets the minimum value of the scrollbar.
setMaximum()	Sets the maximum value of the scrollbar.
setSingleStep()	Sets the single step value.
setPageStep()	Sets the page step value.

Table 8.7   Signals Emitted by the QScrollBar Class

Signal	Description
valueChanged()	Emitted when the scrollbar's value is changed.
sliderPressed()	Emitted when the user starts to drag the slider handle.
sliderMoved()	Emitted when the user drags the slider handle.
sliderReleased()	Emitted when the user releases the slider handle.
actionTriggered()	Emitted when the scrollbar is changed by user interaction.

Sliders

Sliders are generally used to represent some integer value. You can make a slider to represent some value by positioning its handle along a horizontal or vertical groove. You can increase or decrease the represented value by moving the slider handle toward the top or bottom edge. In order to display horizontal and vertical sliders, you use HorizontalSlider and VerticalSlider widgets, which are instances of the QSlider class. The methods used to set and retrieve the value of the slider handle are the same as you saw in ScrollBars. Also, sliders generate the same signals (valueChanged(), sliderPressed(), sliderMoved(), sliderReleased(), etc.) on moving the slider handle as you already saw in ScrollBars. Like QScroll-Bar, QSlider also provides only integer ranges.

The slider handle in scrollbars and sliders represents a value within the minimum and maximum range. If you don't want the scrollbars or sliders to assume default minimum and maximum values, it is better to set the values for the minimum, maximum, singleStep, and pageStep properties before proceeding.

Note

The default values of the minimum, maximum, singleStep, pageStep, and value properties of scrollbars and sliders are 0, 99, 1, 10, and 0, respectively.

We can also display tickmarks in sliders.

The methods used for configuring tickmarks are these:

setTickPosition(): Sets the position of tickmarks.

setTickInterval(): Specifies the number of ticks desired.

tickPosition(): Returns the current tick position.

tickInterval(): Returns the current tick interval.

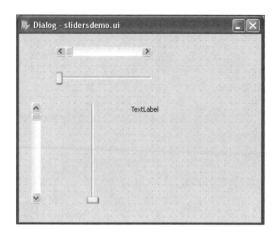

Figure 8.8
Horizontal and vertical ScrollBars and Sliders, along with a Label widget.

Let's create an application in which a horizontal scrollbar is connected to a horizontal slider and a vertical scrollbar is connected to a vertical slider. A connection means that the movement of the slider and the scrollbar's slider handle is synchronized. If you move the slider handle of any scrollbar, the slider handle of the corresponding slider should also move. You want the opposite to be true as well: When the handle of any slider is moved, the slider handle of the corresponding scrollbar also moves in the same direction. You want the value represented by the slider handle to be displayed through a Label widget. Let's create a new application of the Dialog without Buttons template and drag and drop horizontal and vertical ScrollBars and Sliders onto the form. Also, drop a Label widget to display the value of the slider handle. The form will appear as shown in Figure 8.8.

Save the application with the name slidersdemo.ui. The pyuic4 command utility will convert the .ui (XML) file into Python code as shown here:

slidersdemo.py

```
# Form implementation generated from reading ui file 'slidersdemo.ui'

from PyQt4 import QtCore, QtGui

try:
    _fromUtf8 = QtCore.QString.fromUtf8
except AttributeError:
    _fromUtf8 = lambda s: s

class Ui_Dialog(object):
    def setupUi(self, Dialog):
        Dialog.setObjectName(_fromUtf8("Dialog"))
```

```
    Dialog.resize(400, 300)
    self.horizontalScrollBar = QtGui.QScrollBar(Dialog)
    self.horizontalScrollBar.setGeometry(QtCore.QRect(60, 20, 160, 16))
    self.horizontalScrollBar.setOrientation(QtCore.Qt.Horizontal)
    self.horizontalScrollBar.setObjectName(_fromUtf8("horizontalScrollBar"))
    self.verticalScrollBar = QtGui.QScrollBar(Dialog)
    self.verticalScrollBar.setGeometry(QtCore.QRect(20, 110, 16, 160))
    self.verticalScrollBar.setOrientation(QtCore.Qt.Vertical)
    self.verticalScrollBar.setObjectName(_fromUtf8("verticalScrollBar"))
    self.horizontalSlider = QtGui.QSlider(Dialog)
    self.horizontalSlider.setGeometry(QtCore.QRect(60, 60, 160, 21))
    self.horizontalSlider.setOrientation(QtCore.Qt.Horizontal)
    self.horizontalSlider.setObjectName(_fromUtf8("horizontalSlider"))
    self.verticalSlider = QtGui.QSlider(Dialog)
    self.verticalSlider.setGeometry(QtCore.QRect(110, 110, 21, 160))
    self.verticalSlider.setOrientation(QtCore.Qt.Vertical)
    self.verticalSlider.setObjectName(_fromUtf8("verticalSlider"))
    self.label = QtGui.QLabel(Dialog)
    self.label.setGeometry(QtCore.QRect(185, 110, 141, 20))
    self.label.setObjectName(_fromUtf8("label"))
    self.retranslateUi(Dialog)
    QtCore.QMetaObject.connectSlotsByName(Dialog)

def retranslateUi(self, Dialog):
    Dialog.setWindowTitle(QtGui.QApplication.translate("Dialog", "Dialog", None,
QtGui.QApplication.UnicodeUTF8))
    self.label.setText(QtGui.QApplication.translate("Dialog", "TextLabel", None,
QtGui.QApplication.UnicodeUTF8))
```

The next step is creation of a Python script file that imports the code to invoke the user interface design and synchronizes the movement of the slider handles. The script will also display the value of the slider handle with a Label widget. The Python script file will appear as shown here:

```
callsliders.pyw
import sys
from slidersdemo import *

class MyForm(QtGui.QDialog):
    def __init__(self, parent=None):
        QtGui.QWidget.__init__(self, parent)
        self.ui = Ui_Dialog()
        self.ui.setupUi(self)
        self.ui.horizontalScrollBar.valueChanged.connect(self.scrollhorizontal)
```

```
          self.ui.verticalScrollBar.valueChanged.connect(self.scrollvertical)
          self.ui.horizontalSlider.valueChanged.connect(self.sliderhorizontal)
          self.ui.verticalSlider.valueChanged.connect(self.slidervertical)

      def scrollhorizontal(self,value):
        self.ui.label.setText(str(value))
        self.ui.horizontalSlider.setValue(value)

      def scrollvertical(self, value):
        self.ui.label.setText(str(value))
        self.ui.verticalSlider.setValue(value)

      def sliderhorizontal(self, value):
        self.ui.label.setText(str(value))
        self.ui.horizontalScrollBar.setValue(value)
          def slidervertical(self, value):
        self.ui.label.setText(str(value))
        self.ui.verticalScrollBar.setValue(value)

if __name__ == "__main__":
    app = QtGui.QApplication(sys.argv)
    myapp = MyForm()
    myapp.show()
    sys.exit(app.exec_())
```

In this code, you are connecting the valueChanged signal of each widget with the respective functions so that if the slider handle of the widget is moved, the corresponding function is invoked to perform the desired task. For instance, when the slider handle of the horizontal scrollbar is moved, the scrollhorizontal() function is invoked. The scrollhorizontal() function displays the value represented by the slider handle through the Label widget and sets the value of the horizontal slider's handle equal to the value of the horizontal scrollbar's signal handle. The slider's handle of the horizontal slider also moves in the same direction and by the same amount as the horizontal scrollbar's slider handle. In short, you keep setting the value of the slider handle when any scrollbar or slider's signal handle is moved. In Figure 8.9(a), you see that when the horizontal scrollbar's slider handle is moved, the horizontal slider's handle also moves. Also, the value of the slider handle is displayed with a Label control. Similarly, Figure 8.9(b) shows that when the slider handle of the vertical scrollbar or slider is moved, the slider handle of the corresponding widget also moves accordingly.

The next widget that you are going to learn about not only enables you to display different options to the user but also allows you to manipulate them, meaning that you can add options, delete any or all options, and update an existing option.

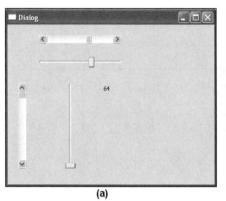 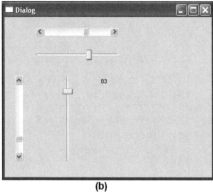

(a)   (b)

Figure 8.9
(a) Movement of the slider handles of the horizontal scrollbar and the slider is synchronized, and their position is displayed through a Label widget. (b) The vertical scrollbar and the slider's handles are synchronized, and their position is indicated through a Label widget.

WORKING WITH A LIST WIDGET

To display a list of items, you use a List widget, which is an instance of the QList-Widget class. You can not only view items, you also can add and remove them. The class provides a classic *item-based interface* for adding and removing list items. Also, it has its own internal model to manage each item in the list. Items in the list are instances of the QListWidgetItem class. The methods provided by QListWidget are shown in Table 8.8.

Signals emitted by the QListWidget class are shown in Table 8.9.

To understand the List widget, you will create two applications. The first will demonstrate the procedure for adding new items to the List widget. When you are acquainted with that concept, you will create another application to demonstrate deleting and editing items in the List widget. Let's see how to add items to the List widget.

Adding Items to a List Widget

The following is an application that is focused on explaining the procedure of adding an item to a List widget. In this application, you will use LineEdit, Push Button, and List widgets. The List widget will be empty initially, and the user is asked to enter a country name in LineEdit and select an Add button. The country name then will be added to the List widget. All subsequent country names will be added below the previous entry.

We begin by creating new application based on the Dialog without Buttons template and dragging and dropping Label, LineEdit, Push Button, and List widgets onto the

Table 8.8　Methods Provided by the QListWidget Class

Method	Use
insertItem()	Inserts a new item with the specified text into the List widget at the specified row.
insertItems()	Inserts multiple items from a list of supplied labels, starting at the specified row.
count()	Returns the count of the number of items in the list.
takeItem()	Removes and returns item from the specified row in the List widget.
currentItem()	Returns the current item in the list.
setCurrentItem()	Replaces the current item in the list with the specified item.
addItem()	Inserts an item with the specified text at the end of the List widget.
addItems()	Inserts items with the specified text at the end of the List widget.
clear()	Removes all items and selections in the view permanently.
currentRow()	Returns the row number of the current item. If there is no current item, it returns the value -1.
setCurrentRow()	Selects the specified row in the List widget.
item()	Returns the item at the specified row.

Table 8.9　Signals Emitted by QListWidget

Signal	Description
currentRowChanged()	Emitted whenever the row of the current item changes.
currentTextChanged()	Emitted whenever the text in the current item is changed.
currentItemChanged()	Emitted when the focus of the current item is changed.

form. Set the text property of the Label and Push Button widgets to Enter Country and Add, respectively. The form will appear as shown in Figure 8.10.

Save the application with the name addtolist.ui. The .ui (XML) file is then converted into Python code through the pyuic4 command utility. The code will appear as shown here:

```
addtolist.py
# Form implementation generated from reading ui file 'addtolist.ui'
```

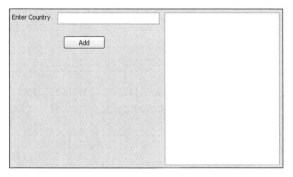

Figure 8.10
The form showing the List, LineEdit, Label, and Push Button widgets.

```python
from PyQt4 import QtCore, QtGui

try:
    _fromUtf8 = QtCore.QString.fromUtf8
except AttributeError:
    _fromUtf8 = lambda s: s

class Ui_Dialog(object):
    def setupUi(self, Dialog):
        Dialog.setObjectName(_fromUtf8("Dialog"))
        Dialog.resize(517, 304)
        self.label = QtGui.QLabel(Dialog)
        self.label.setGeometry(QtCore.QRect(20, 20, 71, 16))
        self.label.setObjectName(_fromUtf8("label"))
        self.listWidget = QtGui.QListWidget(Dialog)
        self.listWidget.setGeometry(QtCore.QRect(290, 20, 201, 261))
        self.listWidget.setObjectName(_fromUtf8("listWidget"))
        self.lineEdit = QtGui.QLineEdit(Dialog)
        self.lineEdit.setGeometry(QtCore.QRect(100, 20, 181, 20))
        self.lineEdit.setObjectName(_fromUtf8("lineEdit"))
        self.pushButton = QtGui.QPushButton(Dialog)
        self.pushButton.setGeometry(QtCore.QRect(110, 60, 75, 23))
        self.pushButton.setObjectName(_fromUtf8("pushButton"))

        self.retranslateUi(Dialog)
        QtCore.QMetaObject.connectSlotsByName(Dialog)

    def retranslateUi(self, Dialog):
        Dialog.setWindowTitle(QtGui.QApplication.translate("Dialog", "Dialog", None,
QtGui.QApplication.UnicodeUTF8))
```

```
    self.label.setText(QtGui.QApplication.translate("Dialog", "Enter Country",
None, QtGui.QApplication.UnicodeUTF8))
    self.pushButton.setText(QtGui.QApplication.translate("Dialog", "Add", None,
QtGui.QApplication.UnicodeUTF8))
```

Let's create a Python script file that imports the Python code to invoke the user interface design and adds the country name entered by the user in LineEdit to the List widget. The Python script file will appear as shown here:

```
calladdtolist.pyw
import sys
from addtolist import *

class MyForm(QtGui.QDialog):
   def __init__(self, parent=None):
      QtGui.QWidget.__init__(self, parent)
      self.ui = Ui_Dialog()
      self.ui.setupUi(self)
      QtCore.QObject.connect(self.ui.pushButton, QtCore.SIGNAL('clicked()'),
self.addlist)

   def addlist(self):
      self.ui.listWidget.addItem(self.ui.lineEdit.text())
      self.ui.lineEdit.setText('')
      self.ui.lineEdit.setFocus()

if __name__ == "__main__":
   app = QtGui.QApplication(sys.argv)
   myapp = MyForm()
   myapp.show()
   sys.exit(app.exec_())
```

The clicked() event of the push button is connected to the addlist() function. Hence, after entering the text to be added to the List widget in the LineEdit widget, when the user selects the Add button, the addlist() function is invoked. The add-list() function retrieves the text entered in LineEdit and adds it to the List widget. The text in the LineEdit is then removed, and the focus is set on it, enabling the user to enter different text.

In Figure 8.11, you can see the text entered by the user in the LineEdit widget is added to the List widget when the user selects the Add button.

We have followed the procedure of adding items to the List widget. Now let's see how to perform other operations such as deleting and editing items in the List widget.

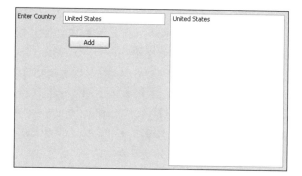

Figure 8.11
The text entered in LineEdit added to the List widget.

Performing Operations on a List Widget

We have seen how new list items can be added to a List widget. Now let's move one step ahead and see how the list item can be edited or deleted.

Using List Items

An item that is inserted or added to a List widget is usually an instance of the QListWidgetItem class. The List widget item represents a single item. Usually, a list item is created without a parent widget and then inserted into a list using the insertItem() or addItem() method. List items may be in text or icon form. List items can be checked or unchecked. Methods provided by QListWidgetItem are given in Table 8.10.

The constructor of QListWidgetItem() constructs an empty List widget item of the specified type with the given parent. If a parent is not specified, the item can be inserted into a List widget by using the insertItem() or addItem() method.

Table 8.10   Methods Provided by the QListWidgetItem Class

Method	Use
setText()	Used to specify the text for the list item.
setIcon()	Used to specify the icon for the list item.
checkState()	Used to see whether the list item is in checked or unchecked state.
setHidden()	Pass Boolean value true to this method to hide the list item.
isHidden()	Returns true if the list item is hidden.

Displaying an Input Dialog Box

To get feedback from the user, you display an input dialog box that is an instance of the QInputDialog class. The data entered by the user can be a string, a number, or an item from a list. If the dialog is accepted, it returns the text entered by the user in the dialog's LineEdit widget. If the dialog is rejected, a null string is returned. You can set the mode of the dialog box to enable the user to enter text, an integer, or a floating-point value using the InputMode property. InputMode is used to set different modes of input for the dialog box. The available options are these:

TextInput: To input text strings.

IntInput: To input integers.

DoubleInput: To input floating-point numbers.

To fetch the string entered by the user in the dialog box, you use the getText() method. Similarly, to get an integer or a double value entered by the user, you use the getInt() or getDouble() method.

In the following application, you will see how list items are added, edited, and deleted in the List widget. You will also see how to remove all list items from the List widget. Unlike the previous application, the List widget in this application will not be empty but will show some list items by default.

Open Qt Designer, create a new application based on the Dialog without Buttons template, and drag and drop a Label, a LineEdit, four Push Button widgets, and a List widget onto the form. Set the text property of the label to Enter Text. Also, set the text property of the four push buttons to Add, Edit, Delete, and Delete All. Set the objectName of the four push buttons to AddButton, EditButton, Delete-Button and DeleteAllButton. The form will appear as shown in Figure 8.12.

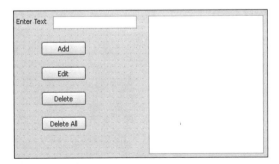

Figure 8.12
The form with a List, a Label, a LineEdit, and four Push Button widgets.

Save the application with the name `listoper.ui`. The Python script generated through the `pyuic4` command utility is shown here:

```python
listoper.py
# Form implementation generated from reading ui file 'listoper.ui'

from PyQt4 import QtCore, QtGui

try:
    _fromUtf8 = QtCore.QString.fromUtf8
except AttributeError:
    _fromUtf8 = lambda s: s

class Ui_Dialog(object):
    def setupUi(self, Dialog):
        Dialog.setObjectName(_fromUtf8("Dialog"))
        Dialog.resize(452, 263)
        self.lineEdit = QtGui.QLineEdit(Dialog)
        self.lineEdit.setGeometry(QtCore.QRect(90, 20, 141, 20))
        self.lineEdit.setObjectName(_fromUtf8("lineEdit"))
        self.DeleteButton = QtGui.QPushButton(Dialog)
        self.DeleteButton.setGeometry(QtCore.QRect(70, 140, 75, 23))
        self.DeleteButton.setObjectName(_fromUtf8("DeleteButton"))
        self.AddButton = QtGui.QPushButton(Dialog)
        self.AddButton.setGeometry(QtCore.QRect(70, 60, 75, 23))
        self.AddButton.setObjectName(_fromUtf8("AddButton"))
        self.label = QtGui.QLabel(Dialog)
        self.label.setGeometry(QtCore.QRect(30, 20, 51, 16))
        self.label.setObjectName(_fromUtf8("label"))
        self.EditButton = QtGui.QPushButton(Dialog)
        self.EditButton.setGeometry(QtCore.QRect(70, 100, 75, 23))
        self.EditButton.setObjectName(_fromUtf8("EditButton"))
        self.DeleteAllButton = QtGui.QPushButton(Dialog)
        self.DeleteAllButton.setGeometry(QtCore.QRect(70, 180, 75, 23))
        self.DeleteAllButton.setObjectName(_fromUtf8("DeleteAllButton"))
        self.listWidget = QtGui.QListWidget(Dialog)
        self.listWidget.setGeometry(QtCore.QRect(250, 20, 191, 221))
        self.listWidget.setObjectName(_fromUtf8("listWidget"))
        self.retranslateUi(Dialog)
        QtCore.QMetaObject.connectSlotsByName(Dialog)

    def retranslateUi(self, Dialog):
        Dialog.setWindowTitle(QtGui.QApplication.translate("Dialog", "Dialog", None,
QtGui.QApplication.UnicodeUTF8))
```

```
    self.DeleteButton.setText(QtGui.QApplication.translate("Dialog", "Delete",
None, QtGui.QApplication.UnicodeUTF8))
    self.AddButton.setText(QtGui.QApplication.translate("Dialog", "Add", None,
QtGui.QApplication.UnicodeUTF8))
    self.label.setText(QtGui.QApplication.translate("Dialog", "Enter Text", None,
QtGui.QApplication.UnicodeUTF8))
    self.EditButton.setText(QtGui.QApplication.translate("Dialog", "Edit", None,
QtGui.QApplication.UnicodeUTF8))
    self.DeleteAllButton.setText(QtGui.QApplication.translate("Dialog", "Delete
All", None, QtGui.QApplication.UnicodeUTF8))
```

Next is to create a Python script file that imports the Python code, enabling you to invoke the user interface design and add, delete, and edit the list items in the List widget. The code in the Python script is as shown here:

```
calllistop.pyw
import sys
from listoper import *
from PyQt4.QtGui import *

class MyForm(QtGui.QDialog):
   def __init__(self, parent=None):
     QtGui.QWidget.__init__(self, parent)
     self.ui = Ui_Dialog()
     self.ui.setupUi(self)
     self.ui.listWidget.addItem('Pizza')
     self.ui.listWidget.addItem('Hot Dog')
     self.ui.listWidget.addItem('French Fries')
     self.ui.listWidget.addItem('Chicken Burgar')
     QtCore.QObject.connect(self.ui.AddButton, QtCore.SIGNAL('clicked()'),
self.addlist)
     QtCore.QObject.connect(self.ui.EditButton, QtCore.SIGNAL('clicked()'),
self.editlist)
     QtCore.QObject.connect(self.ui.DeleteButton, QtCore.SIGNAL('clicked()'),
self.delitem)
     QtCore.QObject.connect(self.ui.DeleteAllButton, QtCore.SIGNAL('clicked()'),
self.delallitems)
     def addlist(self):
     self.ui.listWidget.addItem(self.ui.lineEdit.text())
     self.ui.lineEdit.setText('')
     self.ui.lineEdit.setFocus()
        def editlist(self):
     row=self.ui.listWidget.currentRow()
     newtext, ok=QInputDialog.getText(self, "Enter new text", "Enter new text")
```

```
        if ok and (len(newtext) !=0):
          self.ui.listWidget.takeItem(self.ui.listWidget.currentRow())
          self.ui.listWidget.insertItem(row,QListWidgetItem(newtext))
          def delitem(self):
        self.ui.listWidget.takeItem(self.ui.listWidget.currentRow())
          def delallitems(self):
        self.ui.listWidget.clear()

if __name__ == "__main__":
  app = QtGui.QApplication(sys.argv)
  myapp = MyForm()
  myapp.show()
  sys.exit(app.exec_())
```

To display the initial content of the List widget, four list items with the text Pizza, Hot Dog, French Fries, and Chicken Burger are added to the List widget through the addItem() function. Then the clicked() signal of AddButton, EditButton, DeleteButton, and DeleteAllButton is connected to the functions addlist(), editlist(), delitem(), and delallitems(), respectively. These functions are invoked by the four pushbuttons and are used to add, edit, and delete list items from the List widget.

- In the addlist() function, the text typed by the user in the LineEdit widget is retrieved and added to the List widget. The text in the LineEdit widget is deleted to create space for the new text, and focus is set.

- In the editlist() function, the row number of the selected list item is retrieved using currentRow() and stored in the variable row. An Input dialog box is displayed on the screen asking the user to enter new text. In the dialog box, the user enters new text for the selected list item and then selects OK. The text entered in the Input dialog box is fetched and assigned to the variable newtext. After that, you remove the item from the List widget using takeItem(), whose row number is stored in the variable row, so you delete the list item the user wanted to edit from the List widget, and the new text in newtext is inserted in the List widget.

- In the delitem() function, the row number of the selected list item in the List widget is retrieved using currentRow(), and the list item at that row location is deleted from the List widget using takeItem().

- In the delallitems() function, all list items from the List widget are deleted using the clear() method.

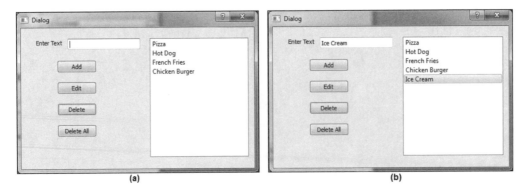

Figure 8.13
(a) The List widget with initial items. (b) Adding Ice Cream to the List widget.

On execution of the application, you get a List widget initially displaying four list items, Pizza, Hot Dog, French Fries, and Chicken Burger, as shown in Figure 8.13(a). To add a new item to the List widget, you enter text in LineEdit and select the Add button. Figure 8.13(b) shows the addition of Ice Cream to the List widget.

To edit a List item, you need to select it from the List widget and select the Edit button. For instance, if you select Ice Cream from the List widget and click the Edit button, an Input dialog box pops up asking you to enter new text to replace the Ice Cream item, as shown in Figure 8.14(a). Enter **Cold Drink** and select OK on the Enter New Text dialog. Ice Cream will be replaced with Cold Drink, as shown in Figure 8.14(b).

We can also delete a list item from the List widget by selecting it and clicking the Delete button. Selecting Delete All will delete all list items from the List widget.

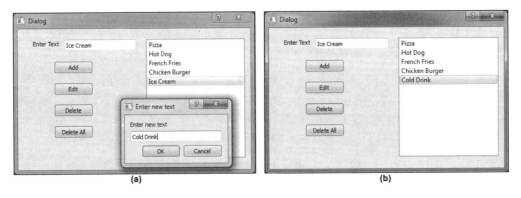

Figure 8.14
(a) Changing "Ice Cream" to "Cold Drink." (b) The List widget displaying the modified content.

SUMMARY

In this chapter you learned to create a GUI application using Radio Buttons, which enable the user to select one option out of several. You learned how to select more than one option by using checkboxes and specify integers as well as float values using spin boxes. Also, you learned to use ScrollBars and Sliders to display large documents and represent integer values, respectively. Finally, you learned to display options with a List widget, add items to a List widget, and delete and edit existing items in a List widget. In the next chapter you will learn to display system clock time, display calendar of the desired month and year and display dates in different formats. Also, you will learn to display options with a Combo Box, display information in tabular format, display web pages, and display graphic images.

CHAPTER 9

ADVANCED WIDGETS

In this chapter you will learn several things that are usually required in a fully featured GUI application. These include accessing and displaying system clock time, displaying Calendar, displaying dates in different formats, displaying options through a Combo Box, displaying information in tabular format, displaying web pages, and displaying graphics images. You will learn to implement these features one by one. This chapter covers the following:

- Displaying system clock time in LCD format
- Working with Calendar and displaying dates in different formats
- Using Combo Box
- Displaying information in a table
- Displaying web pages
- Displaying graphics

Let's begin the chapter with the procedure to display system clock time in LCD format.

DISPLAYING SYSTEM CLOCK TIME IN LCD FORMAT

To display system clock time in LCD format, you need to know how to do the following:

- Display LCD digits (QLCDNumber class)
- Use Timers (QTimer class)
- Fetch and measure system clock time (QTime class)

Table 9.1 Methods Provided by QLCDNumber

Method	Use
setMode()	Used to change the base of the numbers. Available options: Hex for displaying hexadecimal digits. Dec for displaying decimal digits. Oct for displaying octal digits. Bin for displaying binary digits.
display()	To display the specified content as LCD digits.
value()	Returns the numerical value displayed by the LCD Number widget.

Displaying LCD Digits

To display LCD-like digits, you use the LCD Number widget, an instance of the QLCDNumber class. The widget can display decimal, hexadecimal, octal, and binary digits of any size. The methods provided by QLCDNumber are shown in Table 9.1.

You want the system clock time displayed to be updated automatically. For this, you need to implement timers.

Using Timers

To perform a repetitive task, you use a timer. A timer is an instance of the QTimer class. To use timers in an application, you just need to create an instance of QTimer and connect its timeout() signal to the slot that performs the desired task. A timeout() signal can be controlled by these methods:

start(n): Initiates the timer to generate a timeout() signal at n millisecond intervals.

setSingleShot(true): Sets the timer to generate a timeout() signal only once.

singleShot(n): Sets the timer to generate a timeout() signal only once after n milliseconds.

We will be using timers to invoke the function that displays the system clock in our application so that the function will update the system clock every second. Next, you need to know about the class through which you can fetch and measure system clock time.

Table 9.2   Methods Supported by QTime

Method	Description
currentTime()	Fetches the system's clock time and returns it as a QTime object.
hour()	Returns the number of hours.
minute()	Returns the number of minutes.
seconds()	Returns the number of seconds.
msec()	Returns the number of milliseconds.
addSecs()	Returns the time after adding a specified number of seconds.
addMSecs()	Returns the time after adding a specified number of milliseconds.
secsTo()	Returns the number of seconds between two times.
msecsTo()	Returns the number of milliseconds between two times.

Fetching and Measuring System Clock Time

To fetch the system clock time and measure a span of elapsed time, you use the QTime class. The time returned by this class is in 24-hour format. You have the option to use the system clock's time or set the number of hours, minutes, seconds, and milliseconds explicitly. The methods supported by QTime are given in Table 9.2.

Note

The information returned by these methods can be converted into text format with the toString() method.

Now you are ready to create an application that displays system clock time in LCD-like digits. From Qt Designer, create a new application based on the Dialog without Buttons template and drag and drop an LCD Number widget onto the form as shown in Figure 9.1.

Save the application with the name disptime.ui. Use the pyuic4 command utility to convert the .ui (XML) file into Python code as shown here:

disptime.py

Figure 9.1
Form with an LCD Number widget.

```
# Form implementation generated from reading ui file 'disptime.ui'
from PyQt4 import QtCore, QtGui

try:
 _fromUtf8 = QtCore.QString.fromUtf8
except AttributeError:
 _fromUtf8 = lambda s: s

class Ui_Dialog(object):
 def setupUi(self, Dialog):
  Dialog.setObjectName(_fromUtf8("Dialog"))
  Dialog.resize(192, 128)
  self.lcdNumber = QtGui.QLCDNumber(Dialog)
  self.lcdNumber.setGeometry(QtCore.QRect(30, 20, 141, 81))
  self.lcdNumber.setObjectName(_fromUtf8("lcdNumber"))
  self.retranslateUi(Dialog)
  QtCore.QMetaObject.connectSlotsByName(Dialog)

 def retranslateUi(self, Dialog):
     Dialog.setWindowTitle(QtGui.QApplication.translate("Dialog", "Dialog", None,
QtGui.QApplication.UnicodeUTF8))
```

The next step is to create a Python script that imports the code to invoke the user interface design and display the current system clock time through an LCD Number widget. The script must also include a timer to keep updating the LCD display at fixed intervals. The Python script appears as shown here:

```
showtime.pyw
import sys
from disptime import *

class MyForm(QtGui.QDialog):
 def __init__(self, parent=None):
  QtGui.QWidget.__init__(self, parent)
  self.ui = Ui_Dialog()
  self.ui.setupUi(self)
  timer = QtCore.QTimer(self)
  timer.timeout.connect(self.showlcd)
  timer.start(1000)
  self.showlcd()

 def showlcd(self):
  time = QtCore.QTime.currentTime()
  text = time.toString('hh:mm')
  self.ui.lcdNumber.display(text)
```

Figure 9.2
LCD Number widget displaying the system clock time.

```
if __name__ == "__main__":
 app = QtGui.QApplication(sys.argv)
 myapp = MyForm()
 myapp.show()
 sys.exit(app.exec_())
```

In this code, you see that an instance of QTimer is created with the name timer, and its timeout() signal is connected to showlcd(). Whenever timeout() is generated, the showlcd() function will be invoked. Also, via start(), you set the timer to generate a timeout() signal after every 1,000 milliseconds. In the showlcd() method, you fetch the current system clock time, convert it into string data type, make it appear in HH:MM format, and display it with an LCD Number widget as shown in Figure 9.2.

Now let's see how dates are handled. .

WORKING WITH CALENDAR AND DISPLAYING DATES IN DIFFERENT FORMATS

In this section you will learn to display a calendar on the screen and also understand the procedure to display the date selected by the user in the calendar through a Date Edit widget. You will learn three things in this section:

- **Using Calendar:** Displays a monthly calendar.
- **Using the QDate class:** Provides methods to fetch the system date, extract the day, month, and year from a given date, find days between the two dates, and so on.
- **Using the Date Edit widget:** Used to display and edit dates.

Displaying Calendar

To display a monthly calendar, you use the Calendar widget, which is an instance of the QCalendarWidget class. By default, the Calendar widget displays the current month and year, which you can change. By default, the days are displayed in abbreviated form (Sun, Mon, Tue …), and Saturdays and Sundays are marked in red. The grid in the calendar is not visible. The week numbers are displayed, and the first column day is Sunday. Properties of the Calendar widget that you can use to configure its display are given in Table 9.3.

Table 9.3 Properties of the Calendar Widget

Property	Description
minimumDate	Used to specify the minimum date range.
maximumDate	Used to specify the maximum date range.
selectionMode	Set this property to NoSelection to prohibit the user from selecting a date.
verticalHeaderFormat	Set this property to NoVerticalHeader to remove the week numbers.
gridVisible	Set this property to True to turn on the calendar grid.
HorizontalHeaderFormat	Used for specifying the form in which days are displayed. The available options are these: SingleLetterDayNames: The header displays a single letter for days, such as M for Monday, T for Tuesday and so on. ShortDayNames: The header displays a short abbreviation for days such as Mon for Monday, Tue for Tuesday, and so on. LongDayNames: The header displays complete days (Monday, Tuesday and so on). NoHorizontalHeader: The header is hidden.

Table 9.4 Methods Provided by QCalendarWidget

Method	Description
selectedDate()	Returns the currently selected date.
monthShown()	Returns the currently displayed month.
yearShown()	Returns the currently displayed year.
setFirstDayOfWeek()	Used to set the day in the first column.
selectionChanged()	Emitted when the user selects a date other than the currently selected date. The date can be selected using the mouse or keyboard.

Methods provided by QCalendarWidget are given in Table 9.4.

The date that is selected by the user in the Calendar widget is returned as a QDate object. Let's look at the QDate class, which not only enables you to fetch the system date but also extracts the year, month, and day. The class also provides methods that make manipulating dates quite easy.

Table 9.5   Methods Provided by the QDate Class

Method	Use
currentDate()	Returns the system date as a QDate object.
setDate()	Sets a date by specifying the year, month, and day.
year()	Returns the year from the specified date object.
month()	Returns the month from the specified date object.
day()	Returns the day from the specified date object.
dayOfWeek()	Returns the day of the week from the specified date object.
addDays()	Adds the specified number of days to the specified date and returns new date.
addMonths()	Adds the specified number of months to the specified date and returns new date.
addYears()	Adds the specified number of years to the specified date and returns new date.
daysTo()	Returns the number of days between two dates.
daysInMonth()	Returns the number of days in the specified month.
daysInYear()	Returns the number of days in the specified year.
isLeapYear()	Returns true if the specified date is in a leap year.
toPyDate()	Returns the date as a string. The format parameter determines the format of the result string.

QDate Class

For working with dates, you use an instance of the QDate class. A QDate object contains a calendar date with the year, month, and day in the Gregorian calendar. It reads the current date from the system clock. Methods provided by the QDate class are in Table 9.5.

The following expressions are used for specifying the format:

d: Displays the day as a number without a leading zero (1 to 31).

dd: Displays the day as a number with a leading zero (01 to 31).

ddd: Displays the day in abbreviated form (Mon, Tue, and so on).

dddd: Displays the day in long form (Monday, Tuesday, and so on).

M: Displays the month as a number without a leading zero (1 to 12).

MM: Displays the month as a number with a leading zero (01 to 12).

MMM: Displays the month in abbreviated form (Jan, Feb, and so on).

MMMM: Displays the month in long form (January, February, and so on).

yy: Displays the year as a two-digit number (00 to 99).

yyyy: Displays the year as a four-digit number.

Examples:

dd.MM.yyyy will display the date as 15.10.2011.

ddd MMMM d yy will display date as Sun October 15 11.

To display the date that is selected by the user in a Calendar widget, you use a Date Edit widget.

Using the Date Edit Widget

For displaying and editing dates, you use the Date Edit widget, which is an instance of the QDateEdit class.

Properties used to configure the Date Edit widget:

minimumDate: This property is used to define the minimum date that can be set to the widget.

maximumDate: This property is used to define the maximum date that can be set to the widget.

Methods provided by QDateEdit are given in Table 9.6.

Note

If an invalid date format is specified, the format will not be set.

In the following example, you will learn to display the date that is selected by the user in the Calendar widget with the Date Edit widget. Open Qt Designer and create a new Dialog without Buttons application and drag and drop Calendar and Date Edit widgets onto the form. The form will appear as shown in Figure 9.3.

Save the application with the name dispcalendar.ui. The pyuic4 command utility will convert the .ui (XML) file into Python code:

```
dispcalendar.py
# Form implementation generated from reading ui file 'dispcalendar.ui'
from PyQt4 import QtCore, QtGui
```

Table 9.6 Methods Provided by the QDateEdit Class

Method	Description
setDate()	Used to set the date to be displayed in the widget.
setDisplayFormat()	Used to specify the string format that you want to apply to the date displayed in the Date Edit widget. Formats with their outputs are these:

Format	Output
dd.MM.yyyy	15.10.2011
MMM d yy	Oct 15 11
MMM d yyyy	Oct 15 2011
MMMM d yy	October 15 11

Figure 9.3
Form displaying Calendar and Date Edit widgets.

```
try:
 _fromUtf8 = QtCore.QString.fromUtf8
except AttributeError:
 _fromUtf8 = lambda s: s

class Ui_Dialog(object):
 def setupUi(self, Dialog):
  Dialog.setObjectName(_fromUtf8("Dialog"))
  Dialog.resize(285, 223)
  self.dateEdit = QtGui.QDateEdit(Dialog)
  self.dateEdit.setGeometry(QtCore.QRect(90, 180, 110, 22))
  self.dateEdit.setObjectName(_fromUtf8("dateEdit"))
  self.calendarWidget = QtGui.QCalendarWidget(Dialog)
```

```
        self.calendarWidget.setGeometry(QtCore.QRect(30, 20, 232, 141))
        self.calendarWidget.setObjectName(_fromUtf8("calendarWidget"))

        self.retranslateUi(Dialog)
        QtCore.QMetaObject.connectSlotsByName(Dialog)
    def retranslateUi(self, Dialog):
        Dialog.setWindowTitle(QtGui.QApplication.translate("Dialog", "Dialog", None,
QtGui.QApplication.UnicodeUTF8))
```

Let's create a Python script that imports the code to invoke the user interface design and displays the selected date from the Calendar widget in the Date Edit widget. The Python script appears as shown here:

```
callcalendar.pyw
import sys
from dispcalendar import *

class MyForm(QtGui.QDialog):
  def __init__(self, parent=None):
   QtGui.QWidget.__init__(self, parent)
   self.ui = Ui_Dialog()
   self.ui.setupUi(self)
   QtCore.QObject.connect(self.ui.calendarWidget,    QtCore.SIGNAL('selectionChanged
()'), self.dispdate)

  def dispdate(self):
   self.ui.dateEdit.setDate(self.ui.calendarWidget.selectedDate())

if __name__ == "__main__":
  app = QtGui.QApplication(sys.argv)
  myapp = MyForm()
  myapp.show()
  sys.exit(app.exec_())
```

In the code, you see that the selectionChanged() signal of the Calendar widget is connected to dispdate(). Hence, as the user selects a date, the dispdate() function will be invoked. In the dispdate() function, the date selected by the user is retrieved through selectedDate() method and displayed in the Date Edit widget through setDate(). The date is displayed in default date format *mm/dd/yyyy* (see Figure 9.4(a)). You can display the date in a different format with the setDisplay-Format() method. Let's modify the dispdate() function to display the date in *MMM d yyyy* format:

```
  def dispdate(self):
   self.ui.dateEdit.setDisplayFormat('MMM d yyyy')
   self.ui.dateEdit.setDate(self.ui.calendarWidget.selectedDate())
```

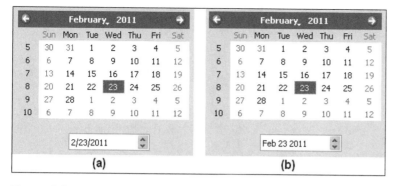

Figure 9.4
(a) Selected date displayed in default format. (b) Selected date displayed in specified format.

Now the date selected from the Calendar widget will appear in the desired format in the Date Edit widget as shown in Figure 9.4(b).

The next widget will enable us to display different items or options to the user using minimum screen space.

USING COMBO BOX

To display a pop-up list (also known as a Combo Box), you use the QComboBox class. With a Combo Box, the items are listed in a minimum of screen space. Besides text, pixmaps can be displayed in a Combo Box. Methods provided by QComboBox are shown in Table 9.7.

Table 9.7   Methods Provided by QComboBox

Method	Use
setItemText()	Used to change the item in the Combo Box.
removeItem()	Used to remove an item.
clear()	Used to remove all items.
currentText()	Returns the text of the current item.
setCurrentIndex()	Used to set the current item.
count()	Returns the number of items in the Combo Box.
setMaxCount()	Used to set the maximum number of items.
setEditable()	Used to allow editing in the Combo Box.
addItem()	Used to add an item to the Combo Box with specified text. The item is appended to the list.

(Continued)

Table 9.7   Methods Provided by QComboBox (*Continued*)

Method	Use
addItems()	Used to add each of the strings in the text to the Combo Box. Each item is appended to the list.
itemText()	Returns the text at the specified index in the Combo Box.
currentIndex()	Returns the index of the current item in the Combo Box. An empty Combo Box or a Combo Box with no current item selected returns −1 as the index.

Table 9.8   Signals Generated by QComboBox

Signal	Description
currentIndexChanged()	The signal is emitted if the index of the Combo Box is changed (through user interaction or via program), and a new item is selected.
activated()	The signal is emitted when the index is changed by user interaction.
highlighted()	The signal is emitted when the user highlights an item in the Combo Box.
editTextChanged()	The signal is emitted when the text of an editable Combo Box is changed.

Signals generated by the Combo Box are shown in Table 9.8.

The next application is a computing application that asks the user to specify the date of a journey, the number of persons traveling, and the class type the user wants to use. Then it computes the fare accordingly. The user can specify the date of his journey with a Calendar widget, the number of persons with a Spin Box, and the class type with a Combo Box. The Combo Box will display four traveling class options: First Class, Second Class, Business Class, and Economic Class. The fare of these classes is assumed to be $40, $30, $20, and $10, respectively. In the application, six Labels, a Calendar, a Spin Box, a Combo Box, and a Push Button are used. The text property of the first four Labels is set to Reservation form, Date of Journey, Number of persons, and Class. Set the objectNames of the fifth and sixth Labels to Enteredinfo and Fareinfo, respectively. The Enteredinfo Label will be used to display the options selected in the different widgets by the user, and the Fareinfo Label will be used to display the computed fare. Also, delete the text

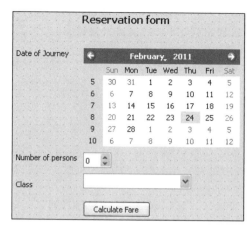

Figure 9.5
Form displaying Labels, Calendar, Spin Box, Combo Box, and Push Button.

property of the two Labels, Enteredinfo and Fareinfo, to make them invisible in the form; their respective text will be assigned through programming. The text property of the Push Button is set to Calculate Fare, the point size of the Label representing the Reservation Form text is increased, and its Bold property is set to make it appear as the header of the application (see Figure 9.5).

Save the application with the name reservform.ui. The pyuic4 command utility converts the .ui (XML) file into Python code as shown here:

```
reservform.py
# Form implementation generated from reading ui file 'reservform.ui'
from PyQt4 import QtCore, QtGui

try:
 _fromUtf8 = QtCore.QString.fromUtf8
except AttributeError:
 _fromUtf8 = lambda s: s
 class Ui_Dialog(object):
  def setupUi(self, Dialog):
   Dialog.setObjectName(_fromUtf8("Dialog"))
   Dialog.resize(462, 401)
   self.label_4 = QtGui.QLabel(Dialog)
   self.label_4.setGeometry(QtCore.QRect(70, 260, 46, 13))
   self.label_4.setObjectName(_fromUtf8("label_4"))
   self.spinBox = QtGui.QSpinBox(Dialog)
   self.spinBox.setGeometry(QtCore.QRect(170, 220, 42, 22))
   self.spinBox.setObjectName(_fromUtf8("spinBox"))
   self.label_2 = QtGui.QLabel(Dialog)
   self.label_2.setGeometry(QtCore.QRect(70, 70, 91, 16))
```

```python
self.label_2.setObjectName(_fromUtf8("label_2"))
self.calendarWidget = QtGui.QCalendarWidget(Dialog)
self.calendarWidget.setGeometry(QtCore.QRect(170, 70, 232, 141))
self.calendarWidget.setObjectName(_fromUtf8("calendarWidget"))
self.comboBox = QtGui.QComboBox(Dialog)
self.comboBox.setGeometry(QtCore.QRect(170, 250, 161, 22))
self.comboBox.setObjectName(_fromUtf8("comboBox"))
self.Enteredinfo = QtGui.QLabel(Dialog)
self.Enteredinfo.setGeometry(QtCore.QRect(10, 330, 421, 16))
self.Enteredinfo.setText(_fromUtf8(""))
self.Enteredinfo.setObjectName(_fromUtf8("Enteredinfo"))
self.label = QtGui.QLabel(Dialog)
self.label.setGeometry(QtCore.QRect(70, 220, 91, 16))
self.label.setObjectName(_fromUtf8("label"))
self.label_3 = QtGui.QLabel(Dialog)
self.label_3.setGeometry(QtCore.QRect(160, 20, 171, 16))
font = QtGui.QFont()
font.setPointSize(11)
font.setWeight(75)
font.setBold(True)
self.label_3.setFont(font)
self.label_3.setObjectName(_fromUtf8("label_3"))
self.Fareinfo = QtGui.QLabel(Dialog)
self.Fareinfo.setGeometry(QtCore.QRect(10, 360, 441, 16))
self.Fareinfo.setText(_fromUtf8(""))
self.Fareinfo.setObjectName(_fromUtf8("Fareinfo"))
self.pushButton = QtGui.QPushButton(Dialog)
self.pushButton.setGeometry(QtCore.QRect(170, 290, 101, 23))
self.pushButton.setObjectName(_fromUtf8("pushButton"))
self.retranslateUi(Dialog)
QtCore.QMetaObject.connectSlotsByName(Dialog)

def retranslateUi(self, Dialog):
    Dialog.setWindowTitle(QtGui.QApplication.translate("Dialog", "Dialog", None,
QtGui.QApplication.UnicodeUTF8))
    self.label_4.setText(QtGui.QApplication.translate("Dialog", "Class", None,
QtGui.QApplication.UnicodeUTF8))
    self.label_2.setText(QtGui.QApplication.translate("Dialog", "Date of Journey",
None, QtGui.QApplication.UnicodeUTF8))
    self.label.setText(QtGui.QApplication.translate("Dialog", "Number of persons",
None, QtGui.QApplication.UnicodeUTF8))
    self.label_3.setText(QtGui.QApplication.translate("Dialog", "Reservation form",
None, QtGui.QApplication.UnicodeUTF8))
    self.pushButton.setText(QtGui.QApplication.translate("Dialog", "Calculate Fare",
None, QtGui.QApplication.UnicodeUTF8))
```

What you need now is to create a Python script that imports the code to invoke the user interface design and that computes and displays the fare on the basis of the number of persons and class type selected. The script will also display the date, number of persons, and class type options selected by the user. The Python script file will appear as shown here:

```
computefare.pyw
import sys
from reservform import *

class MyForm(QtGui.QDialog):
  def __init__(self, parent=None):
   QtGui.QWidget.__init__(self, parent)
   self.ui = Ui_Dialog()
   self.ui.setupUi(self)
   self.classtypes=['First Class', 'Second Class', 'Business Class', 'Economic Class']
   self.addcontent()
   QtCore.QObject.connect(self.ui.pushButton,   QtCore.SIGNAL('clicked()'),   self.
computefare)
  def addcontent(self):
   for i in self.classtypes:
    self.ui.comboBox.addItem(i)

    def computefare(self):
   dateselected=self.ui.calendarWidget.selectedDate()
   dateinstring=str(dateselected.toPyDate())
   noOfPersons=self.ui.spinBox.value()
   chosenclass=self.ui.comboBox.itemText(self.ui.comboBox.currentIndex())
   self.ui.Enteredinfo.setText('Date of journey: '+dateinstring+ ', Number of persons:
'+ str(noOfPersons) + ' and Class selected: '+ chosenclass)
   fare=0
   if chosenclass=="First Class":
    fare=40
   if chosenclass=="Second Class":
    fare=30
   if chosenclass=="Business Class":
    fare=20
   if chosenclass=="Economic Class":
    fare=10
   total=fare*noOfPersons
   self.ui.Fareinfo.setText('Fare for '+ chosenclass +' is '+ str(fare)+ '$. Total fare
is '+ str(total)+ '$')

if __name__ == "__main__":
  app = QtGui.QApplication(sys.argv)
```

```
myapp = MyForm()
myapp.show()
sys.exit(app.exec_())
```

In this code, you see that a `classtypes` list is defined with four elements: `First Class`, `Second Class`, `Business Class`, and `Economic Class`. To make the elements of the `classtypes` list appear as options in the Combo Box, the `addcontent()` function is invoked and adds the elements of `classtypes` to the Combo Box with the `addItem()` function. Also, the `clicked()` signal of the Push Button, `Calculate Fare` is connected to the `computefare()` method, which is invoked when the user selects the Calculate Fare button after selecting the date of his the journey, number of persons traveling, and the class type. In the `computefare()` method, you fetch the date from the Calendar widget, the number of persons from the Spin Box, and the class type from the Combo Box and display them through an `Enteredinfo` Label widget to indicate the options that are selected by the user. Then the fare of an individual is determined on the basis of the class selected and is multiplied by the number of persons to compute the total fare. The total fare is then displayed via `Fareinfo` as shown in Figure 9.6.

How about displaying information in tabular form? The information appears very organized and readable when displayed in a table. Let's learn more.

DISPLAYING A TABLE

To display contents in a row and column format, you use a Table widget, which is an instance of the `QTableWidget` class. The items displayed in a Table widget are instances of the `QTableWidgetItem` class.

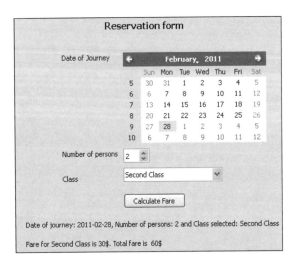

Figure 9.6
The date, number of persons, and class type selected are displayed with a Label widget, along with the total.

Table 9.9   Methods Provided by QTableWidget

Method	Use
setRowCount()	Used to specify the number of rows in the Table widget.
setColumnCount()	Used to specify the number of columns in the Table widget.
rowCount()	Returns the number of rows in the table.
columnCount()	Returns the number of columns in the table.
clear()	Clears the table.
setItem()	Sets the item for a given row and column of the table.

Note

To display a table that uses your own data model, you use the QTableView class.

Methods provided by QTableWidget are given in Table 9.9.

Displaying Items in the Table

The items displayed in the Table widget are instances of the QTableWidgetItem class. A Table Item can be any content: text, an image, a checkbox, and so on. Methods provided by QTableWidgetItem are shown in Table 9.10.

Note

You can use the QTableWidgetItem() constructor to create a Table Item of the specified type that does not belong to any table.

Let's create an application to demonstrate how information is displayed with a Table widget. Open Qt Designer and create a new application based on the Dialog without

Table 9.10   Methods Provided by QTableWidgetItem

Method	Use
setFont()	Used to set the font for the text label of the Table Item.
setCheckState()	Used to check or uncheck a Table Item.
checkState()	Used to determine if the Table Item is checked or not.

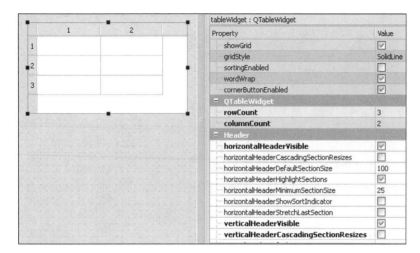

Figure 9.7
The Table widget with `showGrid`, `rowCount`, `columnCount`, `horizontalHeaderVisible`, and `verticalHeaderVisible` properties set.

Buttons template. Drag and drop a Table widget onto the form. To assign it the default size of three rows and two columns, from the Property Editor window, set the value of `rowCount` and `columnCount` to 3 and 2, respectively. To display the row and column headers, the `horizontalHeaderVisible` and `verticalHeaderVisible` properties are already checked by default. The Table widget will appear as shown in Figure 9.7.

Save the application with the name `tables.ui`. The Python code generated through the `pyuic4` command utility is shown here:

```
tables.py
# Form implementation generated from reading ui file 'tables.ui'

from PyQt4 import QtCore, QtGui
 try:
 _fromUtf8 = QtCore.QString.fromUtf8
except AttributeError:
 _fromUtf8 = lambda s: s

class Ui_Dialog(object):
 def setupUi(self, Dialog):
   Dialog.setObjectName(_fromUtf8("Dialog"))
   Dialog.resize(296, 236)
   self.tableWidget = QtGui.QTableWidget(Dialog)
   self.tableWidget.setGeometry(QtCore.QRect(20, 20, 256, 192))
   self.tableWidget.setRowCount(3)
```

```
    self.tableWidget.setColumnCount(2)
    self.tableWidget.setObjectName(_fromUtf8("tableWidget"))
    self.tableWidget.setColumnCount(2)
    self.tableWidget.setRowCount(3)
    self.tableWidget.verticalHeader().setVisible(True)
    self.tableWidget.verticalHeader().setCascadingSectionResizes(False)
    self.tableWidget.verticalHeader().setHighlightSections(True)
    self.retranslateUi(Dialog)
    QtCore.QMetaObject.connectSlotsByName(Dialog)

def retranslateUi(self, Dialog):
    Dialog.setWindowTitle(QtGui.QApplication.translate("Dialog", "Dialog", None,
QtGui.QApplication.UnicodeUTF8))
```

Let's move on to the next step and create a Python script file that imports the Python code and enables us to invoke the user interface design and displays information in the Table widget. The code in the Python script is as shown here:

```
calltables.pyw
import sys
from tables import *
from PyQt4.QtGui import *

class MyForm(QtGui.QDialog):
  def __init__(self, data):
    QtGui.QWidget.__init__(self)
    self.ui = Ui_Dialog()
    self.ui.setupUi(self)
    self.data=data
    self.addcontent()

  def addcontent(self):
    row=0
    for tup in self.data:
      col=0
      for item in tup:
        anitem=QTableWidgetItem(item)
        self.ui.tableWidget.setItem(row,col, anitem)
        col+=1
      row+=1

    data=[]
data.append(('John', 'johny@gmail.com'))
data.append(('Caroline', 'caroline@hotmail.com'))
data.append(('Bintu', 'bintu@yahoo.com'))
```

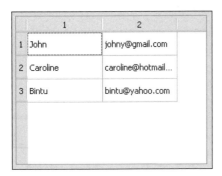

Figure 9.8
The Table widget, displaying information from a list.

```
if __name__ == "__main__":
 app = QtGui.QApplication(sys.argv)
 myapp = MyForm(data)
 myapp.show()
 sys.exit(app.exec_())
```

If you want to display information in three rows and two columns of the Table widget, create a list named `data` that stores three tuples, each of which consists of two elements, `name` and `email address`. In `addcontent()`, you fetch one tuple at a time from the `data` list and assign it temporarily to the `tup` variable. The `tup` variable contains two elements, `name` and `email address`. With the help of another `for` loop, you fetch each element from the `tup` variable; that is, you fetch `name` and `email address` and assign them to the variable `item`. The content of `item` is converted into an instance of `QTableWidgetItem` and assigned to an `item`, which is assigned and displayed in the Table widget at a particular row and column position using the `setItem()` method. With the help of nested `for` loops, you display the information (Figure 9.8) of the `data` list in the Table widget.

DISPLAYING WEB PAGES

To view and edit web pages, you use a QWebView widget, that represents an instance of `QWebView class`. It is the main widget component of the `QtWebKit` web-browsing module. Methods of `QWebView` that are used for displaying web pages are shown in Table 9.11.

Different signals are generated by `QWebView` while loading web pages. Some of them are shown in Table 9.12.

Create a new application of the Dialog without Buttons template and drag and drop Label, Line Edit, Push Button, and QWebiew widgets onto the form. Set the `text` property of the Label and Push Button widgets to `Address` and `Go`, respectively, as shown in Figure 9.9. Also, change the `objectName` property of the Line Edit to

Table 9.11   QWebView Methods for Displaying Web Pages

Method	Use
`load()`	Loads the specified URL and displays it through QWebView widget. The view remains unchanged until enough data is downloaded to display.
`setUrl()`	Same as `load()` method.
`setHtml()`	To view HTML content.

Table 9.12   Signals Generated by QWebView While Loading Web Pages

Signal	Description
`loadStarted()`	Emitted when the view begins loading.
`loadProgress()`	Emitted whenever an element of Web View completes loading, such as an embedded image, video, or script.
`loadFinished()`	Emitted when the view is loaded completely.

Figure 9.9
Form showing Label, Line Edit, Push Button, and QWebView widgets.

siteURL. The URL of the web page to be viewed will be entered in the Line Edit, and the web page will appear in a QWebView widget.

Save the application with the name `webviewdemo.ui`. The `pyuic4` command utility converts the `.ui` (XML) file into Python code:

```
webviewdemo.py
# Form implementation generated from reading ui file 'webviewdemo.ui'
from PyQt4 import QtCore, QtGui

try:
 _fromUtf8 = QtCore.QString.fromUtf8
except AttributeError:
 _fromUtf8 = lambda s: s

class Ui_Dialog(object):
 def setupUi(self, Dialog):
  Dialog.setObjectName(_fromUtf8("Dialog"))
  Dialog.resize(518, 495)
  self.webView = QtWebKit.QWebView(Dialog)
  self.webView.setGeometry(QtCore.QRect(10, 80, 491, 371))
  self.webView.setUrl(QtCore.QUrl(_fromUtf8("about:blank")))
  self.webView.setObjectName(_fromUtf8("webView"))
  self.label = QtGui.QLabel(Dialog)
  self.label.setGeometry(QtCore.QRect(10, 30, 46, 13))
  self.label.setObjectName(_fromUtf8("label"))
  self.siteURL = QtGui.QLineEdit(Dialog)
  self.siteURL.setGeometry(QtCore.QRect(60, 30, 351, 20))
  self.siteURL.setObjectName(_fromUtf8("siteURL"))
  self.pushButton = QtGui.QPushButton(Dialog)
  self.pushButton.setGeometry(QtCore.QRect(430, 30, 75, 23))
  self.pushButton.setObjectName(_fromUtf8("pushButton"))
  self.retranslateUi(Dialog)
  QtCore.QMetaObject.connectSlotsByName(Dialog)

 def retranslateUi(self, Dialog):
     Dialog.setWindowTitle(QtGui.QApplication.translate("Dialog", "Dialog", None,
QtGui.QApplication.UnicodeUTF8))
     self.label.setText(QtGui.QApplication.translate("Dialog", "Address", None,
QtGui.QApplication.UnicodeUTF8))
     self.pushButton.setText(QtGui.QApplication.translate("Dialog", "Go", None,
QtGui.QApplication.UnicodeUTF8))
from PyQt4 import QtWebKit
```

Let's create a Python script that imports the code to invoke the user interface design and loads the web page of the specified URL and displays it through a QWebView widget. The Python script file will appear as shown:

```
callwebview.pyw
import sys
from PyQt4.QtCore import *
from webviewdemo import *

class MyForm(QtGui.QDialog):
  def __init__(self, parent=None):
    QtGui.QWidget.__init__(self, parent)
    self.ui = Ui_Dialog()
    self.ui.setupUi(self)
    QtCore.QObject.connect(self.ui.pushButton,    QtCore.SIGNAL('clicked()'),    self.
openURL)
    def openURL(self):
    if len(self.ui.siteURL.text())!=0:
      self.ui.webView.load(QUrl(self.ui.siteURL.text()))

if __name__ == "__main__":
  app = QtGui.QApplication(sys.argv)
  myapp = MyForm()
  myapp.show()
  sys.exit(app.exec_())
```

In this code, you can see that the clicked() signal of the Push Button is connected to openURL, and when the user selects the Go Push Button, the openURL method will be invoked. In the openURL method, you retrieve the URL of the web page supplied by the user in the Line Edit widget and load and display it via a QWebView widget. On specifying the URL of my website, http://bmharwani.com, in the Line Edit widget, the web page will appear as shown in Figure 9.10.

In the next section, you will learn to display graphics in a GUI application through the Graphics View widget.

DISPLAYING GRAPHICS

Graphics View is used for viewing and managing 2D graphical items. It displays a scene that in turn acts as a container for several graphical items. A Graphics View scene is created with QGraphicsScene, and items are created using QGraphics-Item. Graphics View provides several standard items for typical shapes, such as rectangles, ellipses, and text items.

Figure 9.10
Home page of my website, http://bmharwani.com, displayed with a QWebView widget.

The graphics scene has no visual appearance of its own; its job is to manage graphical items. To visualize the scene, Graphics View is used. Graphics View provides the view widget to visualize the contents of a scene. The view receives input events from the keyboard and mouse and translates them to scene events before sending the events to the scene. When the scene receives a mouse press event at a certain position, it passes the event on to the item at that position. To add items to a scene, you first create a QGraphicsScene object and then add an existing QGraphicsItem object by calling the addItem() function. To remove an item from the graphics scene, the removeItem() function is called.

Note

> Graphics View also provides the transform() method to transform the scene's coordinate system to be used for applying zooming and rotation features.

To understand the Graphics View widget, create an application that displays an image. Create a new application based on the Dialog without Buttons template and drag and drop a Graphics View widget onto it. The form will appear as shown in Figure 9.11.

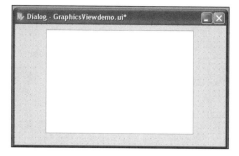

Figure 9.11
Form displaying a Graphics View widget.

Save the application with the name `GraphicsViewdemo.ui`. The `pyuic4` command utility converts the `.ui` (XML) file into Python code as shown:

```
GraphicsViewdemo.py
# Form implementation generated from reading ui file 'GraphicsViewdemo.ui'
from PyQt4 import QtCore, QtGui

try:
  _fromUtf8 = QtCore.QString.fromUtf8
except AttributeError:
  _fromUtf8 = lambda s: s

class Ui_Dialog(object):
  def setupUi(self, Dialog):
    Dialog.setObjectName(_fromUtf8("Dialog"))
    Dialog.resize(400, 300)
    self.graphicsView = QtGui.QGraphicsView(Dialog)
    self.graphicsView.setGeometry(QtCore.QRect(60, 60, 281, 192))
    self.graphicsView.setObjectName(_fromUtf8("graphicsView"))
    self.retranslateUi(Dialog)
    QtCore.QMetaObject.connectSlotsByName(Dialog)

  def retranslateUi(self, Dialog):
      Dialog.setWindowTitle(QtGui.QApplication.translate("Dialog", "Dialog", None,
QtGui.QApplication.UnicodeUTF8))
```

You need to create a Python script that imports the code to invoke the user interface design and loads an image from the disk and displays it through Graphics View. The Python script file will have the following code:

```
callGraphics1.pyw
import sys
from GraphicsViewdemo import *
from PyQt4.QtGui import *
```

```
class MyForm(QtGui.QDialog):
 def __init__(self, pixmap, parent=None):
  QtGui.QWidget.__init__(self, parent)
  self.ui = Ui_Dialog()
  self.ui.setupUi(self)
  self.scene = QGraphicsScene(self)
  item=QGraphicsPixmapItem(pixmap)
  self.scene.addItem(item)
  self.ui.graphicsView.setScene(self.scene)

if __name__ == "__main__":
  app = QtGui.QApplication(sys.argv)
  pixmap= QtGui.QPixmap()
  pixmap.load("bmpic.jpg")
  myapp = MyForm(pixmap)
  myapp.show()
  sys.exit(app.exec_())
```

Note

In the preceding code, I used an image with the file name `bmpic.jpg`. You will need to replace `bmpic.jpg` with the image file name that is available on your disk or else nothing will be displayed on the screen.

These are the methods that are used:

QGraphicsView.setScene (self, QGraphicsScene scene): Sets the current scene to `scene`. If `scene` is already being viewed, this function does nothing. When a scene is set on a view, the `QGraphicsScene.changed()` signal is generated, and the view's scrollbars are adjusted to fit the size of the scene.

addItem(QGraphicsItem * item): Adds the specified `item` to the scene. If `item` is already in a different scene, it will first be removed from its old scene and then added to the current scene.

Note

An `ItemSceneChange` notification is generated by `QGraphicsScene` when an item is added to the scene.

The procedure that you are following in this program is to use Graphics View to display an image. You add a graphics scene to the Graphics View, and you add a `QGraphicsPixmapItem`. If you want to add an image to the graphics scene, you need to provide it in the form of a pixmap item. First you need to represent the image as a pixmap, and then you make it appear as a pixmap item before adding it to the graphics scene. First you create an instance of QPixmap and specify the image that you want to display through its load() method. Then you tag the pixmap as pixmapitem by passing the pixmap to the QGraphicsPixmapItem's constructor. The pixmapitem is then added to the scene via addItem(). If pixmapitem is bigger than QGraphicsView, scrolling is enabled automatically.

You also can add pixmap to the scene directly using the addPixmap() function, as shown in the following program. The addPixmap() function creates and adds a pixmapitem to the scene. The position of the item is initialized to (0, 0).

```
callGraphics2.pyw
import sys
from GraphicsViewdemo import *
from PyQt4.QtGui import *

class MyForm(QtGui.QDialog):
  def __init__(self, pixmap, parent=None):
   QtGui.QWidget.__init__(self, parent)
   self.ui = Ui_Dialog()
   self.ui.setupUi(self)
   self.scene = QGraphicsScene(self)
   self.scene.addPixmap(pixmap)
   self.ui.graphicsView.setScene(self.scene)

if __name__ == "__main__":
   app = QtGui.QApplication(sys.argv)
   pixmap= QtGui.QPixmap()
   pixmap.load("fig1.jpg")
 myapp = MyForm(pixmap)
 myapp.show()
 sys.exit(app.exec_())
```

Note

Remember, you will need to replace fig1.jpg with the image file name that is available on your disk, or else nothing will be displayed on the screen.

Figure 9.12(a) displays an image smaller than the width and height of the Graphics View widget. Figure 9.12(b) automatically includes scrollbars when an image larger than Graphics View is displayed.

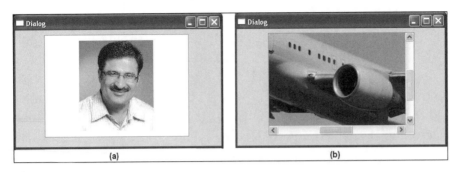

Figure 9.12
(a) A smaller image displayed with Graphics View. (b) A larger image displayed with Graphics View appears with scrollbars.

SUMMARY

In this chapter you learned to access and display system clock time in LCD digits. You also saw how to display a calendar and display a selected date in different formats. You learned to create an application that displays options with a Combo Box, displays information with a Table widget, displays web pages, and displays graphic images.

In the next chapter you will learn to create menus and toolbars. You will learn to store images and videos in a resource file. You will learn how to create dockable windows and display information with the Tab widget and enhance the appearance of a widget with the Style Sheet Editor. Finally, you will learn to convert a Tab widget into a Tool Box or Stacked widget.

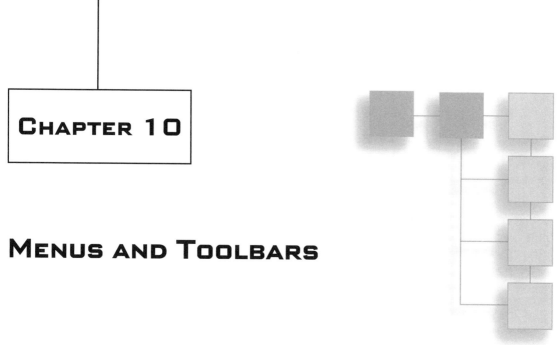

CHAPTER 10

MENUS AND TOOLBARS

Menus and toolbars are handy options for initiating any task in an application. This chapter covers the following:

- Creating a menu
- Creating a toolbar
- Creating a resource file
- Creating dockable windows with the Dock widget
- Displaying a large volume of information with the Tab widget
- Working with the Style Sheet Editor
- Converting a Tab widget into a Tool Box or Stacked widget

Let's begin the chapter with menus.

UNDERSTANDING MENUS

A menu bar consists of several menus, each of which consists of several entries, which in turn may include submenu entries. The Main Window template of Qt Designer provides a main application window that displays a menu bar and a toolbar by default. The default menu bar appears as shown in Figure 10.1. We can always remove the default menu bar by selecting Remove Menu Bar from the context menu. We can also add a menu bar later by selecting the Create Menu Bar option from the context menu. The context menu pops up when you right-click in the main window. An application can have several toolbars but only one menu bar.

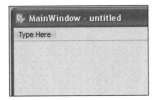

Figure 10.1
The default menu bar in a main window-based application.

The menu and its entries are represented by menu text. Menu entries can be checkable. If a shortcut key is assigned to a menu entry, it appears with the menu text.

Note

A toolbar displays icons instead of text to represent the task that it can perform.

A default menu bar contains Type Here placeholders. You can replace the Type Here placeholders with text to be displayed in the menu bar. Click the placeholder to highlight it and type to modify its text. When you add a menu, Type Here appears below the menu as its entry. Again, just click the Type Here placeholder to select it and simply type the text for the menu entry. If you select the right arrow key on any menu entry, a submenu entry appears with Type Here. When editing the text for a menu or submenu entry, if you add an ampersand character (&) before any character, that character in the menu entry will be displayed as underlined and will be treated as a shortcut key. You also can assign a shortcut key to a menu entry explicitly. You can delete any menu entry by right-clicking it and selecting the option Remove Action `action_name` from the context menu that pops up. You also can access the properties of a menu and menu entries through the Property Editor. The menu and menu entries in the menu bar can be arranged by dragging and dropping them at the desired location.

Note

Menus can also be nested.

You can add separators after a menu entry by double-clicking the Add Separator option in the context menu. To delete a separator, right-click on it and select Delete Item.

The menu entry added to a menu will automatically appear in the Action Editor. You can manipulate the menu text, its shortcut key, and so on through the Action Editor.

Action Editor

An action is an operation that the user initiates through the user interface. Tasks such as saving a file, giving a print command, and aligning text are actions. The action can be initiated by selecting a toolbar button, selecting a menu entry, or pressing a shortcut key. On occurrence of an action, a function is executed to serve the action. In Qt, an action is created as an object of the `QAction` class and can be assigned to a menu or a toolbar button for the user to invoke.

To create and manage actions, use Qt Designer's Action Editor. You can create new actions and delete existing actions through the Action Editor. The Action Editor is usually enabled and displayed below the Property Editor by default. Just click the Action Editor tab to activate it. If you can't see the Action Editor, open the View menu and check if the Action Editor option is not already checked. The Action Editor has two views: Classic Icon view and Detailed view. The Action Editor also provides a Filter search function to filter out undesired actions and display actions that you are interested in. The Action Editor will appear empty at first, as shown in Figure 10.2(a).

To create an action, use the New button in the Action Editor. You get the dialog box shown in Figure 10.2(b) to enter the information of the new action. In the Text box, enter the text that will appear in the menu entry. The object name of the menu entry automatically appears in the Object Name box, with the menu text prefixed by the text `action`. Enter text in the ToolTip box. The action can be represented by an icon. You can provide different icons or pixmaps to represent different states of the action.

An action can be in four states, which can be represented by icons:

Normal: Represents the icon's image or pixmap when the user is not interacting with the action and is in enabled mode.

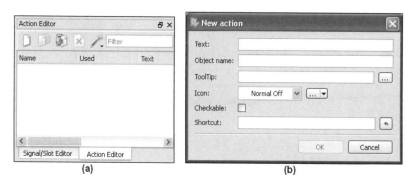

Figure 10.2
(a) Action Editor. (b) Dialog for a new action.

Disabled: Represents the icon's pixmap when the action is in disabled mode.

Active: Represents the icon's pixmap when the action is enabled and the user is interacting with it (moving the mouse over it or clicking it).

Selected: Represents the icon's pixmap when the action is selected.

Select OK to create an action. The action created can be added to the menu or toolbar. To add an action to a menu or a toolbar, select the action in the Action Editor and drag it to the desired place in the menu or toolbar. A thick red line will appear in the menu bar when the action is dropped to indicate where the new menu entry will appear.

Creating a Menu

The tools that you see in the toolbar are basically actions. The entries in the menu bar can be created two ways:

- By creating an action in the Action Editor and dragging and dropping it into a menu. Each action dropped into the menu will act as an individual menu entry.

- By typing text for menus and menu entries in the menu bar replacing the Type Here placeholders. In that case, each menu entry will appear as an individual action in the Action Editor, where you can configure its properties.

Open Qt Designer and create a new application based on the Main Window template. A menu bar and toolbar will be provided by default. The menu bar that you want to create is shown in Figure 10.6(a). There will be two menus, with the text `File` and `Edit`. The File menu will have Open and View entries with a separator between them. The View menu will have two submenu entries, Page Layout Box and Format Box. The Edit menu will contain two menu entries, Cut and Copy. The process to create the menu bar is very simple:

1. Double-click the Type Here placeholder and enter the menu text **File**.

2. The down arrow key on the File menu brings up the Type Here and Add Separator options. Double-click Type Here and type **Open** for the menu entry.

3. The down arrow key on the Open menu provides the Type Here and Add Separator options. Select Add Separator.

4. Below Add Separator, type **View** for the Type Here option.

5. Select the right arrow to add submenu entries to the View menu. Select Type Here and enter **Page Layout Box**.

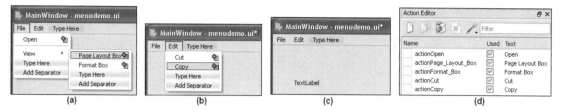

Figure 10.3
(a) Adding submenu entries to the View menu entry. (b) Cut and Copy menu entries added to the Edit menu. (c) A Label widget added to indicate which menu entry is selected. (d) All menu entries represented as actions in Action Editor.

6. Select the down arrow and enter **Format Box** below the Page Layout Box submenu entry as shown in Figure 10.3(a).

7. Select the File menu and click the right arrow to indicate that you want to add a second menu to the menu bar. Replace Type Here with **Edit**.

8. Select the down arrow and add Cut and Copy menu entries, as shown in Figure 10.3(b).

When the user selects any menu or submenu entry, you want a text message to appear on the form indicating which menu entry has been selected. To display a message, drag and drop a Label widget onto the form as shown in Figure 10.3(c). The actions for all menu entries will appear in the Action Editor automatically as shown in Figure 10.3(d). You can see that the action names are generated by prefixing the text action to every menu text and replacing the spaces with underscores. You will use these actions to configure menu entries.

If you want a status bar message to appear when the user hovers over any menu entry, set it through the `statusTip` property. For example, to assign a status bar message to the Open menu entry of the File menu, select `actionOpen` in the Action Editor and set the `statusTip` property to `Opening a file`, as shown in Figure 10.4 (a). Similarly, you can assign status bar messages to other menu entries. To assign a shortcut key to any menu entry, open its action from the Action Editor, as shown in Figure 10.4(b), and click the Shortcut box. When the keyboard focus is at Shortcut, press the key combination that you want to assign to the selected menu entry. For example, if you press Ctrl with the O character in the Shortcut box, Ctrl+O appears in the box, as shown in Figure 10.4(b), indicating that Ctrl+O is assigned to the menu entry. You can have any combination of shortcut keys, such as Shift+key, Alt+key, Ctrl+Shift+key, and so on.

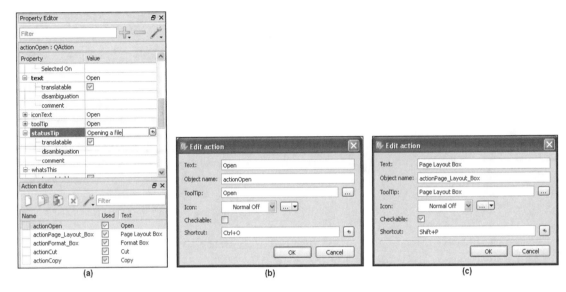

(a)   (b)   (c)

Figure 10.4
(a) Setting a status bar message through `statusTip`. (b) Action dialog box demonstrating application of a shortcut key. (c) Action dialog box demonstrating a checkable menu entry.

Note

Once assigned, shortcut keys will appear automatically with the menu entry text on execution.

Also, you can make any menu entry checkable. All you need is to select the action of the desired menu and check the Checkable checkbox as shown in Figure 10.4(c). The figure shows the action of the Page Layout Box menu entry, which confirms that the shortcut key is Shift+P and is checkable.

The actions of each menu entry along with its action name, menu text, shortcut keys, checkable status, and tooltip appear in the Action Editor as shown in Figure 10.5.

Save the application with the name `menudemo.ui`. The default location where the application will be saved is C:\Python32\Lib\site-packages\PyQt4 folder. Then use

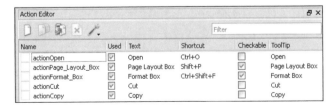

Figure 10.5
All menu entries represented as actions, along with their text, shortcut key, `checkable` and `tooltip` properties in Action Editor.

the `pyuic4` command line utility to convert the `.ui` (XML) file into Python code as shown here:

```
C:\Python32\Lib\site-packages\PyQt4>pyuic4 menudemo.ui -o menudemo.py
```

The generated Python code will appear as shown here:

```
menudemo.py
# Form implementation generated from reading ui file 'menudemo.ui'

from PyQt4 import QtCore, QtGui

try:
    _fromUtf8 = QtCore.QString.fromUtf8
except AttributeError:
    _fromUtf8 = lambda s: s

class Ui_MainWindow(object):
    def setupUi(self, MainWindow):
        MainWindow.setObjectName(_fromUtf8("MainWindow"))
        MainWindow.resize(800, 600)
        self.centralwidget = QtGui.QWidget(MainWindow)
        self.centralwidget.setObjectName(_fromUtf8("centralwidget"))
        self.label = QtGui.QLabel(self.centralwidget)
        self.label.setGeometry(QtCore.QRect(40, 60, 311, 16))
        self.label.setObjectName(_fromUtf8("label"))
        MainWindow.setCentralWidget(self.centralwidget)
        self.menubar = QtGui.QMenuBar(MainWindow)
        self.menubar.setGeometry(QtCore.QRect(0, 0, 800, 20))
        self.menubar.setObjectName(_fromUtf8("menubar"))
        self.menuFile = QtGui.QMenu(self.menubar)
        self.menuFile.setObjectName(_fromUtf8("menuFile"))
        self.menuPreference = QtGui.QMenu(self.menuFile)
        self.menuPreference.setObjectName(_fromUtf8("menuPreference"))
        self.menuEdit = QtGui.QMenu(self.menubar)
        self.menuEdit.setObjectName(_fromUtf8("menuEdit"))
        MainWindow.setMenuBar(self.menubar)
        self.statusbar = QtGui.QStatusBar(MainWindow)
        self.statusbar.setObjectName(_fromUtf8("statusbar"))
        MainWindow.setStatusBar(self.statusbar)
        self.actionOpen = QtGui.QAction(MainWindow)
        self.actionOpen.setObjectName(_fromUtf8("actionOpen"))
        self.actionPage_Layout_Box = QtGui.QAction(MainWindow)
        self.actionPage_Layout_Box.setCheckable(True)
```

```
self.actionPage_Layout_Box.setObjectName(_fromUtf8("actionPage_Layout_Box"))
        self.actionFormat_Box = QtGui.QAction(MainWindow)
        self.actionFormat_Box.setCheckable(True)
        self.actionFormat_Box.setObjectName(_fromUtf8("actionFormat_Box"))
        self.actionCut = QtGui.QAction(MainWindow)
        self.actionCut.setObjectName(_fromUtf8("actionCut"))
        self.actionCopy = QtGui.QAction(MainWindow)
        self.actionCopy.setObjectName(_fromUtf8("actionCopy"))
        self.menuPreference.addAction(self.actionPage_Layout_Box)
        self.menuPreference.addAction(self.actionFormat_Box)
        self.menuFile.addAction(self.actionOpen)
        self.menuFile.addSeparator()
        self.menuFile.addAction(self.menuPreference.menuAction())
        self.menuEdit.addAction(self.actionCut)
        self.menuEdit.addAction(self.actionCopy)
        self.menubar.addAction(self.menuFile.menuAction())
        self.menubar.addAction(self.menuEdit.menuAction())
        self.retranslateUi(MainWindow)
        QtCore.QMetaObject.connectSlotsByName(MainWindow)

    def retranslateUi(self, MainWindow):
        MainWindow.setWindowTitle(QtGui.QApplication.translate("MainWindow", "MainWin-
dow", None, QtGui.QApplication.UnicodeUTF8))
        self.label.setText(QtGui.QApplication.translate("MainWindow", "TextLabel", None,
QtGui.QApplication.UnicodeUTF8))
        self.menuFile.setTitle(QtGui.QApplication.translate("MainWindow", "File", None,
QtGui.QApplication.UnicodeUTF8))
        self.menuPreference.setTitle(QtGui.QApplication.translate("MainWindow", "View",
None, QtGui.QApplication.UnicodeUTF8))
        self.menuEdit.setTitle(QtGui.QApplication.translate("MainWindow", "Edit", None,
QtGui.QApplication.UnicodeUTF8))
        self.actionOpen.setText(QtGui.QApplication.translate("MainWindow", "Open", None,
QtGui.QApplication.UnicodeUTF8))
        self.actionOpen.setStatusTip(QtGui.QApplication.translate("MainWindow", "Open-
ing a file", None, QtGui.QApplication.UnicodeUTF8))
        self.actionOpen.setShortcut(QtGui.QApplication.translate("MainWindow", "Ctrl+O",
None, QtGui.QApplication.UnicodeUTF8))

self.actionPage_Layout_Box.setText(QtGui.QApplication.translate("MainWindow", "Page Lay-
out Box", None, QtGui.QApplication.UnicodeUTF8))
self.actionPage_Layout_Box.setStatusTip(QtGui.QApplication.translate("MainWindow",
"Setting page layout", None, QtGui.QApplication.UnicodeUTF8))

self.actionPage_Layout_Box.setShortcut(QtGui.QApplication.translate("MainWindow",
"Shift+P", None, QtGui.QApplication.UnicodeUTF8))
```

```
        self.actionFormat_Box.setText(QtGui.QApplication.translate("MainWindow",
"Format Box", None, QtGui.QApplication.UnicodeUTF8))

self.actionFormat_Box.setStatusTip(QtGui.QApplication.translate("MainWindow",
"Format toolbox for formatting", None, QtGui.QApplication.UnicodeUTF8))

self.actionFormat_Box.setShortcut(QtGui.QApplication.translate("MainWindow",  "Ctrl
+Shift+F", None, QtGui.QApplication.UnicodeUTF8))
        self.actionCut.setText(QtGui.QApplication.translate("MainWindow", "Cut", None,
QtGui.QApplication.UnicodeUTF8))
        self.actionCut.setStatusTip(QtGui.QApplication.translate("MainWindow", "Cutting
text", None, QtGui.QApplication.UnicodeUTF8))
        self.actionCopy.setText(QtGui.QApplication.translate("MainWindow",  "Copy",  None,
QtGui.QApplication.UnicodeUTF8))
        self.actionCopy.setStatusTip(QtGui.QApplication.translate("MainWindow",
"Copying text", None, QtGui.QApplication.UnicodeUTF8))
```

The next step is to create a Python script that imports the code to invoke the menu
and display the text message with a Label widget when a menu entry is selected. You
want a message to appear that indicates which menu entry is selected. The Python
script will appear as shown here:

```
callmenu.pyw
import sys
from menudemo import *

class MyForm(QtGui.QMainWindow):
    def __init__(self, parent=None):
        QtGui.QWidget.__init__(self, parent)
        self.ui = Ui_MainWindow()
        self.ui.setupUi(self)
        self.connect(self.ui.actionOpen, QtCore.SIGNAL('triggered()'), self.openmessage)
        self.connect(self.ui.actionPage_Layout_Box,  QtCore.SIGNAL('triggered()'),  self.
layoutmessage)
        self.connect(self.ui.actionFormat_Box, QtCore.SIGNAL('triggered()'),
self.formatmessage)
        self.connect(self.ui.actionCut, QtCore.SIGNAL('triggered()'), self.cutmessage)
        self.connect(self.ui.actionCopy, QtCore.SIGNAL('triggered()'), self.copymessage)

    def openmessage(self):
        self.ui.label.setText("Opening a File")

    def layoutmessage(self):
        self.ui.label.setText("You selected Page Layout option")
```

```
def formatmessage(self):
    self.ui.label.setText("You selected Format option")

def cutmessage(self):
    self.ui.label.setText("Cutting a text")

def copymessage(self):
    self.ui.label.setText("Copying text")

if __name__ == "__main__":
    app = QtGui.QApplication(sys.argv)
    myapp = MyForm()
    myapp.show()
    sys.exit(app.exec_())
```

You see that the triggered() signal for each menu entry is connected to a method that performs the desired task when the menu entry is selected. For example, the triggered() signal of the actionOpen action (Open menu entry) is connected to openmessage(). Now, when the user selects the Open menu entry from the File menu, the openmessage() function will be executed. In the openmessage() function, the text Opening a File is displayed with a Label widget. Similarly, the triggered() signals of other menu entries are connected to their respective methods to indicate which menu entry is selected. The status bar messages will also appear (if defined with the statusTip property) while hovering over a menu entry. Figure 10.6(a) shows the Setting Page Layout status bar message when the user hovers over the View, Page Layout Box menu entry. On selecting the Page Layout Box menu entry, You Selected Page Layout appears as shown in Figure 10.6(b). Again, Figure 10.6(c) displays Cutting a Text when the user hovers over the Edit > Cut menu entry. Finally, Figure 10.6(d) displays Cutting a Text when the user selects the Edit > Cut option.

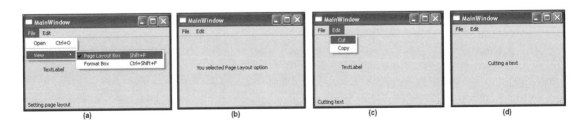

Figure 10.6
(a) Selecting the Page Layout Box of View. (b) The message indicating selection of the Page Layout Box sub-menu option. (c) Selecting the Cut menu entry from the Edit menu. (d) Text message indicating selection of Cut.

CREATING A TOOLBAR

The toolbar represents different tools for tasks the user performs in an application. The tools are usually represented as icons. When placing icons on the toolbar, you can pick icon images either from the disk drive or from the resource file. Before you create a toolbar, let's see how a resource file is created.

Creating a Resource File

Qt Designer allows you to specify resources for an application when you design the form. You can create a separate resource file for each form in the application. To specify a resource file, you need a Resource Browser, which is visible by default below the Property Editor. If you cannot see the Resource Browser tab, open the View menu and make sure that the Resource Browser menu option is checked. You will see the screen shown in Figure 10.7.

The Resource Browser window displays two icons at the top, Edit Resources and Reload. As the name suggests, Edit Resources is used to create and edit new resources. The Reload option is for reloading the current form's resource files and images in case they have been modified outside Qt Designer. On selecting Edit Resources icon, you get the screen shown in Figure 10.8.

The six icons that you see at the bottom of the Edit Resources dialog are explained in Table 10.1.

On selecting New Resource File, you get a dialog that prompts you to provide a name for the new resource file. Enter the filename `tmpresource`. The name will be stored with a `.qrc` extension, and the file will appear in the Edit Resources dialog box. The next step is to add resources to the resource file currently open.

To add a resource, add a prefix to the resource file. A prefix is a section or category name given to a resource. Select the Add Prefix icon, and a prefix will be added with

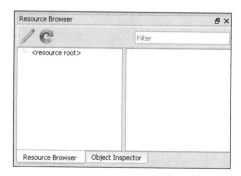

Figure 10.7
The Resource Browser window, showing icons for the Edit Resources and Reload options.

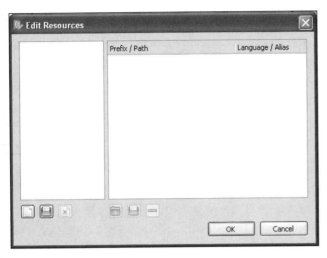

Figure 10.8
Edit Resources dialog to add, edit, and remove resource files and their resources.

Table 10.1   Icons in Edit Resources

Icon	Description
New resource file	Creates a new resource file.
Open resource file	Loads an existing resource file into the Edit Resources dialog.
Remove	Removes the selected resource file from the Edit Resources dialog.
Add prefix	Adds a prefix to the resource file for categorizing resources.
Add files	Adds a resource from the disk drive.
Remove	Removes the selected resource from the resource file.

the default name `newPrefix`. You can change the prefix name to indicate the type of resources assigned to it. Change the prefix name to **icon images**.

Note

You cannot add a resource to the Resource Editor without adding a prefix.

Select the Add Files icon (marked with an ellipse) to add resources to the prefix category. Browse your disk drive to select the resource you want to add. Add an image named `plus.ICO`. The Edit Resources dialog will appear as shown in Figure 10.9(a).

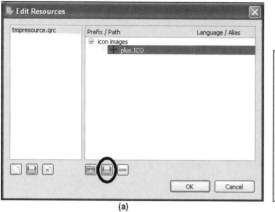

(a)   (b)

Figure 10.9
(a) The Edit Resources dialog showing the resource file and the icon image added to it. (b) The icon image appears in the Resource Browser window.

Select OK, and the resource (image) added appears in the Resource Browser as shown in Figure 10.9(b). You can add more resources to the prefix by selecting the Add Files icon. Also, you can add another prefix to represent another category of resources and add new resources to it.

Note

You can create any number of prefixes and add any number of resources to each prefix.

Let's create a new application to understand the steps involved in creating a toolbar. Open Qt Designer and create a Main Window-based application. To add a toolbar, right-click on the Main Window and select Add Tool Bar from the context menu. A blank toolbar will be added below the menu bar as shown in Figure 10.10.

Toolbar buttons are created with actions. You need to create an action in the Action Editor for each toolbar button you want to display. Then, drag each action from the Action Editor and drop it on the toolbar to represent a button on the toolbar.

Figure 10.10
The default toolbar in Main Window.

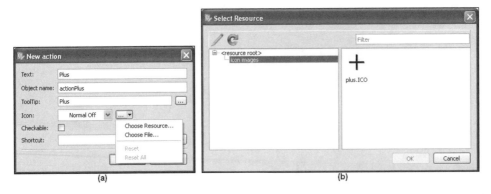

Figure 10.11
(a) Adding a new action. (b) Using Select Resource to specify an icon.

Invoke the Action Editor. To display and enable Action Editor, select View, Action Editor. Let's create a toolbar with icons to represent arithmetical operators such as plus, minus, multiply, divide, and equal to symbols as shown in Figure 10.11(b). Assuming you have the .ico files for these operations, select the New button in the Action Editor to create an action for the first toolbar button. In the Text box, specify the name of the action, **Plus**. In the Object Name box, the name of the Action object automatically appears, prefixed with the text action. In the ToolTip box, enter the action name, though you can enter any descriptive text. The Icon drop-down list shows two options, Choose Resource and Choose File as shown in Figure 10.11(a). Select Choose Resource. You get the Select Resource dialog as shown in Figure 10.11(b).

On the left side of the Select Resource dialog are the prefixes in the current resource file, and on the right side are the resources assigned to the prefix. Remember that you created a prefix named icon images and assigned an image named plus.ICO to it. Select the Plus icon image from the icon images prefix to assign it to the Plus action.

If the prefix doesn't appear in the Select Resource dialog, it means the resource file is not loaded in the current form. In that case, select the Edit Resources icon at the top of the dialog to open the Edit Resources dialog (refer to Figure 10.8) and select the Open Resource File icon to select and load the resource file that you created earlier, tmpresources.qrc. When the resource file is loaded, you can see its prefixes and their respective resources.

Select Choose File to browse your disk drive and select the .ico image to represent the Plus action. The action will appear as shown in Figure 10.12(a). Select OK to create the action. Repeat the procedure to create actions for the minus, multiply, divide, and equal to operators. The Action Editor will appear as shown in Figure 10.12(b).

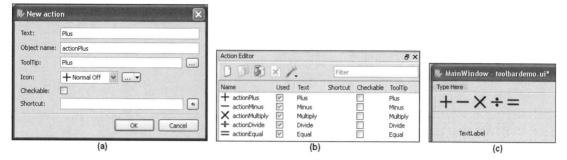

Figure 10.12
(a) Action window showing creation of the Plus icon. (b) All actions listed in Action Editor. (c) Tool Bar with all actions dropped in as toolbar buttons.

Note

To add an icon to an action, you can also drag it from the Resource Browser and drop it onto the action in the Action Editor window.

Now, you can drag an action from the Action Editor and drop it onto the default toolbar below the menu bar. Each action will appear as a toolbar button.

To know which toolbar button is selected by the user, you need to add a Label widget to the form. The Label widget will display a message indicating which button is selected in the toolbar. The Tool Bar and Label (with its default text, TextLabel) widgets will appear as shown in Figure 10.12(c).

Save the application with the name `toolbardemo.ui`. The `pyuic4` command line utility will convert the `.ui` (XML) file into Python code, and the code will appear as follows:

`toolbardemo.py`

```
# Form implementation generated from reading ui file 'toolbardemo.ui'

from PyQt4 import QtCore, QtGui

try:
    _fromUtf8 = QtCore.QString.fromUtf8
except AttributeError:
    _fromUtf8 = lambda s: s

class Ui_MainWindow(object):
    def setupUi(self, MainWindow):
        MainWindow.setObjectName(_fromUtf8("MainWindow"))
        MainWindow.resize(800, 600)
```

```
        self.centralwidget = QtGui.QWidget(MainWindow)
        self.centralwidget.setObjectName(_fromUtf8("centralwidget"))
        self.label = QtGui.QLabel(self.centralwidget)
        self.label.setGeometry(QtCore.QRect(50, 30, 291, 16))
        self.label.setObjectName(_fromUtf8("label"))
        MainWindow.setCentralWidget(self.centralwidget)
        self.menubar = QtGui.QMenuBar(MainWindow)
        self.menubar.setGeometry(QtCore.QRect(0, 0, 800, 20))
        self.menubar.setObjectName(_fromUtf8("menubar"))
        MainWindow.setMenuBar(self.menubar)
        self.statusbar = QtGui.QStatusBar(MainWindow)
        self.statusbar.setObjectName(_fromUtf8("statusbar"))
        MainWindow.setStatusBar(self.statusbar)
        self.toolBar = QtGui.QToolBar(MainWindow)
        self.toolBar.setObjectName(_fromUtf8("toolBar"))
        MainWindow.addToolBar(QtCore.Qt.TopToolBarArea, self.toolBar)
        self.actionPlus = QtGui.QAction(MainWindow)
        icon = QtGui.QIcon()
        icon.addPixmap(QtGui.QPixmap(_fromUtf8("plus.ICO")), QtGui.QIcon.Normal,
QtGui.QIcon.Off)
        self.actionPlus.setIcon(icon)
        self.actionPlus.setObjectName(_fromUtf8("actionPlus"))
        self.actionMinus = QtGui.QAction(MainWindow)
        icon1 = QtGui.QIcon()
        icon1.addPixmap(QtGui.QPixmap(_fromUtf8("minus.ICO")),    QtGui.QIcon.Normal,
QtGui.QIcon.Off)
        self.actionMinus.setIcon(icon1)
        self.actionMinus.setObjectName(_fromUtf8("actionMinus"))
        self.actionMultiply = QtGui.QAction(MainWindow)
        icon2 = QtGui.QIcon()
         icon2.addPixmap(QtGui.QPixmap(_fromUtf8("multiply.ICO")), QtGui.QIcon.Normal,
QtGui.QIcon.Off)
        self.actionMultiply.setIcon(icon2)
        self.actionMultiply.setObjectName(_fromUtf8("actionMultiply"))
        self.actionDivide = QtGui.QAction(MainWindow)
        icon3 = QtGui.QIcon()
        icon3.addPixmap(QtGui.QPixmap(_fromUtf8("divide.ICO")),    QtGui.QIcon.Normal,
QtGui.QIcon.Off)
        self.actionDivide.setIcon(icon3)
        self.actionDivide.setObjectName(_fromUtf8("actionDivide"))
        self.actionEqual = QtGui.QAction(MainWindow)
        icon4 = QtGui.QIcon()
        icon4.addPixmap(QtGui.QPixmap(_fromUtf8("equal.ICO")),    QtGui.QIcon.Normal,
QtGui.QIcon.Off)
```

```
        self.actionEqual.setIcon(icon4)
        self.actionEqual.setObjectName(_fromUtf8("actionEqual"))
        self.toolBar.addAction(self.actionPlus)
        self.toolBar.addAction(self.actionMinus)
        self.toolBar.addAction(self.actionMultiply)
        self.toolBar.addAction(self.actionDivide)
        self.toolBar.addAction(self.actionEqual)
        self.retranslateUi(MainWindow)
        QtCore.QMetaObject.connectSlotsByName(MainWindow)

    def retranslateUi(self, MainWindow):
        MainWindow.setWindowTitle(QtGui.QApplication.translate("MainWindow",
"MainWindow", None, QtGui.QApplication.UnicodeUTF8))
        self.label.setText(QtGui.QApplication.translate("MainWindow",
"TextLabel", None, QtGui.QApplication.UnicodeUTF8))
        self.toolBar.setWindowTitle(QtGui.QApplication.translate("MainWindow",
"toolBar", None, QtGui.QApplication.UnicodeUTF8))
        self.actionPlus.setText(QtGui.QApplication.translate("MainWindow",
"Plus", None, QtGui.QApplication.UnicodeUTF8))
        self.actionPlus.setToolTip(QtGui.QApplication.translate("MainWindow",
"Plus", None, QtGui.QApplication.UnicodeUTF8))
        self.actionMinus.setText(QtGui.QApplication.translate("MainWindow",
"Minus", None, QtGui.QApplication.UnicodeUTF8))
        self.actionMinus.setToolTip(QtGui.QApplication.translate("MainWindow",
"Minus", None, QtGui.QApplication.UnicodeUTF8))
        self.actionMultiply.setText(QtGui.QApplication.translate("MainWindow",
"Multiply", None, QtGui.QApplication.UnicodeUTF8))

self.actionMultiply.setToolTip(QtGui.QApplication.translate("MainWindow",
"Multiply", None, QtGui.QApplication.UnicodeUTF8))
        self.actionDivide.setText(QtGui.QApplication.translate("MainWindow",
"Divide", None, QtGui.QApplication.UnicodeUTF8))
        self.actionDivide.setToolTip(QtGui.QApplication.translate("MainWindow",
"Divide", None, QtGui.QApplication.UnicodeUTF8))
        self.actionEqual.setText(QtGui.QApplication.translate("MainWindow",
"Equal", None, QtGui.QApplication.UnicodeUTF8))
        self.actionEqual.setToolTip(QtGui.QApplication.translate("MainWindow",
"Equal", None, QtGui.QApplication.UnicodeUTF8))
```

Now you need to create a Python script that imports the code to invoke the toolbar and displays the text message with a Label widget when a toolbar button is selected from the toolbar. The script file will appear as follows:

```
calltoolbar.pyw
import sys
from toolbardemo import *
```

```
class MyForm(QtGui.QMainWindow):
   def __init__(self, parent=None):
      QtGui.QWidget.__init__(self, parent)
      self.ui = Ui_MainWindow()
      self.ui.setupUi(self)
      self.connect(self.ui.actionPlus, QtCore.SIGNAL('triggered()'),
self.plusmessage)
      self.connect(self.ui.actionMinus, QtCore.SIGNAL('triggered()'),
self.minusmessage)
      self.connect(self.ui.actionMultiply, QtCore.SIGNAL('triggered()'),
self.multiplymessage)
      self.connect(self.ui.actionDivide, QtCore.SIGNAL('triggered()'),
self.dividemessage)
      self.connect(self.ui.actionEqual, QtCore.SIGNAL('triggered()'),
self.equalmessage)

   def plusmessage(self):
      self.ui.label.setText("You have selected Plus ")

   def minusmessage(self):
      self.ui.label.setText("You have selected Minus ")

   def multiplymessage(self):
      self.ui.label.setText("You have selected Multiply ")

   def dividemessage(self):
      self.ui.label.setText("You have selected Divide ")

   def equalmessage(self):
      self.ui.label.setText("You have selected Equal ")

if __name__ == "__main__":
   app = QtGui.QApplication(sys.argv)
   myapp = MyForm()
   myapp.show()
   sys.exit(app.exec_())
```

You see that the triggered() signal of the action of each toolbar button is connected to a method. The method will be invoked when its toolbar button is selected.
For example, the triggered() signal of actionPlus (the plus icon) is connected
to plusmessage(). When the user selects the plus icon from the toolbar, the plus-
message() method will be executed. In the plusmessage() method, "You have
selected Plus" is displayed with a Label widget. Similarly, the triggered() signal
of the actions of other toolbar buttons are connected to their respective methods. If

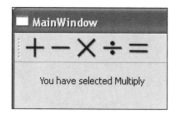

Figure 10.13
The toolbar displaying different toolbar buttons and a Label widget indicating the button that is selected.

the *Multiply* icon is selected, "You have selected Multiply" is displayed, as shown in Figure 10.13.

How about a detachable tool palette? To create a dockable or floating tool palette or widget panel, you use a Dock Widget. Let's see how it works.

DOCK WIDGET

A Dock widget is created with the QDockWidget class. A Dock widget can be used to create detachable tool palettes or widget panels. They can be closed or docked in the Dock area around the central widget inside QMainWindow or floated as a top-level window on the desktop. Allowable dock areas are LeftDockWidgetArea, RightDockWidgetArea, TopDockWidgetArea, and BottomDockWidgetArea, where TopDockWidgetArea is below the toolbar. You also can restrict where a Dock widget can be placed. For example, if you restrict the Dock widget to the left or right, you will not be able to drag it to the top or bottom. A Dock widget has a title bar and buttons that are used to float or close it. The appearance of the title bar and buttons depends on the style being used. Widgets that you want to be available in dock areas or as floating windows are placed in Dock widgets.

The user can drag a Dock window out of the dock area entirely so that it becomes a free-floating window. The properties that control movement of the Dock widget and the appearance of its title bar and other buttons are shown in Table 10.2.

Create a new Main Window application and drag and drop a Dock widget onto the form. We'll drag and drop widgets that you want to be available in dock areas or as a floating window in the Dock widget. To enable all features in the Dock widget, select it and check its AllDockWidgetFeatures property in the Features section of the Property Editor window (see Figure 10.14). The AllDockWidgetFeatures property is to make the Dock widget closable and movable in the Dock and floatable as an independent window. Also, set the title of the Dock window to Dock Window with the windowTitle property. Check LeftDockWidgetArea in the allowedAreas section to restrict the Dock widget to be docked in the left Dock widget area only.

Table 10.2 Properties of a Dock Widget

Property	Description
DockWidgetClosable	If selected, the Dock widget can be closed.
DockWidgetMovable	If selected, the Dock widget can be moved between dock areas.
DockWidgetFloatable	If selected, the Dock widget can be detached from the main window and floated as an independent window.
DockWidgetVerticalTitleBar	If selected, the Dock widget displays a vertical title bar on its left side.
AllDockWidgetFeatures	If selected, automatically selects the DockWidgetClosable, DockWidgetMovable, and DockWidgetFloatable properties, allowing the Dock widget to be closed, moved, or floated.
NoDockWidgetFeatures	If selected, the Dock widget cannot be closed, moved, or floated.

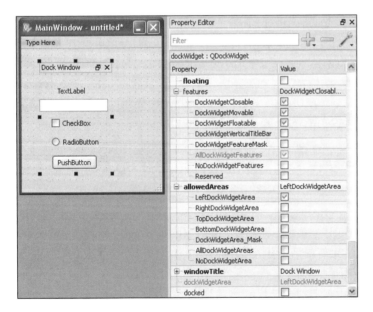

Figure 10.14
A Dock widget with widgets and the Property Editor window showing the Dock widget's properties.

The docked property plays a major role in making a Dock widget dockable. If the docked property is not checked, you will not be able to dock the Dock widget to any of the allowable areas. Though you have checked the LeftDockWidgetArea property, you will not be able to dock the Dock widget to the left Dock widget area because you have not checked the docked property.

Save the application with the name dockdemo.ui. The .ui (XML) file generated with the pyuic4 command utility will appear as follows:

dockdemo.py

```
# Form implementation generated from reading ui file 'dockdemo.ui'
from PyQt4 import QtCore, QtGui

try:
    _fromUtf8 = QtCore.QString.fromUtf8
except AttributeError:
    _fromUtf8 = lambda s: s

class Ui_MainWindow(object):
    def setupUi(self, MainWindow):
        MainWindow.setObjectName(_fromUtf8("MainWindow"))
        MainWindow.resize(212, 253)
        self.centralwidget = QtGui.QWidget(MainWindow)
        self.centralwidget.setObjectName(_fromUtf8("centralwidget"))
        self.dockWidget = QtGui.QDockWidget(self.centralwidget)
        self.dockWidget.setGeometry(QtCore.QRect(40, 10, 111, 191))
        self.dockWidget.setFloating(False)
        self.dockWidget.setFeatures(QtGui.QDockWidget.AllDockWidgetFeatures)
        self.dockWidget.setAllowedAreas(QtCore.Qt.LeftDockWidgetArea)
        self.dockWidget.setObjectName(_fromUtf8("dockWidget"))
        self.dockWidgetContents = QtGui.QWidget()
        self.dockWidgetContents.setObjectName(_fromUtf8("dockWidgetContents"))
        self.label = QtGui.QLabel(self.dockWidgetContents)
        self.label.setGeometry(QtCore.QRect(30, 20, 46, 13))
        self.label.setObjectName(_fromUtf8("label"))
        self.lineEdit = QtGui.QLineEdit(self.dockWidgetContents)
        self.lineEdit.setGeometry(QtCore.QRect(0, 40, 113, 20))
        self.lineEdit.setObjectName(_fromUtf8("lineEdit"))
        self.checkBox = QtGui.QCheckBox(self.dockWidgetContents)
        self.checkBox.setGeometry(QtCore.QRect(20, 70, 70, 17))
        self.checkBox.setObjectName(_fromUtf8("checkBox"))
        self.radioButton = QtGui.QRadioButton(self.dockWidgetContents)
        self.radioButton.setGeometry(QtCore.QRect(20, 100, 82, 17))
        self.radioButton.setObjectName(_fromUtf8("radioButton"))
        self.pushButton = QtGui.QPushButton(self.dockWidgetContents)
```

```
    self.pushButton.setGeometry(QtCore.QRect(20, 130, 75, 23))
    self.pushButton.setObjectName(_fromUtf8("pushButton"))
    self.dockWidget.setWidget(self.dockWidgetContents)
    MainWindow.setCentralWidget(self.centralwidget)
    self.menubar = QtGui.QMenuBar(MainWindow)
    self.menubar.setGeometry(QtCore.QRect(0, 0, 212, 20))
    self.menubar.setObjectName(_fromUtf8("menubar"))
    MainWindow.setMenuBar(self.menubar)
    self.statusbar = QtGui.QStatusBar(MainWindow)
    self.statusbar.setObjectName(_fromUtf8("statusbar"))
    MainWindow.setStatusBar(self.statusbar)
    self.retranslateUi(MainWindow)
    QtCore.QMetaObject.connectSlotsByName(MainWindow)

def retranslateUi(self, MainWindow):
    MainWindow.setWindowTitle(QtGui.QApplication.translate("MainWindow", "MainWin-
dow", None, QtGui.QApplication.UnicodeUTF8))

self.dockWidget.setWindowTitle(QtGui.QApplication.translate("MainWindow",    "Dock
Window", None, QtGui.QApplication.UnicodeUTF8))
    self.label.setText(QtGui.QApplication.translate("MainWindow", "TextLabel", None,
QtGui.QApplication.UnicodeUTF8))
    self.checkBox.setText(QtGui.QApplication.translate("MainWindow",    "CheckBox",
None, QtGui.QApplication.UnicodeUTF8))
    self.radioButton.setText(QtGui.QApplication.translate("MainWindow", "RadioButton",
None, QtGui.QApplication.UnicodeUTF8))
    self.pushButton.setText(QtGui.QApplication.translate("MainWindow",    "PushButton",
None, QtGui.QApplication.UnicodeUTF8))
```

As usual, the next step is to create a Python script that imports the code to invoke the Dock widget. The Python script file will have the following code:

```
calldock.pyw
import sys
from dockdemo import *

class MyForm(QtGui.QMainWindow):
   def __init__(self, parent=None):
      QtGui.QWidget.__init__(self, parent)
      self.ui = Ui_MainWindow()
      self.ui.setupUi(self)

if __name__ == "__main__":
   app = QtGui.QApplication(sys.argv)
   myapp = MyForm()
   myapp.show()
   sys.exit(app.exec_())
```

Figure 10.15
A Dock widget displaying the widgets it contains.

When the application is executed, you get a Dock widget in the Main Window (Figure 10.15), but you cannot move it to any Dock area because you haven't checked the `docked` property of the Dock widget.

To allow the Dock widget to be dockable in all four Dock areas, select `LeftDock-WidgetArea`, `RightDockWidgetArea`, `TopDockWidgetArea`, and `BottomDock-WidgetArea` in the allowedAreas section of the Property Editor (see Figure 10.16). If you want the Dock widget to first appear as docked in the right Dock widget area, check the `docked` property and set the value of the `dockWidgetArea` property to `RightDockWidgetArea`. The Dock widget will immediately shift to the right Dock area as shown in Figure 10.16.

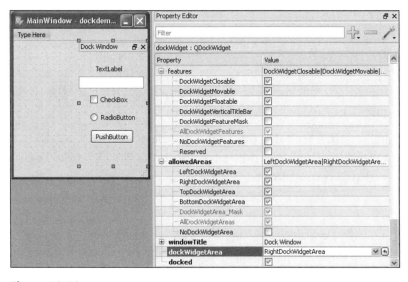

Figure 10.16
Settings properties of the Dock widget to make it dockable and docked to the right Dock area.

Figure 10.17
The Dock widget appears docked in the right dock area.

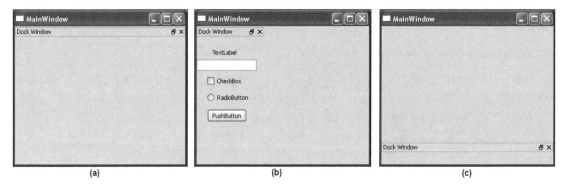

Figure 10.18
(a) Dock widget when docked at the top. (b) Docked on the left. (c) Docked at the bottom.

To see the changes made in properties of the Dock widget, save the file and regenerate the Python code with the `pyuic4` command line utility. The `calldock.pyw` script will pick up the code on execution. The Dock widget appears in the right Dock area as shown in Figure 10.17.

Now you can drag the widget to any area. If you drag it to the top, it will be docked as shown in Figure 10.18(a). If you drag it to the left or bottom, it will be docked as shown in Figure 10.18(b) and (c), respectively.

Note

You can drag the Dock widget outside the Main Window to make it an independent floating window.

If you want the Dock widget to appear as an independent floating window, check its `floating` property, as shown in Figure 10.19.

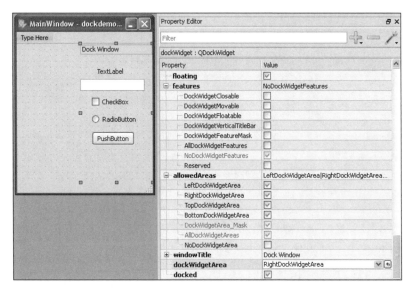

Figure 10.19
Setting properties of the Dock widget to make it a floatable window.

Figure 10.20
Dock widget appears as a floating window.

If you check the floating property of the Dock widget, it will appear as an independent floating window (Figure 10.20) and can be moved anywhere on the desktop. Also, the Dock widget can be docked to any of the four dock areas.

With floating checked and docked unchecked, the Dock widget will initially be floating and can be moved anywhere on the desktop but cannot be docked in any of the Dock areas. With NoDockWidgetFeatures selected, all other properties in the Features section are unchecked automatically; all buttons will disappear from the Dock widget, and you will not be able to close or move it. Similarly, on selecting

NoDockWidgetArea, all other properties in the allowedAreas section are deselected automatically. You can move the Dock window anywhere on the desktop, but you cannot dock it in the Dock areas of the Main Window.

Which widget should you use when you have a lot of information to be displayed? Let's find out.

TAB WIDGET

The Tab widget is used to display information in chunks. It enables you to split information into small sections and display each section when the Tab button is selected. When you drag a Tab widget onto a dialog, it appears with two default Tab buttons labeled Tab1 and Tab2, as shown in Figure 10.21. You can add more Tab buttons to the Tab widget and delete existing buttons if you want.

Let's create a new application based on the Dialog without Buttons template and drag and drop a Tab widget onto the form. Assume that you run a restaurant that sells items in the categories Food, Drinks, and Ice Creams. You will use the Tab widget to display a list of items sold under the three categories. Using the currentTabText property of the Tab widget, change the text displayed on each Tab button. Set the text of two buttons to Food and Drinks. To add a new Tab button, right-click on either Tab button and select Insert Page from the context menu that appears. You will see two suboptions, After Current Page and Before Current Page. Select After Current Page to add a new tab after the Drinks tab. The new tab will have the default text Page, which you will change to **Ice Creams** using the currentTabText property. Expand the Tab widget by selecting and dragging its nodes to provide blank space below the Tab buttons. Select each Tab button and drop the desired widgets into the blank space provided. For example, drop CheckBox widgets onto the first Tab button, Food, to display the items available in the Food category as shown in Figure 10.22. Similarly, place some widgets on the other two Tab buttons.

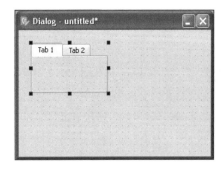

Figure 10.21
A Tab widget with its default buttons.

Figure 10.22
Widgets added to each tab to show content.

To enhance the appearance of the widgets on the form, you can apply fonts, change their background and foreground colors, and so on. Let's learn more about applying styles to widgets.

Working with the Style Sheet Editor

You can apply styles to any widget on a form to customize its appearance. Let's apply styles to the Tab widget through the Style Sheet Editor. To open the Style Sheet Editor, right-click the Tab widget and select Change Style Sheet from the context menu. The Edit Style Sheet dialog box appears that displays four drop-downs: Add Resource, Add Gradient, Add Color, and an Add Font button, as shown in Figure 10.23. The large text box below the drop-downs acts as the Style Sheet Editor; whatever style you apply through this dialog will appear in the form of code in the text box, allowing you to edit the generated code. Clicking a drop-down list shows respective options that you can select, which opens the related dialog for choosing images, gradients, colors, and fonts to be applied to the selected widgets.

Figure 10.23
Options for adding a resource, gradient, color, or a font to the selected widget.

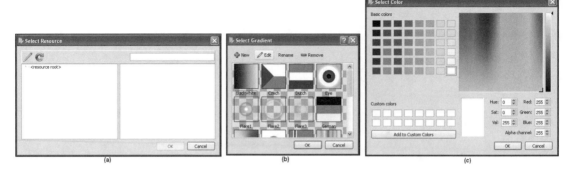

Figure 10.24
(a) Dialog showing resources. (b) Dialog to select a gradient. (c) Dialog to select a color.

On selecting the Add Resource drop-down, three options will be displayed: background-image, border-image, and image. After choosing an option, you get the Select Resource dialog box shown in Figure 10.24(a). The Select Resource dialog box displays two icons at the top, Edit Resources and Reload. Remember that the Edit Resources icon is used for creating and editing new resources (refer to Figure 10.11), and the Reload icon reloads the resources if the resource file or its images were modified outside Qt Designer. Selecting the Add Gradient drop-down shows several options like, color, background-color, alternate-background-color, border-color, border-top-color, border-right-color, and so on. Selecting any of the displayed options brings up the dialog boxes shown in Figure 10.24(b). You can modify a gradient or create a new one by selecting the Edit button.

The Color dialog lets you apply a color to the selected widget. You also can create custom colors by mixing different quantities of red, green, and blue and by setting Hue and Sat values as shown in Figure 10.24(c). The Font dialog is the same as you see in other editors (see Figure 10.25) and can be used to apply a font, style, and size to a widget.

To apply color to the Tab widget, select it in the form and select the `background-color` option from the Add Color drop-down. Select green in the Select Color dialog box and click OK. The background of the Tab widget will turn green, and the code for applying a green background color on the Tab widget will appear in the Style Sheet Editor, as shown in Figures 10.26(a) and (b).

Similarly, on changing the font, font size, or font style with the Font dialog box will cause the Tab widget to appear as shown in Figure 10.27(a), and the code is added to the style sheet as shown in Figure 10.27(b).

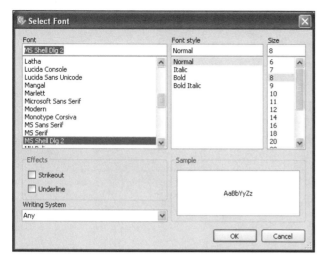

Figure 10.25
Dialog to select and apply font to the selected widget.

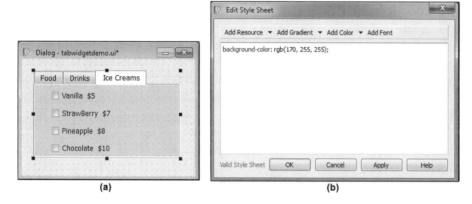

Figure 10.26
(a) The tab contents on application of a green background color. (b) Code in the style sheet that adds green background color.

Save the application with the name tabwidgetdemo.ui. The pyuic4 command utility converts the .ui (XML) file into Python code as follows:

tabwidgetdemo.py

```
# Form implementation generated from reading ui file 'tabwidgetdemo.ui'
from PyQt4 import QtCore, QtGui

try:
    _fromUtf8 = QtCore.QString.fromUtf8
except AttributeError:
    _fromUtf8 = lambda s: s
```

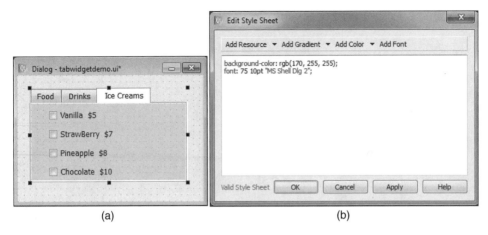

Figure 10.27
(a) The tab contents on changing the font and font size. (b) Code in the style sheet that adds a green background color and font.

```python
class Ui_Dialog(object):
    def setupUi(self, Dialog):
        Dialog.setObjectName(_fromUtf8("Dialog"))
        Dialog.resize(316, 199)
        self.tabWidget = QtGui.QTabWidget(Dialog)
        self.tabWidget.setGeometry(QtCore.QRect(20, 20, 261, 151))
        self.tabWidget.setStyleSheet(_fromUtf8("background-color: rgb(170, 255, 255);
\n"
"font: 75 10pt \"MS Shell Dlg 2\";"))
        self.tabWidget.setObjectName(_fromUtf8("tabWidget"))
        self.tab = QtGui.QWidget()
        self.tab.setObjectName(_fromUtf8("tab"))
        self.checkBox_2 = QtGui.QCheckBox(self.tab)
        self.checkBox_2.setGeometry(QtCore.QRect(20, 50, 91, 17))
        self.checkBox_2.setObjectName(_fromUtf8("checkBox_2"))
        self.checkBox_3 = QtGui.QCheckBox(self.tab)
        self.checkBox_3.setGeometry(QtCore.QRect(20, 80, 141, 17))
        self.checkBox_3.setObjectName(_fromUtf8("checkBox_3"))
        self.checkBox = QtGui.QCheckBox(self.tab)
        self.checkBox.setGeometry(QtCore.QRect(20, 20, 111, 17))
        self.checkBox.setObjectName(_fromUtf8("checkBox"))
        self.tabWidget.addTab(self.tab, _fromUtf8(""))
        self.tab_2 = QtGui.QWidget()
        self.tab_2.setObjectName(_fromUtf8("tab_2"))
        self.radioButton_6 = QtGui.QRadioButton(self.tab_2)
        self.radioButton_6.setGeometry(QtCore.QRect(20, 50, 111, 17))
        self.radioButton_6.setObjectName(_fromUtf8("radioButton_6"))
```

```
        self.radioButton_5 = QtGui.QRadioButton(self.tab_2)
        self.radioButton_5.setGeometry(QtCore.QRect(20, 80, 82, 17))
        self.radioButton_5.setObjectName(_fromUtf8("radioButton_5"))
        self.radioButton_4 = QtGui.QRadioButton(self.tab_2)
        self.radioButton_4.setGeometry(QtCore.QRect(20, 20, 82, 17))
        self.radioButton_4.setObjectName(_fromUtf8("radioButton_4"))
        self.tabWidget.addTab(self.tab_2, _fromUtf8(""))
        self.tab_3 = QtGui.QWidget()
        self.tab_3.setObjectName(_fromUtf8("tab_3"))
        self.checkBox_14 = QtGui.QCheckBox(self.tab_3)
        self.checkBox_14.setGeometry(QtCore.QRect(30, 40, 111, 17))
        self.checkBox_14.setObjectName(_fromUtf8("checkBox_14"))
        self.checkBox_12 = QtGui.QCheckBox(self.tab_3)
        self.checkBox_12.setGeometry(QtCore.QRect(30, 10, 81, 17))
        self.checkBox_12.setObjectName(_fromUtf8("checkBox_12"))
        self.checkBox_11 = QtGui.QCheckBox(self.tab_3)
        self.checkBox_11.setGeometry(QtCore.QRect(30, 70, 101, 17))
        self.checkBox_11.setObjectName(_fromUtf8("checkBox_11"))
        self.checkBox_13 = QtGui.QCheckBox(self.tab_3)
        self.checkBox_13.setGeometry(QtCore.QRect(30, 100, 111, 17))
        self.checkBox_13.setObjectName(_fromUtf8("checkBox_13"))
        self.tabWidget.addTab(self.tab_3, _fromUtf8(""))
        self.retranslateUi(Dialog)
        self.tabWidget.setCurrentIndex(2)
        QtCore.QMetaObject.connectSlotsByName(Dialog)

    def retranslateUi(self, Dialog):
        Dialog.setWindowTitle(QtGui.QApplication.translate("Dialog",  "Dialog",  None,
QtGui.QApplication.UnicodeUTF8))
        self.checkBox_2.setText(QtGui.QApplication.translate("Dialog", "Hot Dog  5$", None,
QtGui.QApplication.UnicodeUTF8))
        self.checkBox_3.setText(QtGui.QApplication.translate("Dialog", "Chicken Burger 10
$", None, QtGui.QApplication.UnicodeUTF8))
        self.checkBox.setText(QtGui.QApplication.translate("Dialog", "Pizza  25 $", None,
QtGui.QApplication.UnicodeUTF8))
        self.tabWidget.setTabText(self.tabWidget.indexOf(self.tab),
QtGui.QApplication.translate("Dialog", "Food", None,
QtGui.QApplication.UnicodeUTF8))
        self.radioButton_6.setText(QtGui.QApplication.translate("Dialog",
"Cold Drink 10$", None, QtGui.QApplication.UnicodeUTF8))
        self.radioButton_5.setText(QtGui.QApplication.translate("Dialog", "Coffee
5$", None, QtGui.QApplication.UnicodeUTF8))
        self.radioButton_4.setText(QtGui.QApplication.translate("Dialog", "Juice
15$", None, QtGui.QApplication.UnicodeUTF8))
```

```
    self.tabWidget.setTabText(self.tabWidget.indexOf(self.tab_2),
QtGui.QApplication.translate("Dialog", "Drinks", None,
QtGui.QApplication.UnicodeUTF8))
    self.checkBox_14.setText(QtGui.QApplication.translate("Dialog", "Strawberry
7$", None, QtGui.QApplication.UnicodeUTF8))
    self.checkBox_12.setText(QtGui.QApplication.translate("Dialog", "Vanilla  5$",
None, QtGui.QApplication.UnicodeUTF8))
    self.checkBox_11.setText(QtGui.QApplication.translate("Dialog", "Pineapple
8$", None, QtGui.QApplication.UnicodeUTF8))
    self.checkBox_13.setText(QtGui.QApplication.translate("Dialog", "Chocolate
10$", None, QtGui.QApplication.UnicodeUTF8))
    self.tabWidget.setTabText(self.tabWidget.indexOf(self.tab_3),
QtGui.QApplication.translate("Dialog", "Ice Creams", None,
QtGui.QApplication.UnicodeUTF8))
```

Let's create a Python script file that imports the code to invoke the Tab widget. The file will have the following code:

```
calltabwidget.pyw
import sys
from tabwidgetdemo import *

class MyForm(QtGui.QDialog):
  def __init__(self, parent=None):
    QtGui.QWidget.__init__(self, parent)
    self.ui = Ui_Dialog()
    self.ui.setupUi(self)

 if __name__ == "__main__":
   app = QtGui.QApplication(sys.argv)
   myapp = MyForm()
   myapp.show()
   sys.exit(app.exec_())
```

On execution of the program, you see that the Food Tab button is auto selected, and the widgets assigned to it are displayed as shown in Figure 10.28(a). If any other Tab button is selected, the widgets assigned to it will be displayed. For example, select Ice Creams and the widget in it will be displayed as shown in Figure 10.28(b).

We can relocate the tabs to appear on any side of the Tab widget through tab-Position, which has four options, North, South, West, and East (see Figure 10.29(a)) to make the Tab buttons appear on the desired side of the Tab widget. Select the West option, and the Tab buttons will appear on the left side of the Tab widget, as shown in Figure 10.29(b). Note that the scroll button appears if all the Tab buttons are not visible in the Tab widget.

Figure 10.28
(a) The tab contents of the Food Tab button. (b) The tab contents of the Ice Creams Tab button.

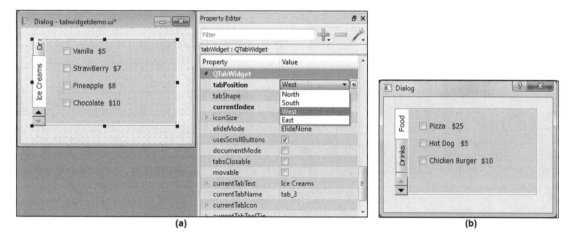

Figure 10.29
(a) The Tab buttons set to appear on the West side of the Tab widget through `tabPosition`. (b) The scroll buttons appear when all Tab buttons are not visible within the size of the Tab widget.

The Tab widget can be converted into a Tool Box or Stacked widget. Let's see how to do so.

CONVERTING A TAB WIDGET

Before you learn to convert a Tab widget into a Tool Box or Stacked widget, let's explain the two terms:

- **Tool Box:** A Tool Box is an instance of the `QToolBox` class and provides a column of tabbed widget items, one above the next. The widgets of the current tab are displayed below it. See Figure 10.31(a).

■ **Stacked Widget:** A Stacked widget is an instance of `QStackedWidget` and provides a stack of widgets where only one widget is visible at a time. Again, it can be used to display large chunks of information in the Tab widget. By default, the Stacked widget doesn't have a way to switch pages, so to switch pages, you must use another widget, such as a Combo Box or a List widget. See Figure 10.32(a) to see a stacked widget.

Converting a Tab Widget into a Tool Box

To convert a Tab widget to a Tool Box, right-click on it and select the Morph Into option. You will see two suboptions: QStackedWidget and QToolBox. Select QToolBox to convert the Tab widget into a Tool Box. The Tab widget will be converted into a Tool Box widget. The Tab buttons of the Tab widget will change to a column of tabs, and the widgets inside each Tab button of the Tab widget will appear as widgets of the respective tabs in Tool Box. The default text of each tab will be Page, as shown in Figure 10.30(a). Change the tab text to Food, Drinks, and Ice Creams, using the `currentItemText` property. The Tool Box will appear as shown in Figure 10.30(b).

Save the application with the name `tabwidgettoolbox.ui`. We don't have to do anything else to make the Tool Box functional. It's already working perfectly. Widgets will be displayed when a tab is selected from the Tool Box. For example, if you select Food, the items or widget displayed will be as shown in Figure 10.31(a). Similarly, select Drinks and the widgets in it will appear as shown in Figure 10.31(b). Select a tab in the Tool Box and the other tabs automatically are collapsed, making their widgets invisible and creating space for displaying widgets.

Now let's convert a Tab widget into a Stacked widget.

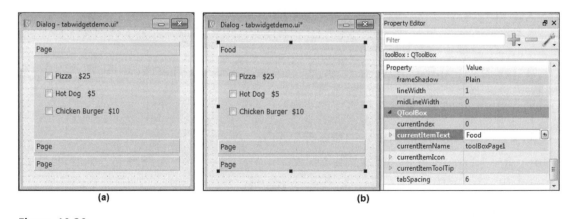

(a)   (b)

Figure 10.30
(a) The Tab widget converted to Tool Box form (b) Setting the text of the tabs through currentItemText property.

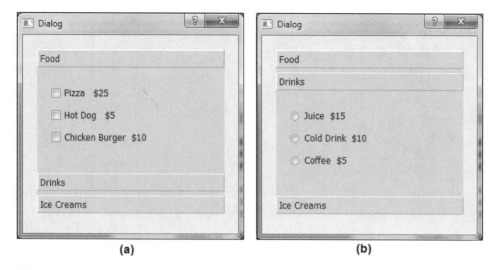

Figure 10.31
(a) The Tool Box displaying contents of Food. (b) Tool Box displaying contents of Drinks. Other tabs automatically collapse.

Converting Tab Widget into Stacked Widget

To morph a Tab widget into a Stacked widget, right-click on it and select Morph Into, QStackedWidget option from the context menu. The Tab widget will be converted into the Stacked widget as shown in Figure 10.32(a). On execution of the application, the Food, Drinks, and Ice Creams Tab buttons are converted into widgets, and the widgets of the first tab are displayed by default. No page switching (or widget switching) is available (Figure 10.32(b)). Recall that a Stacked widget doesn't provide page switching, and you need to use another widget to switch from one page (or widget) to another.

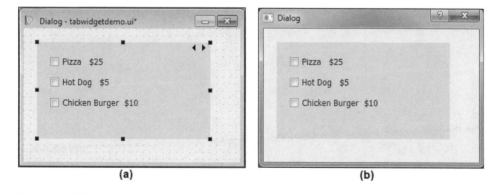

Figure 10.32
(a) The Tab widget converted to a Stacked widget. (b) The first widget appears with no option for page switching.

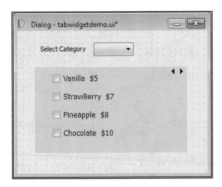

Figure 10.33
Adding a Combo Box above the Stacked widget.

Note

Every widget in a Stacked widget has an index number, and a widget can be accessed through its index number.

Let's use a Combo Box to implement page switching to our Stacked widget. Drag and drop a Combo Box just above the Stacked widget on the form as shown in Figure 10.33.

Save the file with the name `tabwidgetstacked.ui` and use `pyuic4` to regenerate the Python code. The Python code for displaying a Stacked widget and a Combo Box is as follows:

```
tabwidgetstacked.py
# Form implementation generated from reading ui file 'tabwidgetdemo.ui'
from PyQt4 import QtCore, QtGui

try:
    _fromUtf8 = QtCore.QString.fromUtf8
except AttributeError:
    _fromUtf8 = lambda s: s

class Ui_Dialog(object):
    def setupUi(self, Dialog):
        Dialog.setObjectName(_fromUtf8("Dialog"))
        Dialog.resize(316, 223)
        self.stackedWidget = QtGui.QStackedWidget(Dialog)
        self.stackedWidget.setGeometry(QtCore.QRect(20, 50, 261, 151))
        self.stackedWidget.setStyleSheet(_fromUtf8("background-color:  rgb(170,  255,
255);\n"
"font: 75 10pt \"MS Shell Dlg 2\";"))
```

```
self.stackedWidget.setObjectName(_fromUtf8("stackedWidget"))
self.stackedWidgetPage1 = QtGui.QWidget()
self.stackedWidgetPage1.setObjectName(_fromUtf8("stackedWidgetPage1"))
self.checkBox_2 = QtGui.QCheckBox(self.stackedWidgetPage1)
self.checkBox_2.setGeometry(QtCore.QRect(20, 50, 91, 17))
self.checkBox_2.setObjectName(_fromUtf8("checkBox_2"))
self.checkBox_3 = QtGui.QCheckBox(self.stackedWidgetPage1)
self.checkBox_3.setGeometry(QtCore.QRect(20, 80, 141, 17))
self.checkBox_3.setObjectName(_fromUtf8("checkBox_3"))
self.checkBox = QtGui.QCheckBox(self.stackedWidgetPage1)
self.checkBox.setGeometry(QtCore.QRect(20, 20, 111, 17))
self.checkBox.setObjectName(_fromUtf8("checkBox"))
self.stackedWidget.addWidget(self.stackedWidgetPage1)
self.stackedWidgetPage2 = QtGui.QWidget()
self.stackedWidgetPage2.setObjectName(_fromUtf8("stackedWidgetPage2"))
self.radioButton_6 = QtGui.QRadioButton(self.stackedWidgetPage2)
self.radioButton_6.setGeometry(QtCore.QRect(20, 50, 111, 17))
self.radioButton_6.setObjectName(_fromUtf8("radioButton_6"))
self.radioButton_5 = QtGui.QRadioButton(self.stackedWidgetPage2)
self.radioButton_5.setGeometry(QtCore.QRect(20, 80, 82, 17))
self.radioButton_5.setObjectName(_fromUtf8("radioButton_5"))
self.radioButton_4 = QtGui.QRadioButton(self.stackedWidgetPage2)
self.radioButton_4.setGeometry(QtCore.QRect(20, 20, 82, 17))
self.radioButton_4.setObjectName(_fromUtf8("radioButton_4"))
self.stackedWidget.addWidget(self.stackedWidgetPage2)
self.stackedWidgetPage3 = QtGui.QWidget()
self.stackedWidgetPage3.setObjectName(_fromUtf8("stackedWidgetPage3"))
self.checkBox_14 = QtGui.QCheckBox(self.stackedWidgetPage3)
self.checkBox_14.setGeometry(QtCore.QRect(30, 40, 111, 17))
self.checkBox_14.setObjectName(_fromUtf8("checkBox_14"))
self.checkBox_12 = QtGui.QCheckBox(self.stackedWidgetPage3)
self.checkBox_12.setGeometry(QtCore.QRect(30, 10, 81, 17))
self.checkBox_12.setObjectName(_fromUtf8("checkBox_12"))
self.checkBox_11 = QtGui.QCheckBox(self.stackedWidgetPage3)
self.checkBox_11.setGeometry(QtCore.QRect(30, 70, 101, 17))
self.checkBox_11.setObjectName(_fromUtf8("checkBox_11"))
self.checkBox_13 = QtGui.QCheckBox(self.stackedWidgetPage3)
self.checkBox_13.setGeometry(QtCore.QRect(30, 100, 111, 17))
self.checkBox_13.setObjectName(_fromUtf8("checkBox_13"))
self.stackedWidget.addWidget(self.stackedWidgetPage3)
self.comboBox = QtGui.QComboBox(Dialog)
self.comboBox.setGeometry(QtCore.QRect(120, 20, 69, 22))
self.comboBox.setObjectName(_fromUtf8("comboBox"))
self.label = QtGui.QLabel(Dialog)
```

```
        self.label.setGeometry(QtCore.QRect(30, 20, 81, 16))
        self.label.setObjectName(_fromUtf8("label"))
        self.retranslateUi(Dialog)
        self.stackedWidget.setCurrentIndex(2)
        QtCore.QMetaObject.connectSlotsByName(Dialog)

    def retranslateUi(self, Dialog):
        Dialog.setWindowTitle(QtGui.QApplication.translate("Dialog", "Dialog",
None, QtGui.QApplication.UnicodeUTF8))
        self.checkBox_2.setText(QtGui.QApplication.translate("Dialog",
"Hot Dog  5$", None, QtGui.QApplication.UnicodeUTF8))
        self.checkBox_3.setText(QtGui.QApplication.translate("Dialog",
"Chicken Burger 10$", None, QtGui.QApplication.UnicodeUTF8))
        self.checkBox.setText(QtGui.QApplication.translate("Dialog",
"Pizza  25 $", None, QtGui.QApplication.UnicodeUTF8))
        self.radioButton_6.setText(QtGui.QApplication.translate("Dialog",
"Cold Drink 10$", None, QtGui.QApplication.UnicodeUTF8))
        self.radioButton_5.setText(QtGui.QApplication.translate("Dialog",
"Coffee 5$", None, QtGui.QApplication.UnicodeUTF8))
        self.radioButton_4.setText(QtGui.QApplication.translate("Dialog",
"Juice 15$", None, QtGui.QApplication.UnicodeUTF8))
        self.checkBox_14.setText(QtGui.QApplication.translate("Dialog", "Strawberry
7$", None, QtGui.QApplication.UnicodeUTF8))
        self.checkBox_12.setText(QtGui.QApplication.translate("Dialog", "Vanilla
5$", None, QtGui.QApplication.UnicodeUTF8))
        self.checkBox_11.setText(QtGui.QApplication.translate("Dialog", "Pineapple
8$", None, QtGui.QApplication.UnicodeUTF8))
        self.checkBox_13.setText(QtGui.QApplication.translate("Dialog", "Chocolate
10$", None, QtGui.QApplication.UnicodeUTF8))
        self.label.setText(QtGui.QApplication.translate("Dialog", "Select Category",
None, QtGui.QApplication.UnicodeUTF8))
```

Let's modify the calltabwidget.pyw file to display options for the Combo Box and to enable page switching when user selects an option from the Combo Box. The modified Python script will appear as follows:

```
calltabwidgetstacked.pyw
import sys

from tabwidgetstacked import *

class MyForm(QtGui.QDialog):
    def __init__(self, parent=None):
        QtGui.QWidget.__init__(self, parent)
        self.ui = Ui_Dialog()
```

Figure 10.34
The contents of the item selected from a Combo Box displayed in a Stacked widget, enabling page switching.

```
        self.ui.setupUi(self)
        self.ui.comboBox.addItem("Food")
        self.ui.comboBox.addItem("Drinks")
        self.ui.comboBox.addItem("Ice Creams")
        QtCore.QObject.connect(self.ui.comboBox, QtCore.SIGNAL('activated(int)'),
self.ui.stackedWidget, QtCore.SLOT('setCurrentIndex(int)'))

if __name__ == "__main__":
    app = QtGui.QApplication(sys.argv)
    myapp = MyForm()
    myapp.show()
    sys.exit(app.exec_())
```

In the code, you see that the addItem() function adds Food, Drinks, and Ice Creams options to the Combo Box. When any option is selected from the Combo Box, the index location of that option is fetched, and the widget with that index value is opened in the Stacked widget to display its contents. Every widget in the Stacked widget has an index number that can be used to access it. For example, if the Food option is chosen from the Combo Box, its index value is fetched. Being the first option in the Combo Box, its index value will be 0. In the Stacked widget, there are three widgets, Food, Drinks, and Ice Creams, with the index values 0, 1, and 2, respectively. The activated() signal of the Combo Box is connected to set-CurrentIndex() of the Stacked widget, so the widget with index value 0 in the Stacked widget, Food, is accessed and displayed as shown in Figure 10.34.

SUMMARY

In this chapter you learned to create menus and toolbars. Also, you saw the Action Editor and the role it plays in defining actions for menus and toolbars and how to manage resources of an application at one place through a resource file. You saw how to create dockable windows and how to display information in small chunks with the Tab widget. Finally, you learned to convert a Tab widget into a Tool Box or Stacked widget.

The next chapter focuses on MDI and layouts. You will learn to manage multiple documents in a Main Window with MDI and how to organize widgets in different layouts.

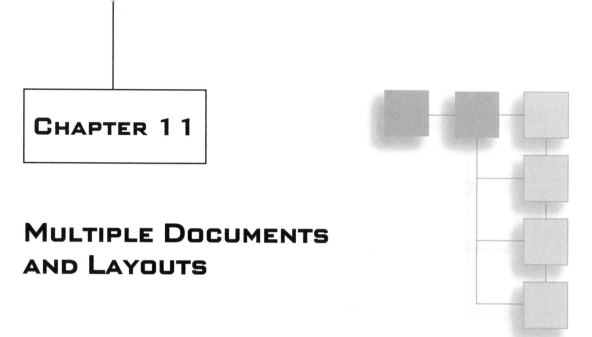

CHAPTER 11

MULTIPLE DOCUMENTS AND LAYOUTS

Until now you have been dealing with a single-document interface. In this chapter you will learn how to manage multiple documents in a main window with MDI. Also, you will learn to organize widgets in different layouts. This chapter covers the following:

- A multiple-document interface
- Layouts
- Displaying widgets collectively through Group Box

Let's begin the chapter with the concept of a multiple-document interface.

MULTIPLE-DOCUMENT INTERFACE

Applications that provide one document per main window are said to be SDI (single-document interface) applications. A multiple-document interface (MDI) consists of a main window containing a menu bar, a toolbar, and a central QWorkspace widget. The job of the central workspace is to display and manage several child windows. The child windows are widgets that are added to the central workspace.

The MDI is a specification that enables you to display multiple documents at the same time, with each document displayed in its own window. One document acts as a parent window, and other documents are its child windows (contained in the parent window). The parent window provides a workspace for the child windows in the application.

To implement an MDI, you will use an MdiArea widget, which is an instance of the QMdiArea class. The MdiArea widget provides an area where child windows (also

317

called *subwindows*) are displayed. It arranges subwindows in a cascade or tile pattern. The subwindows are instances of `QMdiSubWindow`. They are rendered within a frame that has a title and buttons to show, hide, and maximize it. By default, the subwindows are deleted when closed in the MDI area.

First let's look at the methods provided by `QMdiArea`. Table 11.1 shows the methods provided.

Table 11.1   Methods Provided by QMdiArea

Method	Use
`subWindowList()`	Returns a list of all subwindows in the MDI area arranged in the order set through the `WindowOrder()` function.
`WindowOrder()`	Used to specify the criteria for ordering the list of child windows returned by `subWindowList()`. Following are the available options: `CreationOrder`: The windows are returned in the order of their creation. This is the default order. `StackingOrder`: The windows are returned in the order in which they are stacked, with the topmost window last in the list. `ActivationHistoryOrder`: The windows are returned in the order in which they were activated.
`activateNextSubWindow()`	Sets the focus to the next window in the list of child windows. The current window order determines the next window to be activated.
`activatePreviousSubWindow()`	Sets the keyboard focus to the previous window in the list of child windows. The current window order determines the previous window to be activated.
`cascadeSubWindows()`	Arranges subwindows in cascade fashion.
`tileSubWindows()`	Arranges subwindows in tile fashion.
`closeAllSubWindows()`	Closes all subwindows.
`setViewMode()`	Sets the view mode of the MDI area. The subwindows can be viewed in two view modes, SubWindow view and Tabbed view: SubWindow view: Displays subwindows with window frames (default). You can see the content of more than one subwindow if arranged in tile fashion. It is also represented by a constant value 0. Tabbed view: Displays subwindows with tabs in a tab bar. Only one subwindow's content can be seen at a time. It is also represented by a constant value 1.

Note

The `cascadeSubWindows()` and `tileSubWindows()` methods arrange windows in the order determined through `WindowOrder()` function.

To understand the multiple-document interface practically, let's create a new Main Window application and drop an MdiArea widget on the form. Right-click on the widget and select Add Subwindow from the context menu to add a subwindow to the MdiArea. In Figure 11.1 you can see a subwindow inside an MdiArea widget. The MdiArea widget appears in dark background.

Repeat the procedure to add one more subwindow. Drag and drop some widgets in the respective subwindows to show some content. Drop Label and TextEdit widgets in the first subwindow and a Label widget in another subwindow and set their text as shown in Figure 11.2. To change focus from one subwindow to another and arrange them in cascade and tile fashion, you need Push Buttons, so drag and drop seven Push Button controls onto the form and set their text to Show Next, Show Previous, Close All, Cascade, Tile, SubWindow View, and Tabbed View as shown in Figure 11.2.

As previously stated, documents in the MdiArea can be viewed in two modes, Sub-Window view and Tabbed view. SubWindow view is the default view mode. Subwindows can be arranged in cascade or tile fashion, and the content of more than one

Figure 11.1
The MdiArea widget with a subwindow.

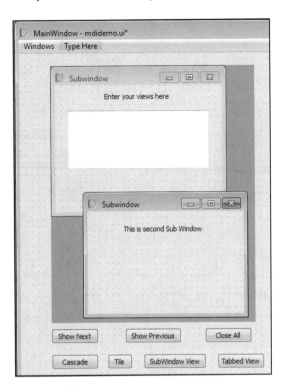

Figure 11.2
A form displaying the MdiArea with two subwindows and seven Push Buttons.

subwindow can be seen simultaneously if arranged in tile fashion. In Tabbed view, several tabs appear in a tab bar. When a tab is selected, the subwindow associated to it is displayed. Only content of one subwindow can be seen at a time.

Since you want to arrange and activate subwindows in the MdiArea through a menu, replace the Type Here placeholder in the menu in the menu bar with Windows and add two entries to it: First Window and Second Window.

Save the application with the name `mdidemo.ui`. The default location where the application will be saved is C:\Python32\Lib\site-packages\PyQt4. Then use the `pyuic4` command line utility to convert the `.ui` (XML) file into Python code as shown here:

```
C:\Python32\Lib\site-packages\PyQt4>pyuic4 mdidemo.ui -o mdidemo.py.
```

The generated Python code will appear as follows:

```
mdidemo.py
# Form implementation generated from reading ui file 'MDIdemo.ui'
from PyQt4 import QtCore, QtGui
```

```
try:
    _fromUtf8 = QtCore.QString.fromUtf8
except AttributeError:
    _fromUtf8 = lambda s: s

class Ui_MainWindow(object):
    def setupUi(self, MainWindow):
        MainWindow.setObjectName(_fromUtf8("MainWindow"))
        MainWindow.resize(775, 600)
        MainWindow.setWindowTitle(QtGui.QApplication.translate("MainWindow",
"MainWindow", None, QtGui.QApplication.UnicodeUTF8))
        self.centralwidget = QtGui.QWidget(MainWindow)
        self.centralwidget.setObjectName(_fromUtf8("centralwidget"))
        self.showNext = QtGui.QPushButton(self.centralwidget)
        self.showNext.setGeometry(QtCore.QRect(50, 430, 75, 23))
        self.showNext.setText(QtGui.QApplication.translate("MainWindow", "Show Next",
None, QtGui.QApplication.UnicodeUTF8))
        self.showNext.setObjectName(_fromUtf8("showNext"))
        self.cascadeButton = QtGui.QPushButton(self.centralwidget)
        self.cascadeButton.setGeometry(QtCore.QRect(50, 470, 75, 23))
        self.cascadeButton.setText(QtGui.QApplication.translate("MainWindow",
"Cascade", None, QtGui.QApplication.UnicodeUTF8))
        self.cascadeButton.setObjectName(_fromUtf8("cascadeButton"))
        self.SubWindowViewButton = QtGui.QPushButton(self.centralwidget)
        self.SubWindowViewButton.setGeometry(QtCore.QRect(200, 470, 101, 23))

self.SubWindowViewButton.setText(QtGui.QApplication.translate("MainWindow",
"SubWindow View", None, QtGui.QApplication.UnicodeUTF8))
        self.SubWindowViewButton.setObjectName(_fromUtf8("SubWindowViewButton"))
        self.closeAll = QtGui.QPushButton(self.centralwidget)
        self.closeAll.setGeometry(QtCore.QRect(300, 430, 75, 23))
        self.closeAll.setText(QtGui.QApplication.translate("MainWindow", "Close All",
None, QtGui.QApplication.UnicodeUTF8))
        self.closeAll.setObjectName(_fromUtf8("closeAll"))
        self.tileButton = QtGui.QPushButton(self.centralwidget)
        self.tileButton.setGeometry(QtCore.QRect(140, 470, 41, 23))
        self.tileButton.setText(QtGui.QApplication.translate("MainWindow",
"Tile", None, QtGui.QApplication.UnicodeUTF8))
        self.tileButton.setObjectName(_fromUtf8("tileButton"))
        self.mdiArea = QtGui.QMdiArea(self.centralwidget)
        self.mdiArea.setGeometry(QtCore.QRect(50, 20, 331, 401))
        self.mdiArea.setObjectName(_fromUtf8("mdiArea"))
        self.subwindow = QtGui.QWidget()
        self.subwindow.setWindowTitle(QtGui.QApplication.translate("MainWindow",
"Subwindow", None, QtGui.QApplication.UnicodeUTF8))
        self.subwindow.setObjectName(_fromUtf8("subwindow"))
```

```
        self.label = QtGui.QLabel(self.subwindow)
        self.label.setGeometry(QtCore.QRect(80, 10, 111, 16))
        self.label.setText(QtGui.QApplication.translate("MainWindow", "Enter your
views here", None, QtGui.QApplication.UnicodeUTF8))
        self.label.setObjectName(_fromUtf8("label"))
        self.textEdit = QtGui.QTextEdit(self.subwindow)
        self.textEdit.setGeometry(QtCore.QRect(20, 40, 231, 91))
        self.textEdit.setObjectName(_fromUtf8("textEdit"))
        self.subwindow_2 = QtGui.QWidget()

self.subwindow_2.setWindowTitle(QtGui.QApplication.translate("MainWindow",
"Subwindow", None, QtGui.QApplication.UnicodeUTF8))
        self.subwindow_2.setObjectName(_fromUtf8("subwindow_2"))
        self.label_2 = QtGui.QLabel(self.subwindow_2)
        self.label_2.setGeometry(QtCore.QRect(60, 20, 141, 16))
        self.label_2.setText(QtGui.QApplication.translate("MainWindow",
"<!DOCTYPE HTML PUBLIC \"-//W3C//DTD HTML 4.0//EN\" \"http://www.w3.org/TR/
REC-html40/strict.dtd\">\n"
"<html><head><meta name=\"qrichtext\" content=\"1\" /><style type=\"text/css\">\n"
"p, li { white-space: pre-wrap; }\n"
"</style></head><body style=\" font-family:\'MS Shell Dlg 2\'; font-size:8.25pt;
font-weight:400; font-style:normal;\">\n"
"<p style=\" margin-top:0px; margin-bottom:0px; margin-left:0px; margin-right:0px;
-qt-block-indent:0; text-indent:0px;\"><span style=\" font-size:8pt;\">This is
second Sub Window</span></p></body></html>", None, QtGui.QApplication.UnicodeUTF8))
        self.label_2.setObjectName(_fromUtf8("label_2"))
        self.showPrevious = QtGui.QPushButton(self.centralwidget)
        self.showPrevious.setGeometry(QtCore.QRect(170, 430, 91, 23))
        self.showPrevious.setText(QtGui.QApplication.translate("MainWindow",
"Show Previous", None, QtGui.QApplication.UnicodeUTF8))
        self.showPrevious.setObjectName(_fromUtf8("showPrevious"))
        self.TabbedViewButton = QtGui.QPushButton(self.centralwidget)
        self.TabbedViewButton.setGeometry(QtCore.QRect(320, 470, 75, 23))
        self.TabbedViewButton.setText(QtGui.QApplication.translate("MainWindow",
"Tabbed View", None, QtGui.QApplication.UnicodeUTF8))
        self.TabbedViewButton.setObjectName(_fromUtf8("TabbedViewButton"))
        MainWindow.setCentralWidget(self.centralwidget)
        self.menubar = QtGui.QMenuBar(MainWindow)
        self.menubar.setGeometry(QtCore.QRect(0, 0, 775, 21))
        self.menubar.setObjectName(_fromUtf8("menubar"))
        self.menuWindows = QtGui.QMenu(self.menubar)
        self.menuWindows.setTitle(QtGui.QApplication.translate("MainWindow",
"Windows", None, QtGui.QApplication.UnicodeUTF8))
        self.menuWindows.setObjectName(_fromUtf8("menuWindows"))
```

```
        MainWindow.setMenuBar(self.menubar)
        self.statusbar = QtGui.QStatusBar(MainWindow)
        self.statusbar.setObjectName(_fromUtf8("statusbar"))
        MainWindow.setStatusBar(self.statusbar)
        self.actionFirst_Window = QtGui.QAction(MainWindow)

self.actionFirst_Window.setText(QtGui.QApplication.translate("MainWindow",
"First Window", None, QtGui.QApplication.UnicodeUTF8))
        self.actionFirst_Window.setObjectName(_fromUtf8("actionFirst_Window"))
        self.actionSecond_Window = QtGui.QAction(MainWindow)

self.actionSecond_Window.setText(QtGui.QApplication.translate("MainWindow",
"Second Window", None, QtGui.QApplication.UnicodeUTF8))
        self.actionSecond_Window.setObjectName(_fromUtf8("actionSecond_Window"))
        self.menuWindows.addAction(self.actionFirst_Window)
        self.menuWindows.addAction(self.actionSecond_Window)
        self.menubar.addAction(self.menuWindows.menuAction())

        self.retranslateUi(MainWindow)
        QtCore.QMetaObject.connectSlotsByName(MainWindow)

    def retranslateUi(self, MainWindow):
        pass
```

Let's create a Python script that imports the code to invoke the MdiArea to display the subwindows created in it with their respective widgets. Also, the script will contain the code for the Push Buttons to do different tasks, such as cascading and tiling the windows, changing the focus from one subwindow to another, changing the view mode from SubWindow view to Tabbed view and vice versa, and closing all subwindows. The Python script will be as follows:

```
callMDI.pyw
import sys
from mdidemo import *

class MyForm(QtGui.QMainWindow):
    def __init__(self, parent=None):
        QtGui.QWidget.__init__(self, parent)
        self.ui = Ui_MainWindow()
        self.ui.setupUi(self)
        self.ui.mdiArea.addSubWindow(self.ui.subwindow)
        self.ui.mdiArea.addSubWindow(self.ui.subwindow_2)
        QtCore.QObject.connect(self.ui.showNext, QtCore.SIGNAL('clicked()'),
self.displayNext)
        QtCore.QObject.connect(self.ui.showPrevious, QtCore.SIGNAL('clicked()'),
self.displayPrevious)
```

```
    QtCore.QObject.connect(self.ui.closeAll, QtCore.SIGNAL('clicked()'),
self.closeAll)
    QtCore.QObject.connect(self.ui.cascadeButton, QtCore.SIGNAL('clicked()'),
self.cascadeArrange)
    QtCore.QObject.connect(self.ui.tileButton, QtCore.SIGNAL('clicked()'),
self.tileArrange)
    QtCore.QObject.connect(self.ui.SubWindowViewButton,
QtCore.SIGNAL('clicked()'), self.SubWindowView)
    QtCore.QObject.connect(self.ui.TabbedViewButton,  QtCore.SIGNAL('clicked()'),
self.TabbedView)
    self.connect(self.ui.actionFirst_Window, QtCore.SIGNAL('triggered()'),
self.displayNext)
    self.connect(self.ui.actionSecond_Window, QtCore.SIGNAL('triggered()'),
self.displayPrevious)

  def displayNext(self):
    self.ui.mdiArea.activateNextSubWindow()

  def displayPrevious(self):
     self.ui.mdiArea.activatePreviousSubWindow()

  def closeAll(self):
    self.ui.mdiArea.closeAllSubWindows()

  def cascadeArrange(self):
    self.ui.mdiArea.cascadeSubWindows()

  def tileArrange(self):
    self.ui.mdiArea.tileSubWindows()

  def SubWindowView(self):
    self.ui.mdiArea.setViewMode(0)

  def TabbedView(self):
    self.ui.mdiArea.setViewMode(1)

if __name__ == "__main__":
  app = QtGui.QApplication(sys.argv)
  myapp = MyForm()
  myapp.show()
  sys.exit(app.exec_())
```

In the code, you can see that the clicked() signals of the showNext, showPrevious, closeAll, cascadeButton, tileButton, SubWindowViewButton, and TabbedViewButton Push Buttons are connected to the, displayNext(), displayPrevious(), closeAll(), cascadeArrange(), tileArrange(),

`SubWindowView()`, and `TabbedView()` functions, respectively. Also, the First Window and Second Window menu entries of the Windows menu are connected to the `displayNext()` and `displayPrevious()` functions. The functions used in the program are these:

`displayNext()`: Activates the next subwindow in the list. The subwindows list is arranged in the order in which they were created.

`displayPrevious()`: Activates the previous subwindow in the list of subwindows.

`closeAll()`: Closes and deletes all subwindows. The subwindows are deleted by default when closed in the MdiArea.

`cascadeArrange()`: Arranges subwindows in cascade fashion.

`tileArrange()`: Arranges subwindows in tile fashion.

`SubWindowView()`: Sets the view of MdiArea to SubWindow view mode.

`TabbedView()`: Sets the view of MdiArea to Tabbed view mode.

The subwindows initially appear in shrinked mode in the MdiArea. You can drag their borders to the desired size. On selecting First Window from the Windows menu, a subwindow becomes active; on selecting Second Window, the next subwindow will become active as shown in Figure 11.3 (a). The same action will take place on selecting the Show Next and Show Previous buttons at the bottom. On selecting Cascade, the subwindows are arranged in cascade mode, as shown in Figure 11.3 (b).

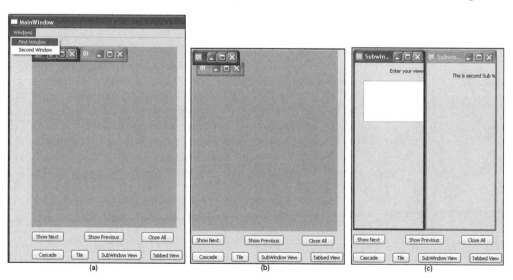

Figure 11.3
(a) Subwindows appear in shrinked form with the first subwindow active. (b) The shrinked subwindows arranged in cascade pattern. (c) Subwindows expanded and arranged in tile pattern.

The subwindows will still be in shrinked mode, though you can drag their borders to expand them. On selecting Tile button, the subwindows are expanded and tiled; both subwindows get equal workspace, as shown in Figure 11.3 (c).

Note

> If windows are maximized, Cascade mode allows the top subwindow to take the whole MdiArea, with other subwindows hidden behind it.

You can drag the boundaries of any subwindow to increase or decrease its size. Figure 11.4(a) shows the first subwindow when its size is increased. You can also minimize a subwindow and drag the boundaries of another subwindow to take the whole width of the MdiArea as shown in Figure 11.4(b). If you select Maximize in any subwindow, it will take up all the space of the MdiArea, making other subwindows invisible as shown in Figure 11.4(c).

On selecting the SubWindow View button, the view mode of the MdiArea changes to SubWindow view, and the border of the maximized subwindow will appear, along with its title and minimize, maximize, and close buttons as shown in Figure 11.5(a). The minimized subwindow behind the maximized subwindow will not be visible. On selecting the Tabbed View button, the MdiArea will change from SubWindow view to Tabbed view as shown in Figure 11.5(b). You can select the tab of any subwindow to make it active as shown in Figure 11.5(c). If you select Close All, all subwindows will be closed.

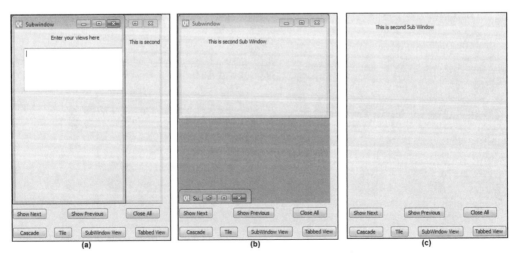

Figure 11.4
(a) Size of first subwindow increased by dragging its boundaries. (b) First subwindow minimized and second subwindow taking up the whole width of the MdiArea widget. (c) Second subwindow maximized, taking up the whole space of the MdiArea widget.

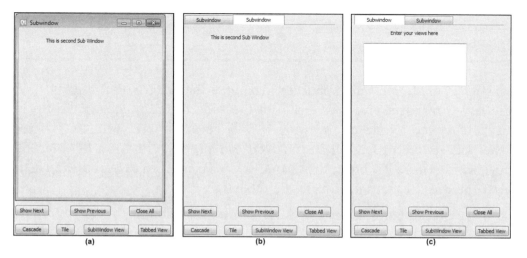

Figure 11.5
(a) Second subwindow in maximized form in SubWindow view. (b) The MdiArea in Tabbed view. (c) The content of the first subwindow appears when the first tab is selected.

LAYOUTS

A layout is used to arrange and manage the widgets that make up a user interface within its container. Qt Designer provides a number of layout managers: Horizontal Layout, Vertical Layout, Grid Layout, and Form Layout. Each widget has a recommended size, and it reports its size requirement to the layout through its $sizeHint$ property. If the layout managers are applied, and you resize the window, the widgets in the layout will also be resized to meet their $sizeHint$. That is, the layout managers automatically adapt to a resize event. You can also set the range for a widget to expand or shrink by implementing widget size constraints through the $minimumSize$ and $maximumSize$ properties. By specifying the values of the two properties in the Property Editor, you can override the default $sizeHint$ property.

On increasing the size of the window, the widgets in the layout also increase in size to use up the increased space, so the widget sometimes may be too wide or long. To avoid excessive spreading of the widgets when window size is increased, you use *spacers*. Spacers expand to fill empty space. Before laying out the widgets, click the form to deselect everything and then select all the widgets you want to be laid out with Shift+click. Once all the widgets are selected, click Layout Manager on the toolbar. The widgets will be laid out in the selected layout, and the layout will be indicated by a red line around the widgets that is not visible at runtime. To arrange more widgets, click the form to deselect again everything and select the widgets you want to arrange in a layout.

Note

Layouts can be nested one inside the other.

When a layout is used, PyQt automatically reparents the widgets that are laid out; that is, the layout manager gives ownership of the widgets and itself to the form in which they are placed. None of the widgets will be a top-level window. To see whether the widgets are properly laid out, you can preview the form by selecting Form, Preview or Ctrl+R. To break the layout, select Form, Break Layout, enter Ctrl +0, or select the Break Layout icon from the toolbar.

Let's look at the procedure of arranging widgets in horizontal box layout.

Horizontal Layout

A horizontal layout arranges widgets next to each other in a row. Let's open the `addtwonum.ui` application in Qt Designer and make a copy with the name `addinlayout.ui`. The application is for adding two numbers entered by the user. Add a Push Button and set its text to **Cancel**. The widgets in the form will now appear as shown in Figure 11.6(a).

Select the Enter First Number Label and a Line Edit widget with Shift+click and select Lay Out Horizontally from the toolbar as shown in Figure 11.6(b). The Label and Line Edit widgets will be laid out horizontally, and a red boundary will appear around them to confirm it.

Similarly, select the Enter Second Number Label and another Line Edit and select Lay Out Horizontally from the toolbar to lay them horizontally.

Repeat the procedure for the Add and Cancel Push Buttons. Now you have three sets of widgets laid out horizontally as shown in Figure 11.6(c).

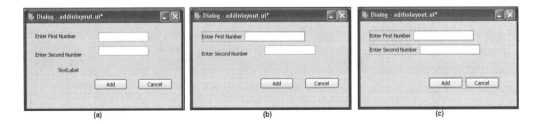

Figure 11.6
(a) Initial layout of the widgets. (b) Label and the first Line Edit arranged in horizontal layout. (c) All widget pairs arranged in horizontal layout.

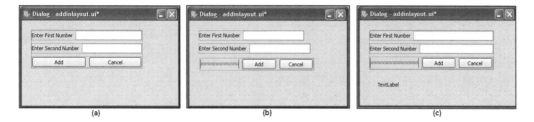

Figure 11.7
(a) The horizontal widgets arranged vertically, allowing the Add and Cancel buttons to spread. (b) Adding a horizontal spacer in front of the buttons. (c) Arranging the widget pairs vertically.

To apply a vertical layout to the three sets of horizontal widgets, select the three sets with Shift+click and select the Lay Out Vertically icon from the toolbar as shown in Figure 11.7(a). The Add and Cancel Push Buttons widen to use the available space. You can control the width of the widgets either by using the `minimumSize` and `maximumSize` properties or by using Horizontal and Vertical Spacer widgets. Let's use the second technique.

Break the vertical layout by selecting its red line boundary and selecting either the Form, Break Layout option, the Ctrl+0 key combination, or the Break Layout icon from the toolbar. Also, break the horizontal layout of the Push Buttons and drag a horizontal spacer from the Spacer section in the Widget Box and drop it in front of the Add button. The spacers appear as blue springs on the form. Adjust the size of the horizontal spacer by dragging its nodes to constrain the width of the buttons. Select all three widgets, the horizontal spacer, and two buttons and place them horizontally, as shown in Figure 11.7(b). Now you can select the three horizontal sets and lay them vertically by selecting the Lay Out Vertically icon. As you can see in Figure 11.7(c), the Add and Cancel buttons will not spread; the empty space is filled by the horizontal spacer.

Save the application with the name `addinlayout.ui`. The `.ui` (XML) file code on converting into Python code with the `pyuic4` command utility will appear as follows:

`addinlayout.py`

```
# Form implementation generated from reading ui file 'addinlayout.ui'
from PyQt4 import QtCore, QtGui

try:
    _fromUtf8 = QtCore.QString.fromUtf8
except AttributeError:
    _fromUtf8 = lambda s: s
```

```python
class Ui_Dialog(object):
    def setupUi(self, Dialog):
        Dialog.setObjectName(_fromUtf8("Dialog"))
        Dialog.resize(346, 183)
        self.layoutWidget = QtGui.QWidget(Dialog)
        self.layoutWidget.setGeometry(QtCore.QRect(21, 21, 276, 85))
        self.layoutWidget.setObjectName(_fromUtf8("layoutWidget"))
        self.verticalLayout = QtGui.QVBoxLayout(self.layoutWidget)
        self.verticalLayout.setMargin(0)
        self.verticalLayout.setObjectName(_fromUtf8("verticalLayout"))
        self.horizontalLayout = QtGui.QHBoxLayout()
        self.horizontalLayout.setObjectName(_fromUtf8("horizontalLayout"))
        self.label = QtGui.QLabel(self.layoutWidget)
        self.label.setObjectName(_fromUtf8("label"))
        self.horizontalLayout.addWidget(self.label)
        self.lineEdit = QtGui.QLineEdit(self.layoutWidget)
        self.lineEdit.setObjectName(_fromUtf8("lineEdit"))
        self.horizontalLayout.addWidget(self.lineEdit)
        self.verticalLayout.addLayout(self.horizontalLayout)
        self.horizontalLayout_2 = QtGui.QHBoxLayout()
        self.horizontalLayout_2.setObjectName(_fromUtf8("horizontalLayout_2"))
        self.label_2 = QtGui.QLabel(self.layoutWidget)
        self.label_2.setObjectName(_fromUtf8("label_2"))
        self.horizontalLayout_2.addWidget(self.label_2)
        self.lineEdit_2 = QtGui.QLineEdit(self.layoutWidget)
        self.lineEdit_2.setObjectName(_fromUtf8("lineEdit_2"))
        self.horizontalLayout_2.addWidget(self.lineEdit_2)
        self.verticalLayout.addLayout(self.horizontalLayout_2)
        self.horizontalLayout_4 = QtGui.QHBoxLayout()
        self.horizontalLayout_4.setObjectName(_fromUtf8("horizontalLayout_4"))
        spacerItem    =    QtGui.QSpacerItem(108,    20,    QtGui.QSizePolicy.Expanding,
QtGui.QSizePolicy.Minimum)
        self.horizontalLayout_4.addItem(spacerItem)
        self.horizontalLayout_3 = QtGui.QHBoxLayout()
        self.horizontalLayout_3.setObjectName(_fromUtf8("horizontalLayout_3"))
        self.pushButton = QtGui.QPushButton(self.layoutWidget)
        self.pushButton.setObjectName(_fromUtf8("pushButton"))
        self.horizontalLayout_3.addWidget(self.pushButton)
        self.pushButton_2 = QtGui.QPushButton(self.layoutWidget)
        self.pushButton_2.setObjectName(_fromUtf8("pushButton_2"))
        self.horizontalLayout_3.addWidget(self.pushButton_2)
        self.horizontalLayout_4.addLayout(self.horizontalLayout_3)
        self.verticalLayout.addLayout(self.horizontalLayout_4)
        self.label_3 = QtGui.QLabel(Dialog)
```

```
        self.label_3.setGeometry(QtCore.QRect(40, 130, 271, 16))
        self.label_3.setText(_fromUtf8(""))
        self.label_3.setObjectName(_fromUtf8("label_3"))
        self.retranslateUi(Dialog)
        QtCore.QMetaObject.connectSlotsByName(Dialog)

    def retranslateUi(self, Dialog):
        Dialog.setWindowTitle(QtGui.QApplication.translate("Dialog", "Dialog", None,
QtGui.QApplication.UnicodeUTF8))
        self.label.setText(QtGui.QApplication.translate("Dialog", "Enter First Num-
ber", None, QtGui.QApplication.UnicodeUTF8))
        self.label_2.setText(QtGui.QApplication.translate("Dialog", "Enter Second Num-
ber", None, QtGui.QApplication.UnicodeUTF8))
        self.pushButton.setText(QtGui.QApplication.translate("Dialog", "Add", None,
QtGui.QApplication.UnicodeUTF8))
        self.pushButton_2.setText(QtGui.QApplication.translate("Dialog", "Cancel",
None, QtGui.QApplication.UnicodeUTF8))
```

You need to create a Python script to import the code to invoke the widgets, compute and display the sum of the numbers entered, and close the application. The file will appear as shown below:

```
callnumadd.pyw
import sys
from addinlayout import *

class MyForm(QtGui.QDialog):
    def __init__(self, parent=None):
        QtGui.QWidget.__init__(self, parent)
        self.ui = Ui_Dialog()
        self.ui.setupUi(self)
        QtCore.QObject.connect(self.ui.pushButton, QtCore.SIGNAL('clicked()'),
self.dispsum)
        QtCore.QObject.connect(self.ui.pushButton_2, QtCore.SIGNAL('clicked()'),
self.reject)

    def reject(self):
        self.close()

    def dispsum(self):
        if len(self.ui.lineEdit.text())!=0:
            a=int(self.ui.lineEdit.text())
        else:
            a=0
        if len(self.ui.lineEdit_2.text())!=0:
            b=int(self.ui.lineEdit_2.text())
```

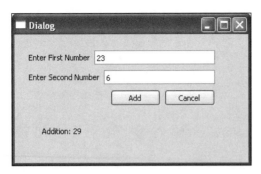

Figure 11.8
The widgets arranged in a combined layout.

```
        else:
            b=0
        sum=a+b
        self.ui.label_3.setText("Addition: " +str(sum))

if __name__ == "__main__":
    app = QtGui.QApplication(sys.argv)
    myapp = MyForm()
    myapp.show()
    sys.exit(app.exec_())
```

The clicked() signal of the Add Push Button is connected to the dispsum() function, and that of the Cancel Push Button is connected to the reject() method. In the reject() method, you simply close the application. In the dispsum() function, you validate the two Line Edit widgets to see if the user left any of them blank. The validation process assumes the value of a blank Line Edit to be 0. The addition of the two values is then displayed through a Label widget after converting it into string data type, as shown in Figure 11.8.

Sometimes you need to collect certain widgets in a frame to show that they are meant to perform similar tasks or belong to the same category. Let's see how to do so.

Using a Group Box

A Group Box is used to represent information that is related in some way. For instance, information about an assortment of laptops, smartphones, or audio CDs can be collected into individual Group Boxes. A Group Box is an instance of the QGroupBox class and appears in a frame with a title. Child widgets within a Group Box can be aligned and enabled or disabled collectively with a Check Box. That is, a Group Box can be set to appear with its title, and all child widgets within it can be enabled or disabled just by checking or unchecking the checkbox. A shortcut key can also be assigned to a Group Box so that the focus of the keyboard can be set to one of the Group Box's child widgets.

The properties of the Group Box are these:

checkable: Enable this property to display a checkbox in the Group Box's title. The child widgets in a checkable Group Box are enabled only when the checkbox is checked. By default, Group Boxes are not checkable. If this property is enabled for a Group Box, it will be checked to ensure that its contents are enabled.

flat: By enabling this property, the space consumed by the Group Box is reduced. The methods supported by the QGroupBox class are these:

isCheckable(): This method returns true if the Group Box has checkbox in its title; otherwise it returns false.

isChecked(): This method returns true if the Group Box is checked.

setChecked(): This method determines whether to display a checkbox in the Group Box's title. A Boolean true value to this method makes the Group Box checkable.

The Group Box generates a clicked() signal when the checkbox is selected or when its shortcut key is pressed.

Let's look at how to arrange widgets in a vertical layout.

Vertical Layout

Vertical layout arranges the selected widgets vertically, in a column one below another. In the following application, you will learn the concept of using Group Box as well as the process of laying widgets in a vertical layout.

Open Qt Designer and create a new application based on the Dialog without Buttons template and drag and drop two Group Box widgets onto the form. Set their titles to Ice Creams and Drinks. Also, set the checkable property of the Drinks Group Box to True, using the Property Editor. Add four Radio Buttons to the Ice Creams Group Box and three Radio Buttons to the Drinks Group Box. Set the text properties of the Radio Buttons in Ice Creams Group Box to Plain Vanilla $5, Black Sunday $10, Chocolate Chips $20, and Strawberry $15. Similarly, set the text property of the Radio Buttons in the Drinks Group Box to Coffee $5, Cold Drink $10, and Juice $15. To display the price of an item from the Group Boxes, drag and drop a Label widget and delete its text property; you will assign text to it, i.e., total price of the items selected, through programming. On deleting text property of the Label widget, it becomes invisible. Drag and drop two Vertical Spacers on the form, one above and

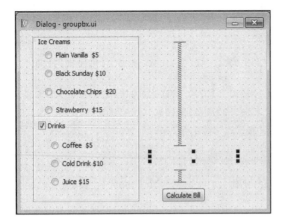

Figure 11.9
The widgets arranged in vertical layout.

one below the Label widget. Finally drop a Push Button on the form and set its text to Calculate Bill. To lay our the two Group Boxes, Ice Creams and Drinks vertically, select both of them through Shift+click and select Lay Out Vertically icon from the toolbar. Both the Group Boxes will be laid vertically as will be confirmed by a boundary of red line that appears around them. After doing all these operations, our form will appear as shown in Figure 11.9.

Note

Vertical spacers are used to avoid vertical spreading of any widgets as they use up the extra vertical space.

Using the Grid Layout

The Grid Layout arranges widgets in a stretchable grid. Select the vertical Group Boxes, vertical spacers, the invisible Label widget (its nodes will appear if you click its approximate location), and the Calculate Bill Push Button with Shift+click and select the Grid Layout icon from the toolbar. All the widgets will be laid in a grid layout and will be surrounded by a red boundary as shown in Figure 11.10. The figure also shows the Object Inspector window.

Save the application under the name `groupbx.ui`. The python code generated on applying `pyuic4` command utility on the `.ui` file will appear as shown below:

`groupbx.py`

```
# Form implementation generated from reading ui file 'groupbx.ui'

try:
    _fromUtf8 = QtCore.QString.fromUtf8
```

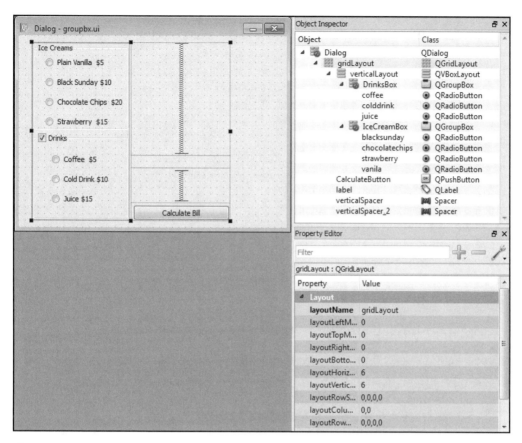

Figure 11.10
Applying Grid Layout to the widgets on the form.

```
except AttributeError:
    _fromUtf8 = lambda s: s

class Ui_Dialog(object):
    def setupUi(self, Dialog):
        Dialog.setObjectName(_fromUtf8("Dialog"))
        Dialog.resize(419, 291)
        Dialog.setWindowTitle(QtGui.QApplication.translate("Dialog", "Dialog", None,
QtGui.QApplication.UnicodeUTF8))
        self.layoutWidget = QtGui.QWidget(Dialog)
        self.layoutWidget.setGeometry(QtCore.QRect(20, 10, 311, 271))
        self.layoutWidget.setObjectName(_fromUtf8("layoutWidget"))
        self.gridLayout = QtGui.QGridLayout(self.layoutWidget)
        self.gridLayout.setMargin(0)
        self.gridLayout.setObjectName(_fromUtf8("gridLayout"))
        self.verticalLayout = QtGui.QVBoxLayout()
        self.verticalLayout.setObjectName(_fromUtf8("verticalLayout"))
```

```
        self.IceCreamBox = QtGui.QGroupBox(self.layoutWidget)
        self.IceCreamBox.setTitle(QtGui.QApplication.translate("Dialog", "Ice Creams",
None, QtGui.QApplication.UnicodeUTF8))
        self.IceCreamBox.setObjectName(_fromUtf8("IceCreamBox"))
        self.vanilla = QtGui.QRadioButton(self.IceCreamBox)
        self.vanilla.setGeometry(QtCore.QRect(20, 20, 131, 17))
        self.vanilla.setText(QtGui.QApplication.translate("Dialog", "Plain Vanilla $5",
None, QtGui.QApplication.UnicodeUTF8))
        self.vanilla.setObjectName(_fromUtf8("vanilla"))
        self.blacksunday = QtGui.QRadioButton(self.IceCreamBox)
        self.blacksunday.setGeometry(QtCore.QRect(20, 50, 121, 17))
        self.blacksunday.setText(QtGui.QApplication.translate("Dialog", "Black Sunday
$10", None, QtGui.QApplication.UnicodeUTF8))
        self.blacksunday.setObjectName(_fromUtf8("blacksunday"))
        self.chocolatechips = QtGui.QRadioButton(self.IceCreamBox)
        self.chocolatechips.setGeometry(QtCore.QRect(20, 80, 141, 17))
        self.chocolatechips.setText(QtGui.QApplication.translate("Dialog", "Chocolate
Chips $20", None, QtGui.QApplication.UnicodeUTF8))
        self.chocolatechips.setObjectName(_fromUtf8("chocolatechips"))
        self.strawberry = QtGui.QRadioButton(self.IceCreamBox)
        self.strawberry.setGeometry(QtCore.QRect(20, 110, 121, 17))
        self.strawberry.setText(QtGui.QApplication.translate("Dialog", "Strawberry $15 ",
None, QtGui.QApplication.UnicodeUTF8))
        self.strawberry.setObjectName(_fromUtf8("strawberry"))
        self.verticalLayout.addWidget(self.IceCreamBox)
        self.DrinksBox = QtGui.QGroupBox(self.layoutWidget)
        self.DrinksBox.setTitle(QtGui.QApplication.translate("Dialog", "Drinks", None,
QtGui.QApplication.UnicodeUTF8))
        self.DrinksBox.setCheckable(True)
        self.DrinksBox.setObjectName(_fromUtf8("DrinksBox"))
        self.coffee = QtGui.QRadioButton(self.DrinksBox)
        self.coffee.setGeometry(QtCore.QRect(30, 30, 82, 17))
        self.coffee.setText(QtGui.QApplication.translate("Dialog", "Coffee  $5", None,
QtGui.QApplication.UnicodeUTF8))
        self.coffee.setObjectName(_fromUtf8("coffee"))
        self.colddrink = QtGui.QRadioButton(self.DrinksBox)
        self.colddrink.setGeometry(QtCore.QRect(30, 60, 101, 17))
        self.colddrink.setText(QtGui.QApplication.translate("Dialog", "Cold Drink $10",
None, QtGui.QApplication.UnicodeUTF8))
        self.colddrink.setObjectName(_fromUtf8("colddrink"))
        self.juice = QtGui.QRadioButton(self.DrinksBox)
        self.juice.setGeometry(QtCore.QRect(30, 90, 82, 17))
        self.juice.setText(QtGui.QApplication.translate("Dialog", "Juice $15", None,
QtGui.QApplication.UnicodeUTF8))
```

```
        self.juice.setObjectName(_fromUtf8("juice"))
        self.verticalLayout.addWidget(self.DrinksBox)
        self.gridLayout.addLayout(self.verticalLayout, 0, 0, 4, 1)
        spacerItem    =    QtGui.QSpacerItem(20,    168,    QtGui.QSizePolicy.Minimum,
QtGui.QSizePolicy.Expanding)
        self.gridLayout.addItem(spacerItem, 0, 1, 1, 1)
        self.label = QtGui.QLabel(self.layoutWidget)
        self.label.setText(_fromUtf8(""))
        self.label.setObjectName(_fromUtf8("label"))
        self.gridLayout.addWidget(self.label, 1, 1, 1, 1)
        spacerItem1    =    QtGui.QSpacerItem(20,    18,    QtGui.QSizePolicy.Minimum,
QtGui.QSizePolicy.Expanding)
        self.gridLayout.addItem(spacerItem1, 2, 1, 1, 1)
        self.CalculateButton = QtGui.QPushButton(self.layoutWidget)
        self.CalculateButton.setText(QtGui.QApplication.translate("Dialog", "Calculate
Bill", None, QtGui.QApplication.UnicodeUTF8))
        self.CalculateButton.setObjectName(_fromUtf8("CalculateButton"))
        self.gridLayout.addWidget(self.CalculateButton, 3, 1, 1, 1)
        self.retranslateUi(Dialog)
        QtCore.QMetaObject.connectSlotsByName(Dialog)

    def retranslateUi(self, Dialog):
        pass
```

Now you need to create a Python script that imports the code to display the user interface design, the widgets that you laid in Vertical and Grid Layout. Also, you need to write code to inspect each Radio Button and compute and display the bill on the basis of the Radio Buttons that are checked. The file will have the following code:

```
callgroupbox.pyw
import sys
from groupbx import *

class MyForm(QtGui.QDialog):
    def __init__(self, parent=None):
        QtGui.QWidget.__init__(self, parent)
        self.ui = Ui_Dialog()
        self.ui.setupUi(self)
        QtCore.QObject.connect(self.ui.CalculateButton, QtCore.SIGNAL('clicked()'),
self.calculatebill)

    def calculatebill(self):
        bill=0
        if self.ui.vanilla.isChecked()==True:
```

```
            bill=bill+5
        if self.ui.blacksunday.isChecked()==True:
            bill=bill+10
        if self.ui.chocolatechips.isChecked()==True:
            bill=bill+20
        if self.ui.strawberry.isChecked()==True:
            bill=bill+15
        if self.ui.DrinksBox.isChecked()==True:
            if self.ui.coffee.isChecked()==True:
                bill=bill+5
            if self.ui.colddrink.isChecked()==True:
                bill=bill+10
            if self.ui.juice.isChecked()==True:
                bill=bill+15
        self.ui.label.setText("The bill is: "+str(bill)+"$")

if __name__ == "__main__":
    app = QtGui.QApplication(sys.argv)
    myapp = MyForm()
    myapp.show()
    sys.exit(app.exec_())
```

You see that the clicked() signal of the Calculate Bill Push Button is connected to the calculatebill() method. When the Calculate Bill button is selected, the calculatebill() method will be invoked. In the calculatebill() method, the status of each Radio Button is checked(). If the Radio Button is checked, its amount will be added to the bill variable. Finally, the value in the bill variable is displayed with a Label widget after converting it to string data type as shown in Figure 11.11(a). Figure 11.11(b) shows how all the widgets contained in the Drinks Group Box are disabled when its checkbox is deselected.

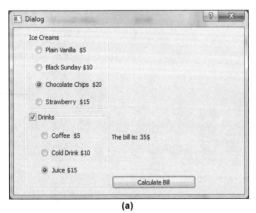

(a)   (b)

Figure 11.11
(a) The widgets arranged in grid layout, displaying the bill of the selected items. (b) All widgets of the Drinks Group Box are disabled on unselecting its Check Box.

SUMMARY

In this chapter, you learned to manage multiple documents in a Main Window through an MDI. You saw how child windows in the MdiArea can be arranged in cascade and tile fashions. You learned to place a collection of widgets that do similar tasks in a Group Box. Also, you learned to organize widgets in different layouts.

In the next chapter, you will learn to save the data entered by the user into a database when running a GUI application. You will learn to install and use the MySQLdb module. Also, you will learn to create Python scripts for creating database tables. You will learn to maintain a database through console-based programs and with GUI programs. Finally, you will learn to insert, fetch, search, delete, and update information in database tables with Python scripts.

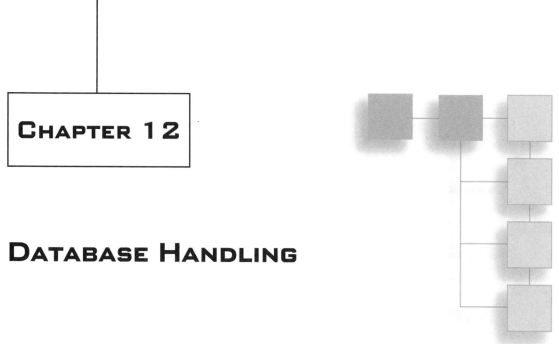

CHAPTER 12

DATABASE HANDLING

Sometimes you need to save data entered by the user for future use. There are two ways to save data that is supplied by the user while running an application. The first way is to use traditional file handling, which you saw in Chapter 6, "File Handling." The second way is to use a database management system. A traditional file system lacks several features, such as indexing, encryption, and joining or merging files. A traditional file handling also is not efficient in handling large volumes of data. A database management system is, and it also provides features such as auto backup, indexing, data sharing, security, and integrity. You will focus on database handling in this chapter, which covers the following:

- Installing and using a MySQLdb module
- Creating databases and tables
- Database maintenance through console-based programs
- Inserting, fetching, and searching rows in a database table
- Updating and deleting information in a database table
- Database maintenance through GUI programs
- Displaying rows in a database table
- Navigating rows of a table
- Maintaining information in a database table

Let's begin with MySQL and MySQLdb. To interface with a database using Python, you need the Python database API, which supports a wide range of database servers, such as MySQL, PostgreSQL, Informix, Microsoft SQL Server 2000, and Oracle. You need to download a separate database API module for each database you want to access. I will explain the procedure to access MySQL Database Server through Python.

WHY MYSQL?

MySQL is one of the most popular relational database management systems in use today. It's open-source software released under the GNU General Public License (GPL) and is fast, reliable, and very easy to learn. Above all, it's free for most uses on all supported platforms. An outline of the benefits of MySQL are as follows:

- MySQL is a very popular database system among web developers. Under the General Public License, MySQL is an open-source system. So that means a developer can work with this server without paying anything.

- MySQL takes less storage space in the disk drive and has remarkable performance.

- It is available for several platforms, including Windows, UNIX, LINUX, FreeBSD, and Mac OS.

- It is easy to maintain and upgrade.

- MySQL is secure. It includes encryption/decryption functions as well as other security measures.

- It has an efficient query engine.

The benefits of storing information in databases are many. Fetching data is much faster than with traditional file systems, as databases use indexing, hashing, and other schemes to quickly find the desired data. Databases usually have auto-backup and restore facilities, encryption for high security, and built-in integrity constraints. For accessing MySQL Database Server through Python, you need to download and install the MySQLdb module.

Note

> Before proceeding with installing the MySQLdb module, make sure that MySQL database server is installed on your computer. You can download the current version from the following URL: http://dev .mysql.com/downloads/. The latest version at the time of this writing is MySQL 5.5. Simply download the file `mysql-installer-5.5.16.0.msi`, and double-click it to initiate the installation procedure. Just follow the Setup wizard, and MySQL server will be installed on your computer. Remember that while installing MySQL, you will be asked to specify the password of the root user of the MySQL server. I have used the root password `mce` in the applications created for this chapter. If you specify some other password for the root, then you will need to replace `mce` in the chapter scripts with your own password.

MySQLdb

MySQLdb is an interface for connecting Python code to a MySQL database server. You can insert, fetch, delete, and update database tables by writing simple SQL statements and executing through Python code. MySQLdb implements the Python Database API v2.0 and is built on top of the MySQL C API. To install a MySQLdb module, download its latest version from the Internet and proceed as explained below. There are many sites that provide a Windows installer file for MySQLdb. I have downloaded the module from http://www.lfd.uci.edu/~gohlke/pythonlibs/.

Installation of MySQLdb

Double-click the downloaded file, `MySQL-Python-1.2.3.win32-py3.2.exe`, to initiate MySQLdb installation. You get a dialog box (Figure 12.1) indicating that the wizard is going to install `MySQL-Python` on your computer. Also, a brief introduction of MySQLdb will appear. Select Next.

The wizard will check your system for all the Python versions that are installed on your computer and display them in list. You will be prompted to select the Python version that you want to use with the MySQLdb module. The wizard will also display

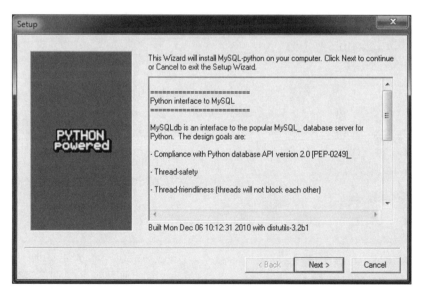

Figure 12.1
The dialog box of the Mysql-Python Setup Wizard with all description of MySQLdb.

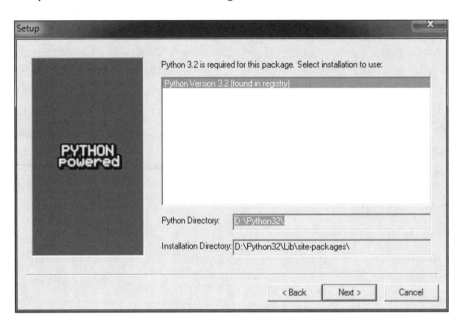

Figure 12.2
Dialog box to select the Python version and specify the installation directory for MySQLdb.

where Python is installed on your machine and where MySQLdb will be installed (Figure 12.2). You can change the directory location if desired. Select Next.

The MySQLdb module will be copied onto your system, and you get a dialog to select Finish to exit the Setup Wizard.

Now you are ready to write SQL-based Python scripts to deal with MySQL Database Server. In the examples you are going to see in this chapter, assume that a dummy database named shopping exists on your MySQL database server. Before you begin to write your first SQL-based Python script, let's first create a database.

CREATING A DATABASE

A database is a collection of information that is organized so that it can easily be accessed, managed, and updated. A database stores tables, their indexes, foreign key constraints, primary key constraints, and other necessary components. A database table consists of columns and rows. Each column contains a single piece of information, and a row is a collection of columns that contains complete information of an object, item, or entity. The database houses all the information stored at the back-end of an application.

To create the shopping database to use in this chapter, launch the MySQL Command-Line Client by selecting Start > MySQL 5.5 Command-Line Client. This

```
mysql> create database shopping ;
Query OK, 1 row affected (0.03 sec)
```

Figure 12.3
SQL command to create a database.

client is an interface that enables you to perform administrative tasks, such as connecting to MySQL server, creating and modifying databases, and executing queries and viewing their results. You will be asked to enter the root's password that you specified while installing MySQL. On entering the correct password, you get the MySQL prompt (mysql>) where you can input SQL commands.

To create a database, you would use the following syntax:

```
create database database_name;
```

Thus to create the example shopping database, enter the following at the MySQL command prompt:

```
mysql> create database shopping;
```

Upon successful execution of the SQL command, MySQL displays a Query OK message, as shown in Figure 12.3. You can, of course, use any other name you like.

Note

The semicolon (;) is essential after every SQL statement to indicate that the statement is finished.

Creating a Database Table

A database table consists of several columns for storing data. For example, a school database table may consist of columns named roll, name, and address that will be used to store roll (student ID) numbers, student names, and their addresses. Each column of the table has to be defined with a specific data type, which determines the type of data it will be able to store. The data types are shown in Table 12.1.

Let's write a Python script that creates a table named products in our shopping database. The products table will have four columns named prod_id, prod_name, quantity, and price. The data type of the columns prod_id and quantity will be smallint, the prod_name column will be of char type with its size set to 50, and price will be of float type. The Python code for creating the table with these four columns is as follows:

```
createtable.py
import sys
import MySQLdb
```

Table 12.1 Data Types in MySQL

Data Type	Stores
`smallint, mediumint, int, bigint`	Integer values
`float`	Single-precision floating-point values
`double`	Double-precision floating-point values
`char`	Fixed-length strings up to 255 characters
`varchar`	Variable-length strings up to 255 characters
`tinyblob, blob, mediumblob, longblob`	Large blocks of binary data
`tinytext, text, mediumtext, longtext`	Long blocks of text data
`date`	Date values
`time`	Time values or durations
`datetime`	Combined date and time values

```
conn=MySQLdb.connect(host="localhost", user="root", passwd="mce", db="shopping")
cursor=conn.cursor()
try:
 cursor.execute ("""
 create table products (prod_id smallint NOT NULL,
 prod_name char(50),
 quantity smallint,
 price float)
 """)
except MySQLdb.Error:
 print ("Error in creating products table")
 sys.exit(1)
cursor.close()
conn.close()
```

Note

Just a reminder: the password of the root user of MySQL server is `mce`. If you specified a different password for the root, then you will need to replace `mce` with your own password.

The methods used are these:

connect(): Connects to the database server. Takes four parameters: host name, user name, password, and database name. The host name specifies the location of our MySQL database server. For the remote database server, you specify its IP address as the host name. For the MySQL Database Server that is locally installed on your computer, you use the term `localhost` for the host name. The username and password of the authorized user are provided, and the name of the database you want is provided as the last parameter.

`cursor()`: Returns the cursor object from the connection. The cursor object is used to traverse the records from the result set.

`execute()`: Used to execute the SQL statement.

`close()`: Disconnects the database connection.

As stated before, using the MySQLdb interface is a better way of working with the MySQL Database Server. So first, import the MySQLdb module. Then connect to the MySQL Database Server with the `connect()` method. Through the `connect()` method, you indicate that you want to connect to the `shopping` database via the authorized user, `root`. When the connection is established, the `Connection` object is returned and saved in the `conn` variable. Through `conn`, you create a `Cursor` object to execute SQL queries. Since you want to create a table named `products` with four columns, `prod_id`, `prod_name`, `quantity`, and `price`, you write a SQL `CREATE` command including the data types and length of the four columns and execute it with an `execute()` method. For exception handling, the `execute()` method is written within a `try` block. If an exception or error occurs while creating the table, an Error in Creating Products Table error message will be displayed on the screen. Finally, you close the Cursor and disconnect the database connection.

The `products` database table will be created in the `shopping` database, and you can confirm by opening the SQL prompt and using the `use database`, `show tables`, and `describe table name` commands.

use database_name

This command loads the specified database into memory. The database loaded in memory is the active or current database, and all SQL commands are executed on that database. Only one database can be in use at any one time. When you use another database, the previous database is automatically closed and unloaded from memory.

```
Syntax:
use database_name;
Example:
use shopping;
```

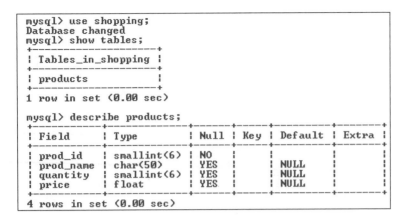

```
mysql> use shopping;
Database changed
mysql> show tables;
+--------------------+
| Tables_in_shopping |
+--------------------+
| products           |
+--------------------+
1 row in set (0.00 sec)

mysql> describe products;
+-----------+-------------+------+-----+---------+-------+
| Field     | Type        | Null | Key | Default | Extra |
+-----------+-------------+------+-----+---------+-------+
| prod_id   | smallint(6) | NO   |     |         |       |
| prod_name | char(50)    | YES  |     | NULL    |       |
| quantity  | smallint(6) | YES  |     | NULL    |       |
| price     | float       | YES  |     | NULL    |       |
+-----------+-------------+------+-----+---------+-------+
4 rows in set (0.00 sec)
```

Figure 12.4
The structure of the `products` database table.

Here, the `shopping` database will be loaded in memory and you get a confirming message, Database Changed (see Figure 12.4).

show tables

This command displays all the tables in the currently open database.

Example:
show tables

If the database is empty and has no tables, an Empty Set message is displayed. Otherwise, the list of tables in the database is shown. Figure 12.4 displays the `products` table, confirming that it was created successfully.

describe table_name

This command displays the structure of the specified table. When executed, a list of columns is displayed, along with their data types. The output also shows if a column can store a `null` value, its default value, and which column is a primary key.

Syntax:
describe table_name
Example:
mysql>describe products;

Figure 12.4 shows the structure of the `products` table.

Now that you have a database table, we will look at database maintenance, such as inserting rows in table, fetching rows from a table, searching rows, updating information in a table, and deleting rows. You will learn database maintenance with two types of programs, console-based and GUI programs. Let's start with console-based programs.

DATABASE MAINTENANCE THROUGH CONSOLE-BASED PROGRAMS

The programs you create in this section are not GUIs, so you won't be able to use your mouse to select or execute actions. You'll need to use the keyboard for all tasks. Let's begin with how rows are inserted into a database table.

Inserting Rows in a Database Table

You learned from the previous program that you can use an execute() method of the cursor object to execute any type of SQL statement. In the following example, you are going to use execute() to insert a row in the products table that you just created. The code is as follows:

```
insertrec.py
import MySQLdb
conn=MySQLdb.connect(host="localhost", user="root", passwd="mce", db="shopping")
cursor=conn.cursor()
cursor.execute("""
INSERT INTO products (prod_id, prod_name, quantity, price)
VALUES (101, 'Camera', 100, 15)
""")
print('One row inserted into the products table')
cursor.close()
conn.commit()
conn.close()
Output:
One row inserted into the products table
```

The program establishes a connection to the MySQL server, creates the cursor object, and executes a SQL INSERT statement to insert a row into the database table. One method that is new here is commit().

commit( )

To apply the modifications to the database table, use the commit() method. Once commit() is executed, then it's not possible to undo the changes.

Confirm if the row is inserted into the products table by accessing it with the MySQL prompt. Use select to retrieve rows in the products table, and you find the newly inserted row, as shown in Figure 12.5.

Let's apply error handling to the program. To handle exceptions in Python, you put code in a try statement and include an except clause that contains the error handling code. To detect database-specific errors, you specify an exception class, MySQLdb.Error, in the except clause. Besides MySQLdb.Error, you might also

```
mysql> select * from products;
+---------+-----------+----------+-------+
| prod_id | prod_name | quantity | price |
+---------+-----------+----------+-------+
|     101 | Camera    |      100 |    15 |
+---------+-----------+----------+-------+
1 row in set (0.00 sec)
```

Figure 12.5
Displaying a new row in the `products` database table.

provide a variable e (any character) in which detailed information of the error such as the error code and description are stored. The previous program with exception handling applied will appear as follows:

```
insertrectry.py
import sys
import MySQLdb
try:
  conn=MySQLdb.connect(host="localhost", user="root", passwd="mce", db="shopping")
except MySQLdb.Error:
  print ("Error in establishing connection")
  sys.exit(1)
cursor=conn.cursor()
try:
  cursor.execute("""
  INSERT INTO products (prod_id, prod_name, quantity, price)
  VALUES (101, 'Camera', 100, 15)
  """)
  conn.commit()
  print('One row inserted into the products table')
except:
  conn.rollback()
cursor.close()
conn.close()
```

You can see that the code for establishing connection is enclosed within a `try` block. If an exception occurs in establishing the database connection, such as database not found or the wrong password is entered, an Error in Establishing Connection error message will appear, and the application will terminate. If no exception occurs in the first `try` block, the program continues to execute. Again, a SQL INSERT statement is written within a `try` block. If an exception occurs because of a bad sector in the disk drive, the disk is full, the table doesn't exist, or something similar, the `rollback()` method will be executed to revert the database table to its last saved version. With exception handling, you get an immediate and detailed message of anything that goes wrong. A brief definition of the `rollback()` method follows in the next section.

rollback()

The `rollback()` method cancels all the modifications applied to the database table. It keeps the database table at the state it was when it was last saved.

The previous program has one drawback: The new row inserted in the `products` table had fixed data; the user was not asked to supply the information for the new row, and instead some dummy data was used. Let's change the program in two ways :

- Ask the user to enter information about the new product
- Instead of just one row, allow the user to insert as many rows as he wants

To apply thesse features, use a `while` loop that inserts rows into the database table until the user wants to stop. Secondly, instead of inserting a dummy product, you will ask the user to enter information of the product to be inserted: the product ID, product name, quantity, and price of the new product. The complete code applying the two features follows:

```
insertrecinput.py
import sys
import MySQLdb
conn=MySQLdb.connect(host="localhost", user="root", passwd="mce", db="shopping")
cursor=conn.cursor()
k="YES"
while k.upper()=="YES" :
  pid=int(input("Enter Product ID: "))
  pname=input("Enter Product Name: ")
  qty=int(input("Enter Quantity: "))
  price=int(input("Enter Price: "))
  try:
    cursor.execute("""
    INSERT INTO products (prod_id, prod_name, quantity, price)
    VALUES (%d, '%s', %d, %f)
    """ %(pid, pname, qty, price))
    conn.commit()
    k=input("Want to insert more products, yes/no: ")
  except:
    conn.rollback()
    sys.exit(1)
cursor.close()
conn.close()
Output :
Enter Product ID: 102
Enter Product Name: Phone
```

```
Enter Quantity: 100
Enter Price: 20
Want to insert more products, yes/no: yes

Enter Product ID: 103
Enter Product Name: Laptop
Enter Quantity: 100
Enter Price: 500
Want to insert more products, yes/no: yes

Enter Product ID: 104
Enter Product Name: Shirts
Enter Quantity: 100
Enter Price: 50
Want to insert more products, yes/no: no
```

You can see in the program that the information of the new product entered by the user is inserted into the `products` table by executing a SQL INSERT statement via the `execute()` method of `cursor`. In case of occurrence of an exception or error, the SQL INSERT command will be cancelled via `rollback()`. After adding three more rows, your `products` table will show four rows as shown in Figure 12.6.

Fetching Rows from the Table

The next step is to learn how to fetch the inserted rows.

When the SQL SELECT statement is executed via `execute()` of the `cursor` object, a `resultset` object is created that contains the rows from the database table that satisfy the specified SQL SELECT criteria. From `resultset`, you can fetch rows with the following two methods:

fetchone(): Fetches the next row in `resultset`.

fetchall(): Fetches all the rows in `resultset`. If some rows have already been retrieved from the `resultset`, the remaining rows will be retrieved.

```
mysql> select * from products;
+---------+-----------+----------+-------+
| prod_id | prod_name | quantity | price |
+---------+-----------+----------+-------+
|     101 | Camera    |      100 |    15 |
|     102 | Phone     |      100 |    20 |
|     103 | Laptop    |      100 |   500 |
|     104 | Shirts    |      100 |    50 |
+---------+-----------+----------+-------+
4 rows in set (0.00 sec)
```

Figure 12.6
Displaying rows in the `products` database table.

You can also use fetchone() in a loop to retrieve all rows from a database table. The following Python script does that. The fetchone() method is used within an infinite while loop to retrieve and display all rows in the products table. Here is the complete code:

```
disprec1.py
import sys
import MySQLdb
conn=MySQLdb.connect(host="localhost", user="root", passwd="mce", db="shopping")
cursor=conn.cursor()
try:
  cursor.execute ("SELECT * from products")
  print ("Product ID\tProduct Name\tQuantity\tPrice")
  while(1):
    row=cursor.fetchone()
    if row==None:
      break
    print ("%d\t\t%s\t\t%d\t\t%f" %(row[0], row[1], row[2], row[3]))
except MySQLdb.Error:
  print ("Error in fetching rows")
  sys.exit(1)
cursor.close()
conn.close()
Output :
Product ID   Product Name   Quantity   Price
101          Camera         100        15.000000
102          Phone          100        20.000000
103          Laptop         100        500.000000
104          Shirts         100        50.000000
```

The steps taken in the program are as follows:

1. Connection to the MySQL Database Server is established.

2. A cursor object is created using the connection object.

3. A SQL SELECT statement is executed using the execute() method of the cursor object, and the result of the SQL QUERY, the resultset object, is created.

4. The column headings for the output are displayed.

5. An infinite while loop is executed.

6. One row from the resultset object is fetched and stored in the row variable. The row variable will become an array with the size equal to the number of columns in the fetched database row: row[0] will contain the data in the first

column of the database row, row[1] will contain the data in the second column of the database row, and so on.

7. If row is None, and all rows from the resultset object are fetched, break out of the infinite while loop.

8. Display the contents of the first four elements in the row array; the information in the prod_id, prod_name, quantity, and price columns of the fetched database row will be displayed.

9. Display error message if an exception error occurs.

10. Close the cursor object.

11. Disconnect the database connection.

This program explains how to use the fetchone() method to fetch rows from a database table. Now let's use another method, fetchall(), for retrieving and displaying all rows of a database table. The program is as follows:

```
disprec2.py
import sys
import MySQLdb
conn=MySQLdb.connect(host="localhost", user="root", passwd="mce", db="shopping")
cursor=conn.cursor()
try:
  cursor.execute ("SELECT * from products")
  print ("Product ID\tProduct Name\tQuantity\tPrice")
  rows=cursor.fetchall()
  for row in rows:
    print ("%d\t\t%s\t\t%d\t\t%f" %(row[0], row[1], row[2], row[3]))
except MySQLdb.Error:
  print ("Error in fetching rows")
  sys.exit(1)
cursor.close()
conn.close()
```

The only difference from the previous program is that here, all the rows from the resultset are fetched and stored in a rows array, where each element represents a row of the products table. Then, one element (row) at a time from the rows array is picked using a for loop, and information in the four columns is displayed. The information of each product in the prod_id, prod_name, quantity, and price columns will be displayed via each element of the rows array. Instead of listing all rows from the table, can you search and retrieve only certain row(s) from the database table?

Searching in a Database Table

Searching can be done in a database table with a SQL SELECT statement. By specifying search criteria in a SQL SELECT statement, you can search and retrieve from the products table. The following program displays a product with a specific product ID:

```
sqlenquiry.py
import MySQLdb
conn=MySQLdb.connect(host="localhost", user="root", passwd="mce", db="shopping")
cursor=conn.cursor()
p=int(input("Enter Product ID: "))
cursor.execute ("SELECT * from products where prod_id=%d" %p)
row=cursor.fetchone()
if row==None:
  print ("Sorry no Product found with ID %d" %p)
else:
  print ("Information of the product with ID %d is as follows:" %p)
  print ("Product ID: %d, Product Name: %s, Quantity: %d, Price: %f" %(row[0], row[1],
row[2], row[3]))
cursor.close()
conn.close()
Output :
Enter Product ID: 105
Sorry no Product found with ID 105
```

Let's run the script again to try another product.

```
Enter Product ID: 103
Information of the product with ID 103 is as follows:
Product ID: 103, Product Name: Laptop, Quantity: 100, Price: 500.000000
```

This program is very simple. The initial steps are as usual, establishing connection with the MySQL Database Server and creating a cursor object using the connection object. Then you ask the user to enter the ID of the product whose information he wants to retrieve. The product ID entered by the user is stored in a variable, p. Then, through the execute() method of the cursor object, you execute a SQL SELECT statement to retrieve the product with the ID specified in p from the products table. The result of the SQL statement is stored in the resultset object. Using fetchone(), you retrieve a row from the resultset object and store it in row, which will now appear as an array, where each element represents a column of the product table's row. You check to see if the value of the row variable is None, which means there was no row found in the database table with the supplied product ID. In that case, you display a Sorry message saying no product with the supplied product ID was found in the table. If the value in row is not None, it means at least one product is found in the database table with the supplied product ID. The product is fetched and stored in row array. Through the elements of the row array, you display the information of the searched product. Finally, you close the cursor object and disconnect the database connection.

Sometimes you need to update the information stored in a database table. Let's look at the procedure for doing so.

Updating Information in a Database Table

To update information in a database table, you will use a SQL UPDATE statement. All you need is to supply the criteria of the rows to be updated and the new information. Let's look at a program that updates product information in the products table:

```
sqlupdate.py
import MySQLdb
conn=MySQLdb.connect(host="localhost", user="root", passwd="mce", db="shopping")
cursor=conn.cursor()
p=int(input("Enter Product ID: "))
cursor.execute ("SELECT * from products where prod_id=%d" %p)
row=cursor.fetchone()
if row==None:
  print ("Sorry no Product found with ID %d" %p)
else:
  print ("Information of the product with ID %d is as follows:" %p)
  print ("Product ID: %d, Product Name: %s, Quantity: %d, Price: %f" %(row[0], row[1],
row[2], row[3]))
  pname=input("Enter new Product Name: ")
  qty=int(input("Enter new Quantity: "))
  price=int(input("Enter new Price: "))
  cursor.execute ("UPDATE products set prod_name='%s', quantity=%d, price=%f where
prod_id=%d" %(pname, qty, price,p))
  print("Information of the Product with ID %d is updated." %p)
cursor.close()
conn.commit()
conn.close()
Output :
Enter Product ID: 105
Sorry no Product found with ID 105
```

Let's run the script again to try some other product ID.

```
Enter Product ID: 103
Information of the product with ID 103 is as follows:
Product ID: 103, Product Name: Laptop, Quantity: 100, Price: 500.000000
```

```
Enter new Product Name: Motor bike
Enter new Quantity: 50
Enter new Price: 400
Information of the Product with ID 103 is updated.
```

The code in this program does the following:

- Establishes connection with the MySQL Database Server.

- Creates a `cursor` object using the `connection` object.

- Asks the user to enter the ID of the product he wants to update. The product ID entered by the user is temporarily stored in variable p.

- Executes a SQL `SELECT` statement through the `execute()` method of the `cursor` object to retrieve the product with the product ID specified in variable p. The result of the SQL statement is stored in the `resultset` object.

- A row is retrieved from the `resultset` using `fetchone()` and stored in `row`.

- It checks to see if the value of the `row` variable is `None`, which means no product with the supplied product ID was found in the `products` table. A Sorry message is displayed saying no product with the supplied product ID was found in the table.

- If the value in the `row` variable (array) is not `None`, a product with the supplied product ID was found in the database table. Then, the existing information of the product is displayed through elements of the `row` array. The `row` array is four elements that represent the information in the `products` table.

- Asks the user to enter new a product name, quantity and price for the product whose product ID was supplied. The information entered by the user is stored temporarily in variables `pname`, `qty`, and `price`, respectively.

- The `products` table is updated by executing a SQL `UPDATE` statement via the `execute()` method of the `cursor` object, and a message is displayed confirming that the product's information is updated.

- The `commit()` method is invoked to apply the modifications to the underlying database table.

- Closes the `cursor` object and disconnects the database connection.

When displaying the `products` table, you find that the information of the product `Laptop` is updated to `Motor bike` as shown in Figure 12.7.

We have seen how to list, insert, search, and update the database table. Now let's see the final task required in database maintenance—deleting rows.

```
mysql> select * from products;
+---------+-----------+----------+-------+
| prod_id | prod_name | quantity | price |
+---------+-----------+----------+-------+
|     101 | Camera    |      100 |    15 |
|     102 | Phone     |      100 |    20 |
|     103 | Motor bike|       50 |   400 |
|     104 | Shirts    |      100 |    50 |
+---------+-----------+----------+-------+
4 rows in set (0.00 sec)
```

Figure 12.7
Displaying updated rows in the `products` database table.

Deleting Information from a Database Table

To delete rows from the database table, you use the SQL DELETE command. The following program deletes a product with the specified ID from the `products` table of the `shopping` database:

```
sqldelete.py
import MySQLdb
conn=MySQLdb.connect(host="localhost", user="root", passwd="mce", db="shopping")
cursor=conn.cursor()
p=int(input("Enter Product ID: "))
cursor.execute ("SELECT * from products where prod_id=%d" %p)
row=cursor.fetchone()
if row==None:
  print ("Sorry no Product found with ID %d" %p)
else:
  print ("Information of the product with ID %d is as follows:" %p)
  print ("Product ID: %d, Product Name: %s, Quantity: %d, Price: %f" %(row[0], row[1],
row[2], row[3]))
  k=input("Confirm, Want to delete this record, yes/no: ")
  if k.upper()=="YES":
    cursor.execute ("DELETE from products where prod_id=%d" %p)
    print("Product with ID %d is deleted" %p)
cursor.close()
conn.commit()
conn.close()
Output:
Enter Product ID: 105
Sorry no Product found with ID 105
```

Let's run the script again to try some other product ID.

```
Enter Product ID: 102
Information of the product with ID 102 is as follows:
Product ID: 102, Product Name: Phone, Quantity: 100, Price: 20.000000
Confirm, Want to delete this record, yes/no: no
```

```
mysql> select * from products;
+---------+-------------+----------+-------+
| prod_id | prod_name   | quantity | price |
+---------+-------------+----------+-------+
|     101 | Camera      |      100 |    15 |
|     103 | Motor bike  |       50 |   400 |
|     104 | Shirts      |      100 |    50 |
+---------+-------------+----------+-------+
3 rows in set (0.00 sec)
```

Figure 12.8
Rows left in the `products` table after performing deletion.

On entering no, the product with ID 102 is not deleted. To confirm this, let's run the script again and enter the product ID 102. If the product information is displayed, it means the product is not yet deleted.

```
Enter Product ID: 102
Information of the product with ID 102 is as follows:
Product ID: 102, Product Name: Phone, Quantity: 100, Price: 20.000000
Confirm, Want to delete this record, yes/no: yes
Product with ID 102 is deleted
```

On entering the option, yes, the product is deleted.

After the usual procedure of establishing connection to the MySQL Database Server and creating a `cursor` object, the user is prompted to enter a product ID that he wants to delete. A SQL `SELECT` statement is executed via the `execute()` method of the `cursor` object to see if the product with the supplied product ID exists in the `products` table. If the product is found, its information is displayed, and user is asked for confirmation to delete the product. If he enters `No`, the product will not be deleted from the `products` table. If he confirms deletion by entering `Yes`, the SQL `DELETE` statement is executed. Also, `commit()` is called to implement the changes in the database table. Finally, `cursor` is closed and the database is disconnected.

After deleting the product with ID 102, the rows that are left in `products` are as shown in Figure 12.8.

The Python code that you saw up until now in this chapter has been console-based. What if you want to create a GUI application that fetches and inserts information in a database table?

DATABASE MAINTENANCE THROUGH GUI PROGRAMS

The database maintenance programs that you are going to create in this section are GUI based. You will creating a user interface with Qt Designer and access Python code with scripts. Before we proceed with developing an application in PyQt, let's first discuss the `QSqlDatabase` class, which will be required to integrate databases to PyQt.

Table 12.2 Methods of the QSqlDatabase Class

Method	Use
addDatabase()	Used to specify the database driver of the database to which you want to establish connection. It is through the database drivers that the database is accessed. **Driver types:** QDB2: IBM DB2 Driver QMYSQL: MySQL Driver QOCI: Oracle Call Interface Driver QODBC: ODBC Driver (includes Microsoft SQL Server) QPSQL: PostgreSQL Driver QSQLITE: SQLite version 3 or above
setHostName()	Used to specify the hostname.
setDatabaseName()	Used to specify the name of the database that you want to work with.
setUserName()	Used to specify the name of the authorized user through whom you want to access the database.
setPassword()	Used to specify the password of the authorized user to access the database.
open()	Opens the database connection using the current connection attributes. The method returns a Boolean true or false value, depending on whether the connection to the database is successfully established or not.
lastError()	Used to display error information that may occur while opening connection with the database through the open() function.

QSqlDatabase Class

To integrate and access databases in PyQt, you use the QSqlDatabase class. To represent connection to a database, an instance of QSqlDatabase is used. Methods of QSqlDatabase are shown in Table 12.2.

Now that you know how to establish connection with the database in PyQt, let's begin the section with the task of displaying information in the database table.

Displaying Rows

To display the rows fetched from the database table, you will use a Table View widget. The Table View widget will display database table information in tabular format. When fetching and displaying information from a database, you want to use a model that is easy to deal with. A model is a mirror image of the database table that the user

Table 12.3 Methods of QSqlTableModel

Method	Use
setTable()	Used to specify the database table you want the model to work with.
setEditStrategy()	Applies the strategy for editing the database table. The available strategies are these: OnFieldChange: All modifications made in the model will be applied immediately to the database table. OnRowChange: All modifications made to a row will be applied to the database table on moving to a different row. OnManualSubmit: All modifications will be cached in the model and applied to the database table when submitAll() is called. Also, modifications that are cached can be cancelled or erased without applying to the database by calling revertAll().
select()	Used to populate the model with the information of the database table specified with setTable().

can use to navigate and edit if required. To create a model, you need to create an instance of the QSqlTableModel class.

QSqlTableModel Class

The class provides a model that can be set to display information of a database table. The class also makes it easy to navigate the model and set editing strategy for the underlying database tables. You can perform modifications in place in the model itself without having knowledge of SQL syntax. The methods of QSqlTableModel are shown in Table 12.3.

Let's create an application that displays rows of the products database table. Open Qt Designer and create a new application based on Dialog without Buttons. Name the application showrec.ui and drag and drop a Table View widget onto the form as shown in Figure 12.9.

Save the application with the name showrec.ui. The Python code of this .ui (XML) file will appear as follows:

```
showrec.py
# Form implementation generated from reading ui file 'showrec.ui'
from PyQt4 import QtCore, QtGui

try:
  _fromUtf8 = QtCore.QString.fromUtf8
```

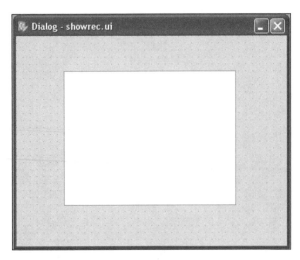

Figure 12.9
Form displaying the Table View widget.

```
except AttributeError:
 _fromUtf8 = lambda s: s

class Ui_Dialog(object):
 def setupUi(self, Dialog):
  Dialog.setObjectName(_fromUtf8("Dialog"))
  Dialog.resize(400, 300)
  self.tableView = QtGui.QTableView(Dialog)
  self.tableView.setGeometry(QtCore.QRect(70, 50, 256, 192))
  self.tableView.setObjectName(_fromUtf8("tableView"))
  self.retranslateUi(Dialog)
  QtCore.QMetaObject.connectSlotsByName(Dialog)

 def retranslateUi(self, Dialog):
     Dialog.setWindowTitle(QtGui.QApplication.translate("Dialog", "Dialog", None,
QtGui.QApplication.UnicodeUTF8))
```

Now let's create a Python script that imports the code to invoke the Table View widget and fetches the rows from the `products` table, creates a model, and displays the information in the model with a Table View widget. The Python script file will appear as follows:

```
callshowrec.pyw
import sys
from showrec import *
from PyQt4 import QtSql, QtGui

def createConnection():
 db = QtSql.QSqlDatabase.addDatabase('QMYSQL')
```

```
db.setHostName('localhost')
db.setDatabaseName('shopping')
db.setUserName('root')
db.setPassword('mce')
db.open()
print (db.lastError().text())
return True

class MyForm(QtGui.QDialog):
 def __init__(self, parent=None):
  QtGui.QWidget.__init__(self, parent)
  self.ui = Ui_Dialog()
  self.ui.setupUi(self)
  self.model = QtSql.QSqlTableModel(self)
  self.model.setTable("products")
  self.model.setEditStrategy(QtSql.QSqlTableModel.OnManualSubmit)
  self.model.select()
  self.ui.tableView.setModel(self.model)

if __name__ == "__main__":
 app = QtGui.QApplication(sys.argv)
 if not createConnection():
  sys.exit(1)
 myapp = MyForm()
 myapp.show()
 sys.exit(app.exec_())
```

The first thing you do is import the QtSql module into the program; it will be required to integrate the database into the PyQt applications. The QtSql module includes classes and drivers that help in accessing and interacting with the database.

Then you provide details of establishing the database connection. Since you want to access the MySQL database, specify its driver with addDatabase(). In the connection, you also specify the database name, user name, and password. Finally, the connection is opened to perform operations on the database. You define a model and set it to display the products table. The edit strategy for the model is set to OnManualSubmit, which means the changes made in the model will not be applied to the database table until submitAll() is called. The model is populated by the rows of the products table with the select() method. To display the content of the model in the dialog box, apply it to the Table view, an instance of QTableView.

The QTableView class is used to create a Table view that displays items from a model. That is, information can be displayed in the Table view through the models that are derived from the QAbstractItemModel class. The rows of the products

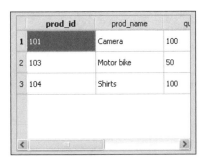

Figure 12.10
`products` table information displayed with a Table View widget.

table will appear in the Table View widget as shown in Figure 12.10. You can navigate to any cell in the Table view by clicking on it or using the arrow keys. You can also use the Tab key to move between cells.

Navigating Through Rows of the Database Table

Now let's create an application that displays the first row of the database table. The application should also display navigation buttons that enable the user to navigate to the next row, previous row, first row, and last row of the database table.

Open Qt Designer and create a new application based on Dialog without Buttons. Drag and drop five Label, four Line Edit, and four Push Button widgets onto the form. Set the `text` property of the five Labels to `List of Products`, `Product ID`, `Product Name`, `Quantity`, and `Price`. Set the `objectName` property of the four Line Edit widgets to `prodid`, `prodname`, `qty`, and `price`. Also, set the `objectName` property of the four Push Button widgets to `FirstButton`, `PreviousButton`, `NextButton`, and `LastButton`. Also increase the point size of the `List of Products` Label and make it bold so that it appears as a heading in the application. Also, set the `text` property of the Push Buttons to First, Previous, Next, and Last. The form will appear as shown in Figure 12.11.

Figure 12.11
Form to display one row of the `products` table at a time.

Save the application with the name `DispProducts.ui`. The Python code of the `.ui` (XML) file generated with the `pyuic4` command utility will appear as follows:

```
DispProducts.py
# Form implementation generated from reading ui file 'DispProducts.ui'
from PyQt4 import QtCore, QtGui

try:
  _fromUtf8 = QtCore.QString.fromUtf8
except AttributeError:
  _fromUtf8 = lambda s: s

class Ui_Dialog(object):
 def setupUi(self, Dialog):
   Dialog.setObjectName(_fromUtf8("Dialog"))
   Dialog.resize(420, 194)
   self.label = QtGui.QLabel(Dialog)
   self.label.setGeometry(QtCore.QRect(140, 10, 131, 16))
   font = QtGui.QFont()
   font.setPointSize(11)
   font.setWeight(75)
   font.setBold(True)
   self.label.setFont(font)
   self.label.setObjectName(_fromUtf8("label"))
   self.label_2 = QtGui.QLabel(Dialog)
   self.label_2.setGeometry(QtCore.QRect(30, 40, 51, 16))
   self.label_2.setObjectName(_fromUtf8("label_2"))
   self.label_3 = QtGui.QLabel(Dialog)
   self.label_3.setGeometry(QtCore.QRect(190, 40, 71, 16))
   self.label_3.setObjectName(_fromUtf8("label_3"))
   self.label_4 = QtGui.QLabel(Dialog)
   self.label_4.setGeometry(QtCore.QRect(40, 70, 46, 13))
   self.label_4.setObjectName(_fromUtf8("label_4"))
   self.label_5 = QtGui.QLabel(Dialog)
   self.label_5.setGeometry(QtCore.QRect(230, 70, 31, 16))
   self.label_5.setObjectName(_fromUtf8("label_5"))
   self.FirstButton = QtGui.QPushButton(Dialog)
   self.FirstButton.setGeometry(QtCore.QRect(20, 130, 75, 23))
   self.FirstButton.setObjectName(_fromUtf8("FirstButton"))
   self.PreviousButton = QtGui.QPushButton(Dialog)
   self.PreviousButton.setGeometry(QtCore.QRect(120, 130, 75, 23))
   self.PreviousButton.setObjectName(_fromUtf8("PreviousButton"))
   self.NextButton = QtGui.QPushButton(Dialog)
   self.NextButton.setGeometry(QtCore.QRect(220, 130, 75, 23))
   self.NextButton.setObjectName(_fromUtf8("NextButton"))
```

```
    self.LastButton = QtGui.QPushButton(Dialog)
    self.LastButton.setGeometry(QtCore.QRect(320, 130, 75, 23))
    self.LastButton.setObjectName(_fromUtf8("LastButton"))
    self.prodid = QtGui.QLineEdit(Dialog)
    self.prodid.setGeometry(QtCore.QRect(90, 40, 71, 20))
    self.prodid.setObjectName(_fromUtf8("prodid"))
    self.prodname = QtGui.QLineEdit(Dialog)
    self.prodname.setGeometry(QtCore.QRect(270, 40, 131, 20))
    self.prodname.setObjectName(_fromUtf8("prodname"))
    self.qty = QtGui.QLineEdit(Dialog)
    self.qty.setGeometry(QtCore.QRect(90, 70, 51, 20))
    self.qty.setObjectName(_fromUtf8("qty"))
    self.price = QtGui.QLineEdit(Dialog)
    self.price.setGeometry(QtCore.QRect(270, 70, 61, 20))
    self.price.setObjectName(_fromUtf8("price"))
    self.retranslateUi(Dialog)
    QtCore.QMetaObject.connectSlotsByName(Dialog)

 def retranslateUi(self, Dialog):
  Dialog.setWindowTitle(QtGui.QApplication.translate("Dialog", "Dialog", None,
QtGui.QApplication.UnicodeUTF8))
   self.label.setText(QtGui.QApplication.translate("Dialog", "List of Products",
None, QtGui.QApplication.UnicodeUTF8))
   self.label_2.setText(QtGui.QApplication.translate("Dialog", "Product ID", None,
QtGui.QApplication.UnicodeUTF8))
   self.label_3.setText(QtGui.QApplication.translate("Dialog", "Product Name", None,
QtGui.QApplication.UnicodeUTF8))
   self.label_4.setText(QtGui.QApplication.translate("Dialog", "Quantity", None,
QtGui.QApplication.UnicodeUTF8))
   self.label_5.setText(QtGui.QApplication.translate("Dialog", "Price", None,
QtGui.QApplication.UnicodeUTF8))
   self.FirstButton.setText(QtGui.QApplication.translate("Dialog", "First", None,
QtGui.QApplication.UnicodeUTF8))
   self.PreviousButton.setText(QtGui.QApplication.translate("Dialog", "Previous",
None, QtGui.QApplication.UnicodeUTF8))
   self.NextButton.setText(QtGui.QApplication.translate("Dialog", "Next", None,
QtGui.QApplication.UnicodeUTF8))
   self.LastButton.setText(QtGui.QApplication.translate("Dialog", "Last", None,
QtGui.QApplication.UnicodeUTF8))
```

Let's create a Python script that imports the code to invoke the user interface design and implements navigation from one row to another. The Python script file will appear as follows:

```
callDispProducts.pyw
import sys
```

```
from DispProducts import *
from PyQt4 import QtSql, QtGui

def createConnection():
 db = QtSql.QSqlDatabase.addDatabase('QMYSQL')
 db.setHostName('localhost')
 db.setDatabaseName('shopping')
 db.setUserName('root')
 db.setPassword('mce')
 db.open()
 print (db.lastError().text())
 return True

class MyForm(QtGui.QDialog):
 recno=0
 def __init__(self, parent=None):
  QtGui.QWidget.__init__(self, parent)
  self.ui = Ui_Dialog()
  self.ui.setupUi(self)
  self.model=QtSql.QSqlQueryModel(self)
  self.model.setQuery("select * from products")
  self.record=self.model.record(0)
  self.ui.prodid.setText(str(self.record.value("prod_id")))
  self.ui.prodname.setText(self.record.value("prod_name"))
  self.ui.qty.setText(str(self.record.value("quantity")))
  self.ui.price.setText(str(self.record.value("price")))
  QtCore.QObject.connect(self.ui.FirstButton, QtCore.SIGNAL('clicked()'),
self.dispFirst)
  QtCore.QObject.connect(self.ui.PreviousButton, QtCore.SIGNAL('clicked()'),
self.dispPrevious)
  QtCore.QObject.connect(self.ui.LastButton, QtCore.SIGNAL('clicked()'),
self.dispLast)
  QtCore.QObject.connect(self.ui.NextButton, QtCore.SIGNAL('clicked()'),
self.dispNext)

 def dispFirst(self):
  MyForm.recno=0
  self.record=self.model.record(MyForm.recno)
  self.ui.prodid.setText(str(self.record.value("prod_id")))
  self.ui.prodname.setText(self.record.value("prod_name"))
  self.ui.qty.setText(str(self.record.value("quantity")))
  self.ui.price.setText(str(self.record.value("price")))

 def dispPrevious(self):
  MyForm.recno-=1
```

```
  if MyForm.recno <0:
    MyForm.recno=self.model.rowCount()-1
  self.record=self.model.record(MyForm.recno)
  self.ui.prodid.setText(str(self.record.value("prod_id")))
  self.ui.prodname.setText(self.record.value("prod_name"))
  self.ui.qty.setText(str(self.record.value("quantity")))
  self.ui.price.setText(str(self.record.value("price")))

def dispLast(self):
  MyForm.recno=self.model.rowCount()-1
  self.record=self.model.record(MyForm.recno)
  self.ui.prodid.setText(str(self.record.value("prod_id")))
  self.ui.prodname.setText(self.record.value("prod_name"))
  self.ui.qty.setText(str(self.record.value("quantity")))
  self.ui.price.setText(str(self.record.value("price")))

def dispNext(self):
  MyForm.recno+=1
  if MyForm.recno >self.model.rowCount()-1:
    MyForm.recno=0
  self.record=self.model.record(MyForm.recno)
  self.ui.prodid.setText(str(self.record.value("prod_id")))
  self.ui.prodname.setText(self.record.value("prod_name"))
  self.ui.qty.setText(str(self.record.value("quantity")))
  self.ui.price.setText(str(self.record.value("price")))

if __name__ == "__main__":
  app = QtGui.QApplication(sys.argv)
  if not createConnection():
    sys.exit(1)
  myapp = MyForm()
  myapp.show()
  sys.exit(app.exec_())
```

Before you start working on the code, let's look at the class and the methods used in it.

QSqlQueryModel class: Provides a read-only model based on the specified SQL query.

setQuery(): Used to specify the SQL query.

record(int): Used to access individual records (rows) from the specified database table.

record.value("column_name"): Used to retrieve the value of the specified column of the current row of the database table.

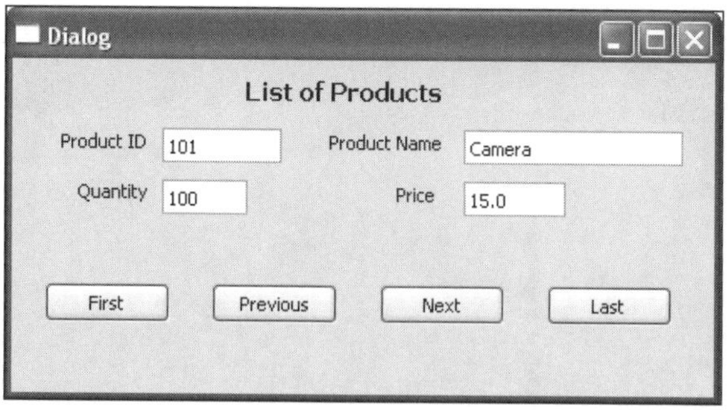

Figure 12.12
First row of the `products` table displayed on startup.

In this code, as usual, you connect to the `shopping` database on the local host through the MySQL driver. When establishing the connection, you specify the user name and password of the user to the database. When the connection is established, you create a read-only model and specify a SQL query to access all the rows of the `products` table and copy them to the model. Since you want the application to display the first row of the `products` table, retrieve the first row of the table with the `record()` method and access the data in the `prod_id`, `prod_name`, `quantity`, and `price` columns and assign it to the Line Edit widgets as shown in Figure 12.12.

The buttons on the form are connected to invoke the respective methods. To retrieve from the database table, you use a static variable, `recno`. The `recno` variable is initially set to 0 to display the first row. When you select Next, the value of the variable `recno` is incremented by 1 to display the next row. If the user selects Next on the last row of the table, the value of the `recno` variable is reset to 0 to display the first row.

Similarly, the value of the `recno` variable is decremented by 1 each time the Previous button is selected to display the previous row. If the user selects the Previous button on the first row, the value of `recno` is set to the value of the last row number of the table to display the last row of the table. The First and Last buttons set the value of `recno` to 0 and `rowCount` to display the first and last rows of the table, respectively.

You have seen how to navigate among the rows in the database table. Now let's look at how to add rows, delete rows, update information in existing rows, and search rows in the database table. These operations are known as maintaining the database table.

Maintaining the Database Table
Let's create an application that displays all the rows of the database table. The application has buttons that enable you to add new rows, delete existing rows, update existing rows, and search the database table.

Figure 12.13
Form to display rows of the `products` table with the facility to add, delete, update, and search.

Open Qt Designer and create a new application based on Dialog without Buttons and drag and drop a Label, a Line Edit, five Push Buttons, and a Table View widget on the form. Set the `text` property of the Label to `Enter Product Name`. Set the `text` property of the Push Buttons to `Filter`, `Update`, `Cancel`, `Add`, and `Delete`. Set the objectName property of the Line Edit widget to `prodname`. Also, set the `objectName` property of the five Push Button widgets to `FilterButton`, `Update-Button`, `CancelButton`, `InsertButton`, and `DeleteButton`. The form will appear as shown in Figure 12.13.

Save the application with the name `MaintainProducts.ui`. The Python code of the `.ui` (XML) file will appear as follows:

```
MaintainProducts.py
# Form implementation generated from reading ui file 'MaintainProducts.ui'
from PyQt4 import QtCore, QtGui

try:
    _fromUtf8 = QtCore.QString.fromUtf8
except AttributeError:
    _fromUtf8 = lambda s: s

class Ui_Dialog(object):
    def setupUi(self, Dialog):
        Dialog.setObjectName(_fromUtf8("Dialog"))
```

```python
        Dialog.resize(479, 317)
        self.tableView = QtGui.QTableView(Dialog)
        self.tableView.setGeometry(QtCore.QRect(20, 40, 441, 221))
        self.tableView.setObjectName(_fromUtf8("tableView"))
        self.UpdateButton = QtGui.QPushButton(Dialog)
        self.UpdateButton.setGeometry(QtCore.QRect(20, 270, 75, 23))
        self.UpdateButton.setObjectName(_fromUtf8("UpdateButton"))
        self.CancelButton = QtGui.QPushButton(Dialog)
        self.CancelButton.setGeometry(QtCore.QRect(140, 270, 75, 23))
        self.CancelButton.setObjectName(_fromUtf8("CancelButton"))
        self.InsertButton = QtGui.QPushButton(Dialog)
        self.InsertButton.setGeometry(QtCore.QRect(260, 270, 75, 23))
        self.InsertButton.setObjectName(_fromUtf8("InsertButton"))
        self.DeleteButton = QtGui.QPushButton(Dialog)
        self.DeleteButton.setGeometry(QtCore.QRect(380, 270, 75, 23))
        self.DeleteButton.setObjectName(_fromUtf8("DeleteButton"))
        self.FilterButton = QtGui.QPushButton(Dialog)
        self.FilterButton.setGeometry(QtCore.QRect(290, 10, 75, 23))
        self.FilterButton.setObjectName(_fromUtf8("FilterButton"))
        self.label = QtGui.QLabel(Dialog)
        self.label.setGeometry(QtCore.QRect(30, 10, 111, 16))
        self.label.setObjectName(_fromUtf8("label"))
        self.prodname = QtGui.QLineEdit(Dialog)
        self.prodname.setGeometry(QtCore.QRect(140, 10, 113, 20))
        self.prodname.setObjectName(_fromUtf8("prodname"))
        self.retranslateUi(Dialog)
        QtCore.QMetaObject.connectSlotsByName(Dialog)

    def retranslateUi(self, Dialog):
        Dialog.setWindowTitle(QtGui.QApplication.translate("Dialog",    "Dialog",    None,
QtGui.QApplication.UnicodeUTF8))
        self.UpdateButton.setText(QtGui.QApplication.translate("Dialog", "Update", None,
QtGui.QApplication.UnicodeUTF8))
        self.CancelButton.setText(QtGui.QApplication.translate("Dialog", "Cancel", None,
QtGui.QApplication.UnicodeUTF8))
        self.InsertButton.setText(QtGui.QApplication.translate("Dialog",    "Add",    None,
QtGui.QApplication.UnicodeUTF8))
        self.DeleteButton.setText(QtGui.QApplication.translate("Dialog", "Delete", None,
QtGui.QApplication.UnicodeUTF8))
        self.FilterButton.setText(QtGui.QApplication.translate("Dialog", "Filter", None,
QtGui.QApplication.UnicodeUTF8))
        self.label.setText(QtGui.QApplication.translate("Dialog", "Enter Product Name",
None, QtGui.QApplication.UnicodeUTF8))
```

The following Python script contains the code to import the Python code to invoke the user interface design that adds, deletes, updates, and searches for information in the database table:

```
callMaintainProducts.pyw
import sys
from MaintainProducts import *
from PyQt4 import QtSql, QtGui

def createConnection():
 db = QtSql.QSqlDatabase.addDatabase('QMYSQL')
 db.setHostName('localhost')
 db.setDatabaseName('shopping')
 db.setUserName('root')
 db.setPassword('mce')
 db.open()
 print (db.lastError().text())
 return True

class MyForm(QtGui.QDialog):
 def __init__(self, parent=None):
  QtGui.QWidget.__init__(self, parent)
  self.ui = Ui_Dialog()
  self.ui.setupUi(self)
  self.model = QtSql.QSqlTableModel(self)
  self.model.setTable("products")
  self.model.setEditStrategy(QtSql.QSqlTableModel.OnManualSubmit)
  self.model.select()
  self.ui.tableView.setModel(self.model)
  QtCore.QObject.connect(self.ui.UpdateButton, QtCore.SIGNAL('clicked()'),
self.UpdateRecords)
  QtCore.QObject.connect(self.ui.CancelButton, QtCore.SIGNAL('clicked()'),
self.CancelChanges)
  QtCore.QObject.connect(self.ui.InsertButton, QtCore.SIGNAL('clicked()'),
self.InsertRecords)
  QtCore.QObject.connect(self.ui.DeleteButton, QtCore.SIGNAL('clicked()'),
self.DeleteRecords)
  QtCore.QObject.connect(self.ui.FilterButton, QtCore.SIGNAL('clicked()'),
self.FilterRecords)

 def UpdateRecords(self):
  self.model.submitAll()

 def CancelChanges(self):
  self.model.revertAll()
```

```
def InsertRecords(self):
  self.model.insertRow(self.ui.tableView.currentIndex().row())

def DeleteRecords(self):
  self.model.removeRow(self.ui.tableView.currentIndex().row())
  self.model.submitAll()

def FilterRecords(self):
  self.model.setFilter("prod_name like '"+self.ui.prodname.text()+"%'")

if __name__ == "__main__":
 app = QtGui.QApplication(sys.argv)
 if not createConnection():
  sys.exit(1)
 myapp = MyForm()
 myapp.show()
 sys.exit(app.exec_())
```

Let's look at the methods that are used in the code:

submit(): Submits the currently edited row; applies the modifications to the underlying database table if the edit strategy is set to OnRowChange or OnFieldChange.

Recall that if the edit strategy is set to OnRowChange, all the modifications done to a row in the model will be applied to the database table on moving on to a different row. If the edit strategy is set to OnFieldChange, all modifications to the model will be applied to the database table. If the edit strategy is set to OnManualSubmit, all modifications will be cached in the model and applied to the database table when submitAll() is called. Also, all cached modifications will be cancelled without being applied to the database if revertAll() is called.

submitAll(): Used to submit all pending changes to the database table if the edit strategy is set to OnManualSubmit. The method returns true if the modifications are successfully applied to the database table; otherwise it returns false.

lastError(): Used to display detailed error information.

revertAll(): Used to cancel all the pending editing of the current database table if the model's editing strategy is set to OnManualSubmit.

revert(): Used to cancel the editing of the current row if the model's strategy is set to OnRowChange.

insertRow(): Inserts an empty row after the specified position in an open database table. If the specified position is a negative value, the row will be inserted at the end.

removeRow(): Removes the row at the specified index from an open database table. You need to call submitAll()to apply the changes to the database table if the edit strategy is set to OnManualSubmit.

setFilter(): Used to specify the filter condition for the database table. If the model is already populated with rows of the database table, the model repopulates the model with the filtered rows.

Note

The model will be repopulated automatically if submitAll() successfully submits the pending changes.

On execution of the application, a model of the products database table is created, and its editing strategy is set to OnManualSubmit. The model is populated with the rows of the products table with a select() method. To display the information of the model on the form, you need to apply it to the Table view. On applying the model to the Table view, it will display all the rows of the products table as shown in Figure 12.14(a). You can select any cell of the Table view to modify its contents. For instance, to modify the quantity of Motor bike to 75, select the cell displaying the value 50 and change it to value 75 as shown in Figure 12.14(b). When you are finished with the modifications, apply them to the database table by selecting Update. The Update button calls the submitAll() method and applies modifications to the database table. The information in the database table will be updated as displayed in Figure 12.14(c).

To insert a row in the products table, select the Add button. A blank row will appear in the model after the row where the cursor was positioned. Enter the information for the new product, as shown in Figure 12.15(a), and select Update. The new row will be appended to the underlying database table, and the Table view will be

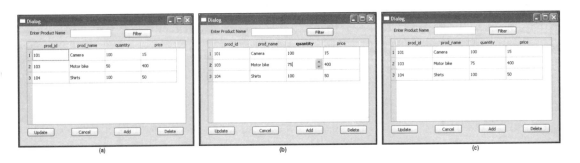

Figure 12.14
(a) All rows of the products table displayed in a Table View widget. (b) Modifying contents of a column with a Table View widget. (c) A Table View widget displaying the updated information.

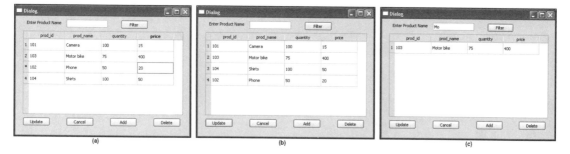

Figure 12.15
(a) Inserting a row with a Table View widget. (b) Table view displaying the new row. (c) Table view displaying the row that satisfies the filter condition "Mo."

repopulated to show the new row, as shown in Figure 12.15(b). When Delete is selected, the row where the cursor is positioned in the Table view will be deleted, and the Table view will be repopulated to display the changes. To filter the rows in the database table with the specified product name, enter the beginning characters of the product you are looking for in the Line Edit widget and select Filter. For example, if you are searching for Motor Cycle, enter **Mo** in the Line Edit widget and select the Filter button. The products that begin with the characters "Mo" will be displayed as shown in Figure 12.15(c).

This finishes our chapter on maintaining a database with console-based Python programs and GUI programs.

SUMMARY

In this chapter you learned to install and use the MySQLdb module, which is required to access MySQL Database Server through Python. Also, you learned to maintain a database through console-based programs and through GUI programs. You learned to write Python scripts to insert, fetch, delete, search, and update rows in a database table.

In this book, I have tried to keep things easy to understand. I hope you agree. You now have all the necessary information to build and maintain your own applications in Python.

Have fun creating your own applications, and thanks for reading!

INDEX

Special Characters and Symbols

!= comparison operator, 31

hash sign, 12

% format codes, 13–14

%c format code, 14

%d format code, 14

%e format code, 14

%f format code, 14

%o directive, 24

%o format code, 14

%s format code, 14

%x directive, 24

%x format code, 14

& (ampersand character), 278

& (intersection) set operation, 74

& bitwise operator, 27–28

(open parenthesis, 12

** double asterisks, 20

.0 component, 25

.py extension, 8–9

.pyw extension, 173

// truncating division operator, 18

; semicolon, 345

@staticmethod decorator, 115–116

[open bracket, 12

\ backslash, 12, 46

\" escape character, 21

\' escape character, 21

\\ escape character, 21–22

\a escape character, 21–22

\b escape character, 21

\f escape character, 21

\n escape character, 21

\r escape character, 21

\t escape character, 21–22

\v escape character, 21

^ bitwise operator, 27–28

__add__ method, 135

__bases__ class attribute, 108

__del__ method, 119

__delattr__ method, 141–142

__delete__ method, 139

__dict__ class attribute, 108

__doc__ class attribute, 108

__get__ method, 139–140

__getattr__ method, 138, 141, 142

__init__( ) method
  defining default value parameters in, 113
  overview, 111–112
  passing arguments to, 112
  string representation of instances, 113–114

__module__ class attribute, 108

__name__ class attribute, 108

__next__( ) method, 96

__set__ method, 139–140

__setattr__ method, 138, 141, 142

__str__ method, 113–114, 136

{ open brace, 12

| (union) set operation, 74

| bitwise operator, 27–28

~ bitwise operator, 27–28

+ plus sign, 13

< comparison operator, 31

<< shifting operator, 27–28

<= comparison operator, 31

== comparison operator
  overview, 31, 136
  polymorphism, 137–138
  properties, 138–139

> comparison operator, 31

>= comparison operator, 31
>> shifting operator, 27–28
>>> Python prompt, 4–5
0j component, 25
0o prefix, 24
0x prefix, 24
, comma, 13

A

A mode option, 145
a+ mode option, 145
access control specifiers
    accessing methods of base classes from derived
        classes, 124–125
    accessing private members, 122–123
    accessing public members, 122
    method overriding, 123–124
    overview, 122
Action Editor, 178–179, 279–280
actionTriggered( ) method, 233
activated( ) method, 260
activateNextSubWindow( ) method, 318
activatePreviousSubWindow( ) method, 318
Active state, 280
add( ) function, 89
Add files icon, 288
Add prefix icon, 288
Add Push button, 332
Add radio button, 218
addDatabase( ) method, 360
addDays( ) method, 255
addItem( ) method, 238, 274
addItems( ) method, 238, 260
addlist( ) function, 245
addMonths( ) method, 255
addMSecs( ) method, 251
addPixmap( ) function, 275
addSecs( ) method, 251
addseq( ) function, 92
addYears( ) method, 255
Adjust Size icon, 188
all( ) method, 75
AllDockWidgetFeatures property, 295, 296
American Standard Code for Information Interchange
    (ASCII), 10
ampersand character (&), 278
AND logical operator, 33
any( ) method, 75
append( ) method, 68
appending file content, 150–151
append(object) method, 67

app.exec_( ) method, 198
applications
    connecting to predefined slots, 193–199
    GUI, 173–175
    in Qt Designer, 191–192
area( ) class method, 123–125, 134–135
area( ) instance method, 109
area of rectangle program (arearect.py), 8–9
area of triangle program (areatriangle.py), 18–19
arguments
    command-line, 102
    function, 80
    keyword, 83–84
    passing to __init__( ) method, 112
arithmetic operations
    coercion (auto conversion), 25
    data types, 23–26
    division operators, 18–20
    escape sequences, 21–23
    exponentiation, 20
    multiple assignment statement, 21
    octal and hexa values, displaying, 24
    overview, 17–18
    user data, getting, 24–25
arithmetic operators, 17–18
arrays
    one-dimensional, 59–60
    overview, 59
    two-dimensional, 60–63
ASCII (American Standard Code for Information
    Interchange), 10
assert statement, 166–167
assertex.py program, 167
AssertionError exception, 161, 166
assignobj.py program, 118
AttributeError exception, 161
attributes
    class, 107–108
    of functions, 90–92
auto conversion (coercion), 13, 25
average of three values program (average.py), 19–20

B

backslash (\), 12, 46
basefunc.py program, 134
bigint data type, 346
binary files
    creating, 156–157
    defined, 144
binaryfile1.py program, 156
bitwise operations, 26–28

`blob` **data type, 346**

block statements, 29-30, 36

blocks

    `try/except`, 160-164

    `try/finally`, 164-165

boolean variables, 11

Booleans, defined, 10

Break Layout icon, 188

`break` **statement, 37-38**

`breakex1.py` **program, 37-38**

`breaking.py` **program, 58-59**

Bring to Front icon, 186

buddies

    overview, 206-207

    setting tab order, 207-211

Buddy Editing mode, 187-188

buttons

    displaying, 190-191

    radio, 213-218

Buttons group, 181

C

`calculate( )` **method, 211, 218, 226**

Calculate Amount button, 207

Calculate Bill Push Button, 338

`calculatebill( )` **method, 338**

`calculation( )` **method, 225**

calendar

    Date Edit widget, 256-259

    displaying, 253-255

    overview, 253

    QDate class, 255-256

Calendar widget, 185

calling functions, 79

`calltwonum.pyw` **script, 204**

`capitalize( )` **method/function, 48**

`cascadeArrange( )` **function, 325**

`cascadeSubWindows( )` **method, 318, 319**

`ceil(x)` **function, 100**

`center(width)` **method/function, 48**

chaining comparison operators program
    (`ifelschaining.py`**), 34**

`char` **data type, 346**

`characterwise.py` **(Displaying first character in**
    string program), 50-51

`checkable` **property, 333**

checkboxes

    initiating actions without using push buttons,
        223-226

    overview, 218-223

`checkState( )` **method, 241, 265**

`checkstr.py` **program, 54**

`choice( )` **function, 42-44**

Choose File option, 290

Choose Resource option, 290

class attributes, 108

class body, defined, 106

class variables, defined, 109

classes

    class methods, 114-115

    `class` statement

        attributes of class objects, 106-107

        built-in class attributes, 107-108

        defining functions in, 108-109

        instances, 109-114

        overview, 105-106

    defined, 106

    derived, accessing methods of base classes from,
        124-125

    descriptors, 139-142

    garbage collection, 118-120

    inheritance

        access control specifiers, 122-125

        multilevel, 128-135

        overview, 120

        single, 120-122

    operator overloading

        comparison operator (==), 136-139

        overview, 135-136

    overview, 105

    QDate, 255-256

    QSqlDatabase, 360

    QSqlTableModel, 361-364

    static methods, 115-118

Classic Icon view, 279

Classic Python (CPython), 2

`classmethd.py` **program, 115**

`classname` **identifier, 106**

`classstr.py` **program, 114**

`cleanText( )` **method, 227**

`clear( )` **method**

    dictionary, 72

    QComboBox class, 259

    QLabel class, 189

    QLineEdit class, 190

    QListWidget class, 238

    QTableWidget class, 265

    sets, 75

Click Me button, 202

`clicked( )` **event, 174, 218, 223, 240**

`clicked( )` **method, 214**

`clicked( )` **signal, 211, 219, 245, 332**

`close( )` **method, 145, 347**

closeAll( ) **function, 325**
closeAllSubWindows( ) **method, 318**
closed **attribute, 147**
CLR; .NET (Common Language Runtime), 2
cls **argument, 114, 117**
coercion (auto conversion), 13, 25
Column View widget, 182
columnCount( ) **method, 265**
columns, two-dimensional arrays, 60
Combo Box, 184, 259–264
comma (,), 13
command line mode
running programs from, 9
working with Python through, 7
command-line arguments, 102
commands, 5, 251, 270, 347–348, 358
commit( ) **method, 349–350**
Common Language Runtime (CLR; .NET), 2
comparison operator (==)
overview, 136
polymorphism, 137–138
properties, 138–139
comparison operators, 31, 34–35
complex numbers, 10, 28–29
compute( ) **function**
globalvar.py program, 85
localvar.py program, 86
concatenating, 13
connect( ) **method, 346–347**
console-based programs, 349–359
constructor.py **program, 113**
containers, defined, 40
Containers group, 183–184
continue **statement, 38–39**
continueex.py **program, 38–39**
copy( ) **method, 72**
copying files, 151
count (value) **method, 67**
count( ) **method**
finding occurrences of substrings in strings, 55
finding substrings in string, 53
QComboBox class, 259
QListWidget class, 238
countvowel.py **program, 53–54**
cPickle **module, 157**
CPython (Classic Python), 2
createfile1.py **program, 146–147**
createiter.py **program, 94**
curly brackets, 71
currentDate( ) **method, 255**
currentIndex( ) **method, 260**
currentIndexChanged( ) **method, 260**

currentItem( ) **method, 238**
currentItemChanged( ) **method, 238**
currentItemText **property, 310**
currentRow( ) **method, 238**
currentRowChanged( ) **method, 238**
currentText( ) **method, 259**
currentTextChanged( ) **method, 238**
currentTime( ) **method, 251**
cursor( ) **method, 347**
custom slots, 199–202

D
data descriptors, defined, 139
data members, defined, 106
data types
converting, 25–26, 202–206
finding, 23–24
overview, 9–10
databases. *See also* **maintenance**
creating, 345–348
MySQL
installation of MySQLdb, 343–344
MySQLdb, 343
overview, 342
overview, 341–342
date **data type, 346**
dates
Date Edit widget, 184, 256–259
displaying calendar, 253–255
overview, 253
QDate class, 255–256
datetime **data type, 346**
Date/Time Edit widget, 184
day( ) **method, 255**
dayOfWeek( ) **method, 255**
daysInMonth( ) **method, 255**
daysInYear( ) **method, 255**
daysTo( ) **method, 255**
dd.MM.yyyy **format, 257**
debugging, 3
def **statement, 80**
default value parameters, 82–83
defaultcons.py **program, 111–112**
del[n] **method, 67**
delallitems( ) **function, 245**
deleting
file content, 152
information from database tables, 358–359
delfilecontent.py **program, 152**
delitem( ) **function, 245**
derived classes (sub-classes), defined, 106

describe table_name **command, 348**
descriptors, 139–142
descript.py **program, 140**
destructor.py **program, 118–119**
Detailed view, 279
Dial widget, 184
dialogs
    creating GUI applications, 173–175
    overview, 172–173
dict1.py **program, 72–73**
dictexample.py **(Merging dictionaries program), 73–74**
dictionaries, defined, 10
difference (-) set operation, 75–76
dir( ) **function, 101–102**
direx.py **program, 101–102**
Disabled state, 280
disp_message( ) **static method, 116**
display( ) **class method, 115, 250**
Display widgets, 184–185
displaying
    buttons, 190–191
    calendar, 253–255
    graphics, 271–276
    input dialog box, 242–246
    items, 265–268
    LCD digits
        fetching and measuring system clock time, 251–253
        overview, 250
        using timers, 250–251
    tables, 264–268
    text, 189
    web pages, 268–271
Displaying first character in string program (characterwise.py**), 50–51**
Displaying list elements program (list1.py**), 63–64**
Displaying list elements program (list2.py**), 64**
displayNext( ) **function, 325**
displayPrevious( ) **function, 325**
dispsum( ) **function, 332**
dispuser( ) **method, 159**
dispvalue( ) **function, 85**
Divide radio button, 218
division operators, 18–20
divmod **function, 35**
Dock widget, 183, 295–302
DockWidgetClosable **property, 296**
DockWidgetFloatable **property, 296**
DockWidgetMovable **property, 296**
DockWidgetVerticalTitleBar **property, 296**

docstr.py **program, 91–92**
documentation string, 91–92
documents. *See also* **multiple documents**
    layouts, 327–338
    multiple-document interface, 317–327
double asterisks (****), 20**
double **data type, 346**
Double Spin Box widget, 184
DoubleInput **option, 242**
double-quoted string, 46–47
downloading Python, 3

E

Edit Buddies icon, 187–188
Edit Resources dialog, 288, 289
Edit Signals/Slots icon, 187
Edit Tab Order option, 188, 208
Edit Widgets icon, 187
editingFinished( ) **method, 190, 227**
editlist( ) **function, 245**
editTextChanged( ) **method, 260**
else **statement, 92–93**
emitted events, 174
endswith ( ) **method, 56**
EOFError **exception, 161–162, 166**
escape characters, 46
escape sequences, 21–23
evenodd.py **program, 35**
event handling, 191
evenval( ) **function, 88**
exceptions
    handling
        overview, 3, 159–160
        using try/except block, 160–164
        using try/finally block, 164–165
    raising
        assert statement, 166–167
        overview, 165–166
exec_( ) **method, 175**
execute( ) **method, 347**
exit( ) **method, 175**
expandtabs([tabsize]) **method, 57**
exponentiation, 20
extend (list) **method, 67**

F

fact( ) **functions, 93**
fetchall( ) **method, 352–354**
fetchone( ) **method, 352–354**
file methods, 145–146
fileanyline.py **program, 155**

fileappend.py **program, 150–151**
fileattrib.py **program, 147–148**
filecopy.py **program, 151**
fileno( ) **method, 147**
filenumerical.py **program, 155–156**
filerandomread.py **program, 154**
fileread2.py **program, 149–150**
fileread.py **program, 148**
filereadtry.py **program, 149**
files
    accessing specific content in, 155–156
    appending content to, 150–151
    copying, 151
    creating binary files, 156–157
    creating resource, 287–295
    deleting content from, 152
    displaying information from file objects,
        147–148
    exception handling
        overview, 159–160
        using try/except block, 160–164
        using try/finally block, 164–165
    opening, 144–145
    overview, 143–144
    performing actions on, 145–147
    raising exceptions
        assert statement, 166–167
        overview, 165–166
    randomly reading content of, 154
    reading from, 148–150
    serialization (pickling), 157–160
    updating content of, 153–154
filetryfinal.py **program, 164–165**
filter( ) **method, 87–88**
find( ) **method**
    displaying substrings in strings, 54–55
    finding substrings in string, 53
FirstApp.py **code, 197**
FirstApp.py **script file, 196**
flat **property, 333**
float( ) **function, 25**
float **data type, 346**
float **values, 226–231**
floating window, 300–301
floating-point numbers
    defined, 9
    using division operator with, 19
floating-point variables, 11
FloatingPointError **exception, 161**
floor(x) **function, 100**
flush( ) **method, 145**

Font Combo Box widget, 184
for **loop**
    choice( ) function, 42–44
    generator expression, 96
    iterators, 94
    membership operators, 41–42
    overview, 40–41
    two-dimensional arrays, 62
forloop.py **program, 40–41**
Form Layout widget, 181
format codes (%), 13–14
Frame widget, 183
from __future__ **statement, 19**
from math import pi **statement, 20**
fruits( ) **function, 95–96**
func1.py **program, 80**
func2.py **program, 83**
func3.py **program, 81**
func4.py **program, 81**
funcattrib.py **program, 90–91**
function call, defined, 79
functionname.__code__ **attribute, 90**
functionname.__defaults__ **attribute, 90**
functionname.__dict__ **attribute, 90**
functionname.__doc__ **attribute, 90**
functionname.__module__ **attribute, 90**
functionname.__name__ **attribute, 90**
functions
    applying to sequences, 87–90
    attributes of, 90–92
    def statement, 80
    default value parameters, 82–83
    defining, 108–109
    differences between methods and, 47–59
    dir( ), 101–102
    global variables, 84–85
    keyword arguments, 83–84
    lambda, 86–87
    local variables, 86
    overview, 79–80
    return statement, 81–82
functools **module, 89**

G

garbage collection, 3, 118–120
General Public License (GPL), 342
generator expression, 96–97
generator iterator, defined, 95
generatorex.py **program, 95**
generators, 95–96

get( ) method
    dictionary, 72
    Merging dictionaries program (dictexample.py),
        73–74
get_name method, 139
getsetattr.py program, 141–142
global variables, 84–85
globalvar.py program, 85
GPL (General Public License), 342
graphical user interface (GUI) applications. *See* GUI
        applications
Graphics View widget, 185, 275
Grid layout, 334–338
gridVisible property, 254
Group Box
    layouts, 332–333
    widget, 183
GUI applications
    creating application with code, 173–175
    database maintenance through
        displaying rows, 360–375
        overview, 359–360
        QSqlDatabase class, 360

H

hash, 71
hash sign (#), 12
hex( ) function, 24
hexa values, displaying, 24
highlighted( ) method, 260
horizontal layout, 328–332
Horizontal Line widget, 185
Horizontal Scrollbar widget, 184
Horizontal Slider widget, 184
Horizontal Spacer widget, 181
HorizontalHeaderFormat property, 254
hour( ) method, 251

I

identifiers in global statements, 84
IDLE (Integrated DeveLopment Environment)
    escape characters, 23
    launching, 8
    working with Python through, 7–8
if statement, 65
if...else statement, 29
if...else statement, 30–32
if-elif-else statement, 32
ifelschaining.py (chaining comparison operators
        program), 34
ifelse4.py program, 30–34, 49–50
imaginary component of complex numbers, 28–29

immutable objects
    defined, 10
    dictionary keys, 71
    tuples, 70
immutable strings, 46
import statement, 97
in membership operator, 41–42
in operator
    accessing list elements, 64–65
    accessing tuple elements, 70
indentation, 36–37
independent floating window, 300–301
index (value) method, 67
index( ) method
    finding substrings in string, 53
    lists, 70
IndexError exception, 161
inherit1.py program, 121
inherit2.py program, 124–125
inherit3.py program, 128–129
inherit4.py program, 130–131
inheritance
    access control specifiers
        accessing methods of base classes from derived
            classes, 124–125
        accessing private members, 122–123
        accessing public members, 122
        method overriding, 123–124
        overview, 122
    multilevel
        multiple inheritance, 131–135
        overview, 125–128
        two classes inheriting from same base class,
            128–131
    overview, 120
    single, 120–122
input dialog box, 242–246
input method, 24–25
Input widgets, 184
insert( ) method, 67
insertItem( ) method, 238
insertItems( ) method, 238
insertRow( ) method, 373
installing
    installation wizard, 3–5
    MySQLdb, 343–344
    PyQt, 170–172
    Python
        Mac, 5–6
        Microsoft Windows, 3–5
        overview, 3
        UNIX, 6

instance methods, 108–109, 115
instance variables, defined, 109
instances
    __init__( ) method, 111–114
    assigning to each other, 117–118
    defined, 106
    overview, 109–110
int( ) function, 25–26, 89, 205
int data type, 346
integer variables, 11
integers
    defined, 9
    entering using Spin Box, 226–231
Integrated DeveLopment Environment (IDLE)
    escape characters, 23
    launching, 8
    working with Python through, 7–8
Interchanging names program
    (interchangenme.py), 58
interfaces, 317–327
intersection (&) set operation, 74
IntInput option, 242
IOError exception, 149, 161
IronPython, 2
isalnum( ) method/function, 48
isalpha( ) method/function, 48
isatty( ) method, 147
isCheckable( ) method, 333
isChecked( ) method, 214, 219, 333
isdigit( ) method, 50
isdigit( ) method/function, 49
isHidden( ) method, 241
isLeapYear( ) method, 255
islower( ) method/function, 49
isReadOnly( ) method, 190
istitle( ) method/function, 49
isupper( ) method/function, 49
item( ) method, 238
Item Views group, 181–183
item-based interface, 237
items, displaying, 265–268
items( ) method
    dictionary, 72
    Merging dictionaries program (dictexample.py),
        73–74
ItemSceneChange notification, 274
itemText( ) method, 260
iter( ) method, 94
iterating_var variable, 40

iterators
    generator expression, 96–97
    generators, 95–96
    overview, 94

J

Java Virtual Machine (JVM), 2
join(sequence) method/function, 48
Jython, 2

K

KeyError exception, 161
keys( ) method
    dictionary, 72
    Merging dictionaries program (dictexample.py),
        73–74
key/value pairs, 71, 91
keyword arguments, 83–84
keywordarg.py program, 83–84
keywords, defined, 11

L

Label widget, 185
lambda functions, 86–87
lastError( ) method, 360, 373
Lay Out Horizontally icon, 188
Lay Out Horizontally in Splitter icon, 188
Lay Out in a Form Layout icon, 188
Lay Out in a Grid icon, 188
Lay Out Vertically icon, 188
Lay Out Vertically in Splitter icon, 188
layouts
    Grid layout, 334–338
    Group Box, 332–333
    horizontal layout, 328–332
    overview, 327–328
    vertical layout, 333–334
Layouts group, 180–181
LCD digits, displaying
    fetching and measuring system clock time, 251–253
    overview, 250
    using timers, 250–251
LCD format, displaying system clock time, 249–253
LCD Number widget, 185
leading zeros, 10
len( ) function
    finding length of lists, 64
    printing count of elements in list, 68
    sets, 75

Length of String program (string1.py), 49
Line Edit widget, 184
list variables, 11
List View widget, 182
List widgets
    adding items to, 237–241
    overview, 237
    performing operations on
        displaying input dialog box, 242–246
        overview, 241
        using, 241
list1.py program, 63–64
list2.py program, 64
list6.py program, 67–68
list7.py program, 69
lists
    defined, 10
    length of, 64–66
    overview, 63–64
    slicing, 66–70
    use of square brackets, 45
literals, 10–11
ljust(width) method/function, 48
load( ) method, 269
loadFinished( ) method, 269
loadProgress( ) method, 269
loadStarted( ) method, 269
local variables, 86
localvar.py program, 86
logical lines, defined, 12
logical operators, 32–34
long integers, defined, 9
longblob data type, 346
longtext data type, 346
loops
    for loop
        choice( ) function, 42–44
        membership operators, 41–42
        overview, 40–41
    overview, 35
    while loop
        break statement, 37–38
        continue statement, 38–39
        indentation, 36–37
        overview, 36
        pass statement, 39
        range( ) function, 39–40
lower( ) method/function, 48
lstrip( ) method/function, 48

M
Mac, installing Python on, 5–6
maintenance
    of databases through console-based programs
        inserting rows in database tables, 349–359
        overview, 349
    of databases through GUI programs
        displaying rows, 360–375
        overview, 359–360
        QSqlDatabase class, 360
make altinstall command, 5
make install command, 5
map( ) method, 88–89
mappings, defined, 71
math module
    command-line arguments, 102
    dir( ) function, 101–102
    overview, 100–101
math.e constant, 100
mathmethod.py program, 100
math.pi constant, 100
matrix1.py program, 61
matter variable, 147
max( ) method/function, 48, 75
maximum( ) method, 232
maximumDate property, 254, 256
maxLength( ) method, 190
MDI (multiple-document interface), 317–327
MdiArea widget, 183, 319
mediumblob data type, 346
mediumint data type, 346
mediumtext data type, 346
member functions, defined, 106
membership operators, 41–42, 54
menus
    Action Editor, 279–280
    creating, 280–286
    overview, 277–278
Merging dictionaries program (dictexample.py),
    73–74
methods. *See also specific method by name*
    __delattr__, 141–142
    __getattr__, 141
    __init__( ), 111–114
    __setattr__, 141
    accessing, 124–125
    class, 114–115
    commit( ), 349–350
    defined, 108

methods (*Continued*)
  differences between functions and, 47–59
  overriding, 123–124
  `rollback( )`, 351–352
  static, 115–118
Microsoft Windows, installing Python on, 3–5
`min( )` **method/function, 48, 75**
`minimum( )` **method, 232**
`minimumDate` **property, 254, 256**
`minute( )` **method, 251**
`MMM d yy` **format, 257**
`MMM d yyyy` **format, 257**
`MMMM d yy` **format, 257**
modal dialogs, 173
`mode` **attribute, 147**
modeless dialogs, 173
modules. *See also specific module by name*
  math module, 100–102
  overview, 97–100
`month( )` **method, 255**
`monthShown( )` **method, 254**
`msec( )` **method, 251**
`msecsTo( )` **method, 251**
multilevel inheritance
  multiple inheritance, 131–135
  overview, 125–128
  two classes inheriting from same base class,
      128–131
`multilevel.py` **program, 126–127**
multiple assignment statement, 21
multiple documents
  layouts
    Grid Layout, 334–338
    Group Box, 332–333
    horizontal layout, 328–332
    overview, 327–328
    vertical layout, 333–334
  multiple-document interface, 317–327
  overview, 317
multiple inheritance
  overview, 131–134
  two base classes having methods with same name and
      signature, 134–135
multiple-document interface (MDI), 317–327
`multiple.py` **program, 132–133**
Multiply icon, 295
mutable objects
  defined, 10
  dictionaries, 71
`myException` **class, 166**
MySQL
  installation of MySQLdb, 343–344

    MySQLdb, 343
    overview, 342
Mysql-Python Setup Wizard dialog, 343

N
`name` **attribute, 147**
nesting, `if...else` **statements, 31–32**
New icon, 186
New resource file icon, 288
newline, embedding in string, 46
newline character, 12–13, 147
`NoDockWidgetFeatures` **property, 296**
non data descriptors, defined, 139
`noOfObjects( )` **method, 119**
`Normal` **state, 279**
`not in` **membership operator, 41**
`not` **logical operator, 33**
`NULL` **character, 47**
numerical arrays, 59–63
`numericarr.py` **program, 59–60**

O
Object Inspector window, 177
objects
  class, 106–107
  file, 147–148
`oct( )` **function, 24**
octal values, displaying, 24
one-dimensional arrays, 59–60
`open( )` **method, 144–145, 360**
open brace ({), 12
open bracket ([ ), 12
Open icon, 186
open parenthesis (( ), 12
Open resource file icon, 288
open source model, 2
opening files, 144–145
`openmessage( )` **function, 286**
operations
  commonly applied to sequences, 46
  performing on List widgets
    displaying input dialog box, 242–246
    overview, 241
    using, 241
operator overloading
  comparison operator (==)
    overview, 136
    polymorphism, 137–138
    properties, 138–139
  overview, 135–136

operatorovr1.py **program, 135**
operatorovr2.py **program, 136**
opr1.py **program, 34–35**
optional parameters, function, 82–83
or logical operator, 33
OSError **exception, 161**
OverflowError **exception, 161**
override.py **program, 124**

P

page control, 232
paramcons.py **program, 112**
parameters
    default value, 82–83
    function, 80
parentheses, tuples, 45
partition( ) **method, 58–59**
partition(separator) **method, 57**
pass **statement, 39, 107**
passex1.py **program, 39**
passex.py **program, 107**
Phonon API, 185–186
Phonon::SeekSlider **widget, 186**
Phonon::VideoPlayer **widget, 186**
Phonon::VolumeSlider **widget, 186**
physical lines, defined, 12
Pickle **module, 157**
pickled files, defined, 144
pickleprog2.py **program, 158–159**
pickleprog.py **program, 157**
pickling (serialization), 157–160
Plain Text Edit widget, 184
Plus icon, 291
plus sign (+), 13
plusmessage( ) **method, 294**
polymorphism, 137–138
polymorphism.py **program, 137–138**
pop( ) **method**
    dictionary, 72
    lists, 67
    sets, 75
pow( ) **function, 20**
predefined slots, 193–199
prefix, finding strings with, 56
prefix=~, **5**
primes.py **program, 43–44**
print( ) **function, 12–14**
private **members, 122–123**
privateaccess.py **program, 123**
prodclasscount( ) **class method, 117**
prodstatcount( ) **static method, 117**

Progress Bar widget, 185
Property Editor window, 177–178
propertyex.py **program, 138–139**
public **members, 122**
publicaccess.py **program, 122**
push buttons, 186, 223–226
PyQt
    buddies
        overview, 206–207
        setting tab order, 207–211
    converting data types, 202–206
    creating GUI application with code, 173–175
    custom slots, 199–202
    event handling in, 191
    fundamental widgets
        displaying buttons, 190–191
        displaying text, 189
        entering single-line data, 189–190
        overview, 188–189
    installing, 170–172
    overview, 169–170
    Qt Designer
        applications, 191–199
        overview, 175–179
        toolbar, 186–188
        Widget Box, 179–186
    Qt toolkit, 170
    Setup Wizard dialog, 171
    window and dialogs, 172–173
Python
    comments, 12
    continuation lines, 12
    data types in, 9–10
    features of, 2–3
    implementations of, 2
    installing
        Mac, 5–6
        Microsoft Windows, 3–5
        overview, 3
        UNIX, 6
    interacting with
        command line mode, 7
        IDLE, 7–8
        overview, 7
    keywords, 11
    literals, 10–11
    overview, 1, 10
    printing, 12–14
    running programs from command prompt, 9
    variables, 11
    writing simple programs with, 8–9
Python Command Line window, 4–5, 7

Python prompt (>>>), 4–5
Python Shell window, 8
pyuic4 command, 251, 270
pyuic4 utility, 196

Q

QAbstractButton class, 219
QAbstractItemModel class, 182
QAbstractItemView class, 181–182
QApplication object, 198
QCalendarWidget class, 253
QDate class, 255–256
QDeclarativeView widget, 185
QDialog superclass, 176
QDoubleSpinBox class, 227
QGraphicsView subclass, 185
QGraphicsView.setScene( )
          method, 274
QRadioButton class, 213
QsciScintilla widget, 184
QSqlDatabase class, 360
QSqlQueryModel class, 368
QSqlTableModel class, 361–364
Qt Designer
    applications
        connecting to predefined slots, 193–199
        overview, 191–192
    overview, 175–179
    toolbar, 186–188
    Widget Box
        Buttons, 181
        Containers, 183–184
        Display widgets, 184–185
        Input widgets, 184
        Item Views (item based), 182–183
        Item Views (model based), 181–182
        Layouts, 180–181
        overview, 179–180
        Phonon, 185–186
        Spacers, 181
Qt toolkit, 170
QTableView class, 265
QTableWidgetItem( ) method, 265
QtCore module, 197
QtGUI module, 197
quit( ) method, 175
quotes, 11, 45
QWebView widget, 185, 272
QWidget superclass, 176, 179

R

R mode option, 145
r+ mode option, 145
radio buttons, 213–218
raise statement, 165–166
raiseexcepclass.py program, 165–166
raising exceptions
    assert statement, 166–167
    overview, 165–166
randomly reading file content, 154
randomnumber.py program, 42
range( ) function, 39–40, 42
range( ) method, 88–89
range(x, y) function, 40
range(x, y, step) function, 40
range(x) function, 39
read([n]) method, 145
reading files, 148–150
readline([n]) method, 145
readlines([n]) method, 145
record(int) method, 368
record.value("column_name") method, 368
rectarea( ) method, 110, 112–113, 118
rectclass1.py program, 107
rectclass2.py program, 107
rectclass3.py program, 110
recurfunc.py program, 92–93
recursion, 92–93
reduce( ) method, 89
reject( ) method, 332
remove ( ) method/function, 75
Remove icon, 288
removeItem( ) method, 259
removeRow( ) method, 374
remove(value) method, 67
replace( ) method, 58–59
replace(s1, s2, n) method, 57
replacing substrings, 57
Resource Browser window, 178, 287
resource file, 287–295
retranslateUi( ) method, 197
return statement, 81–82
returnPressed( ) method, 189
reverse( ) method, 67
reversed( ) function, 48, 51
revert( ) method, 373
revertAll( ) method, 373
rfind method, 53
rjust(width) method, 48
rollback( ) method, 351–352

rowCount( ) **method, 265**

rows
  database tables
    commit( ) method, 349–350
    deleting information, 358–359
    fetching rows from tables, 352–354
    navigating, 364–369
    overview, 349
    rollback( ) method, 351–352
    searching, 355–356
    updating information, 356–358
  displaying
    maintaining database tables, 369–375
    navigating through rows of database tables, 364–369
    overview, 360–361
    QSqlTableModel class, 361–364
  fetching from tables, 352–354
  two-dimensional arrays, 60
rstrip( ) **method/function, 48**

S

Save icon, 186
Scintilla component, 184
Scroll Area widget, 183
Scroll arrows, 231
scroll bars, 231–233
scrollhorizontal( ) **function, 236**
SDI (single-document interface), 317
searching in database tables, 355–356
searchstr1.py **program, 55**
searchstr2.py **program, 55**
seconds( ) **method, 251**
secsTo( ) **method, 251**
seek( ) **method, 154**
seek(offset, location) **method, 146**
select( ) **method, 361**
selected checkboxes, 219
Selected state, 280
selectedDate( ) **method, 254**
selectionChanged( ) **method, 254**
selectionMode **property, 254**
self **parameter, 108, 110**
semicolon (;), 345
Send to Back icon, 186
Sentence splitting program (splitting.py), **57**
sequences
  applying functions to, 87–90
  dictionaries, 71–74
  lists
    length of, 64–66

    overview, 63–64
    slicing, 66–70
  overview, 45–46
  sets
    difference (-), 75–76
    intersection (&), 74
    overview, 74
    union (|), 74
  strings
    arrays, 59–63
    how characters are stored in, 47–59
    overview, 46–47
  tuples, 70–71
serialization (pickling), 157–160
set_name **method, 139**
setChecked( ) **method, 214, 219, 333**
setCheckState( ) **method, 265**
setColumnCount( ) **method, 265**
setCurrentIndex( ) **method, 259**
setCurrentItem( ) **method, 238**
setCurrentRow( ) **method, 238**
setDatabaseName( ) **method, 360**
setDate( ) **method, 255, 257**
setDisplayFormat( ) **method, 257**
setEchoMode( ) **method, 190**
setEditable( ) **method, 259**
setEditStrategy( ) **method, 361**
setEnabled( ) **method, 190**
setexample.py **program, 76**
setFilter( ) **method, 374**
setFirstDayOfWeek( ) **method, 254**
setFocus( ) **method, 190**
setFont( ) **method, 265**
setGeometry( ) **method, 174**
setHidden( ) **method, 241**
setHostName( ) **method, 360**
setHtml( ) **method, 269**
setIcon( ) **method, 191, 214, 219**
setItemText( ) **method, 259**
setMaxCount( ) **method, 259**
setMaximum( ) **method, 227, 232**
setMinimum( ) **method, 227, 232**
setMode( ) **method, 250**
setNum( ) **method, 189**
setPageStep( ) **method, 232**
setPassword( ) **method, 360**
setPixmap( ) **method, 189**
setPrefix( ) **method, 227**
setQuery( ) **method, 368**
setReadOnly( ) **method, 190**
setRowCount( ) **method, 265**

sets
    defined, 10
    difference (-), 75–76
    intersection (&), 74
    overview, 74
    union (|), 74
setSingleShot(true) method, 250
setSingleStep( ) method, 227, 232
setSuffix( ) method, 227
setTable( ) method, 361
setText( ) method, 189, 190, 191
setTickInterval( ) method, 233
setTickPosition( ) method, 233
setTristate( ) method, 219
setupUi( ) method, 197
setupUI( ) method, 198
setUrl( ) method, 269
setUserName( ) method, 360
setValue( ) method, 227, 232
setViewMode( ) method, 318
setWrapping( ) method, 227
shifting operators, 26–28
shopping database, 345
show( ) instance method, 115
show( ) method, 198
show tables command, 348
signals, 191
Signals and Slots Editing mode, 187
Signal/Slot Editor window, 178
signatures, 134–135
single inheritance, 120–122
single-document interface (SDI), 317
single-line data, 189–190
single-quoted string, 46
singleShot(n) method, 250
site-packages folder, 172
sizeHint property, 327
slicing lists, 66–70
Slider handle control, 231
sliderMoved( ) method, 233
sliderPressed( ) method, 233
sliderReleased( ) method, 233
sliders, 233–237
slots, 191, 193–199
smallint data type, 346
sort( ) method, 70
sorted( ) method, 48, 75
spacers, 327
Spacers group, 181
spaces, 36

Spin Box, 184, 226–231
split( ) method, 58–59
splitlines(boolean) method, 57
split(separator, [n]) method, 57
splitting.py (Sentence splitting program), 57
SQL DELETE command, 358
SQL SELECT statement, 355
SQL UPDATE statement, 356
square( ) function, 88
square brackets, 45, 63
Stacked widgets, 183, 309, 311–315
stacks, 92
start(n) method, 250
startswith ( ) method, 56
stateChanged( ) method, 214
stateChanged( ) signal, 219
statements
    assert, 166–167
    class
        attributes of class objects, 106–107
        built-in class attributes, 107–108
        defining functions in, 108–109
        instances, 109–114
        overview, 105–106
    def, 80
    return, 81–82
static methods, 115–118
staticlassmethod.py program, 116–117
staticmethod.py program, 116
stderr variable, 149
stdin variable, 149
stdout variable, 149–150
StopIteration exception, 94
str( ) function, 25, 52, 205
string concatenation program
    (stringconcat1.py), 52
string variables, 11
string1.py program, 49
string2.py program, 50
string3.py program, 51–52
stringfunc2.py program, 56
stringjoin.py program, 52–53
strings
    arrays
        one-dimensional, 59–60
        overview, 59
        two-dimensional, 60–63
    concatenating, 13
    defined, 10
    how characters are stored in, 47–59

length of, 49–59
overview, 46–47
represented by quotes, 11
space between, 13
use of quotes, 45
strip( ) **method, 48**
student grade division program (ifelse.py),
    30–34
Style Sheet Editor, 303–309
submit( ) **method, 373**
submitAll( ) **method, 373**
substrings, 53
SubWindow View button, 326
subWindowList( ) **method, 318**
subwindows, 317–318
SubWindowView( ) **function, 325**
sum( ) **function, 80**
sum( ) **method, 75**
super classes (base classes; parent classes), 106
swapcase( ) **method, 48**
sys.argv **variable, 102**
sys.exit( ) **method, 175**
system clock time, 249–253

T
Tab Order Editing mode, 208
Tab widget
    converting into Stacked widgets, 311–315
    converting into Tool Boxes, 310–311
    overview, 302–303, 309–310
    Style Sheet Editor, 303–309
TabbedView( ) **function, 325**
Table View widget, 182, 364
Table widget, 183
tables
    database, inserting rows in
        commit( ) method, 349–350
        deleting information from database tables,
            358–359
        fetching rows from tables, 352–354
        overview, 349
        rollback( ) method, 351–352
        searching in database tables, 355–356
        updating information in database tables,
            356–358
    displaying
        displaying items in, 265–268
        overview, 264–265
    fetching rows from, 352–354

tabs, 36, 207–211
takeItem( ) **method, 238**
tell( ) **method, 146**
text, displaying, 189
text( ) **method, 190, 227**
Text Browser widget, 185
text **data type, 346**
Text Edit widget, 184
text editors, 8
text files, defined, 144
textChanged( ) **method, 189**
TextInput **option, 242**
tickInterval( ) **method, 233**
tickPosition( ) **method, 233**
tileArrange( ) **function, 325**
tileSubWindows( ) **method, 318, 319**
time **data type, 346**
Time Edit widget, 184
timeout( ) **signal, 250**
timers, 250–251
tinyblob **data type, 346**
tinytext **data type, 346**
title( ) **method/function, 48**
toggled( ) **method, 214**
toggled( ) **signal, 219**
Tool Box widget, 183, 310–311
toolbars, 186–188
toPyDate( ) **method, 255**
transform( ) **method, 272**
Tree View widget, 182
Tree widget, 183
trigarea( ) **method, 121–122**
triggered( ) **signal, 286, 294**
triple-quoted string, 46–47
tristate checkboxes, 219
truncating division operator (//), **18**
try **blocks, 160**
try1.py **program, 162**
try2.py **program, 163–164**
tryelse.py **program, 162–163**
try/except **block, 160–166**
try/finally **block, 160, 164–165**
tup1.py **program, 70**
tup2.py **program, 70–71**
tuple variables, 11
tuples
    defined, 10, 41
    use of parentheses, 45
two-dimensional arrays, 60–63
type( ) **function, 23–24**
TypeError **exception, 111, 161, 164**

U

UnboundLocal-Error **exception, 84**
Unicode, defined, 10
union (|) set operation, 74
UNIX, installing Python on, 6
unselected checkboxes, 219
update( ) method, 72
updatefilecont.py **program, 153–154**
update(set) **method/function, 75**
updating file content, 153–154
updating information in database tables,
    356–358
upper( ) **method/function, 48**
use database_name **command, 347–348**
user data, getting, 24–25

V

value( ) **method, 227, 232, 250**
valueChanged( ) **method, 227, 233**
ValueError **exception, 161**
values( ) **method**
    dictionary, 72
    Merging dictionaries program (dictexample.py),
        73–74
van Rossum, Guido, 1
varchar **data type, 346**
variables
    defined, 11
    displaying values in, 13
    global, 84–85
    local, 86
vertical layout, 333–334
Vertical Layout widget, 181
Vertical Line widget, 185
Vertical Scrollbar widget, 184
Vertical Slider widget, 184
Vertical Spacer widget, 181
verticalHeaderFormat **property, 254**
volume( ) **function, 84**
volume of a sphere program (volsphere.py), **20**

W

W **mode option, 145**
w+ **mode option, 145**
welcomemsg **code, 201**
while **loop**
    break statement, 37–38
    continue statement, 38–39
    indentation, 36–37

overview, 36
    pass statement, 39
    range( ) function, 39–40
whileloop.py **program, 36–37**
white space, 2, 13
Widget Box
    Buttons, 181
    Containers, 183–184
    Display widgets, 184–185
    Input widgets, 184
    Item Views (item based), 182–183
    Item Views (model based), 181–182
    Layouts, 180–181
    overview, 179–180
    Phonon, 185–186
    Spacers, 181
Widget Editing mode, 187
widget toolkit, 170
widgets. *See also specific widget by name;* Widget Box
    calendar and displaying dates in different formats
        Date Edit widget, 256–259
        displaying calendar, 253–255
        overview, 253
        QDate class, 255–256
    checkboxes
        initiating actions without using push buttons,
            223–226
        overview, 218–223
    Combo Box, 259–264
    Display, 184–185
    displaying
        buttons, 190–191
        graphics, 271–276
        system clock time in LCD format, 249–253
        tables, 264–268
        text, 189
        web pages, 268–271
    Dock, 295–302
    entering integer and float values using Spin Box,
        226–231
    entering single-line data, 189–190
    Input, 184
    List
        adding items to, 237–241
        overview, 237
        performing operations on, 241–246
    overview, 188–189, 213, 249
    radio buttons, 213–218
    scroll bars, 231–233
    sliders, 233–237

Tab
    converting into Stacked widgets, 311–315
    converting into Tool Boxes, 310–311
    overview, 302–303, 309–310
    Style Sheet Editor, 303–309
WindowOrder( ) **function, 319**
WindowOrder( ) **method, 318**
windows. *See also specific window by name*
    creating GUI applications, 173–175
    floating, 300–301
    overview, 172–173
    subwindows, 317–318

writelines(list) **method, 146**
write(string) **method, 146**

Y
year( ) **method, 255**
yearShown( ) **method, 254**
yield **statement, 95**

Z
ZeroDivisionError **exception, 161**